PREACHING WITH ELOQUENCE FROM THE HEART

Organize, Internalize, & Extemporize

Nathan Clay Brummel

ISBN-13: 978-1982041526
ISBN-10: 1982041528

Contents

Introduction

As far as I know, I am not dying of cancer. T. David Gordon began his influential book on preaching, *Why Johnny Can't Preach*, while he was undergoing 11 months of treatment for cancer. He tells us in the preface to his book his motivations for writing this prophetic little book:

> I had stage III colorectal cancer, and the various cancer Web sites at the time gave me a 25 percent chance of survival. I'm not a mathematician, but I realized that those numbers were not very encouraging, and I had to face the realistic possibility that I would not survive the year. Having been concerned about the state of preaching for three decades, I believed that it would be irresponsible to leave the world without expressing my thoughts about the matter, in the hope that better preaching might be the result.[1]

I have not received a cancer diagnosis, yet I too have a burden about contemporary preaching. If the Word preached is the Word of God, then the preaching of the Word by ordained ministers plays a crucial role in the life and health of the church.

I have a burden to train prisoners in correctional institutions in Illinois and Indiana to present gospel messages from their hearts at chapel services. I have a burden to equip Reformed and Presbyterian seminary students and preachers to preach the Word with passion, from the heart.

I too feel that I must say something on this important topic during the few years of my life, a life that is as transient as a vapor.

My concerns hover in several areas. First, I have a concern about seminary students and preachers who read their sermons. Hence you will find a developed argument for extemporaneous preaching. I promote extemporaneous preaching and the importance of internalizing one's message so that the preacher can speak from the heart and throw away his

---

[1] T. David Gordon, Why Johnny Can't Preach: The Media Have Shaped the Messengers. (Phillipsburg, PA: P & R Publishing, 2009).

paper.

Second, I am burdened by a lack of passion and rhetoric in the pulpit. Therefore, you will discover an important chapter entitled, "Herman Bavinck on Pulpit Eloquence" where I explore the connection between passion and eloquence.

Third, I am troubled by a lack of simplicity, order, and logic in sermons. I challenge preachers who do not present one "Big Idea" or one main point as the theme in their sermons and, therefore, present sermons with multiple "Big Ideas" or mini-sermons. T. David Gordon was prophetic on the issue of order and logic in sermons. I think that a weakness in homiletics is troubling the churches.

Fourth, I share T. David Gordon's concern about a lack of textual preaching. The preacher needs to communicate the words and ideas of the text. I will argue for the importance of developing the concepts in the text. The minister needs to preach the Word.

Fifth, I disagree with some popular ways of preaching Heidelberg Catechism sermons. Some elders and preachers suppose that what should happen in a catechism sermon is that the preacher only preaches the Lord's Day as the text. I challenge this approach and argue for the importance of doing exegesis of a relevant biblical text and the importance of a poetic interweaving of the text and ideas in both the catechism and the Scripture text.

Fifth, I am troubled by the challenges facing preachers in the 21st century. I am concerned about ignorance on the part of Reformed believers of what Reformed preaching should be like. I am aware of the inability of some elders to evaluate preaching in a balanced way. Therefore, I have included chapters 33 and 34 that are entitled respectively, "Why do the Saints Eat Roast Minister" and "Elders, Wisely Oversee the Preaching."

Sixth, I am disturbed by a lack of authority and power in the pulpit. Preachers do not get up in front of the congregation to dispense advice. They need to bring the Word with the authority of an ambassador and in the power of the Holy Spirit.

We will begin by exploring why Charles Haddon Spurgeon did not preach with an iPad.

Chapter 1

Why Spurgeon Didn't Preach with an iPad

To preach the gospel is not to mumble over some dry manuscript. It is not to speak colorlessly about color or odorlessly about odor.[2]
-C.H. Spurgeon

Charles Spurgeon did not preach with an iPad. He didn't. And he wouldn't have.

Even as a young preacher in his late teens or in his potentially "hip" early 20's, he never preached with an iPad.

Today it is "cool" for hip preachers to walk around on the stage with their iPad in hand. The use of an iPad is a sign of coolness in comparison to the old fuddy-duddy preachers who use paper.

Using an iPad is inferior to the use of paper. I will reject the idea of a preacher writing out his sermon in essay form in order to read it in the pulpit. The difficulty with an iPad is that the screen is smaller than a normal-sized page of paper. Therefore, the preacher with a page of paper in front of him has more room to put material and more to see than occurs on an iPad screen. If the minister is going to use paper in the pulpit he should use an outline at which he only needs to *glance*.

The picture on the cover of this book is mythical. It is ahistorical. It never happened. And it never would have happened.

The "Prince of Preachers", if we dare call anyone that, when our Master "came preaching", did not allow paper to come between his eyes and the congregation. At times he did take a very brief outline into the sermon. But it was brief and he did not depend upon it.

I had the cover artist draw an extra-large iPad on the front cover to symbolize how either paper or an iPad comes between the preacher and the congregation in the act of preaching.

---

[2] Cited by Christian George on Beeson Podcast, Episode 383. March 13, 2018.

How do we know that Spurgeon would not have preached from an iPad? He didn't allow the technology of his day, namely, a paper manuscript, to become a barrier between him and his audience

Spurgeon would not allow paper or an iPad to come between him and his audience because he believed in gaining and keep the attention of his audience. He did not hide behind a pulpit as he preached. He did not stay behind a pulpit so that he could glance down to read a manuscript. The Metropolitan Tabernacle was built with a balcony for the preacher. He was free to walk around as he preached from the heart.

In his *Lectures to My Students*, Spurgeon includes a chapter entitled "Attention!" He admits that an overlooked topic in homiletics is "HOW TO OBTAIN AND RETAIN THE ATTENTION OF OUR HEARERS."[3] He said that the preacher needs "the earnest, candid, wakeful, continued attention of all those who are in the congregation."[4] I have seen from my own experience that Spurgeon is true when he writes: "There are preachers who care very little whether they are attended to or not; so long as they can hold on through the allotted time it is of very small importance to them whether their people hear for eternity, or hear in vain."[5]

In his inimitable style, Spurgeon says of such preachers: "the sooner such ministers sleep in the churchyard and preach by the verse on their gravestones the better."[6] Spurgeon advises the preacher to gain the attention of the congregation by always saying *something worth hearing.*"[7] A minister can lose the attention of his auditors by verboseness: "It is not a severe criticism to say that there are ministers whose words stand in a very large proportion to their thoughts."

Spurgeon is also concerned with something that we shall deal with later: order and logic in the sermon: "*Let the good matter which you give them be very clearly arranged.*"[8] Spurgeon exhorts: "Put the truth before men in a logical, orderly manner, so that they can easily remember it, and they will the more readily receive it."

But what catches our attention at the beginning of this book is what Spurgeon says about how one's manner of address can lead to either losing or catching the attention of the congregation. The Prince of Preachers tells the preacher: Do not read your sermon. If you want to gain and keep the

---

[3] C. H. Spurgeon. Lectures to My Students. Volume 1. (Lynchburg, Virginia: The Old-Time Gospel Hour, 1894), 136.
[4] Ibid., 136.
[5] Ibid., 136.
[6] Ibid., 136.
[7] Ibid., 140.
[8] Ibid., 140.

attention of the congregation, do not read your sermon off paper or an iPad.

Attend also to your manner of address: aim in that at the promotion of attention. And here I should say, as a rule do not read your sermons. There have been a few readers who have exercised great power, as, for instance, Dr. Chalmers, who could not have had a more attentive audience had he been extemporizing; but then I do not suppose that we are equal to a Dr. Chalmers: men of such eminence may read if they prefer it, but for us there is "a more excellent way." The best reading I have ever heard has tasted of paper, and has stuck in my throat.

I have not relished it, for my digestion is not good enough to dissolve foolscap. It is better to do without the manuscript, even if you are driven to recite. It is best of all if you need neither to recite nor to read. If you must read, mind that you do it to perfection. Be the very best of readers, and you had need to be if you would secure attention.

Spurgeon immediately clarifies that he is not recommending radically extemporaneous approaches to preaching or what we might call impromptu speeches.

> Here let me say, *if you would be listened to, do not extemporise in the emphatic sense,* for that is as bad as reading, or perhaps worse, unless the manuscript was written extemporaneously; I mean without previous study. Do not go into the pulpit and say the first thing that comes to hand, for the uppermost thing with most men is mere froth. Your people need discourses which have been prayed over and laboriously prepared. People do not want raw food, it must be cooked and made ready for them.

Spurgeon then tells us what his preferred "manner of address" is:

> The best method is, in my judgment, that in which the man does not extemporize the matter, but extemporizes the words; the language comes to him at the moment, but the theme has been well thought out, and like a master in Israel he speaks of that which he knows, and testifies of what he has seen.

Spurgeon supported extemporaneous preaching, not impromptu preaching. He wanted the minister to study the text, learn from commentaries, preach the message to his own heart, and prepare an outline of the main points of the sermon. Once in the pulpit, the minister should extemporize the words.

Spurgeon internalized the message and with a marvelous extemporaneous ability developed and created his sermon in the act of preaching. He once said that as he preached, his mind was so inventive, creative, and pregnant with ideas that he had 7 ideas presented to his mind simultaneously for what he could say next! He could select from these options the most fitting ideas and words. His marvelous artistry with the Bible message was both his strength and weakness.

With his heart steeped in the Bible, his mind suffused with Calvinistic soteriology, and his marvelous poetic and linguistic gifts; Spurgeon was able to present profound truth with marvelous imagery and symbolism. His sermons are filled with imagery and examples that communicate gospel truth like the light blazes in a multi-faceted gem.

Spurgeon's weakness was that he had such facility in extemporaneous preaching that he did not always do careful exegesis of the Biblical text. As a young minister I learned that I could get some marvelous quotes from Spurgeon, but it was difficult to find careful exegetical insights in his sermons.

Spurgeon's concern for catching the attention of the congregation is evident in his attack on a monotone voice in preaching. One problem I have observed with seminary students who read their sermons is that invariably their voice is reduced to a monotone.

> Do not, for instance, indulge in monotones. Vary your voice continually. Vary your speed as well—dash as rapidly as a lightning flash, and anon, travel forward in quiet majesty. Shift your accent, move your emphasis, and avoid sing-song. Vary the tone; use the bass sometimes, and let the thunders roll within; at other times speak as you ought to do generally—from the lips, and let your speech be conversational. Anything for a change.[9]

It is true that a good reader can vary his delivery. But extemporaneous speaking brings variety to a whole new level.

One great problem with seminary student sermons is a sameness in tone, speed, and loudness. The problem is that too many seminarians learn to read their sermons word for word. The seminarian is focusing on simply communicating what he wrote down. But he is not viewing the preaching moment as an interactive event in which the congregation is responding to him and he to them. He even avoids looking at the congregation because this makes him nervous. He ignores the congregation but expects that they should simply listen to his reading.

The seminarian's emotions are not fired by the latest idea that he is considering. He is simply reciting what he wrote about one idea and then will read the next idea. He does not allow the present idea to sink into his heart. He is not thinking through what it is and what he has learned about it

---

[9] Ibid., 142.

and then using fresh and normal ways of communicating about it. He does not take the time to let the idea impact the congregation by whatever rhetorical methods might cause this. He can't use repetition or variety in speed or volume, because he is simply reading what is before him and now it is time to read the next paragraph. As a reader he is emotionally handicapped.

Often the seminary student simply concentrates on developing an idea in an orthodox way. It is good that he avoids the various heresies that threaten on either side. But he forgets the *dictim* that "those who speak so that children can listen soon find that adults will understand."[10] The seminary student might mention the children in the sermon and even address them. But the children are not fooled. Their attention immediately wanders because the preacher is not really trying to communicate to them in a simple and effective way. He is not trying to communicate to them. He is simply reading what he wrote to read to them. The preacher needs to take the time to stop and make sure that what he is saying is simple and interesting enough to grab the children's attention.

When you have internalized the message, you grasp its relevance and importance. Spurgeon tells the theological student that he must "*be interested*" and then "you will interest others."[11] I have rarely thought that ministers who read their sermons were engrossed in their message. Spurgeon says:

> Your subject must weight so much upon your own mind that you dedicate all your faculties at their best to the deliverance of your soul concerning it; and then when your hearers see that the topic has engrossed you, it will by degrees engross them.

Spurgeon is convinced that the preacher "must *make the people feel that they have an interest in what we are saying to them*."[12] He makes the point that he has never heard of a person going to sleep while a will was being read in which he expected a legacy; neither have I heard of a prisoner going to sleep while the judge was summing up, and his life was hanging in jeopardy. Self-interest quickens attention. Preach upon practical themes, pressing, present, personal matters, and you will secure an earnest hearing.[13]

---

[10] Ibid., 240.
[11] Ibid., 146.
[12] Ibid., 149.
[13] Ibid., 149.

Spurgeon would not have used an iPad because he had a natural understanding of eloquence. Most speakers need to learn how to communicate. Their rhetorical abilities grow and mature. Spurgeon had such native intelligence that from his earliest years he seemed to understand the principles of eloquence. God gave him a mature spirituality as a twenty-year-old. He had a native ability to communicate without having to learn by hard practice the power of pauses, how to affect an audience, and how to wield his marvelous voice.

Spurgeon naturally understood that eloquence involved several matters. He knew how to communicate without taking classes on rhetoric. He knew that communication required eye contact with the congregation. For that reason, he would not have allowed an iPad to come between his eyes and the congregation. Martyn Lloyd-Jones later would talk about the importance of the minister reading the congregation and receiving communication back from them. Preaching is two-way communication between the preacher and individuals in the congregation and the congregation as a whole. Individual saints communicate by a bright smile of joy or by tears of sorrow. Spurgeon knew that eloquence flowed out of passion and spontaneity in the act of preaching.

The "Prince of Preachers" did not read his sermons. He did not write out his sermon as a long essay to read to the congregation. Doing so would have violated principles of communication and eloquence. At times Spurgeon seems to have created sermons in the carriage on the way to church. In such cases he had only a short time to reflect on the text and to think about the main point and divisions of the sermon. He would not have had a lot of time to internalize the message. In such a case he would need to draw upon his understanding of the text, all of Scripture, Reformed theology, his spiritual experience, his understanding of the congregation, the needs of the lost, and the gospel of Christ for the formation of a message in the act of preaching. In the act of preaching his mind creatively drew upon his knowledge of all of these matters. The result was marvelous spontaneity in the act of preaching.

But most of the time Spurgeon worked on the text ahead of time. It does blow my mind that he often selected the text for the Sunday morning sermon on Saturday evening. Sometimes he would become very troubled when his search for a text did not immediately lead to a selection. Sometimes his wife would help with identify a text. Once he had selected a text, we are told that his wife or students would read what the commentators said about the text to him. He began to work on the title of the sermon and the sermon points. He studied the text in the original language. He did careful exegesis. He thought about the sermon. Therefore, he would approach the act of preaching with internalized ideas. The result would be less inventiveness in the act of preaching, although Spurgeon's mind would be able to introduce the ideas he developed ahead of time. Either way, Spurgeon was not dependent on paper.

He did not read out his sermons.

He would not have preached from an iPad.

The problem with a paper manuscript or an iPad is that they come between the pastor and the congregation. They function as a barrier between the preacher as communicator and the congregation as communicators. If a preacher is looking at his iPad, by definition, he is not looking at and reading the congregation.

No one has ever argued that one can communicate better with a congregation by gazing at paper.

If the minister writes out his sermon as a long essay and then reads it, he will spend much time looking at his document. We all know that when someone keeps looking away from us in personal conversation, we feel like he is not giving us his full attention.

Has anyone ever argued that it is better for a person to look away from a person with whom they are engaging in personal conversation? Has anyone ever argued that it is better for a preacher to have his eyes on his manuscript that on the congregation? Has anyone ever argued that it is better for a minister to preach with his eyes closed rather than look at his congregants? Your eyes communicate. Your auditors are looking you in the eye. It is a serious error for a preacher to avoid the eyes of the members of the congregation.

Spurgeon did not preach with an iPad because he knew that the classical rhetoricians never argued that the reading of a prepared document trumped an extemporaneous delivery. By an extemporaneous delivery I do not mean a message that involved no preparation. Spurgeon wanted nothing to do with what we can call "impromptu speech." Impromptu speaking is speaking without preparation.

Spurgeon devotes a lecture to the topic of "The Faculty of Impromptu Speech."[14] In this lecture Spurgeon challenges those who would go into the pulpit without preparation, although he talks about the value of developing impromptu speaking for special occasions. It is unfortunate that Spurgeon never gives us a lecture on the topic of extemporaneous preaching as he conceived it--preaching that involved serious biblical, theological, and spiritual preparation. In this lecture he mentions that he would speak on this topic at a different time, although we do not find records of such a lecture on the four volumes of the published *Lectures to my Students*. This is what Spurgeon says at the end of this lecture on impromptu speaking:

> I might have said much more if I had extended the subject to what is *usually called* extempore preaching, that is to say, the preparation of the sermon so far as thoughts go, and leaving the words to be found during delivery; but this is quite another matter, and although looked upon as a great attainment by some, it is, as I believe, an indispensable requisite for the pulpit, and by no means a mere luxury of talent; but of this we will speak on another occasion.

The subject of his lecture on impromptu speech was "extemporaneous speech in its truest and most thorough form—speech impromptu, without special preparation, without notes or immediate forethought." Thankfully, Spurgeon does actually have things to say about extemporaneous preaching (as he rightly conceives of it) in this lecture as well.

Why does Spurgeon want to lecture his theological students on impromptu speech? Two reasons. First, he rejects impromptu preaching. Second, he believes that practicing and improving one's impromptu speaking abilities can be useful in certain contexts. Spurgeon has in the back of his mind the fact that the practice of impromptu speaking will equip the minister to engage in extemporaneous preaching—where one exercises spontaneity and linguistic freedom in how one communicates the ideas in the text.

Spurgeon rejects what happens in Pentecostal churches where preachers deliberately do not prepare for the sermon, imagining that the Spirit will give them a message apart from them rightly dividing the Word of truth. He observes about radical impromptu speaking, that he *"would not recommend any man to attempt preaching in this style as a general rule."*[15] The result of doing so is that the preacher

---

[14] Ibid., 151.
[15] Ibid., 151.

Would succeed, we think, most certainly, in producing a vacuum in his meeting-house; his gifts of dispersion would be clearly manifested. Unstudied thoughts coming from the mind without previous research, without the subjects in hand having been investigated at all, must be of a very inferior quality, even from the most superior men; and as none of us would have the effrontery to glorify ourselves as men of genius or wonders of erudition, I fear that our unpremeditated thoughts upon most subjects would not be remarkably worthy of attention.[16]

Spurgeon tells us that "The Holy Spirit has made no promise to supply spiritual food to the saints by an impromptu ministry." Yet, Spurgeon does find value in the development of impromptu speaking. "The power of impromptu speech is invaluable, because it enables a man on the spur of the moment, in an emergency, to deliver himself with propriety."[17] He identifies certain lawyers as communicators who have developed extemporaneous speaking abilities "because it would be impossible for them always to foresee the line of argument which the evidence, or the temper of the judge, or the pleadings on the other side would require."[18] Spurgeon shames preachers who will not work at impromptu speech like the "gentlemen of the bar" do:

> What a barrister can do in advocating the cause of his client, you and I should surely be able to do in the cause of God. The bar must not be allowed to excel the pulpit. We will be as expert in intellectual arms as any men, be they who they may, God helping us.[19]

Spurgeon mentions how politicians in the House of Commons "have exercised the faculty of extemporaneous speaking with great results."[20] As a rule, the ability to engage in impromptu speaking is a lost art among American politicians. The livelier environment of the House of Commons today, compared to the United States House of Representatives, continues to value impromptu speeches. Spurgeon once again shames preachers: "Shall the representatives of the nation attain an expertness of speech beyond the representatives of the court of heaven?"

---

[16] Ibid., 150.
[17] Ibid., 155.
[18] Ibid., 154.
[19] Ibid., 154.
[20] Ibid., 154.

Spurgeon tells us that he made a practice of giving a more or less impromptu speech at a weekday evening prayer service. But even here, his speaking was not entirely impromptu, since he spoke on some topic that had interested him of late, on which he had meditated, or about which he had read. He also chose a Biblical text or topic that was not so complex. Spurgeon tells us:

> Ever since I have been in London, in order to get into the habit of speaking extemporaneously, I have never studied or prepared anything for the Monday evening prayer-meeting. I have all along selected that occasion as the opportunity for off-hand exhortation; but you will observe that I don't on such occasions select difficult expository topics, or abstruse themes, but restrict myself to simple, homely talk, about the elements of our faith.

Spurgeon realizes that a preacher might covet the gift of impromptu communication. He challenges the lazy preacher who covets this gift:

> You are all convinced that the ability which we are considering must be a priceless possession for a minister. Did we hear a single heart whisper, "I wish I had it, for then I should have no need to study so arduously"? Ah! Then you must not have it, you are unworthy of the boon, and unfit to be trusted with it. If you seek this gift as a pillow for an idle head, you will be much mistaken; for the possession of this noble power will involve you in a vast amount of labour in order to increase and even to retain it....What the sluggard desires for the sake of ease, we may however covet for the best of reasons.

Not everybody will have the gift of impromptu speaking. Spurgeon admits that "*some men will never obtain it.*"[21] He adds: "There must be a natural adaptedness for extemporaneous speech; even as for the poetic art: a poet is born, not made."[22] Some preachers do not have as intelligent minds as others. Some do not have the ability to think things through deeply for themselves—they depend on the commentators or what their seminary professors taught them. Some are perfectionists who are fearful of saying a wrong word and are therefore tied to their manuscripts with an iron chain. Others are too shy to dare to look into the eyes of the congregation and speak directly to them.

---

[21] Ibid., 156.
[22] Ibid., 156.

If a preacher does not like to read, he will not fill his mind with the pregnant thoughts that could be uttered in extemporaneous speaking. Spurgeon says:

> *If a man would speak without any present study, he must usually study much....*You will not be able to extemporize good thinking unless you have been in the habit of thinking and feeding your mind with abundant and nourishing food. Work hard at every available moment. Store your minds very richly, and then, like merchants with crowded warehouses, you will have goods ready for your customers, and having arranged your good things upon the shelves of your mind, you will be able to hand them down at any time without the laborious process of going to market, sorting, folding, and preparing. I do not believe that any man can be successful in continuously maintaining the gift of extemporaneous speech, except by ordinarily using far more labour than is usual with those who write and commit their discourses to memory. Take it as a rule without exception, that to be able to overflow spontaneously you must be full.

One can only speak effectively in an impromptu manner about a subject if he has wrapped his mind around it. If a preacher doesn't grow theologically, he will lack this gift: "Ignorance of theology is no rare thing in our pulpits, and the wonder is not that so few men are extempore speakers, but that so many are, when theologians are so scarce. We shall never have great preachers till we have great divines."[23] Spurgeon wants the preacher to wrap his soul around spiritual ideas: "Get at the roots of spiritual truths by an experimental acquaintance with them, so shall you with readiness expound them to others."

Spurgeon is convinced that anyone should be able to "speak extemporaneously upon a subject which he fully understands."[24] "Good impromptu speech is just the utterance of a practiced thinker," Spurgeon tells us.[25] Spurgeon almost gives us a proverb when he states: "Do not attempt to be impromptu then, unless you have well studied the them—this paradox is a counsel of prudence."[26]

---

[23] Ibid., 158.
[24] Ibid., 159.
[25] Ibid., 161.
[26] Ibid., 159.

The classical rhetoricians understood that a lawyer or politician would make preparation for giving a speech before the law court or the senate. But the speech would not be an essay written out in detail ahead of time. Rather the speaker would study the issues and consider how to present a convincing argument that would move the court or assembly. But in the act of delivery the speaker would have freedom to develop his argument in response to his audience, new arguments, opposing counsel, and the changing context. No classical rhetorician ever argued that it was better to read a prepared document word for word rather than allow the speaker to develop his message in the act of speaking. Spurgeon agrees with this approach:

> Viewing the whole matter from all quarters, the preacher should think it out, get it well masticated and digested; and having first fed upon the word himself should then prepare the like nutriment for others. Our sermons should be our mental life-blood—the out-flow of our intellectual and spiritual vigour; or, to change the figure, they should be diamonds well cut and well set—precious, intrinsically, and bearing the marks of labour. God forbid that we should offer to the Lord that which costs us nothing.[27]

Spurgeon exhorts the preacher: Don't read your sermon. He does advocate great preparation for the act of preaching. He recommends that the minister write out his sermon ahead of time. Seminary students and preachers need to listen to this strong warning from Spurgeon:

> Very strongly do I warn all of you against reading your sermons, but I recommend, as a most healthful exercise, and as a great aid towards attaining extemporizing power, the frequent writing of them. Those of us who write a great deal in other forms, for the press, *et cetera*, may not so much require that exercise; but if you do not use the pen in other ways, you will be wise to write at least some of your sermons, and revise them with great care. Leave them at home afterwards, but still write them out, that you may be preserved from a slipshod style. M. Bautain in his admirable work on extempore speaking, remarks, "You will never be capable of speaking properly in public unless you acquire such mastery of your own thought as to be able to decompose it into its parts, to analyse it into its elements, and then, at need, to re-compose, re-gather, and concentrate it again by a synthetical process....The pen is the scalpel which dissects the thoughts, and never, except when you write down what you behold internally, can you succeed in clearly discerning all that is contained in a conception, or in obtaining its well-marked scope. You then understand yourself, and make

---

[27] Ibid., 152.

others understand you."[28]

Spurgeon wants nothing to do with a preacher memorizing his sermon word for word so that he can recite it from memory in the pulpit.

> We do not recommend the plan of learning sermons by heart, and repeating them from memory, that is both a wearisome exercise of an inferior power of the mind and an indolent neglect of other and superior faculties.[29]

Spurgeon does recommend extemporaneous preaching. He admits that this approach is the most difficult method of preaching.The most arduous and commendable plan is to store your mind with matter upon the subject of discourse, and then to deliver yourself with appropriate words which suggest themselves at the time. This is not extemporaneous preaching; the words are extemporal, as I think they always should be, but the thoughts are the result of research and study. Only thoughtless persons think this to be easy; it is at once the most laborious and the most efficient mode of preaching, and it has virtues of its own of which I cannot now speak particularly, since it would lead us away from the point in hand.[30]

It is too bad that we do not have a lecture in which Spurgeon speaks more "particularly" on his own method of preaching. It would be nice to see him expand on what he implies in this lecture about extemporaneous preaching.

That Spurgeon does have preaching in mind is evident from a warning that he gives about the danger of a preacher losing the gift of extemporaneous preaching.

Spurgeon tells us that the preacher needs to work at maintaining the power of extemporaneous speech. Spurgeon is talking about extemporaneous preaching (and not merely giving an impromptu talk) when he states:

> If for two successive Sundays I make my notes a little longer and fuller than usual, I find on the third occasion that I require them longer still; and I also observe that if on occasions I lean a little more to my recollection of my thoughts, and am not so extemporaneous as I have been accustomed to be, there is a direct craving and even an increased

---

[28] Ibid., 152-53.
[29] Ibid., 153.
[30] Ibid., 152.

necessity for pre-composition.[31]

If even the Prince of Preachers confesses the danger that he makes his paper into a crutch, how much more do we lesser mortals need to fear this danger. Spurgeon says that "If you are happy enough to acquire the power of extemporary speech, pray recollect that *you may very readily lose it.*"[32] So Spurgeon warns:

> You must continually practice extemporizing, and if to gain suitable opportunities you should frequently speak the word in cottages, in the school-rooms of our hamlets, or to two or three by the wayside, your profiting shall be known unto all men.[33]

But how can the preacher gain the ability to present extemporaneous sermons? How can the preacher who has fallen into the bad habit of reading his sermons, extricate himself from this error? I shall argue that the preacher can learn how to deliver extemporaneous sermons as he learns how to internalize the message of his text.

---

[31] Ibid., 164.
[32] Ibid., 164.
[33] Ibid., 164.

Chapter 2
Internalize, Don't Memorize

You have completed your sermon outline. You translated your text out of the Hebrew or Greek. You reflected on the main point of your text. You prayed that God would give you insight into the text—and the Holy Spirit has helped you to understand the message of God in it. You wrote your exegesis paper. You figured out the homiletics of the sermon. You completed your outline. You developed a unified and organized message. Now what? How do you prepare for delivering your sermon? There is a crucial distinction between the act of writing a sermon and the act of preaching.

On Pentecost Sunday, the Apostle Peter did not recite a speech from memory. Filled with the Holy Spirit, the apostle proclaimed the message of Christ crucified and resurrected. He spoke with freedom---now filled with an amazing understanding of the significance of the crucifixion and resurrection of Jesus of Nazareth.

It is one thing to have a completed sermon outline and it is another thing to preach the sermon. I am concerned with the act of preaching and how the preacher prepares for the act of preaching. If preaching is an oral event that involves live communication with a congregation, then the preparation for it will be different from that of an author preparing to give a book reading at Eerdmans. I once listened to Garrison Keillor do a poetry reading in the gym at Calvin College. He simply read poetry that he had memorized. He repeated it word for word. I far prefer his dynamic, extemporaneous story-telling about Lake Wobegan where the women are strong, the men are good-looking, and the children are far above average.

I am certain that you could have two men work together on exegesis— and work together on putting together a sermon outline—but they would each deliver the sermon in a very different way—one man might communicate very well and in a lively manner while the other man might be boring and making the text seem uninteresting. Why? If the men are both working from good outlines, the difference would involve both their unique personalities, their delivery, and the extent to which they internalized the message. Preaching is not writing an essay or even writing an outline; preaching is communicating the Word of God in a lively manner by a unique person to a specific audience.

Internalization not Memorization

You should not memorize your sermon. The impulse to memorize a sermon might come from the fact that one should not read his sermon to the congregation. You should not read your sermon. Let the philosophers at their academic symposiums read their technically argued papers to one another. I think of the times that I sat through mind-numbingly boring readings of philosophy papers at the University of Wisconsin. I not only needed to endure these boring papers that were presented by philosophers who did not know how to communicate, but then I had to watch these proud philosophers defend themselves. Talk about sensitive egos.

I have only heard one preacher in my life who was able to read a sermon almost like he had internalized it. Astoundingly he was able to get his emotions involved. He was able to sound earnest and lively even as he reads his sermon word for word. Even then the hearer knows that nothing is spontaneous; it is evident that the preacher is bound by what is written on the paper.

Reciting a memorized sermon is a denial of preaching as an oral event. It denies the reality of what should occur: live, personal communication between the preacher and congregation. It involves a caricature of what true preaching is.

Preaching is an oral event. Preaching as an oral event must involve oral communication. A preacher must be above all a communicator of the Word of God. Preaching is the communication of the Word in the power of the Holy Spirit to the congregation through a uniquely gifted man. One is only partially trying to communicate when he reads a sermon. The congregation is not just interested in what the preacher told his computer in the study, but what the preacher wants to tell them in the moment of the encounter between preacher and auditors.

There is another problem with memorization: When the preacher is trying to remember, you can see his eyeballs rolling back in his head! I vividly remember watching a seminary student in practice preaching class at the Protestant Reformed Seminary deliver a sermon by repeating word for word what he installed in his mind through rote memorization. His eyes literally rolled upwards when he came to points where he had a hard time recalling the exact language he had memorized.

Worse yet, the person who just tells you what he memorized is not speaking from his heart!

And what if you lose your place!

Internalize, don't memorize!

In preparation for delivering your sermon, you should not merely memorize what you want to say, but you need to internalize the message. Certainly this does involve memorization. But it is a different kind of memorization from simply trying to remember what words and sentences to say. Smith in *Extempore Preaching* writes: "The best way is, to attempt no memorizing of sentences or words whatever. Let the mind be entirely concentrated on the ideas to be developed, and the end to be accomplished by the sermon."[34]

Internalization involves a personal understanding of the message and how it relates to your life and that of your hearers. The glory and beauty of internalization is that it forces the minister to take the message into his own heart, mind, and soul. Internalize the message as you work hard on the text and concentrate on understanding the meaning so that you have clarity about what God is saying in the text.

Go into the pulpit with the assurance that you have studied the text in the English and Greek (or Hebrew) Bibles so that you have clarity about what God is saying. Know your text well in the original language and in the English translation. If the text is short, memorize it. Hide God's Word in your heart. The more you understand the text, the easier it is to remember what the text is teaching. In a sense we have only hidden God's Word in our hearts when we have done more than memorize it, but also have come to understand what it means and how it applies to our lives. When the Bible tells us to hide God's Word in our hearts it is not referring to the bare memorization that a Tom Sawyer might do just because his Sunday school teacher requires it.

The greater the clarity you have in your own mind about what the text means, the easier to remember and memorize. Even if it is a longer text, become familiar with the key words, phrases, and statements in it. Knowing your text in English translation is like watching a black and white TV. Memorize the passage in English and you will be able to meditate on it. Know it in the Greek or Hebrew and you will have great clarity and a more profound understanding of the meaning and connotations in the passage, like what comes with watching TV on a color television. Our English translations as a rule are quite faithful to the original text. But the original

---

[34] Smith, *Extempore Preaching*, 99.

23

language shed additional light on the English translation. The greater clarity you have about the Scriptures, the better you will be able to communicate the message.

I have learned that I can only preach with confidence after I have digested the meaning of the passage in the original language. Once I have grasped the meaning and connotation of the main verbs and the implication of their tenses, voices, and moods do I comprehend the text.

Do the hard work of concentrating on the text so that you have clarity in your mind about what the text says. Then you will be able to communicate the message with simplicity. Hughes Oliphant Old wrote:

Although Calvin is never thought of as a great orator, he did have some important gifts of public speaking. He seems to have had an intensity which he focused on the text of Scripture which was so powerful that he drew his hearers into the sacred text along with him.

This intensity comes from his tremendous power of concentration. It is this same sort of concentration, of course, which enabled him to preach without notes or manuscript. One can be sure that he carefully studied the text beforehand and consulted the commentaries of others on the passage. His commentaries show how thoroughly he had studied the text. Yet the sermon itself was put together before the congregation.

This was, of course, the way the great preachers of the patristic age had worked. Calvin followed the same method. Concentrating both on the passage at hand and on the congregation before him, he drew out of his well-stocked memory the meaning of the Holy Scriptures for his people.[35]

The more clearly you perceive what God is saying in the text, the better you will be able to internalize the message. You will not just be depending on what the commentators thought the text meant. Hughes Oliphant Olds comments on Abraham Kuyper's preaching:

The value of Kuyper's preaching was the depths of his perception into Scripture. He looked into scripture so much more deeply than his contemporaries. The Enlightenment thought it had thrown new light on the sacred text, but it was a light of its own making. Kuyper understood that the texts possess their own light, an inner light that shines out of them. It is a light not of our making, but a gracious light

---

[35] Hughes Oliphant Old, The Reading and Preaching of the Scriptures in the Worship of the Christian Church: Volume 4: The Age of the Reformation (Grand Rapids: Eerdmans, 2002), 129.

that only God can supply.[36]

The more you understand a text—the easier it will be to communicate it. The more you wrap your mind around it, the greater your ability to communicate about it in your own words. You will not have to depend on how you formulated the ideas in your study.

It is not difficult to prepare a confusing speech. It is simplicity that takes hard work. It is difficult to have a message that is clear, but hard work pays rich dividends. You need to search for accurate expression. The right word can be hard to find. Use brevity of statement in your main points in the outline.

Some preachers deliver sermons with muddled heads. How do I know this? The lack of clarity. The lack of simplicity. The lack of one main point. The lack of clear exegetical answers to the challenging ideas in the text. It is easier to read a muddled sermon than to deliver a muddled sermon extemporaneously. The problem with delivering a muddled sermon extemporaneously is that the preacher does not have a clear and vivid idea of what the text says and doesn't have a clear sense of the logic in the text that needs to come out in the sermon. In plain English: he doesn't know what to say next. There is good reason why muddle-headed preachers need to read their muddled sermons.

It is easier to remember the ideas in a message that is laid out in a clear and simple way. The congregation will not be able to remember a long and complex sentence, even if you tell them at the beginning of the sermon that it is your thesis statement sentence. The title of your sermon must be simple, clear, and memorable. Your divisions (three points) should be simple. A clear and logical organization of your sermon will make it preachable! It is easier to remember a logical development of the message than an illogical and haphazardly organized sermon.

Some preachers preach like they have a radical case of Attention Deficit Hyperactivity Disorder. They swerve off subject at their fancy. I tell my students that they ought not to wander off on side trails. They need to keep to the main trails.

---

[36] Hughes Oliphant Old, The Reading and Preaching of the Scriptures in the Worship of the Christian Church: Volume 6: The Modern Age (Grand Rapids: Eerdmans, 2007), 52.

I admit that there is room for taking the congregation off on little side trails to make some big points or to retain attention, but the whole idea is to take them along on a trip down one central lane. How do you stay on a path that leads logically from the beginning of the sermon to the middle and then to a conclusion? The answer: you have a main point that you are developing logically throughout the sermon. You are taking the congregation from a beginning location to a destination.

The beauty of a logical outline is that it helps you to organize your message so that you deal with the appropriate topic at the appropriate place (and only there!).

Can I repeat that?

You deal with the appropriate topic (and section of the text) at the appropriate time and in the appropriate way. And only there!

And then you move one.

And you don't come back and beat a dead horse.

A good outline will allow the congregation to sense constant forward progress. Retrogression or a lack of logical progress weighs on the minds of hearers. When I am listening to a sermon where the minister talks about one concept in his text for five minutes and then twenty minutes later returns to the same idea, I know what he is doing. He is beating a dead horse. I recognize that there is room for repetition and that one can refer to what he has already developed so that he can later build on that idea. But this is different from a scatterbrained approach to preaching where you deal with a topic, leave it, and then return to the same topic again.

Logic on Fire

John Piper has said that good preaching is "Logic on fire." Even George Whitefield's friends admitted that his sermons were often poorly organized. Hughes Oliphant Olds states that "They lacked structure and meandered from topic to topic."[37] This was a weakness.

Make sure that you do not go to the other extreme of having logic without vitality. This means that you have started giving lectures.

---

[37] Hughes Oliphant Old, The Reading and Preaching of the Scriptures in the Worship of the Christian Church: Volume 5. Moderatism, Pietism, and Awakening (Grand Rapids: Eerdmans, 2004), 153.

An outline also helps you to see where in your message the momentum will build. You can see at a glance what the big points are in your message and what the minor points are. This helps you to keep things in perspective as you present the message. The more organized your sermon outline is, the easier it will be for you to internalize the logic of your message. Charles Koller says: "The better the outline, the greater is the likelihood of its not being needed in the pulpit."[38] As you internalize the logic of your sermon, you are also in a position to burn with the flame of zeal in your presentation. After all, you are making an important argument. You are going somewhere. Plus what you are saying is building on what you have already said. The congregation will know that they are not meandering around in circles.

Repent to Internalize

How do you internalize the message in the text so that you can preach it from the heart?

First, repent of your sins. Pray that the Holy Spirit would use the Scripture text to convict you of your sins and your lack of love for God and man. David Murray writes that: "No amount of theological substance or oratorical skills will make up for a preacher's lack of personal holiness."[39]

I have found that Saturday and Sunday are times of repentance for me. I repent of my sins in preparing the sermon. I repent of my sins and shortcomings in light of what God's law demands in the passage. I have a profound awareness of the fact that I am unworthy to speak the pure and holy Word of the living God. Apply the sermon message to yourself and your own life. Grieve that you do not do what God requires in the text.

The preacher's character is vital for how the congregation will hear his message. Grow in godliness so that you preach as a godly man. Your message is tied up with your identity. Just as you are what you eat, you are spiritually what you eat. Your reading and meditation of Scripture, your life experiences, and your theological growth will shape the person you are.

Seminary cannot make a preacher.

---

[38] Charles Koller, How to Preach without Notes (Grand Rapids: Baker Books, 2007), 92.
[39] David Murray, How Sermons Work (Darlington, England: Publishing with a Mission, 2011), 135.

A preacher is the slow result of the maturation of a covenant boy who begins to grow in grace as a child. He is the result of the loving mentorship of covenant parents. He is the result of loving Christian school teachers and college professors who help to disciple him. A preacher is the result of the godly influence that his wife plays in his life. A preacher is shaped by the rearing of his children. Raising teenagers help to continue the preacher's development.

Martin Luther thought that in order to be a doctor of theology one needed to suffer. God uses the suffering and trials of men to develop them into the preachers that he wants them to be. The love, commitment, and hope of the preacher are virtues that the Holy Spirit develops over time. God uses many obedient choices as a means of building godly character. All of the above goes into the development of the preacher's identity and character. There are no shortcuts to such spiritual maturity.

Sometimes God will save a man as an adult. Yet still all of the man's background was ordained by God in such a way as to prepare the man to preach the gospel of grace. God can cause adult converts to rapidly mature in grace so that they can be equipped for gospel ministry. But this does not challenge my underlying thesis that the boy is father of the man. Christ develops and matures the men whom He calls to gospel ministry.

What preachers preach is what they are.

Preachers are men who have come to know God in the face of Jesus Christ.

They preach out of their maturing Christian experience and their celebration of grace.

You will grow as you apply the Word to your own heart and life.

Pray to Internalize

The second way to internalize the Scriptural message is to pray. Pray that God would enable you to do what He commands. I have found that prayer before preaching is not a difficult thing. My heart cries out to God for help. Away with super confident preachers. I am aware of my weakness and my need for God's help. Hughes Oliphant Old explains why Augustine thinks the minister must pray: "It is because God is ultimately the source of wisdom that in the beginning and in the end we must seek it from him in prayer."[40]

---

[40] Hughes Oliphant Old, The Reading and Preaching of the Scriptures in the Worship of the Christian Church: Volume 2. The Patristic Age (Grand Rapids: Eerdmans, 1998), 393.

When leading congregational prayers, pray from your heart. Do not just write out your prayer—and then read it word for word. You do not talk to your earthly father like this! Yes, make notes about matters that should be included in congregational prayer; but also internalize these issues too so that you pray in an appropriate and fitting way.

Beseech God for help. Pray for the grace to communicate the Word of God. Ask that God would take away your fear about public speaking, your fear of criticism, and the fear of man. Pray for courage if you are preaching a truth that might be opposed.

Pray to be filled with the Spirit so that in your heart and soul you celebrate the realities that you are about to preach.

Doxological preaching will involve a celebration of God, His truth, and what He has accomplished. If you do not rejoice in what the text teaches, why should the congregation? If there is no joy in your heart and no smile on your face, why in the world should they smile with joy in response to your message?

Pray that God would give you joy in Him and His Word. Drink in the grace that Christ has shown to you!

Old explains Augustine's approach: "When the hour is come for the preacher to mount the pulpit, he must lift up his thirsty soul to God, to drink in what he is about to pour forth and to be himself filled with what he is about to distribute."[41]

Edit to Internalize

A third way to internalize the message is by continuing to edit the sermon as you go over it in preparation for preaching. Cheah Fook Ming, a Singaporean who attended seminary with me, once said: "Sermons are best served hot—just like Chinese food!" A preacher will find out that if he preaches a sermon for a second time, he will need to get back into the message in order to communicate it with any passion. As you throw yourself into your message, let your heart burn. Then when you preach, the message will flame forth with burning zeal. And the saints will get a hot meal!

---

[41] Hughes Oliphant Old, The Reading and Preaching of the Scriptures in the Worship of the Christian Church: Volume 2. The Patristic Age (Grand Rapids: Eerdmans, 1998), 396.

To use another food analogy, taste the food before you feed the children. Taste the good news before you feed the congregation. If you have a toddler who will not open his mouth for the spoon of food, what do you do? Dad or Mom can taste the food and show the baby how good it tastes. If Daddy likes the food, then the toddler will willingly open his mouth too. So taste the good news and when the congregation sees that for you God's word is sweeter than honey, they will open their mouths as well.

As you edit your sermon, simplify, simplify, simplify. Old states: "The truth itself, Augustine tells us, when presented in simplicity, gives pleasure because it is the truth."[42]

Clarify. Clarify. Clarify.

Develop metaphors. Metaphors make abstract doctrine concrete. Metaphors connect two fields of discourse. They communicate not just to the mind, but also to the heart. Nathan the prophet was so effective in calling King David to repentance because he used the metaphor of a rich neighbor stealing a poor man's sheep. I like analogies like the following: "You can't merit salvation by good works any more than a spider web can stop a falling rock."

Write with a pen in the margins of your paper outline so that key points in your outline jump off the page even more! I advise you not to use an iPad or a large tablet. The problem with tablets is that you do not have a piece of paper on which you can write, circle things, and underline important ideas. It is true that you can use yellow highlighting on tablets, but you can't usually write in the margins—and if you would, there would be less space for your text.

The biggest problem with a tablet is that you have a limited amount of text in front of you.

You will need to change pages far more than if you use a normal piece of paper. With a normal size of paper you can see a good amount of your outline at a glance. On my printed outline, I never have letters smaller than size 12. I also use Times New Roman because the curves on this font make it readable. Above all you want a font that is large enough and readable so that you can see your notes at the simplest glance.

You need to see what your main points and subpoints are at a glance.

The whole idea is not to depend on your paper.

You want to know what is coming.

---

[42] Hughes Oliphant Old, The Reading and Preaching of the Scriptures in the Worship of the Christian Church: Volume 2. The Patristic Age (Grand Rapids: Eerdmans, 1998), 395.

At a glance you want to see where you need to go next (if, unfortunately, you have not memorized and internalized the next step).

As you work in the word document on your computer, you can use bold print or italics to emphasize important ideas that you might have a hard time memorizing or a statement that you want to say precisely as you wrote it. I place these important ideas in both bold print and italics. They stand out.

Italicize and bold print key words, phrases, or sentences that can jog your memory so that you can communicate in a lively way without being tied to your paper.

Meditate on your sermon so you clearly see more and more what the key points are. Continue to work on the logic and flow of your message—so that you know what should come first and what should come next.

Make sure that your transitions work well. You must avoid awkward transitions like simply announcing "Now we turn to the second point." Any time that you feel the need to announce that you are quitting the first point and starting the second point, it probably is because you do not have a logical transition. Awkward transitions occur when there is a lack of logic in the sermon. I find that when preachers simply announce that they are now turning to the second point it is because the first and second point are actually parallel in value and logic. Instead of the first point being a development of the main idea of the text, the first point probably was half of what should have been in the first point while the second point is the missing half of what should have been back in the first point. I regularly hear sermons where the first, second, and even third points are actually logically parallel and all the material should have been included in a first point.

As you preach, remember that your audience cannot see your outline. They cannot see that you are moving from a major point to a subpoint. So you need to somehow communicate what is central and what is subservient. They cannot see that you are moving from the second point to the third point, so you have to let them know when you are.

The danger is that the minister assumes that the congregation has all of the information that he has. They do not. When you read a text, you can always reread something that you do not understand. The congregation does not have the opportunity to do this as you deliver your oral sermon. They cannot rewind you so that they can listen to what you said earlier. Therefore, there certainly is room for giving emphasis to what needs to be emphasized and using a proper repetition so that the congregation understands what is important and what you want them to remember.

Help the congregation to under the logic of your sermon. Help them to understand the main point. You probably can't announce the main point of your sermon often enough. You want the very language of your main point (theme/title) to sink into their heads. You want them to understand the logic of your argument. When you have demonstrated something and drawn conclusions, there is nothing wrong with summarizing this at the end of a point. John Piper is a master at this.

Chapter 3
The Goal of Internalization: Freedom in the Act of Preaching

The goal of internalization is to communicate the living Word of God in a lively way to a congregation in the act of preaching. To say it another way, the goal of internalization is to enjoy freedom in the act of preaching.

If you internalize, rather than memorize your message, you will be able to enjoy freedom in the act of preaching. This freedom is the liberty of spontaneity.

An iPad screen is a barrier to the live communication that ought to be occurring between the preacher and congregation in the preaching event. When the preacher is dependent on his iPad, the screen functions as a psychological barrier between the preacher and his audience. There is something that is fresh and alive when a man is communicating directly to a congregation, looking at them, reading their response, and doing the hard work of attempting to communicate with them.

A minister enjoys freedom in the act of preaching when he has internalized the message such that he can speak from the heart with authority and power in the Holy Spirit. In the moment of delivery he can speak openly to the congregation. He is able to express his sorrow over sin, his sense of jealousy for the glory of Jesus Christ, or His triumphant celebration of Jesus' victory at the cross.

The congregation automatically knows that the minister is communicating to them. How different it is when a minister's eyes are on his paper. The congregation knows when the minister is just reading what he typed into his computer on Thursday. The congregation notices whether the minister notices that they are getting sleepy and bored. The congregation feels that the message would not change in the least even if every one of them suddenly snuck down into the church basement. They could listen in through the speaker system in the basement nursery and still hear the same message with the same tones and same application. Nothing would change.

View the sermon as an oral event. But it is different from an oral event like a book reading. At a book reading you do not expect anything new from the author. The author simply reads a chapter out of her book. I agree that the author does verbally communicate the gathered readers. But the author communicates with her faithful readers by simply doing her best to read her text in a lively way that best communicates its sense.

A minister is not captive to his prepare notes. Ministers who are prisoners to their prepared notes come across as perfectionists. They are wooden. The congregation wants them to speak from the heart. It appears that the minister has not adequately internalized the message so that he can put it into his own simple words in the act of preaching. But if the minister cannot simply put his message into his own words in the midst of the congregation, how does the preacher ever expect the saints to be able to take this message and share it with their neighbors?

If the minister cannot internalize the message after a week of meditating on it, how can the members of the congregation internalize the message after listening to a 40 minute sermon? It ain't going to happen.

In the act of preaching you are verbally communicating to the congregation. They are not reading your outline! They are not following along in a book. Hughes Oliphant Old writes about the Prince of Preachers:

> Spurgeon had a high respect for preaching as an oral event. When any true orator speaks, there is an encounter that involves people in a way in which they are not involved with a simple reading of a text....As much preparation of the text as he may have made before the entered the pulpit, the actual sermon was worked out between the preacher and the congregation as the sermon progressed.[43]

Spurgeon is right that in the act of preaching there is an encounter between the preacher and the congregation. The actual sermon must be worked out within this dynamic context between the preacher and the congregation. Sermons are dry when the preacher works them out ahead of time in his study and is fearful to work them out in the act of preaching. The sermon seems stale and artificial.

You cannot assume that your audience will listen to you even if you read your sermon. You cannot assume that your audience will pay attention if you treat preaching like the reading of a dry lecture. You need to earn the right to be heard.

---

[43] Hughes Oliphant Old, The Reading and Preaching of the Scriptures in the Worship of the Christian Church: Volume 6. The Modern Age (Grand Rapids: Eerdmans, 2007), 440.

If you do not write well—do not expect that others will want to read what you write. You need to write in such a way that you draw an audience of readers.

For the congregation, the sermon is an oral event. You must speak from the heart. Then the congregation will wake up and listen.

Normally when you talk to someone, you look at them. It is always uncomfortable if you are with a person and they cannot look you in the eye. When someone cannot look you in the eye, you wonder what is wrong. Is there a psychological problem? Is the person afraid of being analyzed? Are they telling the truth? Where there is a healthy bond between parents and children, children can look into their parent's eyes.

If you have a healthy bond with your congregation, you can look at them. They need to know that you are talking to them. If you look at the back of the church instead of your audience, they will know. The very way that you preach will betray that you are avoiding the eyes of the congregation.

If you have internalized the message, you can look at the congregation rather than at your iPad. One thing that stands out with preaching as oral communication rather than reading an essay is that you can repeat yourself. In writing you need to be careful how you repeat yourself. But if you are an author, you know that the person reading your book or article can back up if they want to re-read something. But your congregation cannot hit reverse. So if you want to keep an idea before their minds, feel free to use repetition. Say it again. Say it another way. Say it a better way. Say it in a more memorable way. Work at it.

Communicate with your congregation, but also read what they are communicating back to you and respond by communicating in a contextual way!

View the act of preaching as two-way communication between you and the congregation.

The preaching event needs to be communication between the preacher and the congregation. Hughes Oliphant Old writes about the great Roman and Greek orators:

> During the actual delivery the orator needed to read the audience, and he could hardly do that if he were reading a manuscript. The spontaneous quality of oratory is of its essence. It is fundamentally an encounter between speaker and listener.[44]

Old is correct in saying that "The spontaneous quality of oratory is of its essence." The problem with a preacher who reads his sermon is that he lacks this spontaneity. He is not talking from the heart. He is not formulating fresh ideas as they come to his mind. His preaching lacks spontaneity and, therefore, is missing something that is of the essence of oratory.

Martyn Lloyd-Jones emphasized the necessity of two-way communication:

> Another element to which I attach importance is that the preacher while speaking should in a sense be deriving something from his congregation.

> There are those present in the congregation who are spiritually-minded people, and filled with the Spirit, and they make their contribution to the occasion. There is always an element of exchange in true preaching.[45]

It is precisely for this reason that I enjoy preaching in some churches more than others. In some churches there is a holy expectation and excitement to hear the preaching of the Word.

Lloyd-Jones wondered whether there could be good preaching without a good congregation. The congregation contributes to the act of preaching. They engage in the act of listening and responding.

The act of listening is an act of worship. The worship of the congregation in the act of listening will have an impact on the preacher. It will inspire him. It will rejoice his soul. The gladness of the saints will bring the preacher to greater heights of joy.

When the saints experience a deep sense of the majesty of God, the preacher will enjoy the royal sovereignty of God more than he might have.

The congregation contributes to the preaching event.

Sometimes the congregation contributes by communicating to the preacher that their attention has been lost. Then the preacher can get to work and try to capture their attention again. Again and again I see new

---

[44] Hughes Oliphant Old, The Reading and Preaching of the Scriptures in the Worship of the Christian Church: Volume 2. The Patristic Age (Grand Rapids: Eerdmans, 1998), 395.

[45] Martyn Lloyd-Jones, Preaching and Preachers, (Grand Rapids: Zondervan, 1972), 84.

preachers who lose the attention of the congregation and seem blissfully unaware of it. They do nothing to try to regain attention. They do not seem to know or care whether the congregation is actively listening to their sermon or not. Such ministers could preach as well to sleeping congregations as well as to potentially responsive ones.

All such ministers should be sent off to Randolph, Wisconsin to preach in the Protestant Reformed Church where I once counted 12 men asleep by the time I got finished reading the Scriptural passage before the sermon. It was a 2:00 p.m. afternoon service in the winter. The sleepers were farmers. I don't do well preaching to a church with sleeping people because I am aware of the snoozers. I realize that they are ignoring the Word of God. It bothers me. I know that my calling is to communicate to them and they are making that impossible. I realize that sometimes there are legitimate reasons why people sleep in church. Perhaps they were up half the night with a child who caught the flu. Maybe the person is having problems sleeping. But this is abnormal.

Our calling as preachers is to administer the Word in such a way as to demand the attention of the congregation. God demands their attention. The preacher who does not internalize his sermon will not be in a situation to demand the attention of the congregation and work at obtaining it if he realizes that the people are passive, spiritually dull, and unresponsive.

Godly auditors play a positive role in encouraging the preacher in message. Their interest encourages the minister. When I see saints smiling when they hear the good news that I announce from the pulpit, this encourages me. I want to provide further encouragement and to rejoice with them. Charles Bridges writes:

> The sight of his people in the presence of God—their very countenances—their attention or listlessness—their feeding interest or apparent dislike—suggests many points of animated address, which did not occur in the study; excites many visible impressions, which awakens corresponding sympathy and interest in his congregation.[46]

If you are reading your sermon or reciting it from memory—you cannot do what you need to do to win back the interest of a sleepy congregation. The only thing you can do is read louder and louder. Just don't lose your place in your manuscript when you stop to tell someone to give a peppermint to a sleeping man! I still remember the time that Rev. Herman Veldman exhorted someone in church to wake up the man sitting next to him and give him a

---

[46] Charles Bridges, The Christian Ministry (Edinburgh: The Banner of Truth Trust, 1968), 286-87.

peppermint. Rev. Veldman did not put up with people sleeping in church.

I still remember the time that Rev. Veldman got in trouble with the women at the Protestant Reformed Church in Doon, Iowa. He made the mistake of telling the mother of a crying baby to take her child out of church. Rev. Veldman had a gruff exterior, although he could be a big pushover in personal relationships. I saw a circle of ladies surrounding the dominie. They ganged up on him after church. They took him to task for telling the young mother to take her baby out. Of course, it was self-interest. None of them wanted to be embarrassed before the congregation. They were afraid that they could be the next one called out on the carpet.

I also remember the time that Rev. Veldman visited the church in Edgerton, Minnesota where I grew up. A member of the congregation had been excommunicated, but had repented and returned to the congregation. Rev. Veldman knew about this. When he visited the church sometime after the prodigal returned, he saw the man in the front of church. He gave him a big smooch in the presence of the congregation.

Rev. Veldman read his audience. This was a virtue. He just didn't read the mothers in the congregation all that well.

The Joy of Preaching with Freedom: Freedom in the Pulpit

I appeal to your self-interest. Do you want to have fun preaching?

Do you want preaching to be enjoyable?

Then internalize the message and get rid of as much paper as you can.

One goal of internalizing the message is that you can enjoy the act of preaching. It is one thing to read a manuscript. It is another thing to communicate with the congregation from your heart.

When I was in seminary, my professors, even those who relied too much on paper talked about the importance of freedom in the pulpit.

The glory and beauty of internalization is that it frees up the minister so that he can preach the message without being tied to paper. Perhaps he still needs some paper, but he is freed from the paper and can focus his attention on the congregation and work at communicating the message to them.

Dare to preach the Word with freedom. Freedom means that you are not tied to your iPad. You are not tied to what you wrote and exactly how you phrased things. Fear of not knowing what to say or fear of not saying it right can bind you like an iron chain to your notes.

When you preach with freedom, there is the critical element of spontaneity. Hughes Oliphant Old commentating on the classical orators says: "Spontaneity is another fundamental feature of true oratory."[47]

Augustine did not write out his sermons beforehand, but he also did not preach extemporaneously without careful preparation. Old writes about the church fathers Augustine and John Chrysostom:

> They carefully studied the passage of Scripture on which they were to preach; they meditated on its meaning and application and prepared their material very carefully beforehand; but only when they were in front of their audience did they put it together. They were very much dependent on the reaction of their listeners, and, depending on their audience and the response of their audience, they served up what seemed appropriate from what they had prepared.[48]

How is it that a preacher can enjoy freedom in the pulpit? It is because he has appropriated what is taught in the text into his own heart. He has meditated on God's Word, understood it for himself, and applied it to his own heart and life. Therefore, he can tell you what he learned from God's Word in his own words. He is not dependent on the phraseology of commentators or other preachers.

The preacher can use the linguistic gifts that God the Holy Spirit has given him. He has thought the doctrines in the text through and thought through what the implications are of it—and how Christ is revealed in it. It becomes evident that the preparation of the sermon was not just an academic project, but a spiritual activity.

When the preacher experiences freedom, he can work at communicating the message with force, emotion, and power. He can exercise his gifts of rhetoric. He can use timing, pacing, and voice level to communicate his message in a far more profound way than simply an unemotional reading of it.

You experience freedom as you spontaneously utilize the unique gifts that God has given you. In a natural way, you use your linguistic gifts, voice, and theological insights in a way that serve the message.

---

[47] Hughes Oliphant Old, The Reading and Preaching of the Scriptures in the Worship of the Christian Church: Volume 2. The Patristic Age (Grand Rapids: Eerdmans, 1998), 395.

[48] Hughes Oliphant Old, The Reading and Preaching of the Scriptures in the Worship of the Christian Church:
Volume 2. The Patristic Age (Grand Rapids: Eerdmans, 1998), 395.

Dramatic Pauses

One evidence that a minister is experiencing freedom in the pulpit is that there will be dramatic pauses. Spurgeon says: "A very useful help in securing attention is a *pause*. Pull up short every now and then, and the passengers on your coach will wake up."[49] He adds:

> Know how to pause. Make a point of interjecting arousing parentheses of quietude. Speech is silver, but silence is golden when hearers are inattentive. Keep on, on, on, on, on, with commonplace matter and monotonous tone, and you are rocking the cradle, and deeper slumbers will result; give the cradle a jerk, and sleep will flee.[50]

The minister will sense the power of an effective pause.

He allows the message to sink into the heart of his auditors.

He hurls strong imperatives at the congregation.

And then he pauses.

How few congregations have experienced the thrill and power of dramatic pauses in sermons.

You see, God's pious people love to hear the exhortations of the law and gospel.

They love to have divine imperatives that reveal the holiness and justice of God hurled at their God-fearing hearts.

I love it when this strong earnestness is evident in the imperatives that come from God through the minister impact me.

There is drama in pauses.

They reflect the drama of the gospel.

They communicate something about the exalted grandeur of our transcendent God.

The art of the pause is a lost art.

We are scared of silence.

We hurry forward in our sermons. We don't want empty air time. So we hurry on. Without pauses. And we weary the congregation and stress ourselves.

Dare to pause.

Dare to communicate the drama of the gospel.

You don't need to pause only after imperatives. You should also pause after making a strong point.

Let people know by the pause how important your statement was.

---

[49] C.H. Spurgeon, Lectures to my Students. Volume 1. (Lynchburg, Virginia: The Old-Time Gospel Hour, 1894), 148.

You might need to zip your mouth shut. You are so afraid of silence. Extreme remedies might be necessary.

I sometimes write on the edge of my outline: "Pause". We need to remember to catch our breath.

Composers need to know how to use time. They cannot fill up all of time with their musical notes. Intervals communicate. Pauses communicate. Big time.

Dare to Enjoy Preaching

I know that you are afraid to preach with less paper. But rest in the Holy Spirit who uses the gifts, intellect, knowledge, linguistic abilities, biblical knowledge, theological knowledge, and spiritual experience of His preachers to communicate truth through unique human personalities.

Abraham Kuyper preached with freedom. Old writes:

> Kuyper was a genuine orator. His strongest point was that he had something to say.....His diction was flawless; it flowed effortlessly. Kuyper was a master of the Dutch language. His rich vocabulary, elegant phrases, and sparkling illustrations welled up spontaneously.[51]

You might not have as sparkling illustrations as Kuyper and Spurgeon when you preach extemporaneously. But the Lord can use your vocabulary and life-experiences to provide insights that well "up spontaneously" as occurred with Kuyper.

As you preach with freedom, you will also be able to enjoy the experience of preaching. It is boring to read a sermon. But when you have the Word of God hid in your heart—your heart burns—and you experience the joy and freedom of using your gifts and abilities to communicate as best as you can the gospel to the congregation.

Your infectious excitement about what God is saying and doing will be communicated to the congregation.

---

[50] Ibid., 149.
[51] Hughes Oliphant Old, The Reading and Preaching of the Scriptures in the Worship of the Christian Church: Volume 6. The Modern Age (Grand Rapids: Eerdmans, 2007), 50.

Worship your God in the act of preaching and seek to praise Him as best as you can. Let doxology rise spontaneously from your heart as you preach. Say more than is on your paper. Say better than what is on your paper. What you wrote on paper was prepared for oral delivery, yet it still was written on paper. When you experience freedom, the Lord can lift up your eloquence to a higher level. Remember that even the greatest orators cannot praise God or celebrate His truth as they ought.

The act of preaching is an act of worship by the preacher. Augustine began his *On Christian Doctrine* by discussing the need to love God in "terms of worship, in terms of rejoicing in his praise and enjoying his Wisdom."[52] Let the eloquence of the preacher be shaped by the Wisdom of God. We are not Sophists who care about eloquence as an end in itself. What does it matter if a man can speak with flowery words or if he can maintain interest by his personal charisma? You speak the Word of God from the heart and by God's grace what you say will be interesting and powerful.

Augustine was convinced that there was an eloquence consistent with wisdom. Old explains how Augustine uses a figure of speech to explain how true wisdom is eloquent:

> It is as though Wisdom were going forth from her house, and eloquence, like an inseparable attendant, followed her without having to be summoned.[53]

After Augustine stumbles about with words, mumbling something about the greatness of God in Book 1 of *The Confessions,* he writes:

> But in these words what have I said, my God, my life, my holy sweetness? What has anyone achieved in words when he speaks about you? Yet woe to those who are silent about you because though loquacious with verbosity, they have nothing to say.

So worship God by expressing the eloquent wisdom found in Scripture.

---

[52] Hughes Oliphant Old, The Reading and Preaching of the Scriptures in the Worship of the Christian Church: Volume 2. The Patristic Age (Grand Rapids: Eerdmans, 1998),387.

[53] Hughes Oliphant Old, The Reading and Preaching of the Scriptures in the Worship of the Christian Church: Volume 2. The Patristic Age (Grand Rapids: Eerdmans, 1998), 394.

Preaching with Passion

The goal of internalization of the sermon is so that the preacher can preach with passion. Preach with a heart emotionally affected by the great realities of which you speak. Come to have a strong sense of the reality, wonder, striking nature, and importance of what God requires and the grace of God—so that you can preach with passion. When you believe what you preach, there will be emotion.

John Murray said: "To me, preaching without passion, is not preaching at all."[54] How will the congregation get excited about what God is saying, if the preacher is not? How will the congregation be startled by the grace of God, if the preacher is not surprised? How will the congregation think that they should be deeply affected by the truths of the gospel when the minister before them clearly is not?

George Whitefield "was an orator of pathos, a public speaker who moved the hearts of those to whom he spoke."[55] His heart was on fire when he preached without notes:

But with field preaching came extemporaneous preaching. Once Whitefield disposed of the carefully written manuscript and began preaching to his congregation face to face and eye to eye, somehow a religious of the heart took fire.[56]

Charles Spurgeon is famous for how he could "evoke the full range of emotions."[57] Gardener Spring writes about the preacher:

He must feel his subject. It is as marvelous as it is mournful, that the weighty and thrilling truths of God's Word lose so much of their force from the little interest the preacher himself feels in his theme.[58]

The congregation does not need false emotionalism. It is hard to fake emotions. People can sniff that out. Fake emotion is mere noise. The preacher must feel the power of divine truth. He must believe and must believe spiritual realities strongly. He must believe what he sees by faith as much as what he sees with his natural eyes.

Delight in God and His Christ as you preach! Delight in the Law of God!

---

[54] Cited by David Murray, How Sermons Work, 142.
[55] Hughes Oliphant Old, The Reading and Preaching of the Scriptures in the Worship of the Christian Church: Volume 5. Moderatism, Pietism, and Awakening (Grand Rapids: Eerdmans, 2004), 153.
[56] Ibid., 153.
[57] Hughes Oliphant Old, The Reading and Preaching of the Scriptures in the Worship of the Christian Church: Volume 6. The Modern Age (Grand Rapids: Eerdmans, 2007), 429.
[58] Cited by David Murray, How Sermons Work, 142.

When you internalize your message, you are able to let your method of communicating fit the message. No smiles when speaking about Hell! Do communicate how you feel when you consider the reality of the Lake of Fire. Hughes Oliphant Old discusses how John Calvin's preaching was passionate.

> Although it is hard to speak of this on the basis of a written text, Calvin seems to have spoken with considerable variety of pace and mood. The cool of literary analysis was balanced by both prophetic indignation and mystic rapture. Calvin can speak of God's love for his Church with as much fervor as he can about God's judgment upon the wicked.[59]

Show joy on your face when you speak about Christian joy because you do find joy in your God and what He has done for you!

Communicate how important the truth of God is.

Another reason people listened to Calvin's sermons was that the sermons had a high sense of the authority of Scripture....One of the most amazing things about Calvin's handling of Scripture is that his high regard for the authority of Scripture goes hand in hand with his willingness to regard it as a completely historical document.[60]

Internalize your message so that you can use the oratorical gifts that God the Holy Spirit has showered upon you. As an oral communicator, you have a lot of tools in your toolbox. Rhythm, pace, and timing are tools in the toolbox of the preacher. Charles Spurgeon was a born communicator:

> Another characteristic of his sermons was their sense of rhythm and pace. He knew how to accentuate high seriousness by slow and solemn cadences, and he knew how to excite by rapid delivery. He knew where to pause for reflection and where to hammer his point in by short, rapid sentences. He knew all the tricks the classic rhetoricians had taught, and yet he seems to have known them by instinct.[61]

Good preachers have a superb sense of climax. They know how to work up to a big point. They know that they cannot always keep the congregation in a high state of excitement or they will weary her. They give the congregation breaks. They help the congregation to know when they are talking about something exceedingly important that cannot be missed.

---

[59] Hughes Oliphant Old, The Reading and Preaching of the Scriptures in the Worship of the Christian Church: Volume 4. The Age of the Reformation (Grand Rapids: Eerdmans, 2002),. 129.

[60] Ibid., 131-32.

[61] Hughes Oliphant Old, The Reading and Preaching of the Scriptures in the Worship of the Christian Church: Volume 6. The Modern Age (Grand Rapids: Eerdmans, 2007), 440.

I have rarely heard a sermon preached by a man who reads his sermon where there has been a superb sense of climax.

The ability to develop a sense of climax belongs to a true orator.

An orator knows when to be quiet, when to calm the congregation down with a slower pace and gentle words.

If you are making an important point and there is growing silence and profound concentration on the congregation's part, then emphasize the idea. Do not be quick to move on. Allow the truth to sink in. Develop the idea. While you have a powerful teaching moment, make additional applications. Take advantage of moments when the Holy Spirit is causing the Word to make a deep impression on your heart and that of your hearers.

I think that in every sermon there probably should be a point where the minister's internalization of the message will bring him to an emotional high point during which he stands upon the mountain top of faith. He will be able to celebrate the reality of what he has discovered in God's word that week. He will be deeply convicted by what God requires. He will practically sing about the glory of the grace of Christ.

As you come to the end of the sermon, do not run out of steam. If you are building to a main point of application, save some energy! Your desire is not only to communicate truth to your hearers, but you want their hearts and emotions to be affected by the truth. So pace yourself and be ready to demand the attention of your hearers, so you can bring the Word to them with power.

You have a number of options as you deliver the sermon. You can communicate without emotions. This often occurs if you memorize the message or read the sermon. You can try to fake it. But it will feel fake and you will feel like you are trying to generation emotion. You will wear yourself out. It is better to simply communicate the Word of God from your heart.

When you internalize your message, you will know it through and through. If you merely memorized it, you will be distracted trying to know what to say next. You want to communicate to the mind, will, and emotions of the audience. You can't be reading your notes when you confront the congregation about serious sins. You can't be reading your manuscript when you are extolling the love of Christ and speaking about God with doxologies.

The experts tell us that during the first ten minutes of your sermon, the people are hardly listening to your sermons as they are evaluating you and your character. This sounds like something that especially is the case when you preach in a church for the first time. People who do not know you are wondering whether the preacher is serious or flippant? Is he light-hearted or genuine in his concern? Is he showing off or is he simply trying to communicate the message? But even in your own pulpit, it is true that the congregation is evaluating your interest in the topic and the level of your earnestness and zeal.

Theodore Beza said that what stood out about the preaching of William Farel was the force of his utterance. He said that Pierre Viret's preaching was characterized by eloquence. John Calvin's strength as a preacher was his clarity and the strength of his doctrine. The perfect preacher is a combination of the three. But God gives diverse gifts. And it is important, as we shall see, that you be yourself.

Chapter 4:
Internalize the Logic and Concepts

One can memorize a sermon essay[62] word for word without internalizing the logic or concepts of the message. In this chapter we talk about at least two things that the preacher must internalize. First, he must internalize the logic of the sermon. Second, he must internalize the crucial concepts in the text as well as the imagery related to them. But how does the minister do this? I will share my approach to internalizing a message. In order to get into these topics, it is helpful to look at different ways of preaching and how one prepares to preach in each case.

Michael J. Quicke identifies six ways of preaching:

1) Reading a sermon in essay form.
2) Preaching from notes on notecards—with the notes coming from a completed manuscript.
3) Memorizing a full manuscript and reciting it from memory.
4) Memorizing the logic and structure of the sermon.
5) An interactive approach that involves interacting with the congregation.
6) Impromptu preaching without any preparation.[63]

Quicke evaluates each approach. He writes that a problem with the first approach (reading the sermon) is that "being tied to a script usually limits eye contact and can turn preaching into a lecture rather than a living encounter."[64]

---

[62] By a "sermon essay" I mean a sermon that is written out ahead of time in an essay format that is written to be read in its entirety.
[63] Michael J. Quicke 360-Degree Preaching: Hearing, Speaking, and Living the Word (Grand Rapids: Baker Academic, 2003), 185-86.
[64] Ibid., 185.

The second approach (using notecards) provides greater liberty, "Yet its dependency on paper can still be a barrier."[65]

The third method of preaching (memorizing the entire sermon word for word) "can easily distract with its unnaturalness."[66]

Quicke prefers the fourth method (memorizing the sermon's structure):

> This is my preferred method. Even though I have preached for well over thirty years, I generally write a full stereo draft, which allows me to test for impact and feel confident in its vital language, graceful style, completeness of thought, and ability to engage hearers. But as it is tested and continues to be shaped, its overall structure and certain key expressions eventually become so familiar that I can deliver the sermon without a script and notes. This method does not require total recitation. Of course, certain sequences and phrases should be memorized, such as the introduction and key points, but much is left open, *giving preachers flexibility to respond to the Spirit's prompting.* Obviously, the clearer a sermon's structure, the easier it is to memorize.[67]

What Quicke advocates, namely, memorizing the structure of the sermon while also having a fully prepared essay manuscript (although I recommend an outline) is an example of the internalization that I am commending. The result is extemporaneous preaching. I appreciate that Quicke recognizes that this method of preaching allows the Holy Spirit to lead and guide the preacher in the act of preaching.

The fifth method of delivery is one where the preacher tries to get the church members contributing to the message.

The sixth method (the impromptu) may appear to be without any preparation, although it actually "draws from a reservoir of previous speaking experiences."[68]

---

[65] Ibid., 185.
[66] Ibid., 18
[67] Ibid., 185-86. Emphasis added.
[68] Ibid., 186.

Spurgeon's preaching does not fit into any of these six methods. I think that both Augustine and Calvin, like Spurgeon, prepared for preaching without writing out a full manuscript as methods 1-4 involve. Even those who internalize the logic, main ideas, and structure of the sermon (method 4) still prepare a detailed manuscript or outline. Calvin, Augustine, and Spurgeon would reflect on the passage. Quicke writes that extemporaneous preachers first work "hard on exegesis and interpretation. C.H. Spurgeon, for example, seems to have needed only a few scratched headings for sermons that held thousands enthralled."[69]

Calvin studied the text in the original languages, consulted commentaries, and reflected on the text. He did have an idea of the main points and how they could be developed.

With an encyclopedic memory of the Bible, the Puritans, theology, and church history; Spurgeon was able to draw upon an enormous amount of insights and practical wisdom. As preachers grow in grace and knowledge their minds will become more fertile, which enables them to exercise freedom in the pulpit.

Joseph Webb gives three reasons why preachers should attempt to preach without paper. First, it helps cement a bond between preacher and congregation. "Without notes, human passion is set free, and passion is as close to the cement of human bonding as we ever get."[70] Second, an extemporaneous approach encourages audience participation.[71]

The congregation will rightly sense that the sermon unfolds in the act of communication. They will notice the spontaneity of the preacher and know that this message is being created and communicated to them in the act of preaching. Third, the preaching has the weight of authority because the message comes not from paper or an iPad screen, but from the heart.[72]

Memorizing the Structure of the Sermon

Ministers need to develop their memories. This is important for memorizing Scripture. Your memory is like a muscle that can grow in power through exercise. Quicke describes what occurs in his preferred method of delivery that involves memorizing the sermon structure.

---

[69] Ibid., 186
[70] Joseph M. Webb, Preaching without Notes (Nashville: Abingdon, 2001), 26.
[71] Michael J. Quicke 360-Degree Preaching: Hearing, Speaking, and Living the Word (Grand Rapids: Baker Academic, 2003), 186.
Ibid., 187.

Memorizing the structure of a sermon requires preachers to go over their stereo scripts enough times so that they capture key points mentally. This involves memorizing the introduction, the sequence of major sections, and key points and vital expressions that may need accurate repetition. Rather than aim at total recall (recitation), preachers should retain enough of a script's content and flow to do justice to exegesis and interpretation while still being able to engage listeners face to face.[73]

Fifteen Stages in Internalization

I have found that internalizing the logic, central concepts, and structure of the sermon involves a number of stages. Internalization occurs in at least fifteen stages.

1) I memorize the text.
2) I translate the text from the original language.
3) I study the morphology of the text.
4) I pray over and reflect on the text.
5) I learn from the wisdom of the commentators.
6) I comprehend the them and probably divisions.
7) I prepare the outline and develop the main point and important concepts in a logical way.
8) I edit the outline to improve the simplicity, logic, clarity, and force of the message.
9) I read over the outline.
10) I walk around and read it over.
11) I make sure my transitions work by speaking them aloud.
12) I circle key words and phrases so that they jump of the text (sometimes I put key words and phrases in boldprints and italics).
13) I practice the sermon in an empty church building or on a prayer walk—without using my sermon outline.
14) I add fresh ideas and revisions by pen on the paper outline.
15) I write the main points or ideas on the left side of the page so that I can see them at a glance (without looking at the text).
16) I continue to go over the outline and add notes until it is time to preach. This is in line with Cheah Fook Meng's maxim: "Preaching is like Chinese food. You serve it when it is hot."

---

[73] Ibid., 187-88.

I have not included in these stages anything about the emotions. But internalizing the message means not only grasping the ideas, but also *feeling* them. As I practice preaching I begin to sense the spiritual realities and how they affect my heart. I sense the gravity, euphoria, sorrow, or surprise that will characterize the communication of the concepts. You have not internalized the message if it does not affect your emotions.

Internalization involves spiritual preparation for the delivery of the sermon. One does not prepare to read a written out sermon essay, one prepares for the act of preaching. Quicke writes that "some preachers mistakenly assume that delivery is of secondary importance to content. But this is not the case."[74] This is the understatement of the day. A well-written sermon on paper is not a sermon preached. A paper document is different from a real-life encounter with God and God's people in the act of preaching. David Larsen refers to internalization as "saturation":

> Both Clarence Macartney and Charles Koller have given strong cases for preaching without notes, the latter arguing that this method is 40 percent preparation, 50 percent *saturation*, and 10 percent memorization. Free style requires clear and strong structure, growing vocabulary, and *the hard work of deep saturation.*[75]

Larsen explains how he internalizes a sermon:

> I usually memorize my introduction, rivet the statement of the main points and transitions in and out of my illustrations and my closing sentences. Then I steep my mind and soul in the flow, preach certain sections aloud, and think paragraphically. If I can't get it into my head, it is likely my development is not coherent.[76]

Larsen sets forth extemporaneous preaching as the goal for ministers:

> Preaching without notes or with minimal notes should be our goal, given the contemporary situation in communication. Certainly it is hard work, but few who try it ever leave the method. Ben Hogan practiced six to eight hours a day on his golf game. Albert Schweitzer would practice the musical intricacies of Bach's compositions the whole night long. If we are motivated to put more effort into oral communication we shall begin to see a new effectiveness in the pulpit.[77]

---

[74] Ibid., 188.
[75] David L. Larsen The Anatomy of Preaching: Identifying the Issues in Preaching Today (Grand Rapids: Kregel, 1999), 189. Emphasis added.
[76] Ibid., 189.
[77] Ibid., 189-190.

Why do preachers seem to act as if "delivery is of second importance"? I think that contemporary education rejects the study of rhetoric and ignores the importance of learning how to speak. There is a plain-speak in American culture that is viewed as morally superior to eloquence. Most of our politicians are wretched speakers. They read prepared notes. They speak without spontaneity. Eloquence is not valued in American education. Teachers do not even attempt to communicate well. Seminary students imagine that if they open their mouths without passion, that somehow their message still better grip the hearers. If the law governing the sale of real estate is: Location, Location, Location; then the law governing preaching needs to be: Communicate, Communicate, Communicate. Be fresh, be spontaneous, and look your congregation in the eye!

Chapter 5

The Sermon-Hearing Child is the Father of the Man who Preaches

hey say that the child is the father of the man. I say: the sermon-hearing boy is the father of the grown up man who preaches. God uses child-hood preachers to mold us into the preachers He wants us to become.

The preachers of my childhood preached biblical, exegetical sermons. They identified the main point of the text in a succinct theme. Their sermons were organized into three points. There were two point sermons as well, but they were just as long as the three-pointers (50 minutes to an hour long). The sermons had an introduction followed by three divisions. The first point normally developed the main point. The second point supported and developed the main point. The last point often brought home the significance or application of the text. The sermon had a goal. The minister took us on a logical journey.

The ministers of my childhood and teen years (Revs. James Slopsema, Jon Smith, and Michael DeVries) all preached these types of sermons. Later on I had occasion to hear both Slopsema and DeVries preach when I was a college and seminary student.

All three preachers were serious in the pulpit. No jokes. Rev. Slopsema had a big smile. Not much smiling. No laughter from congregations. They said nothing to provoke vocal "Amens" or clapping. While imminently personable, these pastors were their official selves in the pulpit. It was time for them to speak as ambassadors of Christ. This does not mean that they were not personable in the pulpit. Their personalities were evident in the preaching. Yet there were a lot of serious faces. Rev. Slopsema demonstrated a mature wisdom and spirituality. Rev. DeVries manifested the gravity and seriousness that characterizes the preacher of the gospel. Rev. Smith expressed his excitement at the gospel and the wonder of the covenant of grace. He was willing to engage in polemics with area ministers.

With respect to their preaching styles the men were very different. Rev. Slopsema's height demanded attention. At 6' 8" tall he demanded attention. He had a resonant, effective voice. Hand gestures with arms of that size were impressive! He excelled in a spiritual application. My father mentioned to me how effectively Rev. Slopsema used personal anecdotes. The sermons of my childhood regularly were 50-55 minutes long.

Rev. Jon Smith came to my hometown church fresh out of seminary. He preached with energy. He came from the south and had the passion of a southern Baptist preacher who has discovered the good news of the covenant of grace. He cried at infant baptisms.

Rev. Michael DeVries was one of the least offensive ministers I have ever met. Every word in personal conversation was measured. One could not imagine him saying something inappropriate that could anger anyone. He did not maintain eye contact with the congregation. He depended on his manuscript. Perhaps he felt the need to avoid an extemporaneous statement that could be improper. His preaching was characterized by seriousness.

Rev. James Slopsema was my pastor as a small boy. He served as pastor of First Protestant Reformed Church in Edgerton, Minnesota in the 1970's. Catechism classes for us children were held in the consistory room in the basement of the church. On Wednesday mornings we walked one block from the Free Christian Grade School to the church building for catechism. We sat in the front row of old theater seats in the consistory room. I needed to crane my neck to look up at our towering minister who walked back and forth in front of our seats. He was 6 foot 8 inches. He was a gentle giant. He was a pastor's pastor.

One time I told a joke in class. I was probably 9 years old. It was a joke I heard from my Grandpa Brummel, a farmer. I asked the dominee, "Who was the Chinese inventor of the manure spreader?" When he couldn't tell me the answer, I said: "Fling Shit I." The minister solemnly informed me that the joke was inappropriate for catechism.

Rev. Slopsema was a careful exegete. It is beneficial for young boys who later end up receiving a call to the ministry of the Word to sit under the preaching of good exegetes and homileticians. Both my brother and I received calls to the ministry. We both benefited from good Reformed preaching that taught us Scripture and theology. Slopsema's preaching was biblical, spiritual, theological, practical, and experiential. He had learned the art-homily approach to sermon preparation from Homer Hoeksema and Herman Hanko at the Protestant Reformed Seminary.

Chapter 5: The Sermon-Hearing Child is the Father of the Man who Preaches

God does not make preachers overnight. He uses the ministry of the Word by faithful preachers to prepare the next generation of preachers. We need preachers who can inspire the next generation to desire this holy office.

Early on in his ministry, Rev. Slopsema was bedeviled by his professor's expectations. They sat overlooking his homiletical work in his study. In his mind's eye he kept failing to meet their expectations. The problem was that he struggled with the logic of an art-homily sermon where the theme was the main point and the three divisions logically develop the theme. This was in spite of the fact that Homer Hoeksema, one of his professors, had clearly allowed for greater variety in homiletics.

At times Homer Hoeksema suggested a more analytic or synthetic approach depending on what best fit the text. Slopsema felt that he couldn't live up to the expectations that he set for himself. He couldn't logically lay out or develop a sermon like his professor's modeled for him.

Professor Homer Hoeksema did have high expectations of his students. In his syllabus on Homiletics that he co-wrote with his father, the Rev. Herman Hoeksema, homer set the bar exceeding high for sermon preparation. For example, he taught that the minister ought to do initial exegetical work more than a week prior to writing the sermon. The minister should wrestle with the text for three days himself (doing original analysis of the text) before he looked at commentaries. Then Hoeksema advised much preparatory work before finally writing the exegesis and preparing an outline. He advised that a new minister also write out the sermon in full (although he must not take this into the pulpit).

I first learned of the struggle of my minister on a Sunday morning. I was between 7 and 9 years old. Rev. Slopsema ascended the pulpit, but before the sermon began he announced that he couldn't continue. He returned with a reading sermon for an elder to read. The church learned that he was struggling with depression.

The preacher can be his own worst enemy. Our high expectations for ourselves can undermine our ability to function. The seminary professors counselled the young pastor and he learned to enjoy a greater freedom in homiletics.

The result of this greater freedom allowed the preacher to develop a homiletical style that better fit how his mind worked.

This certainly did not lead to a loss of logic in Rev. Slopsema's sermons. But he enjoyed freedom in the arrangement of his theme and divisions.

His sermons continued to be model Reformed sermons that were characterized by simplicity, spiritual power, doctrine, and practical application. His sermons flowed out of the biblical text. There was clear evidence that he had internalized the message of the sermon.

Oh that all young boys who would later be called to the ministry could grow up under such a preacher! My minister modeled what preaching can be. This is especially important for spiritually-minded young boys who might receive a call to the ministry of the Word.

Preachers should grasp what a gift of grace it is when God raises up preachers from the young boys of the congregation. God Himself emphasizes what a gift ministers of the Word are from God to the church. In Amos 2:6-16 God takes Israel to task for their sins of selling the righteous for silver, violating the seventh commandment, and mistreating the poor. God is incensed at their lack of gratitude for the good things He did for Israel in the past. He recites how He destroyed the Amorite giants before Israel. And then God says:

> And I raised up some of your sons for prophets, and some of your young men for Nazarites. Is it not indeed so, O people of Israel, declares the LORD (Amos 2:11).

God says that the gift of prophets and Nazarites was a marvelous gift to the covenant people. God mentions the fact that the sons and young men of Israel were called to be and appointed prophets and Nazarites. Note that the gift of preachers from among the sons of the congregation is a signal gift of God. God indicts Israel for how ungrateful they were:

> But you made the Nazarites drink wine, and commanded the prophets, saying, 'You shall not prophesy' (Amos 2:12).

So Israel was not only ungrateful for the gift, but they actively undermined the ministry of their sons who were called to speak God's Word.

For the sake of the boys and the young men in the congregation, the churches need ministers who preach the Word. Not just read sermons. But actually preach sermons from the heart in the power of the Holy Spirit. If ministers cannot and do not internalize the message that they are proclaiming, why should they expect the members of the congregation to internalize the message? If ministers are not eloquent, how will they inspire boys and young men to pursue the pulpit ministry? We need preachers whose personality, gifts, and insights are lifted up by the Holy Spirit so that they celebrate the truth, are convicted by their sins, and communicate something of their own excitement about their God.

Chapter 5: The Sermon-Hearing Child is the Father of the Man who Preaches

A Preacher who Influenced my Wife

My wife sat under the preaching ministry of Rev. Carl Haak. She liked him as a preacher because he preached as a man who believed what he was saying. The truth was true for him. He wasn't telling the congregation about somebody in the abstract but about the Jesus whom he loved and worshiped. Haak's sermons helped my wife to be excited about Christ. She wanted to go to church. She wanted to obey the gospel because of how he presented the gospel. She can remember a series of sermons on Psalm 73 that helped her to understand this important Psalm.

Rev. Haak is a little man. Short. But he seemed to tower in the pulpit as he used all of his energy and pasture and facial expressions to communicate the message. His whole person was involved in communicating. His emotions were used in the service of communicating profound realities. He manifests intensity and earnestness. He has a profound biblical theology.

A minister's personal relationship with the sheep plays a critical role in the congregation's reception of the message. Rev. Haak befriended my wife's family. They were covenant friends. My wife appreciated that Rev. Haak's sermons were exegetical. He dug into the passage. He developed the ideas and concepts in the text. His preaching was not abstract and hypothetical, but relevant, concrete, and relevant. He provided precise and specific practical applications. He stood in contrast with other preachers who lack detailed practical application. Others lacked his heart-felt approach to preaching.

As a young pastor, right out of seminary, Carl Haak did an excellent job of relating to younger people. He could tackle issues that were relevant for young people. He was an effective preacher because he preached with gusto and feeling. He did not just preach words, He gave my wife a wider vision of God's work and revelation. She was able to grow in her depth of understanding of Christ, His truth, and how to live a Godward life.

She remembers how Rev. Haak's parents visited the church that their son pastored in Grand Rapids, Michigan. His parents were down to earth people. Like his parents, the preacher was genuine, down to earth—with nothing of the showy. He did not need to be dressed just so. It wasn't about him, but the gospel he proclaimed.

My wife could take a lot of notes when her young pastor preached. There was so much to think about.

Later I heard Rev. Haak preach a sermon at Georgetown Protestant Reformed Church. It was a sermon on the life of Elisha. What stood out to me was the wealth of exegetical insights. They are the kind of insights that you immediately sense are the fruit of the reflections of an entire tradition on the sacred Scriptures. There is in the Reformed tradition a tradition of exegesis as found in commentaries, books, magazine articles (old issues of *The Banner* or *The Standard Bearer*), and in sermons.

There is an unwritten tradition of exegesis that is oral and contained in the manuscript sermons of older ministers. This information is unpublished and yet transferred by conversation and by the hearing of sermons.

There are rich doctrinal and exegetical traditions in the Reformed churches. The newcomer to the churches can be astonished at the exegetical insights that are passed down from preacher to preacher or from preacher to congregant. Many exegetical insights are hidden away in the Latin writings of ministers and theologians of the Reformation (Theodore Beza, for example) and the post-Reformation era, in Dutch, in the French writings of the French Reformed (like Pierre du Moulin), and in the verbose writings of the English Puritans.

Preachers in Grand Rapids, Michigan

In Grand Rapids, Michigan I was able to listen to some notable preachers during my time in college and seminary. I visited Calvary Undenominational with college classmates and heard Ed Dobson preach. This was long before he lived his goofy year like Jesus and then wrote an odd book about it. I was struck by the preacher's poise and self-possession in the pulpit and the precision with which he made his points.

I first heard Charles Krahe's grandfatherly voice on the radio. I visited Seventh Reformed Church in downtown Grand Rapids to hear Krahe preach. In those days Seventh Reformed was known as a conservative, confessional, Bible-believing church in the Reformed Church in America. Krahe's preaching was Reformed and pastoral. After Krahe retired I began to hear the stentorian voice of Dr. John R. DeWitt in the Seventh Reformed pulpit. On my way home from church, I would hear the sermon at Seventh Reformed.

While many people vocally preferred Krahe as a pastor and preacher, I was more impressed by DeWitt's powerful pulpit presence. He sounded like the old school of Dutch Reformed pastors who possessed a more rhetorical approach to preaching. DeWitt spoke with great forcefulness and eloquence. He preached without notes.

He brought a strong personal element into the pulpit and was not afraid to use the first person personal pronoun "I." The strength of this approach is that the congregation notices that preaching is communication of the truth through the medium of a distinct and unique human individual. DeWitt internalized the message he brought and attempted to convey it with all of his eloquence and passion. He preached extemporaneously. The weakness of DeWitt's personal approach was that some in the congregation felt like the preacher was talking too much about his own personal spiritual experience instead of seeking to affect his hearer's emotions.

I also heard Rev. Dale Kuiper preach at Southeast Protestant Reformed Church. He read his sermons. There was a distinct lack of freedom in the pulpit. The content was good, but the sermon was delivered in monotone.

I gravitated towards preachers who showed exegetical originality, logical powers, and had a more lively and extemporaneous method of communication.

While in college I had the chance to hear the four ministers who later would be my professors in seminary. I hear Russ Dykstra preach as a teenager. I only had one class with him in seminary. What struck me about Dykstra's preaching was that he viewed preaching as a teaching moment. He actually taught as a Christian school teacher for a number of years prior to attending seminary. He brought a pedagogical approach to the pulpit. Good preaching must include an educational approach to preaching. Doctrine is teaching. Therefore, we must teach doctrine.

Preaching ought to be theological. The congregation needs to grow in her understanding of Christian theology. I have noticed that some professors who focus on teaching can be terrible preachers. They can lack the prophetic element involved in preaching. But Dykstra demonstrated that preaching involves teaching.

The three main professors that I studied under were Robert Decker, Herman Hanko, and David Engelsma. I was the sole person in my class (year) for all four years (1994-1998) of my seminary education. This meant that I could not hide out in a large class. In exegesis class my exegesis paper was always read and critiqued. In Hebrew and Greek I was the one who had to translate the passage.

Robert Decker stood out to the seminary student body for his humanness. He wore his heart on his sleeve. Yet there was always a great gulf between the seminary faculty and the students. We were in a spiritual boot camp. The faculty members had taught for a good while and were busy throughout the denomination. They were the public face of the denomination. They were taught by old school professors who seemed to have an old-world view of the relationship of professors and students.

Robert Decker could be a moving preacher. He mainly read his sermons. But he was able to read his sermons in a lively and rhetorical way. He evidenced a pastor's heart in the pulpit. His weaknesses were a lack of eye contact and freedom. But he did write a thesis on the preaching of Dr.

Martyn Lloyd-Jones and valued freedom in the pulpit. A strength of his preaching were his exegetical insights. These exegetical insights were the fruit of the exegetical traditions found in the Dutch Reformed churches.

David Engelsma excelled as a preacher. His tall stature and large head added up to an impressive pulpit presence. The striking element in Engelsma's sermons was the logical development of the idea. He often read his sermons without having eye contact with the congregation.

If Engelsma's sermons lacked the freshness and fire that comes with a more extemporaneous preaching, his delivery had a weightiness that came from his voice, exegesis, and logically exhaustive treatment of the main idea. In class he told his students that after a sermon, the congregation should not have any unanswered questions. One felt that the preacher had comprehensively dealt with the topic.

While Engelsma's preaching felt like a logical development of the main point that led inexorably to a logical conclusion, Herman Hanko's preaching was much different.

Of my professors, Herman Hanko's preaching was preeminent. This doesn't mean that he was preeminent as a Christian. Hanko's great fault is his sectarian attitude. This sectarianism affected the content of his preaching. He told the seminary students that every sermon was to be distinctively Protestant Reformed. In practice this translated into a sectarian approach. One problem in the Protestant Reformed Churches is that theology is too often done in the service of the denomination.

Unique theological formulations are majored in because it is felt that this is necessary to protect the right of the denomination to exist as a separatist denomination. Any playing down of differences with other denominations could lead to ecumenism. I certainly have no idea that Reformed sermons should be biblical and within the confessional boundaries of the Reformed confessions. I suspect that many readers would be turned off by how Hanko would handle topics like the covenant of grace when he used a sectarian attitude.

But we are mainly interested in Hanko as a biblical preacher. While Engelsma's preaching could be experienced as involving the hearer in taking one logical step after another, Hanko's was like first exploring one topic in a rounded sort of way and then finishing up with that idea and going on to explore the rich facets of the next idea. I think of this preaching as involving consecutive round metaphorical concepts. The balls are related logically, but an emphasis falls on a metaphor or idea. Hanko's preaching did not lack logic, but that was not what impressed the hearer. Rather it was the clear and profound development of the striking metaphor or idea that struck the hearer's mind.

Chapter 5: The Sermon-Hearing Child is the Father of the Man who Preaches

What was going on here? First, Hanko had memorized the sermon—not word for word—but he had internalized the ideas in the sermon. Since he was not reading a manuscript, he could not read out a careful, logical development of the idea like Engelsma would do. Rather he had to understand the idea itself and have reflected on it from several angles.

In his preaching he was able to introduce the multi-faceted nature of the idea. He did this with freshness because he was producing the words as he preached. I believe that he was effective in doing this partly because he could preach the same sermon in multiple churches. Therefore, after preaching a sermon a couple of times he could have even greater freedom in preaching it the next time. Clearly this approach allowed him to demonstrate his linguistic gifts, rhetorical skill, spirituality, biblical knowledge, and theological insights.

Hanko was eloquent. His eloquence flowed from his passion. He used the pause with great effect. He could preach at a very slow pace, his word count per minute would be below that of most contemporary preachers. This slow pace with greater emphasis on every word characterized both Hanko and some of the older Protestant Reformed ministers like Herman Veldman.

Herman Hanko and John Piper are the two most passionate preachers that I have ever heard.

Both are eloquent.

What Hanko believed, he strongly believed.

When he was righteously angry, he was truly angry.

When he was euphoric over the gospel, he was a poet.

Extemporaneous preaching that is based on careful exegesis, a complete outline, and profound reflection on the text and the main ideas in it has power because it draws on the graces and gifts that God has given to the preacher. In the act of preaching the graces, gifts, and knowledge of the preacher can be used to communicate the message. Extemporaneous preaching draws on the rhetorical gifts that manifest themselves in the act of preaching. It is one thing to search for the right word to place in a written document. It is quite another to have that precise word in one's arsenal as a preacher as you engage in the act of preaching.

Jonathan Edwards' preaching was famous for its seriousness and the preacher's logical, even inexorably logical conclusions. But his preaching was a far cry from the fire, power, and emotion of George Whitefield's extemporaneous preaching.

Charles Spurgeon is not known first as an exegetical preacher. In fact, as anew preacher I often read Spurgeon's sermon on the text I was studying. But it was rare that I found deep and rich exegesis. Spurgeon was logical, but in his own way. His logic was more like Hanko's logic than that of Engelsma's. Spurgeon's sermons are filled with gems. How wonderfully he can take a figure of speech and develop the idea so that it's theological and practical significance become clear. Spurgeon seems to string pearls together—yes logically, but not with the careful logic of Jonathan Edwards, John Piper, or David Engelsma.

Hanko is in a line of Dutch Reformed preachers like Herman Hoeksema, Klaas Schilder, and Abraham Kuyper who wedded together careful exegesis, confessional Dutch Reformed theology, piety, and a highly rhetorical approach. Herman Hanko learned to preach from Herman Hoeksema who advised him to write out his sermons in full during the first five years in the ministry, but to go into the pulpit without notes. Hanko followed this approach. Once a minister has fully written out his sermon he has laid out a safe path to follow. He has developed the main idea and knows where he wants to go. He has carefully considered how Christ crucified is communicated in the passage and what the significance of the passage is for doctrine and life.

When such a preacher goes into the pulpit he is free to work at communicating the message to the congregation. This takes hard work and great effort. If a preacher talks like it is easy and fun to deliver a sermon, this is evidence that he has not given himself to the difficult spiritual task of communicating the gospel. The preacher himself needs to have his own heart influenced by the message. He needs to believe the message with all of his heart. He needs to be convicted by it. The truth needs to have its impact on his emotions. But our emotions are not always impacted by the truth because our sin stands in the way of truth impacting us. We are content to know little of the truth. We do not love the truth and celebrate it when we hear it. So preaching like this is very difficult from a spiritual point of view.

It is easy to read a sermon.

Anybody can read a sermon.

Almost anybody can read a sermon and even provide some proper voice inflection.

But that is not preaching.

It is simply reading a sermon well.

Perhaps this is why I am so strongly in favor of extemporaneous preaching that depends as little as possible on paper. Extemporaneous preaching not merely tells but shows the saints how the truth impacts the Christian.

Chapter 5: The Sermon-Hearing Child is the Father of the Man who Preaches

When a preacher does not use notes, the congregation knows that the minister has wrapped his mind around the idea and understands it. When a minister needs to read his development of an important idea, this means that he has not wrapped his mind around it. It has not sunk through to his heart and mind so that he understands it, comprehends it, and is able to speak about it from his heart.

There is a place for reading notes. For example, there are times when pin-point accuracy is necessary. There is a time for stating a sensitive idea in the careful way that you have prepared. Perhaps an issue is controversial and you want to be careful to avoid controversy. But why do you need to read what you wrote down in your notes about a thousand other ideas that you ought to have your mind wrapped around? If you really have been thinking about the main point of your text during the week in preparation for preaching, why have your meditations and reflections not brought you to the point where you can speak from the heart? If you have mulled the idea over and chewed on it like a cow chews on its cud, why can't you simply explain it in your own words? Why do you need to read out the thoughts that you wrote down?

If the preacher cannot internalize a concept or idea, how can the congregation do so? Listen to me, preacher. This is an important point. If you can't even internalize the concept, how can you expect the members of your congregation to understand it and internalize it?

If the minister needs to read out what he carefully wrote out, does he really imagine that the congregation can simply listen to him orally read out this section of the sermon and then remember it? If it hasn't been impressed sufficiently on your heart so that you have internalized it, how can you expect the idea to be impressed upon their hearts? If the preacher needs to write it out, won't the parishioner have to write it out? But if the parishioner needs to write it out so that he can internalize the truth, he must take detailed notes. He better get things word for word.

But then the minister might as well help the congregants who are going to write their fingers and hands off if they need to record word for word what the preacher said in order for them to get things straight. Why not have the preacher give a hard copy of the sermon to his parishioners before the service? Then they can take the document home after the service and if they want to have the ideas of the sermon impressed on their hearts they can read the exact words of the minister again.

I do not think that it is fair for the minister to avoid internalizing the message while expecting that the congregants will do so. In fact if the preacher thinks that he needs to present the point with great care and with careful qualifications, he will assume that what he is presenting will be too detailed for the congregants to remember. If they cannot remember it due to its complexity and the qualifications involved, then they will not be able to internalize it—especially if they only hear the sermon one time. The preacher needs to internalize the core concepts of his message and then communicate them in such a way that oral listeners can themselves hear, process, and internalize the concepts. If the preacher is making a careful point, then he needs to get to work. If he is making careful qualifications, then he will need to work at making sure that the congregation understands the fine point. He can do this. But he will not do it if he simply reads through what he wrote about the fine point.

Hanko's preaching took individual concepts and simplified and clarified them. He wielded vivid and picturesque metaphors. Hanko's gifts of explaining and developing metaphors reminds one of the gifts of Spurgeon and Edwards.

Hanko was a master of overstatement. He engaged in effective hyperbole. This was a crucial element in his preaching. In other words, he exaggerated certain aspects of a concept in order to make the concept memorable and to impress certain facets of the idea upon the hearers. Perhaps the development of the concept was in some way an overstatement and exaggeration, but it served to make the idea concrete, clear, and memorable. How do I know that Hanko was effective with hyperbole? People often became angry about these overstatements. People thought that he was over the top. He seemed to press matters beyond their logical boundaries. But what is one sign of a limited and parochial mind? It is the inability to understand the use of figures of speech or hyperbole. People would take Hanko's hyperbole as a statement of solemn fact.

Today hyperbole is a lost art. Except in politics. And even there it is not always appreciated as an effective figure of speech. Congregants wrongly view hyperbole as over-the-top. Now it is true that a preacher can make a mistake or teach an error while using hyperbole. Hanko sometimes did that. But this does not undermine the value of hyperbole as an effective mode of communication. We find hyperbole everywhere in Jesus' teachings. To give just one example, Jesus tells the man who is tempted to sin with his eyes to gouge out his right eye. This is hyperbole.

Chapter 5: The Sermon-Hearing Child is the Father of the Man who Preaches

I had the opportunity to listen to Hanko preach when I was in seminary. It was funny that he and the other professors mainly emphasized the necessity of good exegesis and a logical outline in practice preaching. I soon learned that Hanko's actual preaching was quite different from what he was teaching the seminary students to do. In seminary there was little emphasis placed on the communicative aspect of preaching. It is true that students who were very dry (boring) were encouraged to get into their sermons better. But the focus was on the exegesis and homiletics. The development of an ability to communicate was viewed as an art that would be developed once one was in the ministry.

Hanko's actual preaching seemed to violate rules that he taught in seminary. He certainly exercised greater artistic freedom than he allowed his students. Hanko knew that preaching was oral communication. He felt free to move around in the pulpit because he was not tied to paper. His delivery was powerful. He had a strong, deep voice, that was due to his addiction to smoking earlier on in his life. The old Dutch Reformed preachers smoked cigars and pipes. Smoking produced deep voices that carried well. Hanko also used volume effectively; his preaching could be loud or quieter. With the microphone and speaker systems that we have today, ministers should make more use of volume. It simply is a fact that you can communicate quite effectively with a microphone even when you speak quietly. And there are times when the saints need to hear some thunder.

Hanko varied the speed of his delivery. He might preach exceedingly slow at the beginning of a sermon. This enabled him to build up to a crescendo later on when he varied his speed and volume.

Hanko preached from the heart. His knowledge of church history, the Bible, and Reformed theology were placed in the service of the text.

An important element in Hanko's extemporaneous preaching was his power of concentration. Good preaching is a profound exercise in concentration. Reading a sermon requires no absorption in the text. I do not think that preachers who read their sermons are working hard enough. Hanko's preaching could be spell-binding. His hearers enjoyed a sense of excitement and discovery.

John Piper's sermons are effective partly because he explains the logic of the text and how he discovered the logic and arguments in the text. Piper takes us along on his exegetical journey. He might be accused of taking too much of his exegesis paper into the pulpit. In the same way Hanko took the hearers along in his own discovery of the ideas in the text. And he did not present his discoveries as *ho hum* and *humdrum*.

I write this because too many preachers present their own insights in a blasé manner. Hanko shed new light on well-known passages. I am convinced that if you wrote out Hanko's sermons and had someone else read them, they might barely impress—like those of Whitefield. It was the whole man, the whole person, who, in the act of preaching, was able to impact the congregation. It was the emotion, the fire, the concentration, and the purposeful communication with the congregation that created the impact.

I find it remarkable that a preacher can preach on any text without coming into the pulpit with fresh discoveries and insights into the text. Perhaps the preachers learns some new things from the commentators. Well and good. Benefit from past exegetes. But for the preacher the insights he learned (even if some of them might already be known by some of his congregants) are new to him. Why should new insights be treated as if they are old insights that should almost bore the congregation?

When everything in a sermon comes off as the same old thing stated the same old way, the preacher has not wrestled with the text. He has not mined it. If nothing about the passage seems particularly to interest or excite the minister, then he needs to have a break. He needs a time of spiritual recuperation. It is time for a sabbatical.

While God's Word is filled with unexpected insights, some preachers act as if they are like Old Princeton Seminary where supposedly the faculty never developed a new idea. I hate it when ministers flatten out the Word of God. A sermon on a Psalm sounds just like a sermon on Romans. The theme for a sermon on a Psalm is the exact theme hauled out for a Heidelberg Catechism sermon. Every sermon reads into the unique text the same boring formulations that have been used to put the congregation to sleep before.

Since the preachers of my childhood sought to exegete the text and present the main point of the text, their sermons did not bore. Since there is infinite variety and so many wondrous things in God's Word, the preacher who seeks to communicate the meaning of the text of Scripture will not bore the congregation.

As a boy I was impacted by the sermons of my childhood preachers. God used the godly character and the preaching of these men to impress upon my heart the gravity and greatness of the gospel of Christ. He used faithful Reformed preaching to prepare my heart and mind for the gospel ministry. He also used the preachers who I heard as a young man to shape my own understanding of the Scriptures, the gospel, and the ministry of the Word. He used the drama of the weekly preaching of the gospel by gifted men to reveal the drama of the gospel of God. Oh that all young boys and seminary students can heard faithful Reformed preachers who help them to glimpse the glory of God, the love of Jesus, and the gravity of the gospel.

Chapter 6
What I Learned about Preaching by Preaching

As a preacher I learned that Sunday came every third day. My students are astonished that Reformed preachers prepare two sermons each week. They are surprised to learn that Reformed believers keep the Sabbath Day holy by gathering for both morning and evening worship.

And then there was Christmas vacation. If Christmas did not fall on a Sunday, then I would prepare three sermons the week of Christmas. The next week would be Old Years Day and New Years Day. Since the Church Order stipulated that worship services must be held on both Old Years Day and New Years Day, I could preach four sermons that week.

As a preacher who needed to prepare two sermons each week, in addition to many other duties, Sunday came quickly. Monday was usually my day off. I loved to swim at the Indiana Dunes and sit on the beach and read my Greek testament.

On Tuesday morning I identified my texts for the following Sunday and began translating the texts out of the original languages. I began my study of the texts. I made copies of the pages out of relevant commentaries that I could study as the week progressed.

Tuesday night I led a Bible study.

Sometimes on Wednesday morning I led a women's Bible study.

Wednesday afternoons I would teach catechism classes for the first through 7th graders at the local Christian school. Wednesday evenings I taught the high school students catechism classes at church.

I visited sick members in the hospital.

I prepared for leading the youth group that met on Sunday nights.

Consistory meetings took up at least one Thursday night a month.

When the month came for family visitation, I would be out two nights a week for a month visiting the saints in their homes.

Then it was Friday and I needed to submit my sermon titles and their three divisions to the bulletin clerk along with the Psalter numbers for the worship services. Therefore, I needed to know by Friday morning what the main point of the text was. On Friday and Saturday I prepared my outlines. I always prepared outlines. I will argue for the value of using outlines rather than an essay form in preparing a sermon. On Friday and Saturday my studies of the text, the theology in it, the development of the concepts, how the person and work of Christ was communicated in the text, and the practical application needed to come together.

And then it was Sunday morning.

There was no time for writer's block. Writer's block is a luxury for people who do not earn a living by writing. Journalists quickly learn that they do not have the privilege of complaining about writer's block. Try explaining writer's block to your editor when the newspaper needs to be printed at midnight!

Ministers cannot suffer from writer's block.

Sunday is "a comin".

Getting up to Speed on a Text

Only the preachers who are reading this will understand the gravity of what I am going to say next. In six days I needed to become an expert on a new text, a new theological idea, or fresh way of looking at God, salvation in Christ, or His commandments.

The minister constantly explores new passages and new ideas. He must go from zero to 80 miles per hour in six days. Professor Homer Hoeksema advised pastors always to work two weeks ahead of time. I didn't find that this worked for me. Each week had its own texts and sermons. I ran across fresh problems that needed new solutions. I grappled with texts where the commentators provided a wide variety of interpretations, some of them with big implications. How could I choose the right interpretation? In six days?

How could the truth and reality of a text impact me over a period of six days so that I could begin to communicate the beauty, truthfulness, and profundity of the passage?

I had only six days to get the heart and essence of two different Scripture texts into my soul.

It is no wonder that preachers are men of prayer.

Who is sufficient for these things?

The quest begins. What is the main point of the text? What are the most important concepts in it? Is there a logical division in the text itself? How does this text communicate the saving work of the Triune God? How does this Scripture reveal our sin and guilt? What is God requiring of His people? Where does the text fit in the history of the unfolding covenant of grace? What doctrines are being taught?

A crucial question is: What is unique about this text? What is the truth and emphasis that we find alone in this text? Why was this Scripture included in sacred Scripture? How does it contribute to God's revelation in Christ? It should never be the case that a minister preaches on two different texts and makes the same points with the same emphases.

As you begin to perceive the main point of the text this should lead you towards the title or main point of the text. This is also called the "theme" of the sermon.

The sooner I could understand the logic of the text, its application for doctrine or life, and the flow of the argument; the better.

Once I had the bare bone outline of the message, I was able to add flesh to the skeleton and work towards causing the dry bones to live.

I discovered that preaching the main point of the passage probably would not result in a showy, gaudy title. A title that functioned merely as a sign to gain attention would distract the congregation from the big idea in the text.

I found that the theme would not be boring if it expressed the unique revelation found in this unique text. If all of a minister's titles start sounding alike, you probably have a situation where the unique revelation in the texts are being bulldozed. When the minister wrestles with the unique ideas in a text, no two sermon titles or themes will be the same.

I learned that it would not work for me to bring a written-out sermon into the pulpit. I was never taught to write out a sermon in essay form in seminary. In my last three years of seminary I did need to write exegesis papers each week. These were extended essays or term papers, but the exegesis paper provided raw material (and even well-developed material) for the homiletical outline.

One of my professors recommended writing out a sermon in full—but only so one could be prepared to deliver a message without paper.

The problem with a written-out sermon in essay form is that the preacher cannot see the logic of the sermon at a glance. It is true that the first sentence in a good paragraph might be a sort of thesis statement and, therefore, could be equivalent to a main point or at least a more important subpoint in an outline. But the central problem with a fully written out sermon in essay form is that the preacher cannot see the logic of the sermon at a glance. He will not perceive at a glance what the central point is in contrast to supporting arguments.

I speak of the preacher merely taking a "glance" at his paper. This is crucial! I often bring a complete outline into the pulpit. While in seminary, we were limited to using a three-page outline in practice preaching. I would create a 7-9-page outline that included the entire sermon and then pared it down to three pages. Our professors trained us to avoid dependence on paper.

But once out of seminary I felt more comfortable having the crutch of the entire outline with me if I needed it. But my goal was always to use my paper as little as possible. It is here that the benefits of an outline becomes evident. At a glance the preacher can see his main points and main subpoints. He can have a clear idea about what must be emphasized and what is less important.

At a glance the preacher can see where he needs to go.

If a minister feels the need to take paper into the pulpit, the goal is that he merely glance at his outline so that he can look at the congregation and focus on communicating with them. It is far more fun to communicate directly with an audience than to read a sermon. In some sense it is easier to read a sermon if you can put out of mind the problems with this from a social, personal, and communication perspective. In seminary one of my professors emphasized that how you write is important. People will not bother to read someone who writes badly. The same applies to speaking. If you do not speak well or are not communicating well, people will not bother to listen. The minister should not expect that just because words are coming out of his mouth as he reads a sermon that the congregation automatically will listen.

As soon as I begin to read a sermon I feel that I am reading and it seems stilted, awkward, and non-social. I know that there are ministers who, for various reasons do not sense this. Clearly there are social blind spots and communicational blind spots when preachers suppose that it is natural to look at paper rather than the congregation. Ministers spend their entire ministries staring at the back corners and wall of the church building. They find inventive ways to do this, so that it might appear like they are looking at the congregation. But the attentive congregant observes the discrepancy. He knows that the preacher is not even looking at him. A long-established custom of preachers reading sermons written in essay form leads to the impression that this is normative. Some ministers were taught in seminary that the proper way to preach was to prepare a carefully crafted sermon to read.

It is far more fun to preach while focusing on the congregation and working at communicating in the act of preaching. Then a dynamic element is present. The preacher acknowledges that communication dynamics are at work in oral communication. The congregation knows that they have the pastor's attention, just like he seeks their attention!

Why should a preacher require the attention of his congregation if he ignores their presence and communication? I have watched a minister preaching to a sleepy congregation on a hot day without taking their situation into consideration. He droned on and on. If he had recognized the fact that it was very hot in church and that people were getting tired, he would have worked to wake them up. He would have shortened his message. He would have focused on the main things and left out the extraneous details. But he was not watching them. He was clueless. He came across as socially maladjusted, unable to interpret people around him and to communicate in a contextually appropriate way. He had a lot of material and he was going to give it to them. And so he read his sermon to its long conclusion.

If the preacher has no interest in paying attention to the congregation, reading where they are at, and how they are responding to him; why should they care about him? Dr. Martyn Lloyd-Jones emphasized the importance of the preacher receiving communication and feedback from the congregation. Lloyd-Jones is right. This might be as basic as reading that a congregation is apathetic and apparently uninterested or unexcited about hearing the Word preached. Then the preacher knows that he has work to do. He better work at waking up the congregation to the importance of what he is going to say.

I have heard ministers read their sermons on and on while the congregation grows tired, bored, and listless. Yet the preacher motors on. He is clueless. On he goes. I think that many congregants believe that this is just how the thing is done. There is something spiritually attractive about this kind of preaching to confessing Christians. I do not mean spiritually attractive in a good sense. By nature we do not want to hear the gospel proclaimed with sharp and penetrating power. We do not want to hear the strong demands of God that convict us of sin. Because of their old man of sin, many congregants are happy with and complacent about preaching that appears weak and irrelevant. The reading of sermons in a boring manner appeals to the weakness of the flesh. It requires no radical discipleship response from the hearers.

When I sense that the members of the congregation have reached the limits of their concentration, I know that it is time to wrap things up. Now if a preacher is simply reading his sermon in essay form, what is he to do in such a situation? If he is addicted to reading, he cannot provide a summary. If he has not internalized the message, he cannot cut things short. If he doesn't know how to exercise freedom in the pulpit, he must simply keep reading out every sentence until he is done. And the congregation knows that the minister isn't listening to them or taking their concerns seriously. The minister's concern is to read out every sentence in every paragraph until he reaches the conclusion. And ministers often do not realize how long it can take to read out everything that they wrote.

✓ It is hard to express passion while preaching if you are reading your sermon. This is a crucial problem with the mere reading of sermons. *Heartfelt emotion is the mother of eloquence.*

I know that there are exceptions to the rule that provide examples of men who read their sermons and yet do so with great passion. One example is John Piper. He can be quite tied to his manuscript, yet he also explodes with freedom from his manuscript. Piper does possess a unique ability to reengage his passion while reading his carefully composed sermon (that is in essay form). Piper, like Jonathan Edwards, can be effective in reading part of a sermon because of his poetic imagination and logical abilities.

✓ What the congregation wants is passion in the moment of proclamation. It is true that the heart of the minister better contain passion as he writes his sermon outline, but *this passion needs to live again in the act of preaching.* The spiritual minded in the congregation want earnestness and excitement that demands attention.

The reality is that live, living communication by an orator can demand attention far more than the reading of an essay by a good writer. I realize that there is a time for writers to read selections from their published books that they crafted with great care. A good writer knows that it is the ear that must hear the rhetoric of the book. I get easily bored at a book reading unless the author has an exceptionally gifted ability of reading his own works with emphasis. I listen to books on Audible. I find that the worst readers are the authors. The best readers are people who have developed their voices and learned to read with drama.

Ministers who can read their sermons with drama are rare birds. Therefore, you probably are not one of them. If you can read well, you are off the hook with respect to the hard work of gaining your audience's attention. Your internalization of the message becomes expressed in your expressive reading of it.

But you will not be free.

And they will know.

You are not going to experience freedom in the pulpit.

You are chained to your paper and the text. Perhaps you can swerve from the text for a minute here or there. But then you are back to your pre-ordained message and need to toe the party line.

Chapter 5: The Sermon-Hearing Child is the Father of the Man who Preaches

When a man reads a sermon, it is true that the linguistic gifts that he exercised in his study are evident. He can express himself in nice turns of phrase prepared by careful reflection in his study. But the minister's gifts of verbal (and oral) communication are not used or stretched. He is not given the opportunity to express the ideas he has studied in fresh and vigorous language. He does not reveal that he has taken these ideas into his soul.

✓ The minister who has internalized his message owns the ideas. And they own him. He can communicate them in his own heart language. When a minister reads his sermons, the audience has a sense that the minister has not appropriated the insights into his own heart. If he did, he would not need to read the ideas out in a prepared form. He could simply communicate them. The minister should hear his congregation saying, "Just talk from your heart. Tell us what has struck you."

I have found the greatest freedom in preaching in a prison context where I worry less about disseminating all of the information in my outline and more about making sure that I am communicating with the audience members. It helps to have a difficult audience. A challenging audience forces the speaker to recognize the importance of communication. In Dutch Reformed churches a bad communicator can expect that the members will work hard to listen to his message. But in other contexts, the preacher will need to earn the attention of his auditors.

✓ I find that when communication trumps a concern to include all the details and supporting arguments that could be given, the sermon might not be as tightly logical, yet it can have a bigger impact. The logic that comes out is a bigger logic or *a logic that better fits oral communication.* The things that I remember to say in extemporaneous preaching are the big things and the insights that really move me. The congregation knows that even if they ignore me, I will demand their attention back. Men who are not used to concentrating for extended periods of time can sense that I am working with them. By my liveliness, eye contact, variety in tone and loudness, movement around the pulpit; they knew that my focus is on communicating with them and not trying to dot my theological "I's" and exegetical "Q's." The main point is the main thing.

In prison I preach to congregations that include mostly African Americans with a minority of Hispanics and whites. These audiences value liveliness and emotion in oral communication more than Dutch Reformed congregations do. In prison I preach to a large group of men that, as a rule, have a lower educational background than a Reformed congregation on the outside.

Up to 50 percent of prisoners in the Illinois Department of Corrections have a sixth grade or lower reading level. In such a context, oral communication is at a premium. Simplicity in preaching is the gold standard. *Simplicity means that the preacher explains one concept at a time, placing it in rich and variegated perspective, and then gets done and goes on to the next idea.* One simple and clear idea at a time! That is what all the saints want and need.

Simplicity.

Clarity.

One idea at a time.

Developed ideas. Or what I call developed concepts.

Prison congregations have different weakness from Reformed congregations on the outside. Many volunteers who deliver messages in prison are untrained. They never attended seminary. They do not know how to exegete a passage. They do not have a biblical or systematic theology. They do not see Christ in the Old Testament. Their approach to delivering a message includes a lot of hype and emotion with a lot of Christian platitudes.

Emotion and forcefulness of presentation trump the actual message in the text. A Pentecostal spirituality means that the speaker simply draws on his limited spiritual experience and biblical knowledge in the presentation. After a diet of this riveting kind of emotionalistic preaching that involves men in the front row literally dancing and jumping around, what happens when a Reformed preacher shows up and reads his sermon?

The prisoners will commence to have discussions with their buddies.

They will pass notes.

They will trade items.

They will long for the end of the sermon.

A minority will listen and benefit, but they will be a small minority. Twenty-five men out of a crowd of one hundred eighty. The congregation will feel that no preaching actually occurred. There was no passion.

Therefore, it is important that the prison preacher combine exegetical, Christ-centered, theological preaching with lively, passionate communication. And this is what congregations on the outside want too—even if they have become used to something else.

Churches sometimes do not know what bad or good preaching is. But they often know good preaching when they hear it. They learned new things. They feel truth impressed upon their hearts.

Past preachers who wrote on preaching strongly emphasized the importance of passion in preaching. They even dared to say that preaching without passion was not preaching—it was mere lecturing.

Chapter 5: The Sermon-Hearing Child is the Father of the Man who Preaches

Ever notice that when a preacher evidences passion that suddenly heads look up. Ever wonder why that happens? If preachers read their audiences they will quickly learn the importance of passion and earnestness.

You would not believe what a relief it is for me when I am not preaching and the preacher begins to manifest passion. I stop taking notes or examining for myself what the text is saying. I listen transfixed. I know that the preacher is saying something important and even prophetic. Time flies by.

If the preacher is not passionate, what does this communicate about the content of his message? It communicates that he does not believe very strongly what he is saying. If he has not internalized the message, that tells you that he does not deem this topic important enough to have internalized it. If the topic is too complex and unimportant for the minister to internalize, why should you as a hearer work at doing so? If the minister is passionate about something, he has perceived in his own heart how important it is. Then his emotions will be fired as he talks about it.

Some ministers can perform the miracle of being passionate as they read their sermons. John Piper displays a marvelous and poetic use of the English language. As a result, he is able to sacrifice spontaneity on the altar of his prepared message. Piper is a poet. He is like a poet laureate reading his poetry. He does this with meaning and expression. The fire he had in his belly when he wrote his sermon on Friday or Saturday is still present, alive, and burning on Sunday morning. He has a marvelously original mind so that nothing he says is the same old thing spoken the same old way. Piper is the exception to the rule. Lesser preachers who do not have Piper's poetic abilities and his ability to read his messages with passion need to work for freedom and spontaneity in the act of preaching. The moral of the story is that if a preacher can write a sermon with the type of language that flows from an excited heart, he might be able to communicate with excitement. But so far as his written words do not convey this emotion, he will need artificially to manufacture false emotion in the act of preaching. The problem is that it is hard to be yourself when you are reading a prepared statement.

I learned as a preacher that the saints can be very content with the *status quo*. They are very content with "doing church" as they have done it all their lives. If a preacher brings God's Word in a lively way—and in such a way that it cannot be contradicted, he will face opposition. I preached sermons on evangelism, for example, that emphasized the calling of individuals and the church corporately to bring the gospel with deeds of mercy. The younger generation was excited and wanted to know how they could be better witnesses together. But many in the older generation were content with the *status quo* and unwilling to follow pastoral leadership.

✓ The result is that the elders did not want any more sermons on the topic because the younger generation was placing pressure on the older generation. This caused tension. The elders did not want tension. I learned that the greatest sin in a church can be any action whether good or bad that leads to conflict. Conflict is to be avoided at all cost. Elders can be unwilling to stand up for what is right if there is conflict. So the younger generation felt that they were being hindered from carrying out the mission of the church. The older generation was attached to old ways of "doing church". Younger members saw the need for positive change. The elders just wanted to avoid conflict between the two generations. The younger people began to leave the church. The older generation had protected their comfortable way of doing church.

✓ There is a phrase that the Dutch use, "stubborn Dutchmen", and it applies to the life of the church. A preacher can cast a biblical vision for the life of the church that cannot be contradicted because it is biblical, and yet members can dig in their heels and resist the reform that God can use to revive the church and bless her outreach.

✓ I learned that some saints do not want preaching that affects the emotions. They do not want strong, prophetic preaching. I have never understood that. I have always appreciated preachers who say with courage, "Thus saith the Lord." I appreciate preachers who are willing to stand for truth and righteousness and who exhort others to do the same.

I want to be challenged in my Christian life.

I want to grow in godliness.

I want to be convicted of my sins.

✓ But not all church members want to hear prophetic preaching, especially if it steps on their feet. One of my professors used to tell disgruntled parishioners who were offended by a specific application of God's law to their lives: "If the shoe fits, put it on." If they felt that what the minister said rebuked them for a sin in their lives (a sin that they did not want to admit), the minister's response was: "If the shoe fits, put it on." If the rebuke applied to them, they needed to take ownership of that.

✓ If learned that if the preacher presents the biblical message in a boring and expected way, it will be hard for people to feel convicted. If the minister teaches biblical ideas in an abstract and non-personal way, the congregant might disagree, but they will never get worked up about it. But let a minister preach the same doctrine or some precept of God's law with passionate power, a sanctified imagination, and with concrete practical applications; sparks will fly. It has been my goal as a preacher to bring the truth in such a way that it would impact the hearts, minds, wills, and emotions of my hearers.

✓ I consciously think about how a truth impacts or should impact me. I consciously think about how to communicate the biblical concept in a way that is memorable and will make an impact. It is God the Holy Spirit who needs to take His ideas and causes them to impact the whole person. But the Holy Spirit uses the minister who works at communicating the idea in a clear, logical, heartfelt, and powerful way so that it can be used to impact the whole person.

Sometimes I think that preachers do not even think about preparing a message that will have such an emotional and logical impact on the hearers. Jonathan Edwards certainly thought about this ahead of time. The logic in his sermons and his rhetoric was used in the service of a spiritual impact.

In preaching, the minister is engaging in oral communication. The idea is to impact the hearer in the moment of preaching.

✓ If preachers believed that one goal of preaching was to impact the minds of their hearers, preachers would be better teachers. If they believed that their goal was to impact the will of their auditors, they would speak more powerfully to their wills. If they thought that one goal was to have a message that impacted men's hearts, they would try to fire the emotions of their hearers by the ideas in the text. John Piper has described preaching as logic on fire. He is a wonderful contemporary preacher who exegetes the Word and uses a homiletical style that is directed towards using an emotional presentation of the truth to affect the mind and heart of the hearers. If God uses heart change and changes in our desires to turn us towards the truth and godliness, then we need to hear ministers who are concerned to be used by God to impact our hearts.

✓ There are different ways to address the heart and conscience. But it is important that preachers teach God's Law in such a way that it evokes conviction of sin. Some preachers seem shy about bringing God's law to bear in such a way that hearers blush about their guilt. Is the preacher afraid of offending church members? Does he feel that he is a sinner too and, therefore, ought not to call out church members? The preacher simply must preach more to himself and apply the Law to his own life so that the congregation knows that he is under conviction of sin like the pious in the congregation.

It is true that if you bring God's Law in its first use (as a teacher of sin and misery) that there will be people who slander you as a legalist. The preacher meditates on God's Law day and night. He loves God's law. He is sensitive to God's requirements. Not all his auditors will have matured like he has. As the minister legitimately applies God's Law to the lives of the saints, he will step on toes. The minister will not remain abstract. He will rebuke concrete sins. You can guarantee that members will disagree with your application of the Law to specific circumstances.

Remain general and everyone will love you.

Speak in general terms about sin and no one will feel convicted. In fact the congregation will come to pride themselves on their faithfulness.

But as soon as you act like John the Baptist or a godly Puritan and apply God's Law in an accurate way to precise sins, you will be called a Precisionist, a Puritan, and a Pharisee.

That is why pulpits have fallen silent about the Ten Commandments.

Carnal members of the congregation do not come to church to feel uncomfortable. They come to church as pretty good Christians who are comfortable with their level of morality.

However, the members of the congregation with sensitive consciences do want to know their sins. They want to be convicted of their sins. They want to hear about forgiveness and hope—which they will not hear very clearly from ministers who imply that everybody in the church does a pretty good job of being a Christian. Sensitive saints want to be convicted of their sinfulness and then astounded by grace. Where the law is not clearly taught, grace is cheap.

Reformed congregations will put up with preaching that lacks passion. Sometimes I think that congregations imagine that white culture or Dutch-immigrant culture is dignified when there is a lack of passion. Passion is viewed as the opposite of logic and doctrine. Passion is associated with exhortation to godliness, instead of theological faithfulness.

Plain Style Preaching

As a preacher I learned that we need to balance a plain style of preaching with a more emotional and eloquent approach to communication. There is a plain style tradition of preaching that is like the decorations and furniture inside an Amish home. Everything is plain and unadorned.

The Puritan plain style was a rejection of a fancy, baroque approach to preaching in which flowery language replaced clear gospel presentation. In the 17th and 18th century Anglican church, priests were known for their flowery messages. The ministers crafted careful sermons that were literature. They read their essays. The sermons lacked life, emotion, and evangelical truth. During the Victorian era, the same fancy approach to sermons as fine literature characterized pulpits in the Church of England.

In the Dutch Reformed Church during the 17th and 18th century there were ministers who delivered complex, scholastic sermons where the skeleton of the logic overwhelmed the message. The Dutch plain style developed in response to this confusing and mind-numbing complexity. When dead orthodoxy (which really is an oxymoron) infiltrated the Dutch Reformed Church, some ministers were not only scholastic, but overly polemical. Plain speaking is an approach to preaching that values clarity and simplicity over complexity. The Puritans pursued after a plain speak that involved a biblical rhetoric. Within the Dutch Reformed tradition, one can find both plain speak and a more colorful approach to sermon rhetoric. Herman Hoeksema's sermons usually were plain speak. There is a lack of showy rhetoric. At the same time Hoeksema wrote many meditations where he shows a wonderful ear for the English language. But his rhetoric is not as showy as that of Abraham Kuyper. Kuyper showed the best of both traditions. He could preach and write in plain style and deliver messages that were marvelously crafted and revealed his genius at handling the Dutch language. He was a master of metaphors. Klaas Schilder could use a highly rhetorical approach to preaching as will be evident to any reader who peruses his famous sermons on the trials, sufferings, and death of Jesus. You could not characterize Schilder's sermons as Dutch plain-speak!

The gift of language is a gift of God and to be wielded for the glory of God. Let God's ministers balance a simple presentation of the gospel message in ordinary language with the linguistic gifts that can communicate the wonders and marvels of that message.

Ministers defend and justify boring communication on the basis of the fact that they are using the plain style. The plain style is wedded to an emotionless approach to preaching. A lack of emotion and passion leads to colorless plain speak. The fundamental problem with such boring plain speak is that the minister lacks passion. As we shall explore in greater detail, passion is the mother of eloquence.

The minister who does not work at communicating in a lively and interesting way imagines that he can hide under the cover of his plain style because he wrongly imagines that this is a sober, safe preaching method. I know that there are pious Reformed believers who even get upset with their preachers when they use nonbiblical examples or metaphors. Plain style preachers have their supporters in the pews! Plain style preachers laud themselves as people who want to communicate to the common man. But does the common man really lack the aesthetic ability to enjoy good communication? Does the common man want to hear preaching that is abstract instead of filled with concrete ideas and imaginative figures of speech?

Some confessing Christians want a plain style filled with ideas expressed in the same tired, old words. Why? They do not want to feel anything like the full force of the gospel or God's demands. They do not want to hear God's law set forth in a fresh way that will jolt them out of their antinomian complacency. They are content with their present understanding of God and the gospel. They do not want to be roused from their dogmatic slumber. They do not want to be challenged in their calling to be witnesses to the gospel.

Reformed preachers have gone too far down the road in the rejection of eloquence so that the words of the preacher sound mundane and canned.

Where is the fresh presentation of Christian ethics? Where is the vigorous exhibition of what God has done in history? Where is a passionate presentation of Reformed doctrine?

When Stunning Realities are "Ho-hum"

As a preacher, I learned to avoid like the plague the presentation of stunning spiritual realities as ho-hum matters. I am offended when Bible passages that speak of the supremacy and majesty of Christ are communicated in pedestrian language without doxology.

Why do preachers interpret exalted language about God with the same old language and predictable statements?

How is it that Jesus, who battled legalists, is preached to legalistic congregations as if He supports empowering the "weaker brother" who is really a "giant-tyrant." John Calvin wrote about how church members masquerade as weaker brothers when they are in fact giant-tyrants. Why is it that Jesus' unpredictable sayings and actions can turn out to be utterly prosaic and ordinary in the mouths of preachers.

Astonishing miracles are described as if they are events that happen every day and never surprise. Surprising and unique doctrines are presented as utterly predictable. How is it that unpredictable acts of God are presented as old news? Perhaps such a preacher needs to wear a shock collar? Every time he takes what is shocking and makes it pedestrian, every time he takes an astonishing act of divine grace and makes it sound like last years regurgitated news; an elder should press the button. If the minister will not be surprised by God's surprising grace and mighty acts, perhaps the shock will give him a jolt?

Preaching that is predictable is not biblical. It means that the preacher has developed his pet theological and biblical worldview and he will take every marvelous and astounding teaching in Scripture and pass it through his private grid to rob the message of power, grace, life, and beauty. The Holy Spirit gives him the gospel feast for the congregation of T-Bone steak, Kobe beef, and ribeye; but the minister grinds the message into hamburger and feeds the congregation the utterly ordinary meal of Hamburger-helper.

The Preacher Must be Prophetic

As a preacher I learned that the preacher must be a prophet. A good number of people in every congregations do not want a prophet for a preacher. They are content with the status quo in their life and the life of the church. They are unable to see the weaknesses of the church with fresh eyes. They are complacent in their spirituality. They are content with their theological ignorance. They do not want the boat rocked. They do not want to repent.

The local church needs a preacher who is a prophet for ten reasons. First, members of the congregation are walking unrepentedly in sin. Second, the congregants do not understand the Reformed faith as they should. Third, the young people are being blown to and fro by pagan depravity. Fourth, given the rebellion against the seventh commandment in our licentious age, the preacher needs to speak prophetically about sexuality, marriage, and divorce. Fifth, too many members are violating the Lord's Day. Sixth, we live in an antinomian age and this worldliness is rubbing off on Reformed believers. Seventh, our local churches are not carrying out the mission of the church with passion. Eighth, theological heresies threaten and need to be rebuffed in black and white. Ninth, the falsely comfortable need to be prodded awake spiritually. Tenth, the covenant children need to be guarded from demonic attacks.

The congregation needs to hear a prophetic voice from God's preacher.

The Power of Preaching

As a preacher I learned the power of preaching. When a minister is "channeling" the revealed will of God in Scripture, he preaches with power and force.

When one is faithfully preaching the text, he can say with great authority: "Thus saith the LORD."

As a minister one experiences the power of the Word. Then one becomes like Martin Luther. You aren't afraid about thundering out God's truth and message. Like William Tyndale you do not fear the kings of the earth or the high prelates. The English Bible translator dared to speak the word of the eternal God to a rebellious Roman Catholic Church in England. Tyndale feared no man. Therefore, he translated the Scriptures into common English. And he wrote. His pen burned with the flame of passion. He dared to rebuke the highest prelates because he spoke in the name of the living God.

The faithful preacher experiences the power of the Word. He can speak with authority and not like the Pharisees.

I experienced the powerful effect of preaching the truth on my own heart and emotions. When I am wrapped up in a message that I know is the Word and truth of God, my emotions burn. Then I experience what John Piper calls "logic on fire." When you have an irresistible biblical argument to back up what you are calling upon the saints to do (or the unsaved to do), then you speak with great weight. You know that no man can resist the Word that you bring. God is speaking through you. And no one can resist the mouth of the LORD God. Jehovah roars from Zion through his preachers. Men can try to fight the Word, but the Word will break them.

Hypocrites in the congregation oppose the call to love the truth and to pursue after holiness, but the Word will hold them accountable.

A Billy goat in the congregation might oppose and slander the preacher. But the Word stands. And the Word will have its affect. The Word will triumph.

The Billy goat might use family and clan connections to get the minister kicked out of the congregation.

But the Billy goat's win will be a pyrrhic victory.

The Word will triumph. And God will vindicate His preacher. He always does. Be assured, minister of the Word, that Christ loves you. And He speaks through you!

Chapter 7
"The True Method of Speaking is the "*Extempore*"

he very title of this chapter might well arouse opposition in the breast of the preacher. How dare the writer say that the "true method of speaking" (and, therefore, of preaching) is the extemporaneous? I throw this statement out to the reader as a challenge. And notice that I placed the chapter title in quotation marks. This is because I am giving you a quote from an old authority on preaching: Robert Dabney. We shall see that Dabney makes this statement in a context where he promotes extemporaneous *preaching*.

The Ease and Popularity of the Extemporaneous Method

A prominent author who writes about contemporary methods of speech-giving surprisingly can state: "Today most people speak extemporaneously." If even unbelievers are giving speeches extemporaneously, how much more should Christian preachers! Listen to what Stephen Lucas writes: "Today most people speak extemporaneously--which means the speech is thoroughly prepared and carefully practiced in advance, but much of the exact wording is selected while the speech is being delivered."[78] Are preachers willing to do the work of practicing their sermons in advance?

Lucas distinguishes an extemporaneous message from an impromptu: "An impromptu speech is delivered without any immediate preparation whatever."[79] At times the preacher as pastor will need to give impromptu talks. He will suddenly be called out of his busy schedule to visit a parishioner in the hospital. With little or no preparation, he will need to give an impromptu talk. I remember visiting a catechism class taught by Rev. Barry Gritters when I was a seminary student. I surprised him. He forgot that

---

[78] Stephen E. Lucas, The Art of Public Speaking 3rd Edition (New York: Random House, 1989), 198.

a seminary student planned to visit his class that day. He apologized for not having prepared to teach. I thought he did a grant job of teaching. He apologized because his teaching was impromptu. But not even such impromptu speaking is totally impromptu. Gritters called upon his past experiences of teaching the Bible stories that he needed to present on the day I visited class. His teaching was lively and relevant.

Once I attended a funeral at an all-black church. Since I was recognized as a minister, the next thing I knew I was sitting on the platform and speaking during the funeral. My talk was impromptu. But I did have a chance to reflect on the words of a Psalm that I used to give a brief meditation.

Sometimes people use "extemporaneous" to describe an impromptu talk. We want to distinguish between the two. Lucas does so:

> In popular usage, "extemporaneous" means the same as "impromptu." But technically the two are different. Unlike an impromptu speech, which is totally off the cuff, an extemporaneous speech is carefully prepared and practiced in advance. In presenting the speech, the extemporaneous speaker uses only a set of brief notes or a speaking outline to jog his memory. The exact wording is chosen at the moment of delivery.[80]

Seminary students should be encouraged by the fact that extemporaneous speaking is not difficult! Listen to what Lucas writes:

> This is not as hard as it sounds. Once you have your outline (or notes) and know what topics you are going to cover and in what order, you can begin to practice the speech. Every time you run through it, the wording will be slightly different. As you practice the speech over and over, the best way to present each part will emerge and stick in your mind.[81]

What Lucas says is true. As a pastor I often practiced my sermon in church. Maybe you have a study in church like I did. I would ascend the pulpit and present the sermon to an empty church. I would leave my sermon outline in my study. Without the stress of having auditors, I would try to communicate the heart of my sermon. Invariably I discovered new insights. I would incorporate new ideas and better transitions into my written outline. More importantly, I had internalized the new insights and had learned how I could make critical transitions.

Practicing the sermon led to discoveries about what truths caused my

---

[79] Ibid., 234.
[80] Ibid., 235.

heart to burn. I learned when to let the fires of emotion burn out of control and sweep everything before them. It is not enough to have a logical message in a good outline. You need a heart on fire. Passion is necessary. George Campbell writes that "When persuasion is the end, passion also must be engaged."[82]

Lucas, having encouraged extemporaneous speaking, writes that "If you want listeners to do something as a result of your speech, you must arouse their feelings. You must appeal to their hearts as well as their heads."[83] Yet emotion without logic will not work: "Unless you prove your case, careful listeners will not be stirred by your emotional appeals. You need to build a good case based on reason *and* kindle the emotions of your audience."[84]

As I practiced my sermon, I discovered theological insights that brought balance to my message. I thought of fresh ways to apply the sermon.

As we sit at our desks in our studies, we can feel like we have run out of fresh ideas. But our minds are more pregnant and fertile than we are aware. I have found that getting out of my study and taking a walk helps. I can preach through my sermon while praying. The Holy Spirit uses this to give additional insights and add dynamism to the message. I find that preaching a sermon to God as an act of prayer helps me to comprehend the spiritual realities more deeply. If we do not feel truth, we will not become eloquent. When we comprehend God and His truth, we can be used by God the Holy Spirit to impress these genuine realities on the hearts of God's people.

When you practice your sermon in advance, you will have greater confidence when you stand before the congregation. You also will have a better understanding of the verbal fireworks that you can display to make an important point.

The advantage of the extemporaneous method should commend it to preacherThe extemporaneous method has several advantages. It gives more precise control over thought and language than does impromptu speaking; it offers greater spontaneity and directness than does speaking from memory or from a full manuscript; and it is adaptable to a wide range of situations. It also encourages the conversational quality audiences look for in speech delivery. "Conversational quality" means that no matter how many times a speech has been rehearsed, it still *sounds* spontaneous to the audience. When you speak extemporaneously—and have prepared properly—you have full

---

[81] Ibid., 235.

[82] George Campbell, The Philosophy of Rhetoric, ed. Lloyd F. Bitzer (Carbondale, Ill: Southern Illinois University Press, 1988), 77.

[83] Stephen E. Lucas, The Art of Public Speaking 3rd Edition (New York: Random House, 1989), 334.

[84] Ibid., 235.

control over your ideas, yet you are not tied to a manuscript. You are free to establish strong eye contact, to gesture naturally, and to concentrate on talking *with* the audience rather than declaiming *to* them.[85]

I wonder if a better way to talk about the "conversational quality" of extemporaneous preaching is to refer to the "natural quality" of such communication. There is a "conversational" approach to communication that can thrive in the pulpit, but there are also other methods of communication. The crucial thing is that the speaking ought not to come across as artificial or canned.

I think that I have heard enough sermons that were read from manuscripts. My life-time quota has been met. I think of a Protestant Reformed minister who read sermon after sermon from an extended outline while glancing from the left back wall to the right back wall. I think of a mentor on an internship who could not look at the congregation for apparent psychological reasons. He read his manuscript. He couldn't look me in the eye either. I think of an Orthodox Presbyterian minister in Florida who read his sermon word for word while glancing at the opposing walls. I think of a minister at College Church in Wheaton, Illinois who reads his scholarly sermons word for word. I have heard CRC, PCA, and URC ministers and seminary students read their sermons word for word.

I have heard enough read sermons.

If the minister can't internalize the message of the text, why should I? How could I? If the sermon message is so complex that the minister cannot internalize it, how can the auditors?

I do not mind a sermon outline that is a help for extemporaneous preaching. I know that some ministers bring an entire sermon in essay form into the pulpit, but only use it as a help. They treat it like an outline and make notes on the left side of the pages to jog their memory.

I am sympathetic to ministers who do not have the psychological strength to look at their parishioners. God's ministers are often attacked and suffer from a form of Post-Traumatic Stress Syndrome. They can be over-burdened by the expectations and criticisms of congregants. I am not critical of them. Let God's injured ministers read their sermons. Praise God that they can even write a sermon and then get up to read it.

I am not critical of ministers who lack the intellectual gifts to internalize a message. As ministers age, they can lose their short-term memories. Let emeritus ministers read their sermons. They bring a wealth of biblical and pastoral insight along with their written sermons. Not all of

---

[85] Ibid., 235.

God's ministers have as good of minds as others. Some men are limited in their ability to study the biblical languages, engage in careful exegesis, and do their own theological work. Maybe the minister attended a seminary with lowered standards. Recently a minister who graduated from Western Seminary in Holland, Michigan told me that he didn't attend Mid-America Reformed Seminary in Dyer, IN because he couldn't have handled the academic work at the latter institution. Yet he did graduate from Western Seminary and now preaches the Word. I am sympathetic with ministers with limited gifts and have greatly benefited from sermons by such men.

✓Are you spiritually and psychologically strong? Do you have a good memory and a logical mind? Has God given you good linguistic gifts? Then preach extemporaneously. Internalize the message. Bless yourself and God's people by weaning yourself off paper or an iPad.

Iain Campbell on the Use of Paper

Every preacher is different. The extent to which the minister will depend on paper or an iPad will differ. Iain Campbell writes:

> One of the first observations I made in this book is that preachers are individuals, not clones of others. Just as we have different approaches to studying, so we will also have different ways of recalling what we have studied. Some people have better memories than others. Some preachers will rely on copious notes; others will not use notes at all.[86]

The preacher's iPad or paper manuscript can become a third point of reference that distracts from the attention that should be given to the congregation and the text.

> There are two points of reference in any act of preaching: the text of Scripture and the congregation. I am not at all distracted by the preacher's use of notes as long as they do not distract him from these two points of reference. If his notes become a third point of reference, so that he is constantly looking down at them or turning pages, they will be in danger of intervening between him and his audience.[87]

Campbell hopes that the preacher will limit himself to one page of notes.

---

[86] Iain D. Campbell, Pray, plan, prepare, preach: Establishing and maintaining priorities in the preaching ministry (Leominster, UK: Day One Publications, 2012), 87.
[87] Ibid., 87.

Every preacher should aim at having skeleton notes in front of him, contained on one page if possible. The use of electronic notebooks has become popular, and the same principle applies with these as with paper: if we are constantly seen to be turning slips of paper or scrolling down computer screens, we will distract rather than attract our hearers.[88]

Campbell values extemporaneous preaching because of the unpredictability that can occur in it.

The action of preaching the Word is a glorious, remarkably unpredictable event. Who knows what the Holy Spirit might do with a Bible based, Christ-centered and God-glorifying message![89]

Robert L. Dabney: The True Method of Preaching is the *Extempore*

Now we turn to the Southern Presbyterian theologian Robert L. Dabney who is the source of my quotation about how the extemporaneous method of preaching is the true method of preaching. This 19th century theologian authored a widely read book on homiletics called *Sacred Rhetoric*. Dabney writes that the "true method" of preaching is "the *extempore*."[90] Here is the exact quote: "By the last remark I have intimated already my opinion that the true method of speaking is the *extempore*."[91] The Southern Presbyterian theologian then argues for the extemporaneous method in preaching.

Dabney qualifies what he means by the *extempore* method. He does not mean preaching without "premeditation."[92] He distinguishes extemporaneous preaching from an *impromptu* discourse:

I mean by it a discourse in which the thought has been perfectly prearranged, but the words, except in cardinal propositions, are left to the free suggestions of the moment. The preparation of the ideas may even be by reducing them regularly to a written form, provided the words written are not imposed upon the memory.[93]

---

[88] Ibid., 87-88.
[89] Ibid., 88.
[90] Robert L. Dabney Sacred Rhetoric: or A Course of Lectures on Preaching (Edinburgh: Banner of Truth, 1979), 332.
[91] Ibid., 332.
[92] Ibid., 332.
[93] Ibid., 332.

John Calvin rejected an impromptu delivery without prior preparation. The minister who preaches without studying Scripture is a "presumptuous fool":

> If I should step up into the pulpit, without vouchsafing to look upon any book, and fondly imagine to say thus in my self, "Truth, when I come thither, God will give me enough whereof to speak," and in the meanwhile I hold scorn to read, or to study aforehand what I shall speak, and come hither without minding how to apply the Holy Scripture to the edification of the people, by reason whereof I should play the presumptuous fool, and God would put me to shame for mine overboldness.[94]

Dabney admits that extemporaneous preaching is more difficult and takes more preparation than writing and reading a complete sermon manuscript. "I am so far from recommending *extempore* preaching to you as an expedient for saving labour, that I regard it as demanding the most thorough preparation of all."[95]

Although extemporaneous preaching is more difficult than reading a sermon, Dabney believes that the benefits of doing so "are decisive with the man who has a true ideal of oratory."[96]

> The capital advantage is, that the mind is required to perform over again the labour of invention, during the actual delivery of the discourse. It is thus aroused and nerved. The condition of its success is, that it must again represent to itself in a living form the whole thought and emotion of the discourse; that it must, in a word, recreate it in the act of delivering it. It is only such a discourse, actually born in its delivery (if it is a second birth), a living progeny of the soul, that has true movement.[97]

---

[94] John Calvin, Sermons on Deuteronomy, facsimile edition of 1583 (Edinburgh: Banner of Truth Trust, 1987), 292, Column 1. Cited by Derek W.H. Thomas in Derek W. H. Thomas "Expository Preaching" in Feed My Sheep: A Passionate Plea for Preaching, R. Albert Mohler...[et al.], General editor, Don Kistler. (Sanford, Florida: Reformation Trust Publishing, 2008), 37.
[95] Robert L. Dabney Sacred Rhetoric: or A Course of Lectures on Preaching (Edinburgh: Banner of Truth, 1979), 332.
[96] Ibid., 332-33.
[97] Ibid., 333.

Dabney thinks that the problem with a preacher who reads his sermon is that he only delineates "the dead outline of what once feebly lived in his mind."[98] The Southern Presbyterian theologian distinguishes between having a message in your memory—having a certain intellectual understanding of it—and having internalized it in your heart.

> The ill-starred experience of all of us teaches us, that it is possible to do this without having the matter of our discourse penetrate any deeper into our souls than the memory, and therefore they cannot penetrate the souls of our hearers; for the speaker can only affect them with the truth as he affects himself with it.[99]

Dabney, like Herman Bavinck, connects eloquence with the heart and emotion.

> Eloquence is not the mere communication of a set of dry notions; it is a sympathy, a spiritual infection, a communion of life and action between two souls, a projection of the orator's thought, conviction, emotion and will into the mind and heart of the audience. Nothing, therefore, is a true oration which is not a life, a spiritual action, transacted in the utterance.[100]

In extemporaneous preaching

> The mind thus roused, having the advantage of its previous premeditation and thorough knowledge of the subject, grasps it with more vigour than it had ever done in solitude. Indeed, all the powers of the soul are now exalted—reasoning, memory, imagination, suggestion, sensibility. More direct and luminous views of the logical truth now flash athwart the subject, like beams of sunlight. Glowing illustrations and images now teem in the imagination. More appropriate and burning words now arise unbidden than he could ever have excogitated in cold blood. The emotions of the hour dictate an action natural, flexible and animated.[101]

Dabney is convinced that "The natural animation of the orator's mind will deliver him from monotony, give flexibility of style, and protect him from tiresome artifices of intonation."[102]

---

[98] Ibid., 333.
[99] Ibid., 333.
[100] Ibid., 333.
[101] Ibid., 234.
[102] Ibid., 334.

Dabney thinks that an educated man should be able to preach extemporaneously.

> It ought surely to be no impossible thing for an educated man to acquire such a command of his mother-tongue, as to be able to form it readily into simple sentences without error of syntax, especially when the mind is invigorated by the excitement of public address. If you are truly masters of your thoughts, you will have no lack of correct words.[103]

The Challenges and Dangers Facing Extemporaneous Preachers

What are the challenges of extemporaneous preaching? What dangers threaten?

Dabney thinks that the greatest danger is that the preacher will sin against the law of conciseness: "The difficult thing for the *extempore* speaker is to make his words scarce."[104] The orator must avoid "abundant verbiage."[105] You want "to make the style compact, nervous and clear."[106]

While J. Daniel Baumann encouraged the orator to use complex sentences, Dabney argues that concise, shorter sentences will help the preacher avoid excessive verbiage. "But the simple, brief, compact sentence (which is the proper form for oratory) is exacting. It demands the right phrase by its very directness, and demands it at once. It requires to be concluded without dallying."[107]

The greatest danger is that the orator will abuse his quick facility with language. "The fluent declaimer can, for a time, cover his deficiency of matter by his readiness of speech."[108] To safeguard against this danger, the minister should continue to use his pen in the study. Dabney advises that the young minister should write out at least half of his sermon, but not take the document into the pulpit.[109]

---

[103] Ibid., 337.
[104] Ibid., 335.
[105] Ibid., 335.
[106] Ibid., 335.
[107] Ibid., 336.
[108] Ibid., 337.
[109] Ibid., 338.

A second danger of extemporaneous preaching is "becoming confused, and totally losing the thread."[110] This danger "can always be overcome by diligence in preparation and by use."[111] The preacher needs to internalize the main points of his sermon. He should not lose sight of the logical flow of the message. He needs to remember to emphasize what ought to be emphasized and keep in mind that minor points need to be kept in their proper proportion in relation to the big ideas.

Good Eye Contact in Extemporaneous Preaching

When I preach before a congregation, I feel like Andrew Jackson. He told the American soldiers who faced the Redcoats at New Orleans during the War of 1812: "Don't fire till you can see the whites of their eyes." I want to see the whites of the saint's eyes. Jackson didn't want his soldiers to waste their bullets. The American soldiers triumphed over the British, although the War of 1812 technically had been declared over (the news hadn't arrived in New Orleans).

I want the preacher to send forth bullets of truth and love. Haddon Robinson doesn't want preaching to be like shooting shotgun shells so that the message scatters. I bring up Andrew Jackson's exhortation because my concern is with eye contact between preacher and congregation.

I want to be able to see the eyes of the members of the congregation. Then they know that I am speaking to them. My children catch me doing odd things, like blinking my eyes too much while I preach. They realize that this is seen by the congregation and is an odd quirk. We communicate with our eyes.

Both pagan and Christian rhetoricians have recognized the importance of eye contact in communication. Why is it that Christian preachers do not perceive the importance of eye contact? David Larsen writes that "Herbert H. Farmer convincingly argued that the direct encounter with the will is hampered when the sermon is read. *Paper is not a good conductor of heat.*"[112] We have an epidemic of ministers who avoid eye contact with the saints. Larsen writes that "The eye is really an organ of speech. Indeterminate eye focus or too furtive an eye sweep is unsatisfying to listeners."[113]

---

[110] Ibid., 336.
[111] Ibid., 336.
[112] David L. Larsen The Anatomy of Preaching: Identifying the Issues in Preaching Today (Grand Rapids: Kregel, 1999), 188. Emphasis added.
[113] Ibid., 189.

We know that in every day relationships we are uncomfortable when a person cannot look us in the face. If a politician in the House of Commons in Great Britain starts reading a speech and takes his eye off the members, an MP can indict him by announcing: "May I call attention to the fact that the honorable member is reading his remarks."[114] There would be little speaking in the United States Senate if such a policy was enacted. Perhaps one elder in each congregation should be given the opportunity to make this same remark if the minister begins to read a manuscript.

How to Acquire the Ability to Preach Extemporaneously

Dabney provides tips on how to acquire the ability to preach *extempore*. He presents four steps. The first step in learning how to preach without notes is by "careful writing."[115] "The abundant and painstaking use of the pen is necessary to give you correctness, perspicuity and elegance of language, and to make these easy to you."[116] He discusses the symbiotic relationship between the rhetoric of oratory and the use of the pen in the study.

"No man ever learns to compose a sermon at his desk in rhetorical language save by speaking *extempore* under the rhetorical impulse; so no man ever learns to speak well *extempore* save by learning to write well."[117]

The second step towards achieving extemporaneous preaching is by practice. I tell my students to improve the grammatical quality of their sentences in everyday conversation. I want them to become aware of how they use or abuse the Queen's English. Dabney advises the same: "Here let me urge that you make every sentence you utter, in your most familiar conversation, a drill in correctness of speech."[118] He even exhorts his students to practice extemporaneous speaking daily. Are seminary students taking the achievement of eloquence as seriously as Dabney expected of his Southern Presbyterian students? "The man who is training himself for the pulpit should scarcely allow a day to elapse without an exercise in continuous *extempore* speech."[119] Let your audience be the trees in a forest, Dabney suggests.

---

[114] Ibid., 189.
[115] Robert L. Dabney *Sacred Rhetoric: or A Course of Lectures on Preaching* (Edinburgh: Banner of Truth, 1979), 339.
[116] Ibid., 339.
[117] Ibid., 339.
[118] Ibid., 340.
[119] Ibid., 340.

Practice speaking in "clean, simple, and manageable" sentences.[120] "You should speak to your trees audibly and continuously, refusing to yourselves any stoppage, and also consulting propriety of utterance as far as your attention enables you."[121] A third step in achieving extemporaneous preaching is by preparing a logical outline, what Dabney calls a "brief" or "syllabus." In this brief "all important ideas are briefly stated in their intended order, but not in the language which is to be employed in preaching.

The divisions and subdivisions of this brief should then be indelibly fixed in the memory."[122] The idea is to internalize the logic of the sermon. Dabney exhorts: "You must stamp your outline on your memory so deeply, that it will be impossible for you to fail in its prompt recall. And especially must the relation of every part to the central idea and dominant impression of the sermon be distinctly apprehended."[123]

I believe that the best manuscript to take into the pulpit is an outline at which a minister only needs to glance. Dabney expresses the same concern about only glancing at an outline. He gives this practical advice before the advent of typewriters or computers: "You should write remembering that it must be read by a rapid *glance*, and the characters should be large, the ink-strokes strong, the words well separated and blocklike in arrangement, and the capitals marking the beginnings or paragraphs and sentences prominent."[124]

A fourth step in learning how to preach without notes is by doing original exegetical and homiletical work. The preacher's heart and mind must engage in the creative work of what Sinclair B. Ferguson calls "crystalizing" and what Glen C. Knecht calls "intuition." James Stalker wrote that "Originality in the preaching of the truth depends on the solitary intuition of it."[125] I have discovered that it is only when I have wrapped my mind around the text and taken possession of it through hard labor, that I can preach without notes.

---

[120] Ibid., 340-341.

[121] Ibid., 341.

[122] Ibid., 342.

[123] Ibid., 342.

[124] Ibid., 343. Emphasis added.

[125] James Stalker, The Life of St. Paul (Old Tappan, N.J.: Fleming H. Revell, 1950), 47. Cited by Glen C. Knecht, 280.

If preaching is partly truth mediated through the preacher's personality and experience, it is necessary for the preacher to intuit the text. Dabney argues that the preacher will not be able to preach without notes if he borrows his ideas or outline from someone else. "The idea of the plan must be your own conception, or to you it cannot have life. Its invention in your own mind can alone give spirit and interest in your discussion."[126] I fear that this is the reason why preachers do not and cannot preach without paper. They cannot or will not do the hard work of knocking their heads against the text to own it. They have not entered the heart of the text so it does not set their hearts on fire. They feed off the insights of commentators. They might read their own boring insights back into the text and rob it of its originality, beauty, and power.

I think that Dabney's four steps are just as relevant today as when he first suggested them. The reason why Dabney wants the minister to follow these four steps is because the true method of preaching is the *extempore.*

---

[126] Robert L. Dabney Sacred Rhetoric: or A Course of Lectures on Preaching (Edinburgh: Banner of Truth, 1979), 343.

Chapter 8
Be Yourself: The Originality that Enables *Extempore* Preaching

Not Being Yourself

Jerry Clower, the late Baptist Southern comedian, told a story about a young preacher whose education went to his head:

The Lord called an old boy to preach at Route 4, Liberty Mississippi, when I was a youngun growing up. And he went off to college and was gone a year and come home for Christmas holidays and the pastor of our local church said "Do you know, the courteous thing to do is to invite him to fill the pulpit while he's home." Now that feller got up in the pulpit and just gone from East Fork Community just one year and he got up in that pulpit and you would have thought that he was born in a foreign land. He didn't say "God" any more, he said "GAWDDE." He didn't say "morning" he said "moorningg."

My brother Sunny said, "I ain't gonna listennnn!!"

I said, "Sunny, shut up, you are disturbing the worship service."

Sunny said, "Jerry, he ain't being hisself. And the thing that so galls me about it is that he ain't being one of us. Jerry, got no right not to be yourself, Jerry. I ain't gonna listen to him preachin unlessen he goin to talken like he oughta talk."

Sunny said, "The thing that galls me so bad about it is that he was just as poor as we was when we was comin up. If anything he was a little poorer than we was."

Sunny said, "Jerry, don't you remember the one summer that that boy up there in that pulpit preachen right now not being hisself, don't you remember one summer they were so poor that his momma fed him so many turnip greens she had to keep a corrawl rag tied around his ankles to keep the cutworms from gettin him."

That new preacher was not being himself.

There are several ways in which a young preacher might not be himself. He imitates the mannerisms of a professor or favorite pastor. The way he formulates doctrines in his sermons are right out of their systematic theology notes from seminary. Then there is the preek (rhymes with "rake") tone. I am not sure how to write the word "preek" which is a Dutch word that is derogatory to describe a preacher who uses an officious and artificial tone that he thinks makes his speaking sound solemn and important. He tries to sound pious.

Why is it that some young ministers are tempted to imitate some sort of holy language? Are they are trying to sound like a pious Puritan? Are they trying to imitate Sinclair Ferguson's dialect? Sorry, if you were born in the Midwest of the United States you will not sound like Sinclair Ferguson. Charles Spurgeon quoted a Roman Catholic who said: "The instant you abandon the natural and the true, you forego the right to be believed, as well as the right of being listened to." With cutting wit, Spurgeon said:

> You may go all round, to church and chapel alike, and you will find that by far the larger majority of our preachers have a holy tone for Sundays. They have one voice for the parlour and the bed-room, and quote another tone for the pulpit; so that, if not double-tongued sinfully, they certainly are so literally.

The difficulty is that young preachers are trying to develop a style. Naturally they learn from others. Mentors need to encourage young men to display their own personality, gifts, insights, and interests.

Biblical Principles about Being Yourself

The foundation for being yourself in the pulpit is found in the doctrine of creation. God has created and recreated ministers as unique human persons. There is no one else like you in the world. The doctrine of creation and the great diversity of God's works is the biblical foundation for you being yourself. God is a God who celebrates diversity. The Holy Spirit gave you unique gifts. You do not have the same gifts as another man so do not be jealous of the gifts he has. God gave you other and wonderful gifts.

God gives us natural gifts and then uses them for His glory. If you were saved later on in life, there is what we call redemptive continuity. God takes the gifts and abilities that you already enjoyed as an unbeliever, and now directs them to His glory.

✓ The Bible teaches the principle that we are to minister without the fear of man. The fear of man (the desire to impress men by imitating someone impressive) leads to you not being yourself. God frees you to be yourself by warning you not to fear men, but instead minister *coram Deo*. The Bible teaches that you are to be yourself in the face of congregational expectations.

✓ The fear of man bringeth a snare: but whoso putteth his trust in the LORD shall be safe (Proverbs 29:25).

✓ How can ye believe, which receive honour one of another, and seek not the honour that cometh from God only? (John 5:44)

✓ But with me it is a very small thing that I should be judged of you, or of man's judgment: yea, I judge not mine own self. For I know nothing by myself; yet am I not hereby justified: but he that judgeth me is the Lord (I Corinthians 4:3-4).

✓ We need to live free from the desire for human praise. Do not let people stuff you into a mold. We all live with the tension between what we are and what others want us to be. We need to be what God made and remade us to be.

Feel free to let your humanity and uniqueness show.

✓ The Bible teaches that as a young minister you are to be yourself as you rightly divide the word of truth. God wants you to be yourself as you do theology. Paul in I Timothy 4:12-16 tells Timothy "to give attendance to reading, to exhortation, to doctrine." He is not to neglect the gift that is in him. He is to take heed to doctrine. In II Timothy 2:15 Paul says: "Study to shew thyself approved unto God, a workman that needeth not to be ashamed, rightly dividing the word of truth." You need to study the Bible for yourself. You may not live off the research and discoveries of others.

✓ There is a temptation not to be yourself as you do exegesis and theology. The temptation comes from within. By nature we are lazy. It is easier to pluck the exegetical fruits of others. Temptations can come from professors or even the congregation who might want you to fit into some sort of denominational mold. There is the temptation to become sectarian. A theology of fear says that young ministers should not disagree with professors, due to an undue fear of novelty.

✓ A congregation's satisfaction with the *status quo* can express itself in dissatisfaction with anything new and prophetic.

Seminary professors are anxious that when their students begin exhorting in the churches that they avoid heresy.

They teach their students Reformed and Protestant distinctives. Included in this are theological formulations.

Some are historic formulations that are part of the language of the universal church, such as trinitarian formulations. Others are Protestant dogmas, like the doctrine of justification by faith alone. The Apostle Paul writes: "Hold fast the form of sound words, which thou hast heard of me" (II Timothy 1:13). Seminary students who begin to exhort (speak a word of edification) need to hold fast to the form of sound words.

But there are formulations that are more parochial and reflect denominational distinctives that can also reflect theological jealousies. Sometimes influential professors in a denomination teach error. These errors are in conflict with confessional documents. But due to the influence of the professor in the denomination, there is no accountability. Maybe he has convinced a good number of seminary students about the rightness of his views. But you do not need to further the school of a professor. You are not of his party. You are of the party of Jesus Christ.

Do not bore the people of God by spouting formulations that are worn out or that appealed to an older generation.

It takes a rare person to get excited about preaching theological formulations that others have produced.

Be yourself.

Develop fresh arguments and formulations when it is fitting.

Our Master was distinctly unique.

He did not repeat the dry formulations of the rabbinical schools.

Because God's revelation is so multi-faceted you may not rest on the laurels of past insights.

Be yourself as you do exegesis and write your sermon.

Using commentaries and sermons for research is great. They can be helpful and provide you with many good insights. You are what you read. But be yourself. Internalize any good insights that you learn from a commentator.

Translate and meditate upon the Scripture yourself. Try to figure out what the Greek text is saying. Knock your head on the text.

Pray.

Yes, use the insights of others, but use them in your own original way. Make them your own.

In *The Christian Mind*, Harry Blamires laments the loss of the Christian mind in Great Britain in the 1960s. He lamented the fact that Christians were not thinking issues through from a uniquely Christian perspective.

Of course, the Church apart, it is a feature of our culture that as we are rich in scholars so we are poor in thinkers. Occasionally, very occasionally, a man may be both a first-rate scholar and a first-rate thinker. But the nature of our modern educational system is such that this happy combination arises ever more rarely. Potential thinkers are being turned into mere scholars by the pressures of conformity so strong both in the educational world and in society at large. The thinker challenges current prejudices. He disturbs the complacent. He obstructs the busy pragmatists....The thinker is a nuisance.

Blamires says: "But the church is false to itself when it rejects the thinker."

Young pastors must be thinkers. They need to think through exegetical questions themselves. Older pastors need to be thinkers. They need to get the fire of the text in their bones.

New pastors need to think through theological controversies themselves. Sometimes seminary students are fed information on how to interpret theological controversies in the history of the church. The professors have a wrong understanding of the issues and, without thinking, the student spouts the same interpretation from the pulpit. I know of what I speak. I have done battle with sectarians.

In your preaching, be yourself. Use your own examples. It is rather remarkable as you read sermons how often you come across old examples from the 19th or 20th century. They rarely work.

It is a challenge to relax in front of a congregation. It takes time. You might always remain nervous in front of the congregation. Even experienced ministers experience the tension that comes with bringing a new message with an awareness of the expectations of the congregation.

Take advantage of opportunities to speak in rest homes, jails, or rescue missions.

✺ Be Your Sanctified Self

You will best communicate when you are yourself. Being yourself is not the same as being boring. If you are always bored with the Bible, don't be yourself. Repent and start getting excited about the Word so that you can communicate it with excitement.

If you don't find much excitement in talking with God, do not be yourself in the congregational prayer. Repent and begin to get excited about God.

If you do not celebrate God, do not be yourself. Congregations do not need preachers who do not celebrate God. Repent and begin to celebrate the grandeur and glory of the Triune God.

If there is a boring sameness to your talk about the gospel, do not be yourself. Repent.

If you are bored with the Scriptures and find them to be the same old thing, do not bore the congregation by getting up to preach to them. Sit in the pew.

In prayer, be yourself. But your sanctified self. Your old man wants to manifest itself in prayer. But kill it. Mortify it. Otherwise you are really involved in vain repetitions. True prayer needs to come from the heart. If you pray without showing any love for God, do not be that self. Repent and start to show the warmth of your love.

Charles Spurgeon says: "Fine prayers are generally very wicked prayers."

I would add: "Boring prayers are generally very wicked prayers." Why are some congregational prayers so boring? It is because the minister is not enjoying communion with God and is not filled with astonishment at the glory of God. He does not bring petitions with boldness. He does not express much love for God.

Paul prayed out of his personal understanding of Christ and the Christian faith. His prayers were richly doctrinal—make your prayers the same.

Don't try to imitate prayers that moved you—unless the truths or prayers have become your own.

God isn't interested in rhetoric in prayer. But where there is a lack of eloquence, it probably is due to a lack of delightful communion with God. If passion is the mother of eloquence, a lack of eloquence manifests a cold heart. Part of the genius of William Tyndale is that he knew that when ordinary Englishmen talked about high and holy things, their language did become exalted—although it remained simple and clear.

God wants us to talk to Him from the heart.

You are a unique child of God. Therefore, you should not talk to your heavenly Father as if you are just another child. Let the communists try to make unique individuals into a bunch of automatons. God did not save us to deliver us from our unique personalities. You need to develop your own relationship with God and it will be a unique one.

Be yourself.

But your sanctified self.

Iain D. Campbell celebrates the uniqueness of each one of God's preachers:

But long may it be the case that we emphasize that preaching is truth through personality. We rejoice to hear the gospel through a variety of accents, in a variety of cultures, and through a variety of personalities.[127]

The prophetic things that I will have to say about homiletics and extemporaneous preaching is not meant to rob God's unique preachers of their own style and individuality.

> We differ from one another, and preaching remains the filtering of the truth of the gospel through the preacher's personality, precisely because the gospel he preaches has first been preached *to* his personality.[128]

The Originality of One's Own Intuition

Glen C. Knecht argues that *intuition* is the key to order and logic. The only way that you can deliver a sermon *extempore* is if you have internalized the logic of your subject and text. What is this intuition that is the "key to order"?[129] Knecht defines a preacher's "solitary intuition" of a text as his personal grasp of it. The preacher must have this solitary intuition if he is going to internalize the message effectively. How can one internalize a message and perceive it as your own if it a borrowed message from the mind of another? Knecht defines intuition:

> The intuition of a passage is what it means to you after you have pondered it and worked with it and prayed over it. An intuition is original in the sense that it is uniquely yours. You have arrived at it yourself. While your statement of the truth might closely resemble what others have found, nevertheless it is yours. Your intuition of a passage is your particular statement of that interpretation at this time in your own spiritual pilgrimage. *The original grasp of the text or passage is the key to your structure.*[130]

What is this originality that is the key to extemporaneous preaching? Knecht means

---

[127] Iain D. Campbell, Pray, plan, prepare, preach: Establishing and maintaining priorities in the preaching ministry (Leominster, UK: Day One Publications, 2012),19.
[128] Ibid., 20.
[129] Glen C. Knecht, "Sermon Structure and Flow" in The Preacher and Preaching: Reviving the Art in the Twentieth Century Edited by Samuel T. Logan, Jr. (Phillipsburg, N.J.: P & R Publishing, 1986), 280.
[130] Ibid., 280. Emphasis added.

> The flow of truth through you as it would not flow exactly through any other minister of the gospel. A man's sermon ought to have his own soul in it and his own fingerprints on it in the way a great oratorio speaks of its composer in every line....We must be ourselves, for that is the way to Christian originality.[131]

Knecht believes that "the call to originality is a call to the minister to be himself—joyously, thankfully, and creatively."[132] In intuition the preacher's soul confronts the meaning of the text. "Discovering the intuition of a passage brings a man right up against himself. His own inner life is exposed."[133] What I would refer to as part of the process of internalization, Knecht describes as intuition of how the big idea of the text is "displayed...on the screen of his inner life."

> He must be himself, under God, and grasp the solitary intuition of the passage as he sees it displayed in front of him on the screen of his inner life. That is his and that will be the embryo of the sermon.[134]

The preacher intuits the passage through the process of word studies, studying parallel passages, understanding it in the context of all Scripture and Christian doctrine, and grasping the personal application. The minister should write "abundant notes" as he reflects on the text.[135] The preacher intuits the central idea of the text.

> Thus the heart of the sermon is the preacher's intuition of what the passage is saying. A sermon is unfolded from the interior of the text and the inner life of the man....Sermons constructed this way reach to the depths of others' souls.[136]

Knecht argues that this intuition will be expressed in the proposition.

Sinclair B. Ferguson discusses the process of intuiting the main point of the text along with the subsidiary points. The movement from intuiting the main point to composing a unified message, he refers to as "crystallizing." "Crystallization is the process by which the bodies with orderly arrangements of atoms, ions, or molecules are formed or enlarged, generally

---

[131] Ibid., 280.
[132] Ibid., 281.
[133] Ibid., 281.
[134] Ibid., 281.
[135] Ibid., 282.
[136] Ibid., 283.

from the liquid state."[137] Ferguson is not arguing for a uniform monotony.

> The crystallizing process may produce one large and beautiful crystal, but it is that, in turn, because it is composed of other crystals. We are therefore investigating the relationship between the parts and the whole, and seeking to bring those parts (furnished by our *exegesis*) together legitimately in relationship to the whole (the *message*).[138]

Ferguson does not want expository preaching, which he also calls "exegetical" preaching, to be a running commentary on the text.[139] "Exegetical preaching should not be confused with a homiletical running commentary on the text."[140] Far too often it is.

For the sermon to be a unified message and not a running commentary on the text, Ferguson argues that the ideas in the text need to be *restructured*.

> For in expository preaching the material of the text is not only examined; it is also *restructured* in order to become a sermon. Whereas before the text was dismantled in order to unveil the heart of the matter, it is now brought together again on the basis of a new set of principles, the principles of sound rhetoric and communication governed by the identity of our hearers.[141]

The biggest problem I find with seminary students is that they do not perceive this point. Even many established ministers who are known for exegetical preaching do not follow Ferguson's advice. The result is expository sermons that are not a unified message and do not serve the pastoral needs of the congregation. A logical sermon, by definition, will be one where the ideas in the text are restructured in the service of one, unified message.

One reason why ministers do not restructure the message is because they lack gifts of logic and organization. I think that one reason why this doesn't occur is that ministers do not think hard enough about the text so that they can restructure the ideas. Other ministers write out their sermons in essay form and, therefore, are not aware of the lack of restructuring in their message. Seminary students simply haven't learned how to synthesize

---

[137] Sinclair B. Ferguson "Exegesis" in The Preacher and Preaching: Reviving the Art in the Twentieth Century Edited by Samuel T. Logan, Jr. (Phillipsburg, N.J.: P & R Publishing, 1986), 203.
[138] Ibid., 203-04.
[139] Ibid., 192.
[140] Ibid., 193.
[141] Ibid., 205.

material. Preachers can become more logical.

Seminary students and preachers need to learn the benefits of restructuring their material with the goal of presenting a unified message. Many ministers are so used to firing shotgun blasts with three separate mini-sermons in every one of their sermons that they are not aware that it is possible to fire sermons that are a single rifle bullet.

The Strenuous Effort in Extemporaneous Preaching

A lack of strenuous effort or an ignorance of what strenuous work needs to be done stands in the way of true preaching. Peter did not read a sermon on Pentecost Sunday. Jesus did not read a sermon in the synagogues of Galilee. It is the extemporaneous preacher who above all can speak with freshness and authority as Jesus did.

Great labor is involved. Dabney concludes his discussion about the act of preaching with one last "remark" that "is the most important of all."[142] "Whatever may be your method, excellence can only be the result of strenuous effort."[143] But this arduous work needs to be done when we consider the "lofty" goal of the preaching of the Word of God. "He who proposes to sway the souls of a multitude, to be their teacher, to lay his hands upon their heart-strings, to imbue them with his passion and will, makes an audacious attempt. But nothing less than this is true preaching."[144]

Why is there such little passion, emotion, and eloquence in sermons? Why so much time spent reading manuscripts, even if preachers do not read their manuscript with a yad?[145]

The Necessity of a Personal Style

John Broadus argues that every preacher should have his own style. He writes that

> We frequently say of a writer, that he wields a ready, an elegant, or caustic pen. In like manner, the *stylus*, the pointed iron instrument with which the Romans wrote upon their tablets covered with wax, is often employed by Cicero to denote the manner of writing, the manner of expressing one's thoughts in writing, and at a later period was very

---

[142] Ibid., 344.
[143] Ibid., 344.
[144] Ibid., 344.
[145] A yad (which literally means "hand") is a Torah pointer that is used in synagogues to follow along as one reads the Old Testament.

naturally extended to speaking.[146]

Lessing stated, "Every man should have his own style as he has his own nose."[147]

Broadus thinks that "A man's style cannot be separated from his modes of thought, from his whole mental character."[148] He thinks that American preachers have neglected style.

> And the great American fault, in speaking and writing, is an excessive vehemence, a constant effort to be striking. Our style, as well as our delivery, too often lacks the calmness of conscious strength, the repose of sincerity, the quiet earnestness which only now and then becomes impassioned.[149]

Excessive vehemence is often a cover for a lack of preparation.

Broadus argues that even though each preacher should have his own style this doesn't mean that he is "a law unto himself" in the manner of style.[150] He points out that the great classical musicians had their own "characteristic style" but they wrote their music within "the basic laws of music."[151] The style of each unique preacher will operate within certain boundaries, including the laws of grammar. Broadus identifies fault styles: the spacious style, the polished dial, the fine style, or the flowery style.[152]

How can a preacher and improve his style? Broadus thinks that especially the study of the preacher's own language is profitable for improving his style. He thinks that a minister should continue his education by reading good literature:

> The study of literature perhaps contributes still more to the improvement of style than the direct study of language. From reading we gain much in the knowledge of language, especially as to richness of vocabulary, fullness of expression.[153]

---

[146] John A. Broadus, On the Preparation and Delivery of Sermons. (New York: Harper & Row, 1944), 223.

[147] Ibid., 223.

[148] Ibid., 224.

[149] Ibid., 226.

[150] Ibid., 226.

[151] Ibid., 226.

[152] Ibid., 229.

[153] Ibid., 233.

The chief means of improvement in style is careful practice in writing and speaking,--not mere practice without care, for this will develop and confirm what is faulty as well as what is good.[154]

Writing and speaking are two different methods of communication. Broadus writes,

> In addition to writing, one must studiously practice speaking, in order to form his speaking style. A man skilled in both, may closely imitate in writing the style of speaking, but the two are really distinct, and in some respects quite different.[155]

Writers of fiction and nonfiction emphasize that the new author needs to develop his own voice. So must the minister. It is scary that that such an accomplished writer as William Zinsser claims that he did discover his own voice until he was in his early fifties. Prior to this he wrote many articles and books. He was an accomplished writer. It is astonishing that such a prolific writer could say this. He found his mature voice after fifty!

I want to conclude this chapter with a wise statement by a mature minister, the Rev. Wilbur Bruinsma, on how to be yourself in the pulpit:

> In the first place, there is a need soon after seminary to develop our own style. I realize there are some students already begin to do this in seminary. But that is not true for most. And even for those who do begin to develop this already in seminary, they must be aware of their need to continue to develop their style after they have begun their ministry. This is true from the point of view of one's delivery. Students who have graduated from seminary often mimic the stance, facial expressions, and even the voice inflections of one or another of their professors. This is not a bad thing, of course. But there is a need to develop in our delivery in order to reveal to God. Saints who *we* are. The same is true of the *content* of our preaching. Different ministers have different ways of presenting the truth. And that is a good thing. Each of us has our own personality and characteristics. The beauty and wonder of the preaching is that every minister of the gospel leaves the imprint of his own personality and study and what he proclaims. This needs to be evident in our preaching.[156]

---

[154] Ibid., 236.
[155] Ibid., 238.
[156] Wilbur Bruinsma, Protestant Reformed Theological Journal, 7.

Chapter 9
Herman Bavinck on Pulpit Eloquence

Preachers must strive after eloquence. I sense that the 21st century preacher views this as an out of date exhortation.

Isn't eloquence a concept that is wrapped up with a classical education? The study of rhetoric seems to be as old-fashioned as learning Latin and studying the history of the Romans. We no longer advocate learning Latin as teenagers. How many of us have read Cicero?

Given the contemporary bias against the importance of eloquence in preaching (and public speaking), I am glad that I can use a theological heavyweight to counter this trend. The Dutch Reformed theologian Herman Bavinck defended the need for eloquence.

Herman Bavinck on the Need for Eloquence

When Herman Bavinck presented a lecture on preaching to the students at the theological university in Kampen, The Netherlands on November 28, 1889; the subject he chose was eloquence.

I am struck by the fact that this systematic theologian selected eloquence as the topic of the one recorded lecture that he gave on preaching.

In fact, the only developed and lengthy work on preaching that we have from Bavinck's pen is about eloquence.

Why did the Dutch systematic theologian consider this topic important? I get the sense that at the end of the 20th century and the beginning of the 21st century that the subject of eloquence is passé. Bavinck thought that Dutch Reformed preachers in the late 19th century were in self-denial about the value of eloquence.

In the forward to the published booklet of this lecture, which was published under the title of "Eloquence", Bavinck explains why he wants a new edition to be available:

> A new edition was deemed preferable, because the holy eloquence in question is in large part an undiscovered land in our Christian endeavors. Dutch pulpits are not presently overflowing with good, powerful speakers, never mind preachers.[157]

This is a strong criticism of the Dutch pulpit at the turn of the 19th century. Bavinck finds godly eloquence missing from the Reformed pulpits in The Netherlands!

Bavinck considers the lack of holy eloquence a threat to the welfare of the church at a time when the (secular) press was so influential. He writes that in the past the pulpit had a greater influence on the consciences of men. But in his day the newspaper "reaches the furthest parts of the society, in so doing exerting influence on the spirit and dominating public opinion."[158] Bavinck quotes Spurgeon who described the English as "a press-ridden people."[159]

I almost laugh at the naiveté of a Bavinck who thinks that the newspapers and written press were such a challenge to the pulpit.

He gave his lecture on eloquence before the rise of radio, television, the internet, and smart phones. Bavinck was afraid that the newspapers and the press were becoming the masters of Dutchmen's consciences. He writes that if preachers "want to remain master of the people's conscience, they must ensure that they remain masters of the word."[160]

Bavinck understood the high calling of preachers and the power of the Word preached:

> The meaning of preaching cannot easily be overestimated, nor can the worth of the office of preacher. To be a *verbi divini minister,* servant of the Divine Word, one who shares from the hiddenness of God, who declares words of eternal life—which earthly position could be compared to this?[161]

---

[157] Herman Bavinck, Herman Bavinck on Preaching & Preachers. Translated by James P. Eglinton. (Peabody, MA: Hendrickson Publishers, 2017), 17.

[158] Ibid., 17.

[159] Ibid., cited by Bavinck, 18. See C. H. Spurgeon, "Preaching for the Poor," sermon delivered on Sunday, January 25, 1857.

[160] Ibid., 19.

[161] Ibid., 62.

Ministers who wield the sword of the Spirit possess "a power greater than that of monarchs and world leaders" because "He who rules the spirit is mightier than he who captures a city."[162]

If Bavinck believed that eloquence was important for preachers more than 100 years ago, how much more important eloquence is today in the age of the online media! How much harder it is to catch the attention of our hearers today! How many different kinds of media vie for influence on the conscience of our people!

If Bavinck thought that the press in 1889 was such a threat to the conscience of Christians, how can we even begin to describe the threat the media poses today? Sin has developed. The media is omnipresent.

I get the feeling that ministers today suppose that eloquence is a subject best left to the old Romans. With the modern rejection of a classical education, the old Roman emphasis on rhetoric seems old-fashioned and irrelevant. I know that there are a few outposts of classical education in private schools. But preachers feel that the old books they read in seminary (books by old Presbyterian homileticians on sacred rhetoric) were for a different age.

In his lecture, Herman Bavinck felt the need to deal with the charge that the study of eloquence is a study of sophistry. He rebuts these charges. They need to be rebutted today.

Bavinck can best help contemporary preachers by his demonstration of what holy eloquence actually is and why it is vital for the ministry of the Word.

This professor of systematic theology who emphasizes eloquence in preaching just did happen to preach *extemporaneously*. In his first (and only) pastorate in Franker, Bavinck wrote early on in his diary

> Preached in Franeker on Isaiah 53:4-6 and Catechism Question 1 (completely improvised for the first time—it went well).[163]

James Eglinton writes that "This practice of preaching with no, or minimal, notes remained Bavinck's norm and explains why, despite his decades of preaching, only one of his sermons became available in print."[164]

It is crucial that you understand why Bavinck as a preacher was interested in holy eloquence. It was because he viewed preaching as an oral event. The minister who preaches without notes experiences the power of the pulpit.

---

[162] Ibid., 21.
[163] Ibid., 10-11.
[164] Ibid., 11.

✓ The extemporaneous preacher can give free rein to his emotions in the act of preaching. He has an opportunity to express his own faith.

✓ Eglinton tells us that Bavinck as a student began more and more to enjoy preaching: "From then on, Bavinck came to find increasing joy in the act of preaching."[165]

✓ It is especially the extemporaneous preacher who can enjoy the act of preaching. Preaching is a joy as the preacher celebrates the gospel truths that he has internalized.

✓ The preacher delights in the spontaneous expression of his faith and emotions in response to the great gospel truths. The preacher experiences joy when he spontaneously comes up with the right words to express the passion of his heart. There is deep joy in the minister's heart when he speaks about weighty matters in such a way that the congregation experiences the fear of God.

✓ After two short years in Franeker, Bavinck accepted a call to become a professor at the seminary in Kampen. A ruling elder in Franker commented on how the congregation lost a "very valued teacher" and "his glorious preaching."[166] The congregation felt the loss of an eloquent preacher.

The Source of Holy Eloquence

Bavinck begins his speech with a discussion of the value of speaking well. "Speaking well is an adornment for each person, and for the Christian, man or woman, it is an exquisite virtue."[167] He divides his lecture into three parts.

The Principle of Eloquence

The Essence of Eloquence

The Form of Eloquence

In the first part of this speech, he develops the principle of eloquence. The most important insight in this part of the speech is his understanding of the source of eloquence. The source is the heart (or the emotions of the heart).

Bavinck feels the need in the first part of his speech to distinguish between the use and abuse of language. Wicked men abuse language.

---

[165] Ibid., 10.
[166] Ibid., 12.
[167] Ibid., 21.

This does not mean that language is not important or that preachers shouldn't strive to be eloquent. Human language is corrupted due to sin. For this reason, the Bible warns that God will hold us accountable for every idle word. "Indeed, a considerable authority is exerted over us all in view of phraseology, hollow sounds, meaningless words, and conventional terms."[168] Fallen man misuses language.

Bavinck gives three examples of the misuse of language and truth. First, he writes that "There is truth in Goethe's remark that "a man lies as soon as he becomes polite."[169]

Second, he mentions Talleyrand: "As we also pay attention to the dark side of our human nature, it seems that Talleyrand was certainly right to say: "Language was invented in order to conceal our thoughts.""[170]

Third, he mentions the misuse of the French language in Talleyrand's time: "At that time, the French were the undoubted masters of conversation, which is to say, the art (as it is rightly named) of carrying out the most *gallant* conversations on the most *frivolous* subjects in the *finest* forms."[171] Wicked people can speak with eloquence. But in the end their eloquence is sophistry, because it is done in the service of lies, evil, and vanity.

Yet Bavinck affirms that the origin of eloquence in ungodly men is their heart and emotions.

Bavinck makes some insightful comments about the source of eloquence. The source of holy eloquence is the burning heart of the redeemed preacher.

> As with language, the source of true eloquence does not lie in the reasoning mind; indeed, it lies much less in an act or decision of the will, but rather lies behind both in his heart or spirit, from which life goes forth, also from the life of eloquence.[172]

Bavinck's crucial insight is that eloquence finds its origin in the heart and emotions. He cites the proverb: "It is the heart that inspires eloquence."[173] This is the point I want you to take away from this chapter. *If you would be eloquent, you need to experience the truths of the gospel.* If you are not eloquent in the pulpit, you need to fan into flame holy emotions.

---

[168] Ibid., 25.
[169] Ibid., 26.
[170] Ibid., 26.
[171] Ibid., 26.
[172] Ibid., 27.
[173] Ibid., 27. Pectus est quod disertos facit.

Preachers who are lukewarm will not produce eloquence. Bavinck states that "those who sell tolerance and neutrality" "know no passion."[174]

The secret of eloquence "lies in the soul. Let the heart's passion come to the word, and eloquence will be born."[175]

Bavinck helps us to understand why we do not hear enough eloquence in the pulpit. We do not have passionate preachers. We do not have preachers who believe strongly and, therefore, speak with eloquence. They believe, but they do not believe strongly enough. They do not help us to see invisible spirituality realities. We do not have much eloquence because we do not have enough passion, ardency, and fervency.

When the heart is overcome by emotion, holy eloquence is unleashed:

> And if our heart becomes so affected, so touched, or when our beautiful distraction is brought to the fore, and our heart is carried by it, and thus is awoken in passion, regardless of which one (love, hate, sorrow, compassion, indignation, shock, fear, angst, terror), if our conscience is touched and the waves of the life of the soul are set heaving, if our spirit is driven, and is set in motion and delight, then the real source of eloquence is unlocked within us). Deep, inner feeling is the principle of oratory; it is the soul's sensitivity to be jarred and aghast.[176]

Preachers are eloquent as they deeply experience the emotions of sorrow for sin, love, hate, compassion, indignation, fear, or wonder.

We know when a minister is experiencing emotion. It wakes us up. We pay attention.

Who is your favorite preacher? He probably is eloquent. He is eloquent because he *celebrates* the Triune God and His saving work in Jesus Christ.

When a minister preaches with emotion, the saints are inexorably carried along by his passion. When the minister considers something to be of great moment, we tend to consider it important as well. When the minister is excited about a glorious truth, we want to have the same emotion. When a minister is grieved by sin, we also grieve over our own sins. Bavinck mentions how Jesus experienced emotions, like compassion. He became angry. The Apostle Paul's heart was moved by the idolatry in Athens. Bavinck argues that the eloquence of orators flow from emotion:

---

[174] Ibid., 27.
[175] Ibid., 28.
[176] Ibid., 28.

The fury of Achilles, the faithfulness of Andromache, the patriotism of Demosthenes, the fervor of Cicero for the well-being of the city; all these are eloquent.[177]

Bavinck is convinced that "History supplies ample proofs that eloquence, as well as language, is a creation of feeling."[178]

If eloquence is the creation of feeling, then we need to experience the truth. Our emotions need to be affected by what we discover in Scripture.

Bavinck lists four things as necessary for the unlocking of eloquence: "a powerful emotional condition, a moved spirit, an affected heart, and an undeniable impulse to voice these feelings."[179] He quotes 2 Corinthians 4:13: "I believed, therefore I have spoken." "Whoever believes firmly and deeply cannot keep silent."[180] I have seen and heard this. When a minister believes strongly and is able to communicate the reality of what he believes, he becomes eloquent. When a minister believes weakly and, therefore, does not communicate what he believes with much eloquence, we remain unaffected.

Herman Bavinck struggled with his faith while at a liberal university. Afterwards he lamented the loss of a simple, childlike faith. He wrote:

> Now, I can't help but wish that I believed as they did, so happy and joyous, and then I feel that if I were so, I could preach, animated, warm, always full of conviction about what I say; then I could be useful. I would be alive, living for others. But I know full well that this is in the past, it is no longer possible.[181]

He laments how his attendance at the unbelieving Leiden University undermined his childhood faith. He needed to struggle against unbelief and felt like in the process this had somewhat undermined his simple faith. Bavinck recognizes the need for the preacher to preach in faith. I have found that I must exercise my faith, just like a muscle is exercised. We need to grow in faith. We need to become more and more convinced of the concrete reality of spiritual realities.

Bavinck's great insight about holy eloquence is that it finds its source in the heart and emotions of the preacher. The implications of this for the preacher are profound. He must feel the truth of what he speaks. He must enter into the message with his emotions.

---

[177] Ibid., 28.
[178] Ibid., 29.
[179] Ibid., 29.
[180] Ibid., 29.
[181] Ibid., 8.

The preacher will best experience proper emotions that create eloquence as he delivers his sermon extemporaneously and spontaneously. The minister can sit in his study and prepare words that express his feeling about the issue as he sits in front of his computer screen. This is distinct from the spontaneous and extemporaneous communication of emotions in the act of preaching. If the minister wants to experience the emotions of the Christian life as strongly as possible, he needs to internalize the message. The written sermon read will in itself express past emotion. The preacher needs to communicate present emotions. He is not an essayist; he is a preacher.

The Essence of Eloquence

Bavinck turns from the principle of eloquence to the essence of eloquence. He asks: "What is eloquence in itself, and in what does its essence consist?"[182] Bavinck defines eloquence "as the gift developed by the art."[183] He adds that eloquence is "the power of the word to convince the mind, touching the conscience and persuasively affecting the will of the people."[184] Eloquence has three aspects: "argument, description, and persuasion."[185]

The first aspect of eloquence is that the eloquent orator must have "a solid knowledge" of what he wants to persuade his auditors. This means that the preacher must know his Bible, systematic theology, and the unfolding covenant of grace (redemptive history).

The second aspect of eloquence is that the orator must provide description. He must describe the topic or present it in an imaginative way that captures the conscience and imagination of his auditors. The preacher must tell the story of Scripture in all of the drama it possesses. Bavinck believes that the preacher "also focuses on the conscience and the imagination."[186] Bavinck states that the sermon "is an argument, but it is also a drama, a spectacle. It describes what sin is, for example, not only in dogmatic terms. It also lets us see it in its awful guilt, in its devastating power."[187] The Dutch theologian says something very important when he writes that "The orator must make us perceive what he is saying."[188] We need to perceive the truth as the minister perceives and experiences it. Just as the minister perceives the truth with his intellect and experiences it with his emotions, so must the congregation.

---

[182] Ibid., 32.
[183] Ibid., 32.
[184] Ibid., 32.
[185] Ibid., 32.
[186] Ibid., 36.
[187] Ibid., 37.
[188] Ibid., 37.

Bavinck believes that the Bible is wonderfully concrete. God uses narratives to reveal Himself. Therefore, the preacher must know the Biblical narratives if he would be eloquent. Bavinck states that "true eloquence illustrates thought."[189] He appeals for preachers to use their *sacred imaginations*. "Born of feeling, it [eloquence] makes itself known in the language of imagination."[190] The third aspect of eloquence is that the orator "must persuade and move the hearers' will."[191] The goal of the sermon is changed choices by the members of the congregation. "It tries to go through the intellect and heart in order to move the will of the person. The orator may not be satisfied until his hearers think, feel, and act as he does."[192]

The good news is that as Calvinists Reformed preachers have a bearable task. Ultimately it is God the Holy Spirit who needs to regenerate, illumine, and convert elect sinners. Let semi-Pelagian preachers be overwhelmed by the idea that if they are not eloquent enough many people will not decide (with the help of their supposedly 'free wills') to become Christians. The Calvinistic preacher can rest in the fact that God sovereignly uses the persuasive power of the minister to accomplish His ends.

The Form of Eloquence

The third part of Bavinck's speech on eloquence is entitled "The Form of Eloquence." Here he comes down to earth and talks about the harmony that is necessary in the act of preaching between verbal eloquence and what he calls "bodily eloquence." He is concerned that the preacher uses his voice, gestures, and body in a way that serves the content of the message.

Bavinck recognizes that Reformed preachers do not value rhetoric and the drama of presenting a message as an end in itself. He writes that

> We may not value the presentation as highly as Demosthenes and des Amorie van der Hoeven, who considered it the first, second, and third, the be all and end all, of eloquence. And yet, it is surely of great and more than secondary worth. Many public speakers not lacking in natural gifts undervalue it sorely in its power and meaning. In comparison to it, an indefensible nonchalance often dominates.[193]

---

[189] Ibid., 38.
[190] Ibid., 39.
[191] Ibid., 32.
[192] Ibid., 42.
[193] Ibid., 46.

Bavinck feels the need to defend a lively and eloquent presentation of the sermon. He begins a bit defensively by first taking issue with "unnatural mannerisms that disfigure the speech of so many."[194] Hopefully every preacher will see that he should get rid of elements in his presentation that distract from the message.

Develop the Gift of Public Speaking

Bavinck admits that each preacher is unique. Christ gives different gifts to each preacher. Ministers will have different ways of communicating.

Bavinck emphasizes that preachers not only receive gifts for communication, but they also have imperfections that undermine communication. We are not born as perfect communicators. Charles Spurgeon was a rare bird. As a young preacher, he had a natural gift for and innate understanding of oratory. But he also self-consciously developed his gifts.

> While each person is unique, Bavinck argues that "we are not born with this single [kind of] speech ready-made."[195] The preacher needs to engage in "a serious struggle" to overcome "coarseness, banality, and triviality on the one hand, and stiffness, affectation, artificiality, and unnaturalness on the other."[196]

He then makes a crucial statement: "All sorts of enemies lurk in the development from what we are to what we must become."[197]

He states that the "royal law of preaching" is that as a preacher, you must "give yourself, not as you are, but as you can be and must become."[198]

This warns us of resting on our laurels as preachers and simply being ourselves in an "authentic" way that is actually a manifestation of our laziness, lack of spirituality, and unwillingness to overcome our weaknesses.

We must not excuse or justify bad grammar. We must not justify the lazy use of our voice. If you are doing odd things with your face, eyes, or hands that distract from the message, you need to stop these practices. If we are constantly saying "um" every three minutes, we need to work on putting a stop to this distracting mannerism.

---

[194] Ibid., 46.

[195] Ibid., 48.
[196] Ibid., 48.
[197] Ibid., 48.
[198] Ibid., 51.

We must not preach in unbelief, although we often struggle with faith. We may not preach without hope, although at times our hope is weak. We must not preach without love, even though we often are unloving. The authenticity that we need in the pulpit is a preacher who is struggling and fighting to live and grow in faith, hope, and love.

It is no virtue to get into the pulpit and to be influenced by your old man of sin. You are being "authentic" when you sin the pulpit. But it is no virtue to manifest your old nature in the pulpit. It is no virtue to manifest your lack of faith. It is no virtue to show no joy. It is not virtuous to preach as if the gospel is a boring and expected message.

Eloquent as a Whole Person

If preaching is an oral event, it is hard to understand why preachers play down the importance of the act of preaching. I get the sense that ministers think that once the sermon is written in their study, their main work is finished. All that is left is to read the sermon in the pulpit and try to inject some emotion in the process.

Bavinck acknowledges the challenges facing ministers of the Word compared to other orators. First, they speak to the same audience week after week. Second, they preach in churches with bad acoustics. Third, in The Netherlands the ministers often preached from elevated pulpits that limited their movement. The fact that you preach to the same congregation week after week is both a strength and a weakness. The strength of this is that congregations can become addicted to their minister. I am struck by how congregations become attached to and used to their minister so that they do not enjoy having guest ministers. They become resentful of the elders lining up seminary students to bring a Word of edification. They are used to their minister and would rather have him in the pulpit. But the weakness of the minister preaching in the same pulpit week after week is that the congregation can become used to and bored with his delivery.

Bavinck tells us that "Eloquence is produced by the whole person."[199] Your voice, gestures, and dress all contribute to your eloquence. "A good voice is a precious gift."[200] You should develop your voice and use it in the most effective way.

---

[199] Ibid., 51.
[200] Ibid., 51.

Germans who could not even understand Bernard of Clairvaux still wept when they heard him speaking.[201] "There must be harmony between body and soul, speech and voice, word and gesture, between what one says and how one says it."[202]

Bavinck exhorts the preacher: "What we say, we must say with all of our souls, and with all of our bodies, and all of our strength. Everything must speak to us, from us, within us."[203]

Bodily Eloquence

Bavinck even speaks of "bodily eloquence."[204] The entire body of the preacher should "illustrate, support, and confirm" his thoughts and words. His "posture, movement, and countenance" must be in harmony with his message. Bodily eloquence includes how you dress. How you dress can undercut your message. If you dress in a flippant way, you will communicate that your message is frivolous. If you dress to be hip, you will communicate a lie about the gospel. The gospel is not hip.

Bodily eloquence includes eye contact. You must look at the congregation. This is not optional. Bavinck writes that "The hearers rightly demand that they see the speaker, and that he sees them, and that he speaks to them not only with sound, but also with eye contact."[205]

The Perfection of the Sermon

The perfection of the sermon is reached when the emotions, words, content, and the minister's body are in harmony. After discussing the significance of eye contact, Bavinck speaks about "the perfection of the sermon":

> And in so doing the perfection of the sermon is reached, when the preacher utters the same thought and speaks the same language with the content of his words, the sound of his voice, the gaze of his eye, the position of his head, the posture of his body, the gesture of his hand, even the color and cut of his clothes; when all dualism of soul and body, of internal and external, of voice and tone, of language and gesture, is caught up in perfect harmony.[206]

---

[201] Ibid., 52.
[202] Ibid., 50.
[203] Ibid., 50-51.
[204] Ibid., 52.
[205] Ibid., 53.
[206] Ibid., 53.

True Eloquence not Sophistry

Bavinck takes issue with the Sophists who "made eloquence into a form of trickery."[207] He indicts contemporary preachers: "The generation of the Sophists did not die out in the time of the orators."[208] Sophistry manifests itself in the pulpit:

> Pompous voice, blaring speech, drawn out tone, empty sentences, and flattering terms must compensate for what is lacking in sound content and real study.[209]

The antidote to sophistry in the pulpit is "hard study, solid knowledge, and real science."[210]

Sophistry occurs when preachers reject the inerrancy of sacred Scripture. "To the extent that we lose the conviction of the Divinity of the Word that we bring, our preaching loses influence and power."[211] As a pre-seminary student I grasped this fact. My first semester at Calvin College I took a religion class with a professor who denied the inerrancy of Scripture on the first day of class. He proceeded to shred the Scriptures throughout the semester. He was a higher critic. He claimed that the Bible was only infallible with respect to some redemptive message. Whatever this redemptive message might be was exceedingly vague—since my professor would not submit to the authority of the Scriptures as written.

If the preacher tries to scratch itching ears, he will preach in unbelief. The preacher needs to preach the Word. He must teach: "Thus saith the LORD." Otherwise his rhetoric is in the service of vain philosophy.

The Vice of Learnedness

 It is vital that the orator who speaks with eloquence possesses a solid knowledge of the Scriptures and the truth of God. But Bavinck warns of the danger of turning a sermon into an academic lecture. "One must not fall into the other extreme and make the oratorical speech an arsenal of learning."[212]

It is also sophistry to try to look smart and sophisticated. Learnedness in the pulpit is no virtue. "Solid knowledge includes, rather than excludes, simplicity."[213] Bavinck then gives a good description of what Reformed preaching should be like:

---

[207] Ibid., 32.
[208] Ibid., 33.
[209] Ibid., 33-34.
[210] Ibid., 34.
[211] Ibid., 34-35.
[212] Ibid., 35.
[213] Ibid., 36.

But just as in Holy Scripture, the highest ideal in solid preaching is to speak out the deepest thoughts so simply and so naturally that even the casual laborer understands you.[214]

If William Tyndale thought that the Bible should be translated with such simplicity that a plowboy could understand it; should not God's preachers also proclaim the profundities in the Word with simplicity, so the same farm boy can comprehend the sermon?

Eloquence is Passionate Reason

Herman Bavinck tells his audience of seminary students that eloquence is passionate reason: "Rightly has eloquence been named *la raison passionnee* ("passionate reason")."[215]

Bavinck quotes Luke 6:45: "From the overflow of the heart speaks the mouth." This relates to John Piper's idea that preaching should be logic on fire. Good preaching will involve a passionate argument for the main point of the sermon being the truth of God. The preacher will argue for things and draw conclusions. But he must do this with zeal, for true eloquence is passionate reason.

A Dynamic Interaction between the Whole Preacher and Whole Persons

The orator communicates as a whole person to the intellect, emotions, and will of his auditors.

> The word that must go out in order to be eloquent must come from the whole person, it must bear his image and likeness, it must also be directed to the whole person, to understanding, heart and will.[216]

Eloquence does not occur in a vacuum. What is "the secret of all popular eloquence"? The orator "must constantly turn to his hearers, see them, appeal to them, pose questions, set objections in their mouths, clear away resistance."[217] Bavinck speaks of the dynamic interaction that must occur between speaker and auditors: "There must be exchange, intercourse, business done from eye to eye, hand to hand, and soul to soul. The speech must be a single dramatic act."[218]

---

[214] Ibid., 36.
[215] Ibid., 31.
[216] Ibid., 32.
[217] Ibid., 40.
[218] Ibid., 41.

The character of the preacher is intertwined with his message. Bavinck mentions how Cicero thought that "to be a true orator" one "must be a virtuous person."[219] I am also struck by how a preacher can be a terrible communicator; but if people in the church are good friends with him, they can listen to his sermons. You might have noticed that when a church member doesn't like a specific minister; that no matter how eloquent the preacher is, the sermons will not be well received. How people view the preacher shapes how they hear sermons.

Wicked men can be good communicators. But "eloquence can only reach its highest triumph when it is free and, according to its own nature, stands in service of truth and holiness."[220]

Mastery of Your Language

The eloquent preacher has a heart on fire. He masters the language in which he preaches. Bavinck believes that "Real eloquence, is, therefore, inconceivable without mastery of language."[221] He tells how Prof. De Vries in 1849 described the importance of the preacher mastering his language:

> If the speaker has so internalized the content of the language that they are almost united in being, if the language itself has so become his possession in its matter and spirit that all its treasures are available to him on cue; if every thought that arises within him, and every sensation that he feels, causes the best word and expression with which it can be vividly portrayed to spring to mind immediately....Then language has found its master.[222]

This mastery will enable the preacher to master the consciences of his hearers: "The mastery over language assures us first of dominion over the conscience and, as such, over the will of the people."[223] Bavinck says that "Eloquence is a plea, a drama, and an act; and finally, it is more than all of those things together: it is a fight and a struggle."[224] The preacher uses eloquence to persuade his hearers; just as the Apostle Paul explained, reasoned, and persuaded his auditors whether in the synagogue or marketplace.

You may not identify eloquence with sophistry. Godly eloquence flows out of holy emotions.

---

[219] Ibid., 43.
[220] Ibid., 44.
[221] Ibid., 42.
[222] Ibid., 42.
[223] Ibid., 42.
[224] Ibid., 42.

Chapter 10
Don't Preach Dull Sermons in Boring Plain Speak

eter Y. De Jong wrote a syllabus to teach preaching at Mid-America Reformed Seminary. He hammers boring preachers and preaching that lack eloquence.

He begins his section on "Formal Homiletics" with the warning: "Preaching, contrary to what many church members suppose, does not come easy."[225] Sermon making "demands not only an understanding of and commitment to the gospel, it requires skill to bring that Word in its most precise, effective and elegant form."[226] De Jong quotes the old adage: "Genius is one tenth inspiration; nine tenths perspiration."

De Jong believes that much criticism of sermons comes from the fact that ministers do not look at the text with fresh eyes and do not discover personal insights in the text.

> Undoubtedly one of the chief reasons why sermons are frequently criticized lies not so much in their length as it does in their insufferable dullness. Altogether too often a sermon contains the perfectly obvious, an old truth which everybody knows altogether too well, but little that is new, refreshing, and stimulating. Even when new insights into a biblical passage are stated, this is done in such a matter-of-fact manner that its urgency fails to register on the mind and heart of the hearer.[227]

De Jong cites Camerer who lamented dull preaching: "Preachers often fear that their hearers may find their message too hard to believe. Actually a more immediate problem is that they find preaching dull, non-essential to life, and aimless."[228]

---

[225] Peter Y. De Jong, Homiletics, 229.
[226] Ibid., 229.
[227] Ibid., 230.
[228] Ibid., 234. Cited by De Jong.

Preachers will not be eloquent if they do not engage in fresh exegesis, do not get thrilled about the biblical message, and preach with an unexcited heart.

Born a Preacher, Yet Cultivate Your Gifts

One can teach preaching, but there is something to what De Jong says about the production of preachers: "Preaching, when all is said and done, is a gift from God. In the deepest sense preachers are born; not made."[229] While the Holy Spirit alone can empower a qualified man to preach and open the eyes of congregants to see beautiful things in the Word, yet the preacher is "under solemn obligation to cultivate whatever gifts" he has been given in "prayerful dependence" on God.[230]

Eloquence a Gift and an Art

Herman Bavinck emphasizes that eloquence is a gift of God. The apostles "were eloquent, not by their own practice, but by divine gift."[231] God gives to every minister his linguistic gifts. But eloquence "is also an art", Bavinck argues.[232] The Dutch theologian writes that "The gift demands and calls for the art."[233] The minister may not be lazy. He may not claim that since eloquence is a gift, he either has it or doesn't. No, the minister must develop his gift. Bavinck gives us an example of the need to develop the gift from classical orators:

> The orators whose names are passed down from generation to generation, such as Demosthenes and Cicero, spared themselves no effort in developing and perfecting their latent talents.[234]

---

[229] Ibid., 231.
[230] Ibid., 231-32.
[231] Herman Bavinck, Herman Bavinck on Preaching & Preachers. Translated by James P. Eglinton. (Peabody, MA: Hendrickson Publishers, 2017), 30.
[232] Ibid., 30.
[233] Ibid., 31.
[234] Ibid., 31.

Preaching an Oral Event

Preaching is an oral event. De Jong writes that the minister must "cultivate the "art" of communication with ever-greater diligence and delight."[235] I regret that too many ministers and seminarians regard preaching as an oral event in which one reads the sermon essay they wrote the week before. De Jong explains that a sermon is an oral event:

> To be sure, a sermon is ordinarily first put down on paper. It may be written down either in outline form or in full. But the message on a text is intended to be spoken. Only once, under ordinary circumstances, will that sermon be heard by the hearers. Within a comparatively brief time span it must make its impact.[236]

I appreciate this statement about the sermon needing to make an impact. A sermon is an oral event that has as its goal an impact on the heart, mind, and will of the hearer. There are too many sermons where the preacher does not seem to perceive that the goal is to have the truth make an emotional impact on the hearers.

Truth through a Human Personality Experiencing Emotions

Preaching has been called "truth communicated through unique human personality." The preacher must be himself. "A man's style is always his own," says De Jong.[237] I wish they always were! The fact is that goofy ministers imitate and mimic their favorite preacher or theologian. In the Protestant Reformed Churches there are multiple younger ministers who give laughable imitations of David Engelsma's distracting mannerisms. They suppose that this impersonation creates *gravitas*. Some of their hearers are naïve enough to celebrate the caricature. How odd it is to see ministers who ape the mannerisms and delivery of someone else. I can think of at least two ministers who even move their lips with the same distracting mannerisms as Engelsma. They utter guttural sounds like their professor does. They should perceive that acting like someone else is wrong-headed and prideful. It presents a lie about who they actually are as unique individuals. A minister who imitates his professor in order to carry a sectarian mantle, needs to listen to what Lloyd Benson said to Dan Quayle in a vice-presidential debate. He cut down Quayle by saying: "I knew John F. Kennedy and you are no JFK."

---

[235]Peter Y. De Jong, Homiletics, 235.
[236] Ibid., 235.
[237] Ibid., 235.

Finding Your Preaching Voice: Not a Borrowed Eloquence

Just like the writer needs to find his voice, the minister should cultivate his distinct style that results in a unique eloquence. He "should cultivate that *style* which is most appropriate to his high calling on the pulpit."[238] You need to develop your own approach to eloquence. My seminary professors placed a high emphasis on using dignified language that was appropriate for a Reformed worship service. We do need to avoid an imbalance where church becomes a place for formal communication. Luther did not use a high and mighty style when preaching or writing. He used earthy language. It is highly effective to use earthy or colloquial language in preaching. This helps the saints understand that the Word of God is not divorced from real life.

A preacher's style is "his unique way of expressing thoughts whether in writing or in speaking."[239] The Roman word "stylus" referred to "a sharp iron instrument with which they wrote on tablets covered with wax. This made an impression which could be read and understood by those who saw it."[240]

The minister's style will come out in his "choice of words, arrangement of sentences and paragraphs, movement or progress towards the goal of turning the minds and hearts and lives of those who hear to God."[241]

In good communication there is always a symbiotic relationship between form and content. The method of communication becomes the message. Bad content affects the way in which the message is communicated. I am always struck by the fact that when a seminary student does boring exegesis and puts his message together in an illogical way, that he finds it impossible to communicate his message in a lively way. Boring content does not fire the emotions of the preacher.

The old homileticians (in the 18th and 19th centuries) perhaps focused too much on beauty of diction and good rhetoric. I think that the danger today is that preachers and seminary students do not focus enough on developing a style that is interesting, exciting, and absorbing. Do preachers even try to avoid stuttering? Do they even try to enunciate properly?

Broadus long ago warned against bad styles of public communication in the United States.

---

[238] Ibid., 235.
[239] Ibid., 235.
[240] Ibid., 235.
[241] Ibid., 235-36.

And the great American fault, in speaking and writing, is an excessive vehemence, a constant effort to be striking. Our style, as well as our delivery, too often lacks calmness of conscious strength, the repose of sincerity, the quiet earnestness which only now and then becomes impassioned.[242]

Godly Oratory

The ancient church understood the importance of faithful preaching that spoke to men's hearts, wills, and minds. In the preaching of John Chrysostom you find a concern to explain and teach what the text says. He emphasized the use of a godly oratory so that the congregants would be affected by the message. He viewed the sermon as a dynamic event in which God Himself spoke to His people through the preacher.

Because Augustine was concerned with preaching, he wrote "Doctrina Christiana" in 427 A.D. This book discusses rhetoric and style. He argued that one should not learn how to preach from the Roman orators, but from the Holy Spirit. He drew on Cicero and talked about the importance of clarity, simplicity, and a beautiful style. He also understood that one would fall short if he did not have a godly character aligned with his message.

Truth Needed

True passion is always connected to content that inspires and moves the emotions. The minister must know when to attempt to fire the emotions of his hearers and when to give the congregation a rest. He needs to speak with variety in tone, speed, and loudness. There needs to be a rhythm to the message. For example, the minister might start slowly as he, as it were, sets the table for the coming feast. As the minister begins to deal with astonishing realities, the rhythm should speed up. Just like a musical piece should have a variety of rhythm, an oral event should have rhythm.

Most seminary students seem to have little clue about the role of rhythm in communication. They do not use their voices effectively so that there is variety of tone, speed, rhythm, and loudness. They leave the impression that what they are saying does not greatly excite their own souls and that they are not on an exciting journey as they communicate their message.

---

[242] Ibid., 236. Cited by De Jong.

The preacher who does not try to communicate with his audience is not trying to take them along with him on a journey that should impact their mind, heart, soul, emotions, and will. "Since every sermon should have a goal, the minister not only moves towards this throughout his discourse but also makes certain that the audience can follow where he leads."[243]

De Jong warns of two extremes to be avoided: being too concise or too prolix. The danger is that the preacher understands the text and its concepts so well after studying it all week long that he forgets that he is taking the congregation from zero miles an hour to 70 miles an hour in 40 minutes. The topic is new to them. "Saying the same thing in two or even three different ways allows opportunity for the truth to register upon the mind."[244]

The opposite danger is prolixity. Don't use too many words. "It creates the impression of filling up time without having anything worthwhile to say."[245] When the minister says vague things that seem to be irrelevant to the subject at hand the sermon "sins against the law of movement."[246]

De Jong argues for the value of "elegance." The minister should use "good taste" in how he speaks about a subject. His talk of Hell will not be lively and upbeat. His talk of Heaven and the glories of Paradise will not be somber and slow. "Creative imagination, bound indeed by the limits set by the text of Scripture itself, plays an important role in sustaining interest."[247]

Dull language is a threat. "Divine truth can easily become shop-worn. What he speaks may well be true; the manner in which he brings it week after week can at times render it quite ineffective."[248]

De Jong looks for beauty and elegance in the theme and divisions. "Here beauty or elegance of expression will enhance clarity."[249] "True elegance usually dresses itself in simple style."[250]

The eloquent preacher will speak with beauty and eloquence at times and thunder like a prophet at others. But what he will always do is speak truth from the heart. And then he will not be dull.

---

243 Ibid., 244.
244 Ibid., 241.
245 Ibid., 241.
246 Ibid., 241.
247 Ibid., 242.
248 Ibid., 242.
249 Ibid., 242.
250 Ibid., 242.

Chapter 11
Manifest the Joy of Fearing God

Youtube viewer asked John Piper: "Where and how did you learn to preach?"

Piper responded that He received his lowest grade in seminary, a C-, in his preaching class at Fuller Seminary. He disagreed with his professor, James Daane, on almost everything except the principle that "every sermon should have one point." Piper did not learn how to preach in homiletics class. Rather "I think the way I became a preacher was by being passionately thrilled by what I was seeing in the Bible in seminary." He says: "I don't think that there is much you can do to become a preacher except know your Bible and be unbelievably excited about what is thee; and love people."

Note the connection between Piper's heart and affections being affected by the Bible message and the desire to preach. God gave him the desire to preach in exegesis classes on Philippians, Galatians, Romans, and the Sermon on the Mount. Piper says that "Everything in me was saying, I want to find a way to say this, because this is awesome, it is incredible."

God equips men for preaching by giving them a delight in and excitement about the gospel message contained in the sacred Scriptures. Why is John Piper eloquent? He is eloquent because God has fired his heart and emotions with the power, glory, and beauty of the gospel of Christ.

Preaching with Gravity and Gladness

John Piper values gravity and seriousness in preaching. He is not the sort of preacher who feels the need to crack jokes before a sermon or a conference message. His own preaching is characterized by high seriousness. He explains what the marks of a godly gravity in preaching are: Intensity of feeling, the weight of argument, a deep and pervading solemnity of mind, a savor of the power of godliness, fervency of spirit, zeal for God—these are the marks of the "gravity of preaching." If there is one thing we can learn from [Jonathan] Edwards, it is to take our calling seriously, not to trifle with the Word of God and the act of preaching.[251]

Piper writes about the earnestness that characterized Jonathan Edwards' preaching. "Edwards had an overwhelming conviction of the realities of the glories of heaven and horrors of hell that made his preaching utterly earnest."[252] You will not find "one joke in the 1200" extant sermons of the Northampton preacher.[253] Sereno Dwight attributed the impact of Edwards' sermons on "the deep and pervading solemnity of his mind. He had, at all times, a solemn consciousness of the presence of God."[254]

Edwards lacked Whitefield's fiery eloquence. But Dwight writes:

> But, if you mean by eloquence, the power of presenting an important truth before an audience, with overwhelming weight of argument, and with such intenseness of feeling, that the whole soul of the speaker is thrown into every part of the conception and delivery; so that the solemn attention of the whole audience is riveted, from the beginning to the close, and impressions are left that cannot be effaced; Mr. Edwards was the most eloquent man I ever heard speak.[255]

Gravity characterized the preaching of Thomas Chalmers, even though this preacher read his manuscripts. Chalmer's preaching might have been without effect. He even followed along where he was reading with his finger! Andrew Blackwood said that Chalmers was in "bondage to the manuscript and use of long sentences."[256] John Mason explained why Chalmer's preaching still had an effect: "It is his blood-earnestness."[257]

Today there is not enough preaching that is done with "blood-earnestness." Ministers come across as wanting to be seen as nice people. They will not preach with gravity. In fact, if a preacher does preach with earnestness, seriousness, and gravity; congregants will misinterpret what is occurring. John Piper writes:

> Most people today have so little experience of deep, earnest, reverent, powerful encounters with God in preaching that the only associations

---

[251] John Piper, The Supremacy of God in Preaching (Grand Rapids: Baker Books, 1990), 50.

[252] Ibid., 48.

[253] Ibid., 47.

[254] Ibid., 49. Cited by Piper. See Memoirs, S. Dwight, ed., The Works of Jonathan Edwards, (1834; repr. Ed., Edinburgh: Banner of Truth, 1974), 1.clxxxix.

[255] Ibid., 49. Cited by Piper. See Memoirs, S. Dwight, ed., The Works of Jonathan Edwards, (1834; repr. Ed., Edinburgh: Banner of Truth, 1974), 1.cxc.

[256] Ibid., 50. See Andrew W. Blackwood, ed., The Protestant Pulpit (Grand Rapids: Baker Book House, 1977), 311.

[257] Ibid., 51. See James W. Alexander, Thoughts on Preaching (Edinburgh: Banner of Truth, 1975), 264.

that come to mind when the notion is mentioned are that the preaching is morose or boring or dismal or sullen or gloomy or surly or unfriendly.[258]

Solemnity, earnestness, and gravity are misunderstood and mischaracterized as producing an "unfriendly or cold" environment.[259] Piper has warned preachers about the lack of gravity and seriousness in the pulpit. He doesn't feel the need to tell a joke at the beginning of a sermon. Piper argues that a solemn gravity is consistent with high spiritual joy. "Since they have little or not experience with the deep gladness of momentous gravity, they strive for gladness the only way they know how—by being light-hearted, chipper, and talkative."[260] This "verbal casualness" results in "a preaching style plagued by triviality, levity, carelessness, flippancy."[261]

Piper's thesis statement is that "Gladness and gravity should be woven together in the life and preaching of a pastor in such a way as to sober the careless soul and sweeten the burdens of the saints."[262] He wants a "holy gravity."[263] Such gravity in preaching is fitting because of the utter seriousness of the matter that we proclaim. I find that when I am preaching a sermon, it is my job to convey the seriousness of the matter to the congregation. I must get them to stop treating the Christian life lightly. I need to recall them from the trivialities of many of their concerns to weighty spiritual realities that demands their attention. "God saves people from everlasting ruin through preaching."[264] "This is simply stupendous to think about—that when I preach, the everlasting destiny of sinners hang in the balance!"[265]

Robertson Nicoll mentions that many people thought of Charles Spurgeon as a "humorous preacher." Nicolls' response is that "As a matter of fact there was no preacher whose tone was more uniformly earnest, reverent and solemn."[266] Spurgeon himself said: "We must conquer—some of us especially—our tendency to levity. A great distinction exists between holy cheerfulness, which is a virtue, and that general levity, which is a vice."[267]

I have found that if I enter the meaning of the text, the holiness, love,

---

[258] John Piper, The Supremacy of God in Preaching (Grand Rapids: Baker Books, 1990), 51.
[259] Ibid., 51.
[260] Ibid., 51.
[261] Ibid., 52.
[262] Ibid., 52.
[263] Ibid., 54.
[264] Ibid., 55.
[265] Ibid., 55.
[266] Ibid., 58. Cited by Piper. Quoted in Iain Murray, Forgotten Spurgeon, 38.
[267] Ibid., 58. Cited by Piper. See Charles Spurgeon, Lectures to My Students, 212.

or justice of God displayed in it results in a display of utter seriousness, reverence, and solemnity. The gospel and the gospel hope in the text fills my soul with joy, euphoria, fear, and gladness. The gravity of our sins and the utter holiness of God needs to be reflected on our faces and in our souls as we preach. The joyful gladness found in the good news needs to be manifested in your smile and in your style. The message, messenger, and the method of communication must all be in harmony.

There needs to be more gravity, seriousness, and earnestness in the pulpit. There needs to be more celebration, joyful smiling, and gladness as well. I do not think that there can be too much emotion in the pulpit when the religious affections are responding to the truths and realities in the text.

John Piper exhorts the preacher to "Be Intense."[268] "Compelling preaching gives the impression that something very great is at stake."[269] He believes that "Lack of intensity in preaching can only communicate that the preacher does not believer or has never been seriously gripped by the reality of which he speaks—or that the subject matter is insignificant."[270]

I fear that too many people leave church thinking that what they heard was not really so important. We need to cure them of that idea. I want the solemn attention of the congregation. The preacher needs to work at this. I find that when the Holy Spirit helps me to communicate the serious importance of what I am saying, I gain an audience.

I believe that the preacher must demand the attention of the congregation. Since God is to be feared, His Word must be treated with respect. There is a reason why the ancient prophets said: "Thus saith the LORD." They said this to let the people of God know that the message they brought was not their private interpretation but a message from God. God has the right to demand attention to his Word. God wanted the Israelites to understand why the Word preached must be received with joy, fear, and trembling.

If you are bringing God's message to God's people, you have the authority to demand attention. In many Reformed churches, much of the congregation will give the preacher their attention. But there is always a minority in a congregation that have no desire to do so. I have preached in churches where a majority of the congregation seem passive and uninterested in hearing the Word of God. They have low expectations of preaching or they have lost the first love. As a preacher you cannot assume that you will have the attention of the congregation. When I preach at

---

[268] Ibid., 103.
[269] Ibid., 103.
[270] Ibid., 103.

Westville Correctional Center in Westville, Indiana I cannot assume that I will have the attention of the 200 men who gather. In fact, I know ahead of time that about half of the men come to hear the Word of God, while the others come to talk to their buddies who are housed in different dorms. I also know that the majority of the men are not living as Christians. Since these prisoners come to the worship service and I have a message from God for them, I demand their attention. God does not just speak to confessing Christians. God's Word has something to say to all men, including unconverted men. God has a right to be heard. Not only must genuine Christians listen to the Word of God, but unbelievers must listen to the Word of their Creator as well.

When God speaks through His ministers, men must listen.

The Word preached is the Word of God.

Therefore, it is not optional whether the members of the congregation or unbelievers listen to the Word of God.

God has a right to be heard.

Men must tremble before God's message.

If, as a preacher, you act as if it is OK whether people listen to your message or not; you are consciously and subconsciously communicating to people that your message is not as important, authoritative, and relevant as it is.

Your correct attitude must be that there is nothing more important for your hearers than to hear the Word of God. What a boyfriend is whispering to a girlfriend is not more important than God's Word. What a prisoner is talking to his buddy about is not more important than what God says. I have had to rebuke men numerous times for talking with their buddy while I read God's Word. I call out to them and ask them whether what they are saying has more weight than the Word of God.

God's Word trumps all human words.

You must demand the attention of the congregation. Ambassadors have the authority to demand that citizens listen to the Word of the king.

Chapter 12
R.C. Sproul on Dramatic, Emotional Preaching

Dramatic, Emotional Preaching

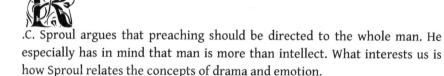

.C. Sproul argues that preaching should be directed to the whole man. He especially has in mind that man is more than intellect. What interests us is how Sproul relates the concepts of drama and emotion.

> Preaching calls forth an emotional response. It is not merely an exercise in the transfer of information. The pulpit is the setting for *drama*. The gospel itself is dramatic....The preacher doesn't make the gospel dramatic—it already is. To communicate the gospel dramatically is to fit preaching with the context. Dispassionate preaching is a lie—it denies the content it conveys.[271]

Sproul mentions several things that convey drama. "Timing is crucial to drama."[272] He mentions "the classic pattern of *pause, punch, pause*."[273] He shows from Jonathan Edwards how "concrete images" and powerful metaphors are "the stuff of which drama is made."[274]

Why does Sproul value extemporaneous preaching? He advocates for it because it is the best method for communicating the drama of the gospel.

> Perhaps the greatest catalyst to dramatic preaching is the extemporaneous sermon. This style of preaching releases the preacher

---

[271] R. C. Sproul, "The Whole Man" in The Preacher and Preaching: Reviving the Art in the Twentieth Century ed. Samuel T. Logan, Jr. (Phillipsburg, N.J.: P & R Publishing, 1986), 113.
[272] Ibid., 114.
[273] Ibid., 114.
[274] Ibid., 115.

from the barriers to communication that stifle so many sermons. Free from a prepared manuscript the minister's body and mind enter fully into communication.[275]

Sproul takes the value of eye contact with the congregation so seriously that when he was once asked to evaluate a preacher, he kept track of how many times the minister took his eyes off the congregation. He counted 127 times. The preacher was "terrified" when Sproul suggested that he move to extemporaneous preaching.[276]

Sproul does not advocate "speaking off the cuff" or "on the spur of the moment."[277] "Effective extemporaneous preaching combines two elements: serious preparation and free-style delivery. It requires two vital factors: knowledge and facility of vocabulary or verbal skills."[278]

Robert J. Lamont taught Sproul the "rudiments of preparation for extemporaneous preaching."[279] Lamont immersed himself in the text and fixed in his head a brief outline. Sproul tells us that

> As the moment of preaching drew near, he would fix in his mind the starting point, the conclusion, and the key points he wanted to include; then he trusted his mind and his verbal skills to add the flesh to the skeleton.[280]

The problem with reading a sermon is that it contradicts the principle that preaching is an oral event. Sproul tells us

> The spoken word differs clearly from the written word. The danger of prepared manuscripts is that few pastors can write in a spoken style. What works in writing almost never works in speech. The forms of communication are different. Preaching is a speaking skill, not a literary one. Memorization is also a barrier to effective communication and inclines toward the mechanical.[281]

Why is it vital to internalize the message of a text? "Of course, it is virtually impossible to communicate to another person what one doesn't first understand himself."[282] But an understanding of a topic "is only half the recipe for communication. Passion must be added to understanding for the

---

[275] Ibid., 116.
[276] Ibid., 116.
[277] Ibid., 116.
[278] Ibid., 116.
[279] Ibid., 117.
[280] Ibid., 117.
[281] Ibid., 117.
[282] Ibid., 117.

magic of communication to take place."[283]

Sproul thinks that "Understanding plus dramatic, effective, and, as Edwards would say, affective passion is the oldest and simplest formula for communication."[284]

The preacher would do well to listen to what Sproul says about communication and simplicity. Sproul is well known for his ability to translate what dogmaticians teach to the ordinary Christian. Sproul argues that a professor who speaks over his audiences' heads might well be a fraud. "He is *transferring* information, not translating it."[285] Read John Frame's *Systematic Theology* and you will be struck by how this gifted theologian knows how to translate theological concepts of the first order into language that a first-year seminary student can understand. Frame comprehends his material.

When a preacher internalizes the message, he should be able to present it with simplicity. He should be able to present the message to children. He should be able to deliver the message in 20 minutes rather than 40 minutes if the situation calls for it. Sproul thinks that a teacher who comprehends his material should be able to translate it to a five-year-old.[286] "The essence of effective teaching is found in the ability to simplify without at the same time distorting. That requires understanding. The deeper the level of understanding, the easier it is to communicate simply."[287]

It is the Holy Spirit who empowers a preacher to convey the drama of the gospel. Sproul mentions the role of the Holy Spirit in extemporaneous preaching.

> A close link between the preacher and the Holy Spirit must be maintained for effective preaching. The Spirit is the energizer, the dynamite (*dunamis*) of powerful preaching. We need the unction, the anointing of the Spirit, lest our words, eloquent or otherwise, bounce off recalcitrant hearts and evaporate.[288]

---

[283] Ibid., 117.
[284] Ibid., 118.
[285] Ibid., 122.
[286] Ibid., 122.
[287] Ibid., 122-23.
[288] Ibid., 125.

Have you experienced in the act of preaching what Sproul here describes? "It is a glorious sensation to feel the Spirit moving while we are preaching. It is exhilarating."[289] As the Holy Spirit works, the preacher and the congregation can experience a deep sense of spiritual realities, the weightiness of the gospel, a conviction of sin, or heavenly joy.

---

[289] Ibid., 125.

Chapter 13

Preach the Psalmist's Emotions in Psalm 119

hy is there a lack of passion, emotion, and eloquence in the pulpit? It is not because the Biblical authors lack religious affections. How can ministers read sermons about the Psalms in the same pleasant tone the entire time? I don't understand how a preacher can suppose that he communicates a text that is filled with emotional eloquence in a conversational, passionless way. How can the preacher give the congregation a sense of the text if he will not personally and experientially enter the holy emotions of the biblical writer? How can you understand the eloquence of the Psalmist if you do not communicate with emotion the emotions that fire his linguistic gifts?

I want you to look at one chapter in the Bible to see how central emotion, passion, and feeling are to the biblical text and writers. I also want to provide some direction about how the minister must enter the emotions of the biblical writer. If the Psalmist has holy emotions, we probably ought to experience the same sacred passions when we are in similar situations. The beauty of the Psalms is that they connect with a wide variety of challenges and experiences that we have in the Christian life. It is nonsense to suppose that the Psalms are not relevant for New Testament Christians. A Christian who thinks this and does not want to sing the Psalms is either ignorant of the Psalms or has a severe spiritual lack.

I still remember the extended Brummel family crowding into a surgical waiting room in the hospital in Sioux Falls, South Dakota. We were crammed into a little room because my cousin Steve, at my age (19) was in a car accident. He went into cardiac arrest when his throat swelled shut. We read Psalms and prayed. My Dad said: "The Psalms are so precious and meaningful in times like this." He was correct. The Psalms are not precious to the saints because they are emotionless songs to be sung without passion and preached without spiritual affections.

I want you to look at Psalm 119 and observe the variety of religious affections that are felt and communicated by the song writer.

First, observe that Psalm 119 is a song. It was written to be sung. The ideas in this song were meant to be expressed with emotion and feeling. Why did the saints chant or sing? The modulation, variation, and variety of tone found in singing are meant to convey heightened emotion. When we sing a song, we feel the words even more deeply than when we read them.

Second, observe that Psalm 119 is poetry. Poetry compresses thought. The poet uses conciseness, metaphor, and clarity to make a maximum impact on the will, mind, and emotions of the reader. Poetry is pregnant thought. The poet is not seeking to share logical information with a reader, to make him smarter in his brain. The poet certainly wishes to communicate ideas, but they are meant to come with feeling and as an expression of what it is like to experience a truth and see it from a fresh perspective that impacts your mind, heart, and will. Since Psalm 119 is song and poetry, we should expect that the intent of the song writer was to communicate truth, feeling, and experience to impact the mind, heart, and will of the children of God. That is exactly what our Hebrew poet does.

We may not push aside the emotion of the eloquent Psalmist by pigeon-holing him as an emotional Jew. It is true that different cultures experience, manifest, and convey emotion in different ways; but there is a catholicity to covenant emotions. No matter what your ethnic or cultural background, you are an emotional creature. God made man as an emotional creature. God loves. God hates. God delights. God celebrates. Even fallen men continue to be emotional persons, even though they now love the wrong things and delight in sin. The catholicity of Christianity is evident in the fact that the Psalms can be translated into any language and the experience of the Psalmists are also the covenant emotions that believers experience today.

The Psalmist expresses powerful emotions. He sings about love and hate. He sings about his love for God's law: "O how I love your law!" (vs. 97) "Therefore I love your commandments above gold, above fine gold" (vs. 127). I cannot begin to develop the emotions involved in love. The Psalmist sings about his "delight in the law" (vs. 92). Delight is included in this love for the law.

The Psalmist shares his hatreds. "I hate every false way" (vs. 128). He says that he hates "every false way" (vs. 104). The poet tells us how he looks at the wicked: "I look at the faithless with disgust" (vs. 158). He experiences burning anger when he sees covenant breakers: "Hot indignation seizes me because of the wicked, who forsake your law" (vs. 53). The song writer isn't afraid to express his emotions. And they are strong!

The preacher needs to understand the truths and feel the emotions that the song writer communicates. If you do not feel the truth of the Psalmist's loves, hates, and hot indignation; how can you communicate the meaning of the text? The saints today should have the same religious affections as the poet. To the extent that they do not, they are not loving the Law as they ought. In our antinomian age Christians need to love the Law and hate sin.

The Psalmist's expressions of love, hate, and indignation are only the beginning of the emotions that he experiences and shares. He expresses his zeal "My zeal consumes me, because my foes forget your words" (vs. 139). He cries: "My eyes shed streams of tears, because people do not keep your law" (vs. 136). I have a problem with a minister who feels no sadness over people breaking God's Law. How can you preach this text without realizing why the Psalmist weeps and experiencing the same grief as you see disobedience saints and the effect this rebellion has on their lives and relationships?

The Psalmist expresses fear and distress: "Let my cry come before you, O LORD" (vs. 170). He cries out to God for salvation. He expresses a desire to be vindicated. He praises God and expresses his commitment to doing so in the future: "My lips will pour forth praise" (vs. 171). He mentions that God comforts him: "Let your steadfast love comfort me" (vs. 73). He writes about singing: "My tongue will sing of your Word" (vs. 172). He expresses the emotion of awe: "my heart stands in awe of your word" (vs. 161). He expresses the emotion of hope: "deliver me according to your word" (vs. 170). He rejoices: "I rejoice at your word" (vs. 162). He expresses longing: "I long for your salvation, O LORD" (vs. 174). These are a few of the emotions expressed by the Psalmist. We have not mentioned his emotional expressions of confidence in God, trust, pain at being persecuted, or how he feels "like a wineskin in the smoke" (vs. 83).

But you get the idea.

The Psalmist possesses a swirl of emotions.

So do we. The only question is: Are they holy emotions? Another vital question is: Are we responding to our experiences and emotions as the Psalmist did?

The eloquence of Psalm 119 rises out of the swirl of mind, will, and emotions in the poet who penned these lyrics.

Why does Psalm 119 have so many memorable statements? Why so many powerful phrases that lend themselves to expository preaching? The answer: the Psalmist is honestly communicating the powerful emotions he experiences in the midsts of the trials and triumphs of life.

Emotion is the mother of eloquence.

Writer's writers tell aspiring authors: "Write what you feel." That is what the Psalmist did. This poetry finds an echo in the heart of the New Testament Christian. We experience many trials and the same covenant love of God. We grieve when we are attacked and celebrate when God delivers us. I would say: "Preach what you feel." Then the truth will be on fire. You will reach heights of eloquence. Then the hearts of the pious will burn with the flame of covenant emotion, which is one of the blessings of the covenant. You will feel and experience the faithfulness of God as you continue to love His law and meditate on it day and night.

Chapter 14

The Role of the Holy Spirit
in the Act of Preaching

he minister experiences freedom in the pulpit as the Holy Spirit equips him. Pierre Ch. Marcel argues that vitality in the pulpit results from the Holy Spirit's sovereign freedom in guiding the preacher in the act of preaching.

> The preaching of the word should be done according to the spirit with the assistance and in the freedom of the Spirit of the church. All the results of preaching should be made dependent on the Spirit.[290]

Marcel argues that *"everything depends, in the last analysis, on the preacher's, the believer's, and the Church's relationship with the Spirit. Preaching, which is, properly speaking, the word preached, depends entirely on the Spirit."*[291]

Vitality in preaching results from the sovereign and gracious freedom of the Holy Spirit. *"The word of God must be preached with the vitality of the Holy Spirit, who is the Spirit of Christ and of the Church. We must let the Spirit be free to intervene in the course of preaching."*[292] Marcel quotes John Calvin in support of this idea. The Genevan reformer wrote a letter in which he criticized English preachers for reading their sermons. Calvin argues that this approach to preaching quenches the Spirit:

> It seems to me that there is very little *ardent* preaching in the kingdom, and that most of it is *recited* as if *read*. I readily see the necessity which leads to such, for, in the first place, there are not, as I believe, any good and fit pastors who could supply this deficiency. It is very possible that there are many fickle spirits which fly off the hinges, sowing inane fantasies, as is often done by way of fanciful innovation.

---

[290] Pierre Ch. Marcel The Relevance of Preaching (New York: Westminster Publishing House, 2000), 90.
[291] Ibid., 91.
[292] Ibid., 92-93.

But all these consideration do not present Jesus Christ's command concerning the preaching of the gospel from having its effect. To be sure, the preaching must in no way be dead, but *alive*, for teaching, reproving, correcting, as Paul tells Timothy (II Tim. 3), indeed so much so that if an unbeliever enters he may be heartrent and convicted and so give glory to God, as he says in another passage (I Cor. 14). You know also how he speaks of the vitality which must be in the mouth of those who desire to be approved as good and faithful ministers of God, who must not make a parade of rhetoric in order to be highly esteemed. *Rather the Spirit of God must resound in their voices.*

All the dangers which one can fear must not prevent the Spirit of God from having his freedom and his effect in those to whom he has distributed his graces for the edification of the Church.[293]

It is by the power of the Holy Spirit that the Word of God preached by a human preacher can be the Word of God. Marcel writes that "If the word which is going to be uttered is to be the *preached* word of God, it must be uttered with the assistance and power of the Spirit."[294]

Only the intervention of the Spirit can lift that word to make it neither a lecture, a recitation, a discourse, an allocution, nor a meditation, but a *preaching*, a word spoken in the vitality of the Spirit, and therefore *preached*. If the Spirit is absent, there is, in a manner of speaking, a *sermon*, but no *preaching*."[295]

He adds:

Preachers and believers alike must pray that the Spirit, who alone can turn the word of man into a word of God, may work forcefully, that nothing in their lives and from the beginning of the service may interfere with the action of the Spirit.[296]

The preacher can pray for the Holy Spirit, but the Heavenly Dove is sovereign and free in dispensing His gifts. "*The Spirit is a living and free person.* It is *necessary*, therefore, when invoking his presence, *to allow him freedom of action.*"[297] Jesus speaks about how in times of persecution Christians will experience "the Spirit of your Father speaking through you" (Matthew 10:18-20).

---

[293] Ibid., 93. Cited by and italics added by Marcel,
[294] Ibid., 94.
[295] Ibid., 94.
[296] Ibid., 94.
[297] Ibid., 94.

Preparation and even redaction constitute only a *preliminary* part of preaching. It means rather that the preacher, in church, is to yield himself a malleable and living organ. For what Christ by the Spirit wills him to say to those who hear. If Christ is left free, he will constrain the preacher to add, delete, and modify (in form or even in content) such and such portion of that which he had intended to say, but which *he cannot now say.* If the preacher is and remains dependent upon his manuscript or upon his memory, there is not *just one* prisoner—there are two: the preacher and the Spirit, and through the Spirit Christ. The written or memorized text of the sermon at this moment exercises its dominance; Christ through the Spirit is not free.[298]

Spurgeon on the Role of the Holy Spirit in Preaching

In April 1891 Charles Spurgeon gave a significant inaugural address to the Pastor's College Conference. He was speaking to fellow pastors. This speech, which Spurgeon gave after 36 years of preaching, has been called one of his most forceful addresses. He spoke about the importance of minister's affirming and submitting to God's authoritative revelation in Sacred Scripture.

What interests us is that he spoke to the issue of the role of the Holy Spirit in the act of preaching. He spoke to the gathered preachers about how the minister can depend upon the Holy Spirit to empower him in the act of preaching.

In the pulpit do we really and truly rest upon the aid of the Spirit. I do not censure any brother for his mode of preaching, but I must confess that it seems very odd to me when a brother prays that the Holy Ghost may help him in preaching, and then I see him put his hand behind him and draw a manuscript out of his pocket, so fashioned that he can place it in the middle of his Bible, and read from it without being suspected of doing so. These precautions for ensuring secrecy look as though the man was a little ashamed of his paper; but I think he should be far more ashamed of his precautions. Does he expect the Spirit of God to bless him while he is practicing a trick? And how can He help him when he reads out of a paper from which anyone else might read without the Spirit's aid? What has the Holy Ghost to do with the business? Truly, he may have had something to do with the manuscript in the composing of it, but in the pulpit his aid is superfluous. The truer thing would be to

---

[298] Ibid., 95.

thank the Holy Spirit for assistance rendered, and ask that what he has enabled us to get into our pockets may now enter the people's hearts. Still, if the Holy Ghost should have anything to say to the people that is not in the paper, how can he say it by us? He seems to me to be very effectually blocked as to freshness of utterance by that method of ministry. Still, it is not for me to censure, although I may quietly plead for liberty in prophesying, and room for the Lord to give us in the same hour what we shall speak.[299]

Marcel writes: "Spurgeon is right. It is impossible in the act of preaching to limit the action of the Spirit to the one he employed during preparation."[300] The French preacher warns:

We must tend to allow the Spirit the widest possible liberty, that he may act personally and according to his purposes. God forbid that we imprison the Spirit in a rigid scheme! Far be it from us to invoke his presence and forthwith behave in such a way as to restrict his liberty and the vital relevance of the word.[301]

How does the Holy Spirit "interfere" in the act of preaching? "The Spirit does not interfere so far as doctrines are concerned, but as concerns the opportuneness, forcefulness, simplicity, and vitality with which we proclaim the gospel."[302]

Marcel is correct in saying that the Holy Spirit empowers us to speak with forcefulness and simplicity. But this is not done in isolation from the doctrines that the Holy Spirit is empowering us to preach. It is true that the Holy Spirit does not give us new revelations like the Apostle Paul experienced. But He does enable us to see, understand, and communicate doctrines better than we might have thought that we were able to do. He is the one who leads us into the truth and illuminates our minds. Even in the act of preaching, the Holy Spirit is our Teacher and Illuminator.

Spurgeon makes clear that he does not support impromptu preaching. Such preaching is the escape of the lazy preacher. We must not expect preaching without preparation to have the Spirit's blessing.

Remember, again, that *he will never encourage idleness*. The Holy Ghost will not come in to rescue us from the consequences of willful neglect

---

[299] C. H. Spurgeon, The Greatest Fight in the World (Final Manifesto) (Toronto; New York; London: Funk & Wagnalls, 1891), 51–52.
[300] Pierre Ch. Marcel, The Relevance of Preaching (New York: Westminster Publishing House, 2000), 96.
[301] Ibid., 97.
[302] Ibid., 99.

of the Word of God and study. If we allow ourselves to go up and down all the week doing nothing, we may not climb the pulpit stairs and dream that the Lord will there and then tell us what to speak. If help were promised to such, then the lazier the man the better the sermon. If the Holy Spirit worked only by impromptu speakers, the less we read our Bibles and the less we meditated on them the better. If it be wrong to quote from books, "attention to reading" should not have been commanded. All this is obviously absurd, and not one of you will fall into such a delusion. We are bound to be much in meditation, and give ourselves wholly to the Word of God and prayer, and when we have minded these things we may look for the Spirit's approbation and co-operation. *We ought to prepare the sermon as if all depended upon us, and then we are to trust the Spirit of God knowing that all depends upon Him.* [303]

Spurgeon emphasizes how the preacher needs to rely upon the Holy Spirit in the act of preaching.

> *Be yourself clothed with the Spirit of God,* and then no question about attention or non-attention will arise. Come fresh from the closet and from communion with God, to speak to men for God with all your heart and soul, and you must have power over them. You have golden chains in your mouth which will hold them fast. [304]

Spurgeon acknowledge that the minister who preaches extemporaneously has a special need to depend on the might of the Holy Spirit. The minister must study and work hard at preparing the message, but then depend on the might of the Holy Spirit in the act of preaching.

> We say to you, perfect yourselves in oratory, cultivate all the fields of knowledge, make your sermon mentally and rhetorically all it ought to be (you ought to do no less in such a service), but at the same time remember, "it is not by might, nor by power," that men are regenerated or sanctified, but "by my Spirit, saith the Lord." [305]

Spurgeon believes that the preacher "must cultivate a childlike *reliance upon the immediate assistance of the Holy Spirit.*" [306] When a preacher is put into a position where he must give an impromptu talk, "then he may with fullest

---

[303] C. H. Spurgeon, The Greatest Fight in the World (Final Manifesto) (Toronto; New York; London: Funk & Wagnalls, 1891), 61–62. Emphasis added.

[304] C.H. Spurgeon, Lectures to my Students. Volume 1. (Lynchburg, Virginia: The Old-Time Gospel Hour, 1894), 150.

[305] Ibid., 150.

[306] Ibid., 163.

confidence cast himself upon the Spirit of God."[307] Spurgeon tells us that in such a situation "The divine mind beyond a doubt comes into contact with the human intellect, lifts it out of its weakness and distraction, makes it soaring and strong, and enables it both to understand and to express divine truth in a manner far beyond its unaided powers."[308]

Marcel deals with objections to extemporaneous preaching. The first objection is that this approach allows the preacher to be lazy. The French pastor's response is that extemporaneous preaching requires harder work than writing out a sermon to be read. "To preach the word in this way demands more spiritual labor than to write sermons to read or to learn....There is a renewed struggle each time to cast oneself on the specific promises of Christ, to abandon oneself to the Spirit."[309]

Extemporaneous preaching involves all of the exegesis and preparation that goes into writing a sermon, but it involves more. The minister must internalize the message and plant its' central ideas and main points in his memory.

A second objection to extemporaneous preaching goes to the opposite extreme. Instead of extemporaneous preaching being caricatured as a method for lazy preachers, it is said to be too difficult. "Perhaps others will object that they do not have the necessary talents, that they do not have facility of language, that they fear failing in this undertaking."[310]

Marcel responds by quoting Calvin to the effect that Christ will equip His preachers: "Besides, Christ never directs his ministers to undertake any charge without at the same time furnishing them with integrity and fortifying them with faculties to administer their office."[311]

Marcel writes that "The Spirit endows his word, his expression, with a natural freshness and vitality which give the word a new and original appearance *and which belong only to the spoken style.* The strain on the memory and the servitude to a manuscript hinder this direct communion with Christ and the congregation."[312]

As the Holy Spirit empowers the minister to preach, "The Spirit begins to speak a language suited to each soul he cherishes, and for everyone present he makes the preaching of the word relevant."[313]

---

[307] Ibid., 164.

[308] Ibid., 164.

[309] Pierre Ch. Marcel, The Relevance of Preaching (New York: Westminster Publishing House, 2000), 99.

[310] Ibid., 99.

[311] John Calvin, Commentary on John 20:22. Cited by Marcel, p. 99-100.

[312] Pierre Ch. Marcel, The Relevance of Preaching (New York: Westminster Publishing House, 2000), 100-101.

[313] Ibid., 101.

Spurgeon tells us that the Holy Spirit uses the means of the hard work of the preacher in empowering the minister to preach. The Holy Spirit does not usually bless the lazy minister.

> Remember, again, that *he will never encourage idleness.* The Holy Ghost will not come in to rescue us from the consequences of willful neglect of the Word of God and study. If we allow ourselves to go up and down all the week doing nothing, we may not climb the pulpit stairs and dream that the Lord will there and then tell us what to speak. If help were promised to such, then the lazier the man the better the sermon. If the Holy Spirit worked only by impromptu speakers, the less we read our Bibles and the less we meditated on them the better. If it be wrong to quote from books, "attention to reading" should not have been commanded. All this is obviously absurd, and not one of you will fall into such a delusion. We are bound to be much in meditation, and give ourselves wholly to the Word of God and prayer, and when we have minded these things we may look for the Spirit's approbation and co-operation. We ought to prepare the sermon as if all depended upon us, and then we are to trust the Spirit of God knowing that all depends upon Him. [314]

Spurgeon concluded his message:

> Lastly, remember *the Holy Ghost will only bless in conformity with His own set purpose.* Our Lord explains what that purpose is: "He shall glorify me." He has come forth for this grand end, and he will not put up with anything short of it. If, then, we do not preach Christ, what is the Holy Ghost to do with our preaching? If we do not make the Lord Jesus glorious; if we do not lift him high in the esteem of men, if we do not labour to make him King of kings, and Lord of lords; we shall not have the Holy Spirit with us. Vain will be rhetoric, music, architecture, energy, and social status: if our one design be not to magnify the Lord Jesus, we shall work alone and work in vain.[315]

---

[314] C. H. Spurgeon, The Greatest Fight in the World (Final Manifesto) (Toronto; New York; London: Funk & Wagnalls, 1891), 61–62.

[315] C. H. Spurgeon, The Greatest Fight in the World (Final Manifesto) (Toronto; New York; London: Funk & Wagnalls, 1891), 63–64.

Chapter 15

Preachers must Read, Interpret, and Comprehend Texts

How can you internalize a message if you cannot read, interpret, or comprehend texts? You can't. You can act as if you have a message, but it will not be profound and will not be the fruit of exegetical labors if you cannot interpret texts.

Hopefully you have read *Why Johnny Can't Preach: The Media Have Shaped the Messengers* by T. David Gordon. Gordon wrote this book as he battled cancer. He thought that he might die. He had one burden on his conscience that he wanted to relieve in case he was on his death bed. He felt the need to address weaknesses in the preaching in confessional Presbyterian churches. He was burdened by the weaknesses in the pulpits of the Orthodox Presbyterian Church, the Presbyterian Church in America, and other "conservative" churches. The book is prophetic.

Gordon argues that Johnny can't preach because he hasn't learned how to decipher and interpret texts. He argues that the American media has shaped young men so that they are not good at reading and analyzing texts.

Gordon is clear that he does not require great preaching from local pastors. He simply wants adequate preaching. But he couldn't even hear adequate sermons in many "conservative" Presbyterian churches that he attended.

We live in odd times. Most Americans can read, but they are functional illiterates. They can read, but they do not. If you gave them a book, they could read it; but they simply have no desire to read. Why read books or literature when they can watch television, listen to the radio, watch Youtube, flip through Facebook, or read short news accounts on your smart phone?

My parents did a good job of loving and encouraging God's ministers. They often invited them into our home. My parents and grandparents loved to show hospitality to visiting ministers. The place for after church coffee was Grandpa and Grandma Brummel's house. It was an established custom that after church our family, my uncles and aunts, and cousins all converged on my grandparent's home. Any guest pastor would be invited over as well.

The ministers lived on the other side of church from our home. Therefore, my siblings and I became friends with the minister's children. Our parents often invited the minister's family to our home and we visited at their place.

My parents were committed to their local church. This commitment showed itself in their commitment to the ministry of the Word. My father also became a local distributor for books published by the Reformed Free Publishing Association, the (unofficial) denominational publisher for the Protestant Reformed Churches. I am not sure how many farmers read books back in the 1970s, but I suppose that percentage-wise a larger percentage read Reformed literature than today. The earlier generations of Dutch Reformed immigrants read theology. They were the offspring of Abraham Kuyper's "kleine luyden"[316] who grew biblically and theologically as they read the writing of Reformed ministers and those of Abraham Kuyper in Dutch periodicals and newspapers. Kuyper wrote on theology, godly living, and Christian faithfulness in society. The Dutch immigrants who moved to Grand Rapids, Michigan and southwest Minnesota were committed to the life of the mind. Farmers believed it necessary to be biblically faithful and theologically orthodox. They eagerly read denominational periodicals where theological issues were discussed and often debated by polemical editors.

My parents grew up in this milieu. My mother's family, the Kuipers, were from Grand Rapids, Michigan where there was a high level of biblical and theological knowledge in the 1960's.

My father was a reader. He grew up in a family where reading was encouraged. He was not a good student in high school; he dropped out after his sophomore year. He was drafted into the army and fought in Vietnam. After returning home and marrying my mom, he worked for the local newspaper, the Edgerton Enterprise. He wrote columns about hunting, fishing, or sports. He helped with editing the newspaper. He worked with words.

---

[316] Little people

Dad taught me the value of reading. My father led by example. He read. He was the first man voted onto the board of the local library. The librarians knew that he read. My siblings learned to read well.

I had a jumpstart on reading compared to my peers—although I do not remember my parents teaching me to read at home. I must have learned to read in kindergarten and first grade at the Free Christian School, a two-room schoolhouse.

Today the curriculum and pedagogy in the school might be viewed by the elites at the National Board of Education as backwards and sectarian. School was not a time to be indoctrinated in the latest social justice craze. No sex education. No fancy, expensive textbooks. No well-paid teachers. We had five grades in one classroom: kindergarten through fourth grade. One teacher. No assistants. I had Carol DeJong for kindergarten.

But since she got married to Harold Brands, the board would not renew her contract for the next year. Miss Beverly Hoekstra moved to town and taught 20-25 students in grades kindergarten to fourth grade. A couple of years later the school did add a kindergarten teacher. Our classroom was large with chalkboards on two sides. In the back, behind the piano, there was thick, shag green carpet. The kindergarteners took their nap back there daily—surrounded by the classroom library.

Miss Hoekstra kept a lemon bush in the classroom.

She loved to write the names of the kings of Judah and Israel on a supersized notebook. She used permanent markers that squeaked across the page. We memorized the kings in historical order.

At Christmas time we spent countless hours preparing for the annual Christmas program. Miss Hoekstra took this event seriously and had high expectations for all of the student body. We all memorized Bible passages that we would recite from the platform at church. Each year we would memorize all the verses for 12-15 Christmas carols. From second grade on, I directed the rhythm band—an undisciplined group of students who slammed and crashed their instruments together.

The curriculum for reading class was *The Programmed Reader*. We also had a phonics workbooks that taught pronunciation and grammar. But the heart of the reading curriculum centered on *The Programmed Reader*. The geniuses behind this series provided a 22-book series filled with marvelous and wonderful pictures of Sam, Ann, Walter, Nip the dog, the Roundabouts, and in the last crucial books, wonderful stories and paintings of Hercules and the Greek (and Roman) gods.

The Programmed Reading Books seized my imagination. The beauty of the system is that children started on the series in first grade and could work through the books at their own speed. The student had a plastic insert that he placed over each page. He used crayons to fill in missing letters or words or to circle correct answers.

Kids in public schools probably had fancy erasers to remove the crayon from the plastic insert. We used toilet paper. We erased the words, letters, and circles we had made on the plastic insert and slipped it over the next page. On the left side of each page a piece of paper ran from the top of the plastic insert to the bottom, hiding the correct answers. You could pull the paper insert down and see the answer or just lift the side of the plastic. The student only worked on the right side of the page—since the left was upside down.

The idea was to reach the end of the first side and then flip the book over. When you came to the end of one side, Miss Hoekstra would oversee you taking the test on the last pages. The test pages had bright-red lines running along the edge. If Miss Hoekstra passed you, the student could flip the book over and work on the second side. So the curriculum came with inbuilt accountability.

In graduate school in philosophy I would find myself in a seminar i

The adventures of Sam and Ann and later Hercules made reading fun. I learned the joy of discovery and how reading fired my imagination.

Usually students worked on this curriculum through fourth grade. I finished it in the second grade. I set a record.

Learning to read is an important element in learning how to interpret texts. Looking back, I now see the value of studying philosophy because philosophy professors press their students to interpret difficult texts. I was a pre-seminary student while at Calvin College and needed to fulfill a lot of pre-seminary requirements that included two years of Dutch, two years of Latin, two years of Greek, and additional classes in history and English.

T. David Gordon talks about the value of a pre-seminary student majoring in English. He points out that gifted preachers like Phil Ryken or John Piper had a strong English background. Dr. Ryken's father was the well-known English professor at Wheaton College, Leeland Ryken. John Piper's poetic and linguistic gifts stand out as crucial to his writing and preaching ministries. In English literature classes there is a focus on reading, interpreting, and critically interacting with the literature. But the same is true in philosophy.

I decided to major in philosophy mainly through the influence of philosophers Mark Talbot and Bill Dennyson. Both men loved Reformed theology and did not divorce the life of the mind from a Reformed world-view. A group of pre-seminary students referred to Mark Talbot as "The Philosopher". Since Dennyson defended the infallibility of the Bible, we called him "The Inerrant One". The challenge in my philosophy classes was that I would encounter a new philosopher and would need to wrestle with comprehending the texts. I spent a semester reading Immanuel Kant's *Critique of Pure Reason*. Due to the difficulty of the text and how foreign Kant's worldview was to mine, it was exceedingly difficult to interpret the text. I learned that to comprehend a philosopher like Kant or Hegel it is necessary to find both points of contact and contrast between their horizons and mine. Philosophers also study Gadamer and Heidegger and, therefore, engage issues of hermeneutics and interpretation which are also important subjects for the theological student.

In which I would be presented by the texts of a thinker like Ludwig Wittgenstein. Starting from scratch, I would need to enter into the thought of this volatile philosopher. I found that a comprehension of some of Wittgenstein's ideas about how language functioned affected how I in turn read texts and interpreted what theologians were doing. If words are defined in use, then this has implications for the theological formulations of theologians who deny this. If a theologian dares to imply that words always have one exact and almost mathematical meaning (like you find Wittgenstein advocating for in his early *Tractatus Logico-Philosophicus*) he will make theological mistakes.

In graduate school I would have exceedingly difficult texts thrust into my hands. I would need to explain what Hegel teaches about being and non-being within his dialectic. I discovered internal contradictions within Hegel's basic presuppositions and marveled at his blind spots. I was not always prepared at age 23 to engage and interpret philosophical texts. At other times I was able to wrap my mind around the thought of a thinker like Jean Jacques Rousseau.

After I wrote a paper on some of the theistic assumptions that underpinned Rousseau's thought, my 60's era hippy, atheistic professor expressed chagrin that I might have undermined the appropriation of Rousseau's thought by atheists. I also learned how secular atheists viewed evangelical Christians. In a graduate seminar, comments were made that the only way to obtain a just society in Wisconsin was to get rid of the Lutherans. I realized that this was a wish to do away with evangelical Protestants. I was included in this wish!

Homeschooled children can benefit from the fact that they have time and freedom to pursue areas of personal interest. Homeschooled children who do not want to learn and are only interested in completing necessary assignments are not included in this.

Students who need to be pressed to complete assignments and are constantly headstrong do not develop the life of the mind. But a psychologically healthy homeschool student will develop areas of interest and with parental support will have the time and energy to pursue their passions. For example, one of my home-schooled children is exceedingly interested in animals and will read difficult textbooks about animals and zoology. The same student has a desire to write stories.

At age 13 he wrote a nice short story about a Japanese boy who helps to save his town from a ninja attack. My son did research on Japanese history and customs for this story. This type of learning is far superior to the parent or teacher assigning a textbook about Japanese history. The crucial element in this learning is that the student is teaching himself. He has learned how to do research, how to appropriate material that is relevant for his work, and then is able to synthesize what he has learned into a unified story.

This student was taught how to think, do research, and apply what he learned. In some sense this was the crucial element in his education. He learned how to read and interpret texts and then incorporate what he learned into his worldview and the cultural product that he produces.

Why is my son able to write at the level he does now? I taught him how to read when he was three years old. By ages five and six he was reading literature far beyond his years—and comprehending much of it. My younger daughter took longer to learn how to read. What is striking is that when my daughter was seven-years-old she was just learning how to read, but her ability to interpret a text that was read to her went far beyond her reading skills. I could read a novel with complex humor and she would get the joke. Even though she had just learned how to read the Bible and stumbled over difficult words, she was able to read the text with understanding.

The moment she began to take off in her Bible reading, she was able to read with expression! This striking ability was due to her comprehension of the text.

She had heard the stories. Many biblical texts were explained to her before. She developed a biblical worldview shaped by the stories of biblical characters. She could understand new texts in light of texts she had already grasped.

My daughter's reading ability needed to catch up with her ability to comprehend. The moral of the story is that in an oral culture, the future preacher will learn how to interpret texts first of all through oral interpretation of texts. Don't be surprised when such a student displays a comprehension of the text that was not learned through careful reading of the text or commentaries. Rather the student learned to interpret by listening to the teaching and interpretation of other speakers.

Chapter 15: Preachers must Read, Interpret, and Comprehend Texts

At Divine Hope Reformed Bible Seminary where I teach (a dedicated prison seminary), sometimes our faculty discover that students who are challenged at reading texts carefully can produce an exegesis paper that does not appear to explain the heart of the text, but when the professor sits down with the student and talks about the meaning of the passage; he will discover that the student can verbalize the heart of the text and its proper application.

Why can the student do a better job of explaining the verse verbally than writing about it? The student is an oral learner. We have students who came to prison as illiterates. You can imagine the challenges that such a student faces in carefully interpreting biblical texts. It is a wonder when I meet a Hispanic student who taught himself English in prison and after a good number of years can translate theological works from English into Spanish. Translating work involves remarkable abilities at interpreting and comprehending texts in two different languages!

Clearly the student who can communicate more verbally about a passage than he can write down about it has resources to draw on that are not dependent his writing abilities. I have had students who never saw or used a biblical commentary before in their life. Yet they could interpret Scripture due to listening to preachers and being involved in Bible studies.

It is interesting that in prison there is a unique approach to the Bible. A lot of prisoners read their Bibles and initially appear biblically literate. Visitors to prison can leave surprised by the Scripture knowledge of prisoners. Yet time and again students have told me, "I thought I knew the Bible, but I didn't."

Prisoners lacked a systematic theology that could have enabled them to read and interpret Scripture as a unity. They lacked a biblical theology that would have allowed them to understand the unfolding covenant of grace. They could not understand texts in their redemptive-historical context. This explains why prisoners can buy into religious views that reject the correct relationship between the old and new testaments. Prisoners are tempted to follow Old Testament dietary requirements due to this fact.

Other students tell me that they knew the words in the Bible and had memorized a lot of texts, but they had not wrestled with the meaning of the texts to grasp their true significance. They were lazy exegetes. They read into texts whatever they thought was there or whatever interpretation was provided through the prison grape-vine.

At Cook County Jail in Chicago I discovered that the prison grape-vine led to strange interpretations and to an undue emphasis on certain texts or biblical characters. This was because various odd interpretations by the cults found their way into the jail. Passages that fit into the category of genealogies that Christians ought not to major in were heatedly discussed.

More fundamental passages that reveal the heart of the gospel were not so eagerly discussed. In prison I kept hearing people discuss who Melchizedech was. Some thought he was an angel. Who was Michael the archangel? Following the interpretations of Jehovah Witnesses, prisoners wondered whether Michael was Jesus. Who were the sons of God who wed the daughters of men, as mentioned in Genesis 6? I was asked whether devils fornicated with human women? This odd interpretation did not originate in prison, but it is interesting that discussions of these type of passages were common.

I found that new seminary students in prison campuses are tempted to waste energy discussing odd interpretations. This is not surprising because the devils want to distract Bible readers from seeing the fundamental teachings of Scripture.

Devils would rather have prisoners argue about goofy interpretations that teaching nothing about godly living than to see them humbled before what the Bible teaches about God's moral will and the great doctrines of the Christian faith.

Few prisoners are well equipped to interpret crucial passages that teach the deity of Jesus, the doctrine of justification by faith, sovereign election, the personhood and divinity of the Holy Spirit, and the Ten Commandments.

Both prisoners and preachers need to grow in their ability to read, interpret, and comprehend texts.

As a preacher, you need to be a student of the Word. This means that your calling involves the study and interpretation of texts. If you do not like reading and do not like the hard work of deciphering texts, the ministry is not for you.

We all fall into habits of reading and interpretation. We need to be shaken out of our habits. We need to learn new ways to approach and interpret texts. We need to learn what better questions to ask of a text. And we need to know the texts. Therefore, we need to read our Bibles in private devotions.

How can you preach, if you cannot interpret texts? Mortimer Adler's famous book *How to Read a Book* grew out of his support of the Great Books curriculum. Adler found that in the first third of the twentieth century too many college graduates in the United States were not receiving a liberal arts education. Students were not being taught how to read and interpret texts.

To counter this trend Adler advocated that students read the "Great Books" of western civilization.

The result is that the president of the University of Chicago co-led a discussion of the Great Books with Adler. The only students allowed in the discussion were college freshmen. After two years of reading the Great Books together, the students who were entering their junior year, asked that they read through the same Great Books a second time. Adler's approach to a liberal arts education (which included encouraging adults to form study groups to read the Great Books) encouraged the reading and interpretation of texts. It is no wonder that Adler's *How to Read a Book* is still used in hermeneutic or exegesis classes in seminaries. The preacher needs to evaluate the nature of his own liberal arts education. And he needs to explore how he can continue to mature as an interpreter of texts.

Chapter 16
Genuine Expository Preaching

oday it is popular to do "Expository Preaching." Everyone claims that they are doing it. John MacArthur and other prominent evangelicals are set forth as models of Expository preaching. Fundamentalist and evangelical churches advertise on their websites that one can hear expository preaching from their pulpits. I have listened to and read enough sermons to know that the messages of those who imagine that they are engaging in expository preaching are not necessarily genuine instances of "Expository preaching." T. David Gordon wrote *Why Johny Can't Preach* because he did not hear expository preaching in confessional Presbyterian churches in the Pittsburgh area.

So what is genuinely expository preaching? What ideal approach to preaching is referred to by the *cognomen* "Expository Preaching"?

Definitions of Expository Preaching

Let's look at some good definitions of expository preaching. Bryan Chapell defines expository preaching as preaching that expounds

> Scripture by deriving from a specific text main points and subpoints that disclose the thought of the author, cover the scope of the passage, and are applied to the lives of the listeners.[317]

Alan M. Stibb's defines expository preaching in the following way:

> The business of the preacher is to stick to the passage chosen and to set forth exclusively what it has to say or suggest, so that the ideas expressed and the principles enunciated during the course of the sermon plainly come out of the Written Word of God, and have its authority for their support rather than just the opinion or the

---

[317] Bryan Chapell, Christ-Centered Preaching: Redeeming the Expository Sermon (Grand Rapids: Baker, 1994), 129.

enthusiasm of their human expositor.[318]

Haddon Robinson defines expository preaching as follows:

> Expository preaching is the communication of a biblical concept, derived from and transmitted through a historical, grammatical, and literary study of a passage in its context, which the Holy Spirit at first applies to the personality and experience of the preacher, then through the preacher, applies to the hearers.[319]

I like what Robinson says about how the Holy Spirit first applies the truth to the "personality and experience of the preacher."

Sinclair Ferguson describes expository preaching:

> Preaching to the heart, then, is not merely a matter of technique or homiletic style. These things have their proper place and relevance. But the more fundamental, indeed, the more essential thing for the preacher is surely the fact that something has happened in his own heart; it has been laid bare before God by His Word.

> He, in turn, lays his heart bare before those to whom he ministers. And within that context, the goal he has in view is so to lay bare the truth of the Word of God that the hearts of those who hear are opened vertically to God and horizontally to one another.[320]

Derek Thomas writes that the minister needs to have a "sense of the reality of God's presence."[321] J.I. Packer said about Dr. Martyn Lloyd-Jones:

> I have never known anyone whose speech communicated such a sense of the reality of God as did the Doctor in those occasional moments of emphasis and doxology. Most of the time, however, it was clear, steady analysis, reflection, correction and instruction, based on simple thoughts culled from the text, set out in good order with the minimum of extraneous illustration or decoration. He knew that God's way to the heart is through the mind (he often insisted that the first thing the gospel does to a man is to make him think), and he preached in a way designed to help people think and thereby grasp truth—and in the process be grasped by it, and so be

---

[318] Alan M. Stibbs. Expounding God's Word (London: Inter-Varsity Press, 1970), 17.

[319] Haddon Robinsons, Biblical Preaching: The Development and Delivery of Expository Messages 2nd Edition (Grand Rapids: Baker, 2001), 21.

[320] Sinclair B. Ferguson, "Preaching to the Heart" in Feed My Sheep: A Passionate Plea for Preaching, R. Albert Mohler...[et al.], General editor, Don Kistler. (Sanford, Florida: Reformation Trust Publishing, 2008), 104.

[321] Derek W. H. Thomas "Expository Preaching" in Feed My Sheep: A Passionate Plea for Preaching, R. Albert Mohler...[et al.], General editor, Don Kistler. (Sanford, Florida: Reformation Trust Publishing, 2008), 48.

grasped by the God whose truth it is.[322]

Sinclair Ferguson writes that "A leading characteristic of preaching to the heart will be the humbling, indeed, the prostration of hearts before the majesty of God on high."[323]

Bad Expository Preaching

Derek Thomas identifies bad approaches to expository preaching:

> It cannot be denied that bad expository preaching exists. Much of it is in the form of a running commentary, with little attention to structure and form. As one who now teaches homiletics at a seminary, I find myself needing to distinguish a sermon from something that sounds like the fruits of culling several commentaries (even if they are *good* ones).[324]

Bad expository sermons are running commentaries on the text. The revival of expository preaching has too often led to sermons that are really not unified messages but rather running commentaries on a rather long passage. The preacher gets caught up in the details of the particular passage and doesn't step back to think about what the main message of the text is or how to drive that home to the congregation with a clear message that can be remembered. The sermon does not contain a logic.

The auditor leaves church with a multitude of ideas in his head. He heard several shorter messages that were tacked together. The sermon contained no real logic unless by accident the minister picked a text where the chronology of the narrative led logically from point to point.

The people of God are forgiving towards a minister who does not provide unified messages. If the preacher exegetes God's word and brings it home in a lively manner, they might not even notice that when they get home from church that it is hard to discuss the sermon. No one will have in their minds a clear sense of the main point.

A great failing of many sermons is that they end up as three sermons in one. I can look at the three divisions in a sermon and immediately grasp whether it is one or three messages. I regularly hear three messages

---

[322] J. I. Packer, "David Martyn Lloyd-Jones," in Collected Shorter Writings of J.I. Packer (Carlisle, U.K.: Paternoster, 1999), 4:85.

[323] Sinclair B. Ferguson, "Preaching to the Heart" in Feed My Sheep: A Passionate Plea for Preaching, R. Albert Mohler...[et al.], General editor, Don Kistler. (Sanford, Florida: Reformation Trust Publishing, 2008), 105.

[324] Derek W. H. Thomas, "Expository Preaching" in Feed My Sheep: A Passionate Plea for Preaching, R. Albert Mohler...[et al.], General editor, Don Kistler. (Sanford, Florida: Reformation Trust Publishing, 2008), 38.

masquerading as one. You simply need to ask of a sermon: Could the second point simply stand by itself and be lengthened into a message that would be in no way dependent on the first and third points? One way you often find three messages parading as one is when you find the same word used three times (once in each of the three divisions). Here is an example of a three-message sermon:

The Good Shepherd Calling His Sheep
I.   A Radical Calling
II. A Necessary Calling
III. A Blessed Calling

The logic of this message (really messages) would involve the preacher developing the concept of "calling" in each of the three points. Since the first point is "A Radical Calling", by definition, this point should discuss the nature of this calling and how it is radical. But the second point is entitled "A Necessary Calling" and, therefore, logically would include a development of the concept of "calling" and how it is necessary. When the third point arrives, logically the minister must develop the concept of "calling" all over again and then talk about how it is blessed. If the minister is really going to teach what is going on in each point as he states them, this is the logical outcome.

But we all know what actually happens.

The minister never actually develops the idea of "calling" in any of the three points.

This crucial idea in his message remains undeveloped.

You certainly will not find the minister actually developing the idea of calling in each of the three points.

Everyone would have a sense that this would involve vain repetition. If you have talked about the nature of this calling in the first point, why would you beat a dead horse in the second and third points? This all points to the fact that there is a lack of logic and movement in the sermon. The first point is logically parallel to the second and third. There is no development.

The solution to this problem is to have a title that contains the idea of calling. The first point would be a development of the main point of the text that should be contained in the theme (or sermon title). In this first point the minister would develop the idea of "calling". In the second and third points he would logically move on to subsidiary points that logically build on the first point. Perhaps the minister could have a theme and division as follows:

The Good Shepherd Calling His Sheep
  I.   The Meaning
  II.   The Necessity
  III. The Goal

In this message there would be a logical progression from the first point to the second and third. In the first point the minister would develop the idea of "calling". Having accomplished this, he would be free to develop another concept, namely, that it is necessary for the Good Shepherd to call His sheep. In the final point the preacher would develop what Christ's goal is in doing so.

Do not preach a commentary. There is a big difference between a running commentary on a text and a unified, logically developed message that communicates the main point (the big idea) of the text. Genuine exegetical preaching involves the presentation of a message that is a harmonious whole.

Chapter 17
Preach with Authority

Jesus preached: "But I say unto you." He preached with authority as the Son of God and as the Messianic king. The apostles preached with authority. I do not hear enough authoritative proclamation from the pulpit. Have you ever gone to church and hear a minister preach in such a way that the last thing you would say about his preaching is that it is authoritative. He submits things to you for consideration. His preaching is weak. He will not take strong stands or make strong statements. His preaching is merely that of a friend giving advice. I hear too much conversational style pulpit communication that purposely avoids any hint of authority. Don Kistler wrote:

> Jesus preached with authority. Why? Because He had authority. Likewise, the preachers of old preached with authority. They preached, "Thus saith the Lord." We have lost that today, I'm afraid. Our preaching reflects it and the lives of our people reflect it. They live as if the pastor has no authority, as if the elders have no authority, and, even more appalling, as if the Word of God itself has no authority.[325]

The Apostle Paul did not tell Titus to be a namby-pamby. He exhorted him: "These things speak and exhort and reprove with all authority. Let no one disregard you" (Titus 2:15). Paul told Timothy to "Reprove, rebuke, exhort, with great patience and instruction" (2 Timothy 4:2b).

Be a man!

Ministers have a derived authority from the Head of the church. Don Kistler explains what Paul means in Romans 10:14-15a when he asks the Romans "And how shall they believe in Him whom they have not heard?"

> Notice that Paul does not ask how they shall hear *about* Christ, but how they shall hear *Him* without a preacher! Do you see what Paul is saying here? When the faithful minister is properly exegeting the Word of

---

[325] Don Kistler, "Preaching with Authority" in Feed My Sheep: A Passionate Plea for Preaching, R. Albert Mohler...[et al.], General editor, Don Kistler. (Sanford, Florida: Reformation Trust Publishing, 2008), 117.

God, it is God Himself who is speaking to His people, drawing them to Himself! Failure to hear the faithful minister is a failure to hear God Himself![326]

Ministers can preach with authority, because Christ speaks through His ambassadors. That is why Jesus could tell His disciples: "The one who listens to you listens to Me, and the one who rejects you rejects Me" (Luke 10:16a).

When you preach, do not act like you are simply asserting your private, personal opinions? You need to convey Christ's Word with the authority that it deserves. It is a message that must be believed and obeyed.

A Puritan preacher, Thomas Taylor, told how both preachers and congregations need to acknowledge the authority of the Bible. First, he says to the preacher:

> The word of God must be delivered in such a manner that the majesty and authority of it shall be preserved. The ambassadors of Christ must speak His message even as He himself would utter it.[327]

As to the congregation, they must humble themselves under the Word of God:

> To withstand this authority, or to weaken it, is a fearful sin, whether in high or low men....Hearers must...not refuse to yield subjection to this authority, nor be angry when it bears down upon some practice which they are loath to part with.[328]

Dare to preach: "Thus saith the LORD!"

Preach with authority. Not because you possess any authority in yourself, but because Christ has delegated to you *the right* to speak the Word of the High King.

---

[326] Don Kistler, "Preaching with Authority" in Feed My Sheep: A Passionate Plea for Preaching, R. Albert Mohler...[et al.], General editor, Don Kistler. (Sanford, Florida: Reformation Trust Publishing, 2008), 120.

[327] Cited by Don Kistler, "Preaching with Authority" in Feed My Sheep: A Passionate Plea for Preaching, R. Albert Mohler...[et al.], General editor, Don Kistler. (Sanford, Florida: Reformation Trust Publishing, 2008), 121.

[328] Cited by Don Kistler, "Preaching with Authority" in Feed My Sheep: A Passionate Plea for Preaching, R. Albert Mohler...[et al.], General editor, Don Kistler. (Sanford, Florida: Reformation Trust Publishing, 2008), 121-22.

Chapter 18
Preach the Text *and* a Shorter One

You need to preach the text. This means that you need to engage in careful exegesis of each word, every phrase, and the important concepts in your text.

You not only need to preach the text, but you need to preach a shorter text. You are preaching on too long of passages and as a result you are not doing justice to the Scriptural text.

You need to preach the text. You don't need to preach the parallel passage. Yes, there are other texts that shed light on your text but keep your nose in your text.

Worry the bone of your text.

Exegete your text.

I hear preachers using parallel texts as a crutch to avoid explaining and exegeting their actual text. I find that a preacher who too quickly runs off elsewhere to allow Scripture to interpret Scripture does not actually interpret his text. Yes, do compare Scripture with Scripture, but this needs to be done in the service of interpreting your text. It is easy to mention a bunch of parallel passages. It is hard work to exegete your text. And when you quote a parallel text, provide exegesis of it. Be brief, clear, and simple. Define the central concepts. Remain on point. Quickly summarize the insight from the parallel text. And then get back to your text.

And stay there.

You need to preach the text, but you will not do so effectively if you do not select an appropriate one. I find that one of the biggest problem with new preachers is that they select too large of a text.

If you select too long of a text the result will be that you do not dig down into any part of your text. You will be stuck on the surface of the text because there will be so much that you must cover. Your message will be all over the map instead of a unified message.

You need to pick shorter texts. I am astonished how ministers will try to preach on 10-15 verses in Paul's writings. Are these ministers suicidal? Such ministers are trying to imitate John Calvin's commentaries where a good number of verses are listed and then there is an explanation of them. But Calvin's commentaries do not provide a good model for preaching. His commentaries do not synthesize Calvin's comments into a unified message. He simply works his way through the text one verse at a time. Your job in a sermon is to provide one, unified message. Your job is always to dig into the text and bring out the multifaceted beauty of the text. You need to bring out the unique accents in the text. Help the saints to see the beautiful facets of the text—rather than just showing them the whole forest again.

The reality is that if you teach in generalizations, many of the mature saints in the congregation will not learn much. But if you do careful exegesis and bring out the unique concepts in the text, they will learn and grow.

For textual sermons, the preacher needs to select an appropriate text that will normally be shorter rather than longer.

I know that the exception to this will be historical material.

You might want to preach one sermon on the life of King Manasseh. You will have an entire chapter of information in one book of the Bible and more information in a parallel account. But then you need to take into consideration the other piece of advice that I am sharing: prepare a unified message.

You will need to synthesize the information in the text so that you are not repeating yourself and so that the sermon moves from a beginning to an end. It will be all the more important that there will be logic in your sermon. I do not mean a scholastic logic that becomes an end in itself, but the logic of the story better be present in the logic of your homiletical outline. The longer your text, the more important it is to have a unified, harmonious message.

It can be useful to preach on longer texts, just for the practice of learning how to major in the majors and minor in the minors. The younger preacher might not have learned yet how to balance off major and minor points in the text. When you preach on a larger text, you get an exercise in logic and in identifying what is of homiletical importance (what is relevant for the congregation both theologically and practically).

What a Textual Sermon Is

The church where I pastored for a decade was not so supportive of longer series of sermons. This was a weakness in the congregation. They did not have a history of preachers preaching through longer books of the Bible. Therefore, the elders were not enthusiastic about me preaching longer series through books of the Bible. The church preferred small series or preaching on a variety of texts. Therefore, I either knew the next text in a short series and could begin to analyze this text or I needed to identify the text that I would preach on the following Sunday.

If I needed to identify a new text, I considered the pastoral needs of the congregation, world events, or a text that recently had jumped out at me. On Mother's Day I knew that covenant mothers would love a sermon on biblical motherhood. Theological weaknesses or besetting sins in the congregation directed me to specific texts. Perhaps my own reading had excited me about a certain portion of Scripture. My studies in missions and evangelism gave me a passion for communicating what the Bible said about the mission of the church.

But I knew that I could not afford to waste too much time identifying a text.

There came a point when I simply needed to select a text, even if it did not excite me too much. I could not waste an extra day trying to identify a relevant text. I would check my records to see whether I had preached on the text before.

Once my texts were chosen, the dye was cast! There was no turning back. I might discover that the text took me in a direction that I had not anticipated. Perhaps I thought that the text was teaching one thing, but it turned out to be emphasizing quite another idea. But I needed to be a servant of the Word. Perhaps I got excited about a text because I thought that it taught one thing, when in fact it taught something else. Sometimes the text would turn out to be more difficult that I realized upon further inspection. I would need to knock my head against the text.

Each week meant fresh research.

That is one of the challenges of the ministry. Always and weekly the preacher needs to chart new territory. That will be the case if the minister is actually exegeting the passage. If the minister struggles to understand the unique ideas taught in a specific text, he will always chart new territory. If the minister is not charting new territory, he has not learned how to exegete Scripture, but rather brings what he already knows to the text and is unable to understand the unique insights in it. The sign of a minister who does not know how to engage in fresh exegesis is that his sermons will major in vague generalities. You will learn his theology and understanding of the Bible from his various sermons until they begin to sound alike.

Commentators can take years of study to conclude their research on difficult passages. But the preacher must preach in six days. He cannot engage in indefinite research. He cannot read doctoral dissertations on the text. He does not have the leisure to research his topic until he thinks that he can make an original contribution. Sunday is "a comin." So the minister needs to dive into the text, wrestle with its meaning, make quick judgments about alternative interpretations, and be prepared to say, "Thus saith the Lord" six days later. Sometimes you will need to say that there are several good possibilities about how to interpret the text and lay them out for the congregation. If you have a favored interpretation mention it, but let the congregation know that you are not being dogmatic.

It is important to remember that there is a big difference between teaching heresy and simply engaging in erroneous exegesis. It is one thing to misinterpret a text of Scripture to teach a truth that is taught elsewhere. It is a whole different story to teach heresy from a text. It is not that I am encouraging weak exegesis. When I hear a minister who repeatedly brings unconvincing exegesis into his sermons, I begin to wonder about how much of his teaching can be trusted. But we must still recognize that an exegetical mistake is on a whole different plane from teaching heresy.

Preaching Through Books of the Bible

The challenges involved with doing fresh research are an argument for preaching series through books of the Bible. When you engage in expositional preaching through books of the Bible, at least you continue to build on your understanding of the context of your text. If you preach on Habakkuk one week and Jonah the next, you are moving from one context to another. If you decide to preach a single sermon out of Romans chapter 2, you will need to figure out that week the flow of Paul's argument in the chapter. But if you are preaching a series on Romans, by the time you come to a later verse in Romans chapter 2, you have already done research the previous weeks on what Paul has been teaching and how he is developing his argument. When a minister is preaching a series, it is easier for him to decide his text for the next Sunday. He does not need to search all the Scriptures for a text, but rather can simply explore where there is a complete thought in the verses he is up to that will provide him with the material for a unified message.

I found it easier to preach on a shorter text because I had a better chance of mastering the text. In a longer text I would need to focus on key verses because I would not have time to do in-depth analysis of each verse. It is difficult to go into the pulpit if you have not wrapped your mind around your text. But once you have mastered the text you can allow it to master you. Then you can internalize the very distinct meaning of the text.

Faithful preaching is textual preaching. Textual preaching is delivering sermons that expositor a specific text in the Bible. In the early church the best preachers would provide textual sermons. In the high Middle Ages Aquinas delivered exegetical sermons on the gospel accounts. John Calvin preached textual sermons that involved preaching through entire books of the Bible.

Spurgeon did not preach in long series. He custom was to preach on a text from a different portion of Scripture each week. While Calvin loved to preach through entire books of the Bible, that was not Spurgeon style. In his best sermons Spurgeon is explaining the idea and thought in the actual text. I realize that because Spurgeon had such felicity of thought and such a pregnant mind and imagination. Some of his sermons do not show careful exegesis of the Bible passages. It was almost like public communication was too easy for him and his knowledge of the Bible and theology was so broad that he did not take the care of thinking through the meaning of the text. That is why you will find him coming up with marvelous metaphors that he builds on images in the text, but that don't necessarily express the intention of the original author. But in Spurgeon's best sermons you do find that he not only selects a certain passage as his text, but he explains the text and allowing the ideas, logic, argument, and application in the text to determine his homiletics.

With John Calvin we find the use of textual sermons, but they do not demonstrate the same level of organization that we find in Spurgeon. Calvin's sermons seem to be more like a commentary. In contrast one finds a unified message in Spurgeon's sermons. Nevertheless, both Calvin and Spurgeon provide textual sermons. They explain the sense of the text and then applying it to the people of God. They are concerned to see Christ and His gospel in the passage.

Defining a Textual Sermon

The language of a "textual sermon" comes from the Latin word *textus* which comes from a verb which means "to weave". The original use of the word "text" points to weaving together words into a message. The language of a text implies that there are several connected words or sentences or paragraphs it all together are weave together into a complete, logically developed thought.

The minister chooses a text that is a single verse or a number of verses that contain a complete idea. He might need to deal with an entire chapter in a narrative account. What is crucial is that the text is a unified body of material that can be addressed and communicated in a unified way. There are some passages of Scripture that by themselves do not provide a very useful text for a sermon. The biggest mistake that I find ministers or seminary students doing is choosing too large of a text. The result is that they are unable to dig into their text in a meaningful way. The sermon lacks careful exegetical insights. The sermon is not a unity.

Preach Old Testament Texts Too

Peter Y. De Jong recommended that the minister preach from both Old Testament and New Testament texts. He writes: "We do not deny that the New Testament texts will receive the larger share of a faithful preacher's attention. No longer do we live in the dispensation of the shadows."[329] He writes that "The two testaments (or: "covenants") constitute the one, indivisible, comprehensive Word given as a lamp to our feet and a light to shine on our path."[330] When one preaches on the Old Testament, one is aware of the "fact that he is dealing with salvation-history in a time of shadows and preparations."[331]

De Jong traces textual preaching back to the synagogue. Textual "preaching has an ancient and honorable history."[332] He writes that "already in synagogue--worship, which apparently sprang up during, or somewhat after the days of Ezra, it was customary to follow the readings from the law and the prophets with a 'message.'"[333] De Jong writes that

> The Reformed in their best days have always committed themselves to textual preaching. They insisted that text to be carefully chosen, also with regard to their length, so that the unique message contained in each text might be dealt with as clearly and convincingly and comprehensively is the time allotted to a sermon would allow.[334]

De Jong identifies some of the problems with non-textual preaching. "This method soon delivers the congregation into the power of the preacher."[335] He also recognizes that just because the preacher is trying to engage in textual preaching does not mean that the word of God in text will actually be a explained. "Always the danger remains that the words will not be adequately explained or properly applied."[336] When the preacher does not engage in "solid exegesis" then he can fall into "the error of accommodation" in which he interprets the passages as teaching other than what it does. Another way in which a text is "grossly abused" is when the preacher ignores the context. Remember the proverb: "A text without a

---

[329] Peter Y. De Jong, Homiletics (Class Syllabus: 1983), 120.
[330] Ibid., 120.
[331] Ibid., 121.
[332] Ibid., 122.
[333] Ibid., 122.
[334] Ibid., 123.
[335] Ibid., 124.
[336] Ibid., 125.

context is a pretext."

Each generation of expositors needs to be warned about the evils of allegorical exegesis. Peter De Jong provides the example of a minister who preached on the Apostle Paul's shipwreck on Malta as recorded in Acts 27:39-44. The allegorical exegete claimed that the day in the passage referred to the day of grace which signifies the whole New Testament era. The ship stood for the visible church that can never save anyone. The two seas that battered the ship represent the temptations that come from within and without. Such allegorical preaching can sound pious and spiritual, but it is a flight of fancy.

The Reformed pastor must be a "minister of the Word." The word "minister" means that the preacher is a servant of the Word. De Jong writes that the "preacher must be a servant to his text."

Choose a Text that Includes a Complete Thought

De Jong identifies the characteristics of a fitting text. First, it should "contain a complete thought."[337] Second, it should "contain a message which is of direct significance for the life of believers today."[338] Third, the text should "not be burdened with so much historical, archaeological or ceremonial material, that involved in lengthy explanations or need needed to make it plain."[339] Fourth, the preacher should avoid a text that is too short or too long.

De Jong also advises a new preacher to "make use of texts which are fully clear to himself."[340] This is easier said than done. I often find that a text of which I had a general understanding becomes on closer analysis, profound and deep. One of my professors advised me not to preach on the Song of Solomon until I had been in the ministry for many years. This probably wasn't the best advice. I would suggest that the minister not only choose texts that he thinks that he understands, but also choose texts that will stretch him. A minister might feel more at home in doctrinal portions of Scripture, but he ought to stretch himself and bless the congregation by preaching on the poetic Psalms.

The preacher must not take too long to select his text. He will waste time that should be spent on exegesis. De Jong recommends that preachers avoid long series, but instead preach through several shorter series throughout a year.

---

[337] Ibid., 130.
[338] Ibid., 131.
[339] Ibid., 132.
[340] Ibid., 134.

Studying the Text

You have selected your text. What next? De Jong advises that it "takes time, occupied with quiet study and meditation and prayer, to distill a worthy sermon from Scripture truth."[341]

You need to memorize and reflect on the text. You need to do this in dependency upon the Holy Spirit. De Jong writes

> Not the preacher's intellectual abilities are creative imaginations, but only the guidance of the Holy Spirit can unveil the true meaning of what is written down for the high purpose of bringing men to an ever-richer understanding and experience of salvation.[342]

Working on a text takes time and concentration. "All this requires a time of quiet."[343] De Jong, writing before the rise of the internet, warned about the "tyranny of the telephone and the doorbell."[344] We could only wish these were the only tyrannies in our lives. Now we face the tyranny of email, Facebook, the Internet, and Twitter.

How can the minister begin to understand the text? He has five or six days before he will need to preach on the text. The text is new to him. How can the preacher begin to interact with the text so that he can later on the week begin to put together a sermon?

De Jong advises the preacher to follow several steps. First, he must reread the text and pay "attention to every word, to every phrase."[345] Second, the preacher needs to study the context. Third, the minister needs to identify the important words and ideas in the passage and then begin to ascertain what their significance is. Fourth, the preacher should examine the figures of speech found in the passage.

Fifth, the preacher must identify the main idea or subject of the passage that will become the theme of his sermon. "Every true text has one central and all-controlling thought."[346] De Jong wonderfully emphasizes a matter that is a great concern to me. He writes that "each text has its own unique message."[347] "Even when one Bible writer quotes another, the focus will show shades of difference. We do well to remember that the Holy Spirit wastes no words; he never engages himself in any need this repetition."[348]

---

[341] Ibid., 138.
[342] Ibid., 138.
[343] Ibid., 139.
[344] Ibid., 139.
[345] Ibid,. 141.
[346] Ibid., 142.
[347] Ibid., 142.
[348] Ibid., 142.

Sixth, the preacher will engage in a "serious dialogue with his text."[349] The minister must throw questions at the text and then attempt to answer them.

Seventh, De Jong argues that the minister should do his research with pen in hand. The problem is that we can't always remember important insights we discover in the text or learn from a commentator. John Piper argues that one value of having your pen in hand is that as you read things you can write down an argument that you can better follow on paper than in your head. It is easier to follow a train of thought when you write it out, than if you let ideas flit through your brain. Writing forces you to think more carefully. You write to learn.

Eighth, the minister must place his text within the whole of Scripture. De Jong thinks that too many Reformed preachers do not take this next step because it is difficult, even though it is the "most intriguing and necessary aspect of proper interpretation."[350] This necessary aspect relates to the necessity of doctrinal preaching:

> The text must be explained or interpreted theologically. The special message of the text is to be placed consciously and clearly in the study not only of the chapter book in which appears, but in the total self-revelation of God in Christ.[351]

De Jong concludes by emphasizing once again the importance of discovering the unique message in the text. "We must attain clarity on its unique meaning before we are able to teach his people what they are to believe and how they are to live."[352]

What about the use of commentaries? De Jong argues that the preacher should use the commentaries after he has first interacted with the text himself. Even the best commentaries "are not to be used as crutches with the result that soon the preacher dares no longer walk in his own mental and spiritual legs."[353] Do not become "a superficial preacher who can bring only the warmed-over servings of other men's efforts."[354] De Jong advises: "Use commentaries only after you have patiently and persistently studied the text directly from Scripture for and by yourself."[355]

But for all of this to be successful, choose a small enough text. And then dig into it.

---

[349] Ibid., 142.
[350] Ibid., 143.
[351] Ibid., 143.
[352] Ibid., 143.
[353] Ibid., 144.
[354] Ibid., 144.
[355] Ibid., 144.

Chapter 19
Gather Raw Material by Writing Your Exegesise Paper

Does a carpenter start building a house without first stockpiling the raw materials? Can he build a house without having lumber delivered? Doesn't he need a nail gun and nails at the building site before he can begin to put up the frame?

Did James Michener write a novel (at the youthful age of 80) without doing research? No, he gathered the raw material. He even hired researchers.

Yet the preacher imagines that he can start putting his sermon together without gathering raw material?

William Clair Turner on Sermonic Building Blocks

William Claire Turner Jr. compares the preparation of a sermon to making a recipe or building a home.[356] Turner uses the same carpentry metaphor that I use with my students.

I find that seminary students can have a hard time preparing a message because they do not know how to get their building supplies. A student stares at an empty document in Microsoft Word on his laptop computer screen and doesn't know what to type. The problem: The student has not gathered raw material. Turner writes that "Nothing is more frustrating in attempting to craft the sermon than attempting to write without having something to say."[357]

He compares making a sermon to gathering the ingredients that one needs to bake something.

---

[356] William Clair Turner Jr. Preaching that Makes the Word Plain: Doing Theology in the Crucible of Life (Eugene, Oregon: Cascade Books, 2008).
[357] Ibid., 30.

Like making bread, creating a sculpture, etc., one gets everything in place, and then they begin to work. This is the work of mixing, blending, with intention and proportion. Or, one can make the comparison to building a house: before the work gets started there must be the assembling of the supplies.[358]

Turner identifies five building blocks for sermon-making. First, the minister must prepare block one which is exegesis. He says,

Dare I say it; dare you believe it? The heart and soul of Christian preaching is exegesis. This is the work that "brings out" what is given in the text. Another way of putting the matter is that, as preachers, we have no more to give than what has been given to us.[359]

The second block is the thesis statement. "The thesis is what makes the sermon stand up and go somewhere. Without it, the sermon lies like a jellyfish--limp, lifeless."[360]

"The thesis is what makes the argument worth advancing."[361] It "makes all the difference in the sermon. It serves like a spine to distribute the content throughout the sermon. It prevents content from "hanging off" the sermon, like clothes that won't fit."[362] The thesis statement "grows out of the struggle for clarity."[363] The thesis statement cannot be fully written out until the whole sermon has been written.

The third block is theological issues. Turner correctly argues that "preaching is a theological task."[364]

The fourth block that must be prepared is an analysis of the contemporary setting. The preacher needs to evaluate what the Scripture says for Christians in the present context.

The fifth block is proclamation. "The sermon should make clear and direct proclamation of the gospel of God."[365]

The initial notes that you make as you reflect on your text is the first raw material that you gather for your sermon. If you begin to study your text with pen in hand, you will soon have pages of written material about your text. After you look at the commentators, you will have more raw material. Think of this raw material as the wood, nails, boards, and other basic

---

[358] Ibid., 30.
[359] Ibid., 31.
[360] Ibid., 37.
[361] Ibid., 38.
[362] Ibid., 38.
[363] Ibid., 38.
[364] Ibid., 39.
[365] Ibid., 52.

material you will need for the project.

The next step it to prepare your exegesis paper. Think of how a carpenter takes his two by fours and nails and begins to put up parts of the frame. He organizes the raw material. When you are finished with a good exegesis paper, it is like you already have the entire frame for your sermon finished and have even crafted some of the fine details in the house. Work remains, but much of the preparatory work is finished. If you did good work on your exegesis paper, you will be able to take much of the information over into your sermon.

So once you have your exegesis paper finished, it is time to complete the whole house. Your finished sermon is like a completed home.

In your exegesis paper you should have already figured out what the main point of the text is. You might continue to clarify your theme as you finish your sermon. You should have discovered what the logical divisions (your three points) might be. You have written down insights about the practical application of the text. But now you need to take your research and develop it into the homiletical form necessary for preaching. You need to put it together into a clear, concise, logical, Christ-centered message that can grab the congregation's attention and that is relevant for your hearers.

In your exegesis paper you are focusing on the meaning of the text and are beginning to lay out its implications for the Christian life. In your sermon you must have your congregation more and more in front of your mind. Your text might have a several emphases and you will need to choose what emphases are of pastoral relevance.

While your exegesis paper followed the text word by word and phrase by phrase, your sermon needs to deal with your text in a more logical way. You need to synthesize what your text teaches. You might have a couple of different places where your text deals with the same topic. Perhaps these places are verses apart. But in your sermon it will be wise and logical to deal with the issue in one place. You need to synthesize the material so that you do not talk about an issue, get finished, and then return to it.

Examples of Raw Material

Jay E. Adams provides examples of the raw material that the preacher needs to gather prior to writing his sermon:

1. Notes on the meaning of the passage, with cross references, word studies, etc. You may have made your own translation of it. All this is recorded on several sheets of paper, note cards, or in a notebook.
2. Jottings of various sorts, including
   a. Ideas suggested by the exegetical study;

    b. Initial outlines, or bits of outlines, that occurred to you during the study;

    c. Illustrations;

    d. Possibly a suggested title or two.

3. A crisp, one-sentence *telic* statement.
4. Individual ideas about how to introduce and/or close the sermon.
5. Extraneous materials (not always seen as such at first) that will best be laid aside and filed for future use.
6. A list of problems and questions yet unresolved and unanswered.[366]

I face too much stress on Friday and Saturday if I do not have enough raw material for my Sunday sermons. If I did not write an exegesis paper or had not written out the equivalent of one on notebook paper, I would be afraid that I had nothing to say.

New students want to go from 0 to 70 mph in five seconds. They want to go directly from research on a text to writing an Adult Sunday School message. They need to learn how to do research. Research is the act of gathering raw materials and beginning to organize them.

Why do ministers avoid writing exegesis papers or at least writing out their exegetical discoveries as they study the passage throughout the week? I think that it is easier to read than to take notes. So laziness is involved. Sometimes the minister is a perfectionist and feels that he cannot write anything down until he has everything just right.

It is a mistake to put off taking notes and writing an exegesis paper. It is a mistake to be a perfectionist. What perfectionist has ever written a perfect first draft? Why should you begin to take notes early on?

A fundamental insight pressed upon us by experts on writing non-fiction is that you must sit in your chair, take up your pen, and begin to write. One must simply begin to write. You need to work on the first draft.

The same applies for fiction writers. They simply need to start putting pen to paper. The minister may feel that he is not yet ready to write down any insights, so he puts off what is actually his first draft until too late. Then he becomes paralyzed by fear because his sermon is his functional first draft. He senses that this is inadequate. It is. What first draft ever was adequate?

What writers call the "first draft" is part of what I mean by "raw material."

Technically your first draft will be your notebook pages where you write out the Greek or Hebrew text. On this page you will begin to figure out

---

[366] Jay E. Adams, Preaching with Purpose (Phillipsburg, NJ: P & R Publishing, 1982), 47-48.

the morphology of the grammar, discover the meaning and connotation of the words, and translate the text. This first draft will include your own reflections on the meaning and application of the text. Then will come your reflections on the insights of the commentaries. Once you have looked at the commentaries you will have additional insights of your own. These should be written down while you remember them. You should study with pen in hand.

Technically your second draft will be an exegesis paper where you now synthesize your exegetical discoveries. In seminary I was taught to select a single word or a phrase and then exegete it. I would write out the word or phrase in bold print and then dig into it. After developing the concepts, I would hit return a few times and type in bold print the next word or phrase. Doing this keeps your attention in the text and on the nouns, prepositions, and verbs. It is hard to do exegesis at 70,000 feet over the terrain of the text when you are staring at a couple of words (or a phrase) and realize that you need to explain what they mean. Too many preachers do not carefully interpret the words and phrases in the text. They ignore connecting words like "for", "and", or "but." Work your way through the text, making sure not to pick too large of a part of the text at a time, or you will find that you do not carefully exegete the words or phrases.

Once you are finished with your exegesis paper; you should be able to identify the main point of the text, the logic of the text, and what your potential theme (title) should be.

You should also have a sense of what your second and third points will be. The first point normally should be the development of the theme. You will refer to it as "The Meaning." Your exegesis paper should also begin to show lines of relevant application that flow out of the text. As we will see later, you have only understood a text properly when you understand what its' application is.

Having finished your second draft (your exegesis paper) you are now ready for your final draft—the writing of your sermon. While the exegesis paper can be written as an essay, I am a firm believer that your sermon should be written out in outline form. You will begin working on a first draft of your sermon outline. I edit my outline until I preach. I am never finished editing and internalizing my sermon until the moment I get up to preach.

Chapter 20

Heidelberg Catechism Sermons Need Fresh Biblical Exegesis

rofessors who over-emphasize that Reformed preachers must preach the text of the Heidelberg Catechism need to listen to William Perkins. He instructs the preacher:

> The Word of God alone is to be preached, in its perfection and inner consistency. Scripture is the exclusive subject of preaching, the only field in which the preacher is to labour.[367]

Heidelberg Catechism Sermons

It is a custom in the Reformed churches that one of the Sunday sermons teaches the subject matter found in one of the Lord's Days in the Heidelberg Catechism. The Heidelberg Catechism was written as a teaching tool. It includes questions and answers. The catechism includes teaching on three writings: The Apostle's Creed, the Ten Commandments, and the Lord's Prayer. The catechism is divided up into 52 parts, one for each Lord's Day. This catechism is famous for its experiential warmth and how it teaches what the Christians only comfort is in life and in death.

As a Reformed pastor, I knew each Tuesday one of the subjects that I would preach on at the Sunday morning service. I might be on the Lord's Day that teaches about the doctrine of the Trinity. Preaching on the Heidelberg Catechism is topical preaching. My sermon on the Lord's Day 8 would deal with the truth of the holy Trinity. Along with this topical preaching come all the inherent dangers found in this form of preaching that has experienced a fair share of criticism. Supporters of expository preaching rightly take issue with a kind of topical preaching where a minister picks a topic and speaks on it without exegeting Scripture.

---

[367] William Perkins, The Art of Prophesying (Edinburgh: Banner of Truth Trust, 1996), 9.

It remained for me to identify a biblical text that I would exegete for the catechism sermon. If I held to the naïve view that a pastor should just "preach the catechism" and not exegete and proclaim the Word of God in the sermon my job would have been easier. I could have majored in generalities. Once I prepared a catechism sermon the first year, I could have basically repeated it for however many more years I spent in the church. Instead I needed to identify a text that was relevant and that would shed light on the topic in the Lord's Day.

If I was preaching on one of the ten Lord's Days that dealt with the Ten Commandments, the actual text of the commandment would be one text that would grab my attention. If I was preaching on the Lord's Day that covered the seventh commandment, I would focus in on the meaning of the text of the commandment: "Thou shalt not commit adultery." This would mean that I would need to do research on the meaning and connotation of the Hebrew word that is translated as "adultery." If I was preaching on the sixth commandment, "Thou shalt not kill," I would need to examine the meaning of the Hebrew word that is translated as "kill." I would have to pay attention to the fact that newer translations translate this: "You shall not murder."

I might also notice that in Hebrew you have the future tense in these commandments and explain to the congregation that the future tense carried the idea of the imperative. Notice what I am doing. Preaching on the Heidelberg Catechism must lead us to study the biblical texts to which they refer.

How can you preach on the 2nd commandment that forbids the making of graven images without dealing with the actual language of the commandment? Yet ministers do this. Instead of studying the text of the second commandment, they only explain the Heidelberg Catechism's explanation of the 2nd commandment. *Ad fontes.*

The final Lord's Days in the Heidelberg Catechism are a discussion of the Lord's Prayer. Once again, the minister should do exegesis on the actual language of the Lord's Prayer. Yet I have heard sermons that do not even delve into the meaning of the word "Hallowed" that is used in the first petition. Or a minister preaches on the Lord's Day that discusses the petition, "Give us this day our daily bread" and never carefully explains the concepts in this brief petition which certainly include 1) give, 2) us, 3) this day, and 4) daily bread. Instead the minister explains what the catechism says about the petition without studying the text himself.

But my greater concern is sermons on the first part of the catechism where the minister is dealing with Lord's Days that, for example, take him through each phrase in the Apostle's Creed. The minister comes to the Lord's Day that discusses what we mean when we confess: "I believe in the Holy

Spirit." The Heidelberg Catechism has a brief discussion of the doctrine of the Holy Spirit in Lord's Day 20. What should the minister do? Should he just explain the language of the Heidelberg Catechism? Many rich passages teach about the person, divinity, and work of God the Holy Spirit. Must the congregation endure another sermon that is vague, general, and boring? Or will the minister engage in fresh exegesis that will bring the person and work of the Holy Spirit to life?

I knew on Tuesday what Lord's Day I was scheduled to preach on the following Sunday. The big challenge was to find a fitting biblical text to exegete in relation to the topic of the Lord's Day. For example, if I was preaching on the Lord's Day that explains the person and work of the Holy Spirit, I might select a passage from the book of Acts where we see the Holy Spirit at work. I would make sure that I was not studying a text that I had preached on before in connection with the Lord's Day.

Then the work would begin. I would do research on the Lord's Day. I might explore whether there were any differences in nuance between the original German text of the catechism and our English translation. I would read commentaries on the catechism. I would translate the biblical text I had chosen and begin the process of exegesis.

What should be the origin of your sermon? The basic answer is that it should be the text of the sacred Scriptures. The Apostle Paul exhorted Timothy to preach the word. That is the basis for textual preaching. I am an opponent of catechism preaching that becomes topical and exclusively involves exegesis of the catechetical text. I have effectively delivered catechism sermons using the Heidelberg catechism, where, yes, it is true that I am communicating what Reformed Christians confess and believe in the Heidelberg Catechism, but I also always do original exegesis on a text related to the topic.

When ministers just preach the text of the Heidelberg catechism, they are not preaching the text of the Word of God (unless the Lord's Day includes a quotation from the Bible). We all agree as Reformed believers, that the Heidelberg catechism does express the truths that are found in the word of God. There are Lord's days that even have direct quotes from Scripture. For example, Lord's Day 2 provides Jesus' own summary of the Law of God (which is found in sacred Scripture).

But the odd thing I discover is that when ministers buy into this wrong kind of catechism preaching, they do not even exegete Jesus' statements about the need to love the Lord our God with all our heart, soul, mind, and strength. You will not find them explaining and developing the concepts of "love", "heart", "soul", "mind", or "strength." Also, I find that when ministers perceive themselves to be preaching on the 10 Commandments, they do not even engage in careful exegesis of the text of the commandment.

When I was in seminary, David Engelsma emphasized that when the minister delivers catechism sermons, he must engage in fresh exegesis of a Bible passage. I have found that this is what brings power to catechism preaching. It is the authority of the Word of God that provides power. It is true that Zacharius Ursinus said many good and true things. But what he writes in the catechism is not the word of God. It is a human word about the word of God. It is an interpretation of a doctrine or a commandment. It is true that he is trying to summarize what the Bible teaches on a certain topic, like the doctrine of the Holy Spirit. But his description of the person and work of the Holy Spirit is limited and does not come close to reflecting all that the Bible says about the glory and beauty of the Holy Spirit. The Word has much more to say about the doctrine of the holy Trinity than Ursinus and Olevianus did.

The gospel minister knows, just like Ursinus and Olevianus did, that the authority of our message flows out of the authority of the Word of God. So, preach the Word! Bring fresh and powerful insights from the Word that come with divine authority to the congregation.

Sometimes elders are at fault for a wrong approach to catechism preaching. The elders naïvely command their pastor to just preach the text of the catechism. The congregation senses that something is lacking. What is lacking is spiritual power and authority. Ministers who just "preach the catechism" in this naïve way teach like the scribes and Pharisees. There is a lack of spiritual power and authority in their sermons. Their sermons are lectures.

Many copies of the Heidelberg Catechism even provide multiple Scriptural texts that teach a specific truth. But preachers do not even do fresh exegesis on these Scriptural texts. They quote them.

Yes, they quote them.

And they quote a lot of other Bible passages.

But they do not do exegesis on them.

They do not discover any fresh insights.

They think that their only job is to explain the text of the catechism.

So, they bring up passages that the members of the congregation know, but there is nothing new. The same old way of saying the same old things.

Another massive problem with this kind of "just preach the catechism" mentality is that catechism preaching becomes boring and repetitive. This should not surprise anyone. This is exactly what one might expect. While the word of God is profound and deep, no human confession possesses that same depth and profundity. Therefore, once a minister has allegedly exegeted the Heidelberg catechism, he runs out of new insights. Once he has figured out the original German and Latin text, there will be a sameness in subsequent sermons. All the minister needs to do is pull out the sermon on the Lord's Day that he preached a few years back and there he will have everything that he needs. And ministers do this.

Decade after decade.

The preacher might need to pick out some new proof texts, but he will not spend time digging into them. And he imagines that he brings variety into the pulpit.

Heidelberg Catechism preaching that turns into a lecture on the concepts and ideas in the Lord's Day, while using only the language of the catechism, is not expository preaching. It is not biblical preaching. It is a form of topical preaching disconnected from the power found in the fountain. Back to the sources. Back to the fountain. Ministers need to drink from the fountain of Scripture as they develop Heidelberg Catechism sermons.

The Form of Sound Words

It is important that the preacher exegete the language of the Heidelberg Catechism. Here we find the form of sound words. Reformed Christians should know what their confessions say and should be familiar with not only the ideas, but the wording in them. If a minister knows Latin or German he can examine the original texts in which the Heidelberg Catechism was written to perceive the intent of the original authors. The authors of the Heidelberg Catechism were human, not divine. Their names are Zacharius Ursinus and Caspar Olevianus.

Just like the preacher needs to interpret and exegete Scripture, the Reformed minister needs to interpret the language of the catechism. But this may not be the end of his labors. He is a minister of the Word of God.

He is not a minister of the Heidelberg Catechism.

He is not a minister of the Nicene Creed.

He is not a minister of the Council of Chalcedon.

He is a minister of the Word of God.

If our preacher falls into the error of exegeting only the language and text of the catechism, he might be saved when he preaches on certain Lord's Days, if they contain the actual text of Scripture.

One might also get his hopes up when a preacher who will not exegete Scripture for a catechism sermon comes to the Ten Commandments.

One might hope that since the minister is dealing with the Ten Commandments that he will at least exegete the language and text of the Ten Commandments as found in Exodus 20 or Deuteronomy 5. Alas, the hearer will once again be disappointed.

Even longer commandments, like the fourth, will go without careful explanation of the language of the commandment.

And when the preacher addresses briefer commandments, like the first or eighth, the same glaring lack will appear. The very language of the commandments and the concepts in them will go unexplained.

What it means to "serve" and how the word is used in the first commandment will be ignored.

It is probably in the last section of the catechism where the Lord's Prayer is explained that the preacher who resists doing fresh exegesis on a Scripture passage might begin to preach the Scriptures. Since the catechism deals with each petition of the Lord's Prayer in detail, the preacher will be forced to deal with the text. But even here do not be surprised if the preacher avoids looking at the texts of the Lord's Prayer in the gospel accounts and does not bring the congregation face to face with the text, the main concepts in it, and the relationship between them. Variant readings will go ignored. The congregation will not learn that some texts contain the petition about our need to be delivered from "evil" while others speak of the need to be delivered from the "evil one" (de Bozer), as the old Dutch Bible reads.

David Engelsma exhorted me to prepare catechism sermons that contained fresh, legitimate, deep exegesis of a text that taught the truth or topic contained in the Lord's Day. A sermon on Lord's Day 7, which deals with the nature of true faith, must include exegesis on a passage or passages that speak about faith. Engelsma also wanted the catechism exegeted and its themes communicated in the sermon.

I have tried to follow this approach of exegeting both the catechism and a relevant Scripture text. The great danger of preaching is the danger of generalization. Sermons that are vague and deal with generalities are usually ineffective. Sermons that say the same thing, the same old way, are often general and generic.

A Poetic Weaving Together of the Catechism and a Scripture Text

Do not give into the temptation to exegete more than one Scripture passage in detail for a catechism sermon. Resist the impulse. It will undermine the unity of the sermon. It is challenge enough to interweave a sermon that communicates the language and ideas in the catechism while at the same time doing fresh exegesis of a passage that teaches the same truth.

What I say next is of great importance. *Already the preacher is dealing with two texts and needs to weave them together in a logical and poetic way.* He will want to use the *rhetoric of the catechism* and the *sacred rhetoric found in the biblical text.* It is true that the preacher might need to refer to parallel passages, but if he does deep exegesis on the biblical passage that he chose, he will have a rich harvest for the congregation. And the harvest will not be vague and general, but will be a harvest with depth and specificity.

Preaching a catechism sermon is an art. You need to weave together two texts into a harmonious whole. You need to teach the main idea in the confessional document. You want the congregation to know what they confess as a confessing church, but you also want them to know the language of the catechism. Therefore, you need to teach and use the language of the catechism.

The language of the catechism can be incorporated into the sermon title (which is the theme or main point of the sermon). The unique light shed on the truth by the biblical text that you are exegeting also can shape the title. In addition, the language of both the catechism and the biblical text should shape the three divisions (three main points) of the sermon.

I am implying that a Heidelberg Catechism sermon involves a careful duet or dance between the confessional document and a text of sacred Scripture.

That is why creating a catechism sermon is more complex from an homiletical perspective than preaching on a Scripture text. When you preach a catechism sermon your title, the three divisions, your practical application, and rhetoric are shaped by the catechism *and* the biblical text.

Therefore, a catechism sermon involves a careful intertwining of the ideas and rhetoric of two texts.

The parallel to this would be selecting two passages from the New Testament that teach the deity of Jesus and using both passages to present a unified sermon. I have done something like this before. I chose two statements of Jesus that appeared to be contradictory and preached on both of them. In doing something like this, the main point, divisions, rhetoric and application need to be shaped by both texts. Both need to be carefully exegeted. By careful exegesis I include careful analysis of the language, grammar, and meaning that would involve the original language and then the crucial development of the chief concepts by doing word studies and comparing Scripture with Scripture.

Preaching a Heidelberg Catechism sermon is an *art* because there needs to be a unified interplay between two texts.

Peter Y. De Jong on Preaching the Word

Peter Y. De Jong emphasizes the importance of a preacher preaching on a biblical text. He asks,

> On what, then, is preaching to be based, and from where does it drive its content? The only defensible answer is: from the *text of holy Scripture.*[368]

De Jong has catechism sermons in mind: "We are not to preach the catechism; we are called to preach, 'the sum of doctrine' is arranged in the catechism as a confession which sets forth in order the teaching of holy writ."[369] De Jong makes a careful distinction: we do not preach the catechism *per se*, but, "the sum of doctrine" arranged in it. He writes that "such preaching, when rightly done, is not a theological lecture or an inspirational address; it is administration of the word."[370]

Why do Fresh Exegesis on a Biblical Text?

You will want to do fresh exegesis on Scripture for your catechism sermon or it will devolve into a lecture more fit for the catechism classroom or Sunday School.

You must do fresh exegesis or your preaching will lack authority and power. Homer Hoeksema explains where the authority of preaching originates:

> In the sermon the preacher approaches the congregation with the authoritative, "Thus saith the Lord!" We may note in this connection that the content and character of a sermon are very closely related—in fact, inseparably related. Materially, the authority of the sermon is derived from the fact that its content is the content of the Word of Christ.[371]

It is inappropriate to say: "Thus saith Caspar Olevianus."

It is true that the content of the catechism is the truth contained in the law and gospel. But this is also the case with a biblical sermon.

It is also the case with a good Christian book that faithfully teaches God's Word. But this may not be used as an excuse by a lazy preacher who, therefore, will not investigate where and how Scripture teaches the truths and topics contained in a Lord's Day.

---

[368] Peter Y. De Jong, Homiletics, 116.
[369] Peter Y. De Jong, Homiletics, 119.
[370] Ibid., 119.
[371] Homer Hoeksema, Homiletics, 14.

The catechism contains human formulations of truths and topics of which we have divine formulations in sacred Scripture.

The preacher himself will experience the lack of authority in his preaching when he proclaims, "Thus saith Zacharius Ursinus." I always have a sense of a clear *lack* of authority and power in catechism preaching if I am not saying, "Thus saith the LORD."

I have learned that catechism preaching must obey the *dictum* of the Humanists: *ad fontes*. We need to go back to the well and spring of sacred Scripture.

The preacher will bore both himself and his hearers if he only exegetes the language of the catechism. Astonishingly, graduates of the Protestant Reformed Seminary once were told that for their first time preaching through the Heidelberg Catechism they should basically use Herman Hoeksema's commentary on it (*The Triple Knowledge*). New ministers were given a license to plagiarize this commentary to preach their first good, doctrinal catechism sermons. But this robs catechism preaching of power and authority. It does help the preacher to say: "Thus saith Herman Hoeksema." The orthodox Reformed didn't even like it when people quoted John Calvin in sermons. The early French Reformed preachers resisted the idea of quoting human authorities in their sermons. They wanted to preach the Word.

Human formulations do not contain the depths and multi-faceted beauty that is found in Scripture. The second time that a minister preaches through the Heidelberg Catechism he will discover a few more insights into the meaning and intentions of Zacharius Ursinus. But by the 5th or 6th time he preaches through the catechism his sermons will become calcified interpretations. He most certainly will bore himself and his hearers.

It will be the biblical exegesis of a fresh new biblical text each time that the preacher goes through the Lord's Days that will provide freshness and variety to his sermons.

Do I even need to address the preacher who will not listen to this advice because he is content to quote various Scripture passages throughout his catechism sermons without any helpful or profound reflection on them. He brings them in to support the topic. He even senses that he must show that the idea in the catechism is found in Scripture. But his references to these passages is mere padding. He will not carefully explain the text or even develop the concepts in it. He assumes that the congregation will see how the text proves the point without bringing out the beauty and riches of the text. He will not emphasize the unique light that the text sheds on the truth.

I am afraid that the preacher who uses the excuse that he must only exegete the catechism text because the sermon is a catechism sermon simply does not understand the power of the Word or the riches of the exegetical insights that can be mined when a minister pores over a biblical text.

It is true that there are ministers who lack the ability to identify the one main point of a text and who lack the ability to preach with simplicity. For these preachers it will be all the more difficult to take the catechism text and the biblical text and then develop one coherent, unified, simple message where there is balance between the catechism and the text as well as a poetic interplay between the two.

I can guarantee that there will be a deadly sameness in catechism sermons if the minister will not engage in fresh exegesis of Scripture. Many ministers try to get by with the hope that the people will not remember the sermon that they preached 1 ½ or 2 years ago on the same Lord's Day. As a pastor I was able to preach through the catechism every 1 ½ years. A lack of biblical exegesis will result in sermons that have a deadly, boring sameness. The minister might be able to wax noisy and convey false emotion with a sense of authority, but the preaching will lack authority and freshness.

Some ministers read through a different commentary on the catechism or a different sermon series on the catechism each time that they preach through it. But then the originality of the new sermon comes from the insights of the commentator or old preacher and not from the Word. They basically exegete the catechism and do research on a commentary or old catechism sermon. They might as well say: "Thus saith Herman Veldkamp." Now I better be careful here. Since there is nothing wrong with exegeting the text of the catechism, if you can learn from Herman Veldkamp about the meaning and significance of the text, that is great. Veldkamp might point you to a Scripture text that you should exegete for your sermon. Many of the older Reformed preachers were gifted at intertwining exegesis of a biblical text with their explanation of the catechism. You can learn from their past good examples.

Homer Hoeksema made the point that a preacher ought not to preach his dogmatics, but Scripture. He warns that a minister who preaches his doctrine (as derived from a commentary on the catechism) will lack variety.

> In order to achieve this variety, it is essential that the preacher faithfully exegete Scripture. Not his dogmatics, but the exegesis of the Scriptures must furnish him with material for preaching.[372]

He states that "Such exegetical labor will guarantee, without doubt, variety in the preaching."[373]

---

[372] Homer Hoeksema, Homiletics, 22.
[373] Ibid., 22.

This speaks to my concern about a "dogmatic" preaching of the catechism that lacks freshness, originality, variety, and power because the minister wants to just preach the catechism (in a wrong sense).

You can tell that a Reformed preacher is on the wrong path when he begins a series on the Heidelberg Catechism by emphasizing his plan to preach and exegete the catechism. I remember a small church in New Jersey where a new attendee heard this message and never came back. I am sure that the minister could have saved the day if he had emphasized that he would preach the word of God and exegete Scripture as he explained the topic in the Lord's Day. He probably didn't emphasize or exegete a biblical text as he preached on Lord's Day 1. He should have emphasized a biblical passage that taught the idea of the Christian's only comfort in life and in death.

Sometimes ministers get themselves in trouble by how they make such a big deal about the value and use of confessions and then emphasize the fact that they will preach through a confession (or catechism). There is a wise way to introduce saints to catechism preaching and the value of confessions.

Instead of hammering home that you are going to preach a confession, which is by definition a human document, you need to emphasize what will be covered in a series of sermons on the Heidelberg Catechism. You need to let the congregation know that this means that you will study the Apostle's Creed and two biblical texts, the Ten Commandments and the Lord's Prayer. I would emphasize in a church plant context that what the preacher is doing is not novel. I would explain the long custom, ever since the early church, of preparing new converts for baptism by using three documents: the Apostle's Creed, the Ten Commandments, and the Lord's Prayer. I would also explain that catechism sermons are topical sermons in which the Scriptural teachings in the Apostle's Creed are covered. Christians who have come to see the value of expositional preaching might be wary of topical preaching— but if they know that your topical preaching through the Apostle's Creed will be richly grounded in Scripture, they will see the benefit of the series. The power and authority of the sermons will flow from the fact that what we confess is taught in the sacred Scriptures.

Teach what we confess in the Heidelberg Catechism. And preach the Word!

Chapter 21
The Necessity of Developing Concepts
Developing Concepts

n seminary Herman Hanko, David Engelsma, and Robert Decker impressed upon me the importance of developing concepts as I engaged in exegesis. As a pastor I learned how important and difficult it could be to develop the concepts in the text. I find that it is hard to communicate the significance of developing concepts to seminary students. When students listen to sermons they do not automatically grasp what a good exegete is doing. The preacher explains the concept in the passage, for example the idea that Jesus is the only begotten Son. In another passage the minister explores the idea of a hope that makes one unashamed. A good preacher will do word studies to figure out the meaning and connotation of the Greek word for "only begotten" or "hope". He will look up the Hebrew word for "hope." He will compare Scripture with Scripture to determine the central meaning of the word "hope" and its various connotations. Then he will develop the various facets of hope. Of the greatest importance, the preacher will develop the unique slant on "hope" that is found in his text. He will need to see the contribution that this text provides for the Christian to understand the multi-faceted nature of the Christian hope.

Then the preacher will relate hope to other ideas in the text, not least of all the person and work of Christ. He will explore what unique light the text throws on the idea of the Christian hope. The preacher has just developed and communicated a sort of biblical theology and systematic theology of hope. He has communicated something of the richness of the biblical idea of hope. This is what I mean by developing a concept.

Developing concepts is crucial for preaching. The bad exegete and, therefore, bad preacher will just assume that everybody knows what hope is. He will use the word numerous times in his sermon without ever defining it or developing the facets of the Christian hope. If he defines it, he will use an old and weary definition of hope that he mentioned in previous sermons. He might tell the congregation that hope is a confident expectation, but he does not lend wings to what this means. He does not develop for himself the riches of the concept by showing what new, fresh, bright light the text sheds on the idea of hope.

The future preacher needs to grasp the importance of doing proper exegesis that explores the ideas in the text. This will result in fresh exegesis and fresh preaching. The preacher will continue to discover for himself (by the Spirit's enlightening work) what central biblical concepts mean. He will come to have a deeper understanding of the biblical idea of justification. He will use Hebrew or Greek dictionaries or concordances that enable him to trace the development of a biblical idea. As the minister does this fresh work, he will internalize the rich concepts in Scripture. In time this will greatly benefit his exegetical work and preaching. The biblical concepts will appear deeper, profounder, and brighter and be seen in ever richer perspective as he develops various concepts that are all part of the unified message that God has revealed in Jesus Christ.

Bad preaching fails because it remains shallow.

When a minister does not develop concepts, his preaching remains thin.

Rich biblical concepts are presented as one-dimensional by the preacher who does not know how to exegete and develop concepts. Such preaching never does justice to the text.

Blank Looks

My students initially have blank looks when I begin to talk to them about the importance of developing concepts. They soon discover that whatever I mean by "developing concepts" is certainly an important concept to me. They learn that if it is important to me, it better become important to them!

For years Rev. Dale Kuiper wrote a rubric in *The Standard Bearer* entitled "A Word Fitly Spoken." The rubric was limited to a single page. Each rubric involved just a single word that was the title of the write-up. What was Kuiper doing in this rubric? He was developing the concept of the biblical word. He would search throughout the Bible for the meaning and connotation of the word. Then he would develop the concept, define the word, and provide the theological meaning.

This is hard work. The minister needs to know his Bible and Christian theology. I am sometimes astounded by how Reformed preachers develop a concept in a sermon. For example, there are important concepts like "kingdom" that need to be developed in a sermon where the word or idea is in the text. What is the kingdom of God?

If a preacher decides to preach on John 1:1 he will need to deal with the concept of the "logos." What was the meaning of the word "logos" among the Greeks? What connotations does the Apostle John give to this word that he borrows from the Greeks? You could investigate whether Gordon Clark was right to think that the word "logos" primarily refers to logic. What you want to do is teach the meaning and connotation(s) of the biblical word. Then you should attempt to define what it means. What does the title "Logos" tell us about Jesus Christ? What does it add to God's other revelations about the glory of His Son? How does the idea of the second person of the Holy Trinity being the Logos relate to Him being the eternal Son?

I find that in many sermons the ministers do not carefully develop concepts. Even though there are words or concepts like "sanctification" in their text, they never explain what they mean. They just assume that everybody understands what sanctification is. They never define it. They say the word a thousand times in their sermon. But they never tell us what it means. They never develop the concept. They never carefully explain what is unique about the Christian sanctity. They do not show what is uniquely said about sanctification in the text that they are preaching on. They do not show how other passages that mention holiness bring out slightly different connotations. It is apparent to me that some ministers are not even aware of the need to develop concepts.

On the other hand, ministers who do try to develop concepts can right away recognize when it is happening in a sermon preached by another man. You see what is happening and appreciate how the minister is developing the concepts in ways that you have not done. *I find that some of my most enjoyable times in listening to sermons is when a minister exceeds my expectations in developing the richness of a concept.* The minister has done me a favor by bringing fresh insights to bear on a word and concept with which I have been familiar from my childhood. You cannot underestimate the importance of ministers doing fresh work and bringing new insights into the pulpit. It is like feeling the warmth of refreshing spring breezes when you live in Fairbanks, Alaska.

I find that seminary students take for granted that everyone understands the meaning and connotation of biblical words. Everywhere they take concepts for granted. So they feel no need to define and develop them. I exhort my students that they need to act like their auditors are little children. If they define the words and develop the concepts so that children can understand the meaning of them, then they will also be beginning to communicate effectively the meaning of the text to adults.

How Herman Bavinck Developed Concepts

We have only one published sermon of Herman Bavinck. It is entitled "The World-Conquering Power of Faith" and was preached on June 30, 1901. His text was I John 5:4b: "And this is the victory that has overcome the world—our faith." On this occasion, the president of the South African Republic was present in church. This sermon is exegetical. It possesses an internal logic. His theme and divisions are as follows:

> The World-Conquering Power of Faith
> The *opposition* that this faith experiences.
> The *character* that this faith bears.
> The *victory* that is promised to this faith.

Let us look at Bavinck's homiletics and then at his exegesis and development of concepts.

First, let us look at his homiletics. Bavinck has a long introduction. He does relate his text to the context, but in his introduction he already begins to say an awful lot about faith—something he probably should save for the meat of the sermon. He does make a nice point about John, the Apostle of Love, also teaching much about faith.

Before we analyze his development of concepts, I have criticisms of his homiletics. His theme (or title) unfortunately covers what is contained in all three of his divisions. He puts too much in his title: "The World-Conquering Power of Faith." The result is that the three divisions could be separate sermons. It would have been better for him to have a theme or main point that he would begin to develop already in his first point. There is a lack of synthesizing in this sermon. In the first point our preacher talks about the opposition that faith experiences without even defining what faith is. But what he is doing is developing the concept of the "world" in the first point. In the second point he discusses the nature of true faith—especially that it is centered on Jesus Christ. In the third point he develops the idea of how our faith overcomes the world—although since he developed the idea of the world back in point 1, he focuses on the victory of faith.

Technically Bavinck should have covered the three ideas of the identity of the world, the nature of faith, and its conquering power in the first point, if his main point is "The World-Conquering Power of Faith". In the second point he could have discussed the way faith overcomes the world. The final point would deal with the implications of this for our lives. He does have a short conclusion where he tries to do what he should have been doing in the entire third point—applying the message.

But what Bavinck does well is develop the various concepts in the text. Our chief concern now is with his development of concepts. The first concept with which he interacts is his development of the idea of the world. He talks about the positive connotation of the Greek word "cosmos" that has to do with "harmonious order and regularity."[374] You will know that the word "cosmos" has a number of connotations and sometimes is used to refer to the physical creation. Bavinck then provides us with a definition of the sinful world:

> The existing order of created beings, in its entirety, the whole orrery that is God's creation, that fixed whole in all its visible and invisible parts, insofar as it is an instrument of unrighteousness, is summed up by the apostle John under the name "the world." And he can name it as such, in *one* name, with *one* word, because sin has damaged the whole world and makes it (in its entirety) live from *one* principle, inspired by *one* spirit, pointed toward *one* goal, namely, enmity and rebellion against God, its Creator and Lord.[375]

I want my students to see what is going on when a preacher provides us with a nice definition like this. Bavinck is defining and developing the concept of the word "cosmos" when it is used to refer to the sinful world. He provides us with a concise and clear description. He develops the concept. He explains the connotation of the word.

In the second point of his sermon, Bavinck defines what faith is. He is concerned to point out that faith has as its object the Son of God. The believer confesses that Jesus of Nazareth is Messiah and Savior. He also provides us with descriptions and even a definition of what true faith is:

> But it is firm certainty, unshakeable conviction, ineradicable confidence, not of blood or of the will of the flesh, not of the will of a man, but coming from God and worked in the heart by his Spirit. It is the bond that the soul binds to the Mediator and holds fast to him as seeing the Unseen.[376]

True faith involves conviction. It is a bond that unites the believer to Christ.

In the third point of the sermon, Bavinck develops the idea of the victory of faith. He discusses the nature of our spiritual weapons. Whereas the world uses the weapons of intimidation and persecution, the church

---

[374] Herman Bavinck, Herman Bavinck on Preaching & Preachers. Translated by James P. Eglinton. (Peabody, MA: Hendrickson Publishers, 2017), 71.
[375] Ibid., 72.
[376] Ibid., 78.

triumphs through faith "that Jesus is the Christ."[377] He very nicely develops the certainty of the believers conquering by faith. Since Christ has conquered the enemies of the saints, they will triumph through faith in the victorious King.

Bavinck does a nice job of identifying the main concepts in the text and developing them. He develops them biblically and theologically. He has a sense of the drama of the great story of redemption and brings this into his message. He traces the victorious work of Christ in salvation history. He preaches Christ and Him crucified.

Even though I pointed out some homiletical shortcomings to Bavinck's sermon, there is logic to it. First, he deals with the enemy or threat that the Christian must overcome. Second, he discusses the faith in Christ that overcomes the world. Third, he moves to how as believers we triumph over our enemies.

These are the two critical things we want in sermons. We want to have teaching that flows out of the text and develops the concepts in it. And we want there to be a logic that involves the preacher taking us from somewhere to a destination. Bavinck poses the problem, provides us with the resolution, and then shows us the victorious consequence of Christ's death.

Russ Dykstra on Developing Concepts

Russ Dykstra (from the Protestant Reformed Seminary) has some important things to say about the importance of developing concepts for preaching.

> Concepts are the substance of the text. Concepts are the ideas, the thoughts, and the doctrines of the text. A few of the concepts found in the Bible include the love of God, the forgiveness of sins, the hope of glory, our high priest--merciful and faithful, eternal life, justification by faith.[378]

Developing concepts involve *defining* and *explaining* them:

> The main message of the text arises out of the central concepts. For this reason, the exegesis gives much attention to concepts, is very careful in explaining them, and works hard at clear definitions and explanations of them. The main element for exegesis is accurately *defining* and then carefully *explaining* the concepts. This is what it means to "develop the

---

[377] Ibid., 83.
[378] Russell Dykstra, "Developing God-Honoring, Faithful, and Effective Preaching." Protestant Reformed Theological Journal. Vol. 48. April 2015. Number 2., p. 44.

concepts" of the text.[379]

The reason why Reformed pastors can develop biblical concepts because of the organic unity of the Scriptures, which are inspired by God. Dykstra writes that "The significance of this doctrine of Scripture for exegesis is that the Spirit determines the meaning of each word in the Bible, and thus, He determines the meaning of the concepts."[380]

One needs to interpret Scripture with Scripture to understand the meaning of words and the idea that certain concepts have. Dykstra writes, "But the Spirit uses the basic Hebrew or Greek word, and often elevates it to a higher meaning. The Spirit can even change the meaning of the word to one degree or another."[381] Therefore, the developing of concepts includes word studies.

> In concrete terms, the preacher engages in "word study" to understand how the Bible uses a given word. How does the Bible explain the word? What are the various elements that are part of the concept? The exegete then brings together all the various elements of the Bible gives a concept, and sets forth the clear (biblical) definition.[382]

Dykstra relates the development of concepts to preaching Christ and Him crucified. Just as every road led to Rome and from every little hamlet in England a road led to London (as Charles Haddon Spurgeon pointed out) every concept in Scripture leads to Christ and Him crucified. Dykstra writes,

> This method of developing concepts from Scripture is the connection to the discussion on preaching Christ--every concept leads back to Jesus Christ! Christ crucified! Christ risen and exalted! The exegete cannot be confident that he has captured the meaning of the concept until he is able to explain how this concept is related to Christ crucified, and how it reveals Christ crucified.[383]

---

[379] Ibid., 44.
[380] Ibid., 44.
[381] Ibid., 44.
[382] Ibid., 44-45.
[383] Ibid., 45.

Dykstra writes that "the proper way to develop biblical concepts" is to show "their full meaning in Jesus Christ."[384] Dykstra connects exegesis with the development of concepts in their relation to the Savior:

> Exegesis involves, first, defining and explaining the concepts. The second part of exegesis is setting forth the relationship between the various concepts. Each concept individually points to Christ. Together, the concepts give the theme, the main message of the text. That theme will show the way that the text reveals God in the face of Christ crucified and exalted.[385]

I hope that you are beginning to grasp the importance of developing the concepts in your text. In some sense the rubber hits the road in exegesis when it comes to developing concepts. If you are not developing the concepts in your text, you will not have good raw material to use in constructing your sermon.

On the other hand, if you do a good job in developing the concepts, your sermon will brim with fresh insights and you will grow in your understanding of Christian doctrine.

---

[384] Ibid., 45.
[385] Ibid., 45-46.

Chapter 22
The Sermon Must be a Unified, Logical, Organic Whole
The *Big Idea* of Biblical Preaching

he *Big Idea of Biblical Preaching* is a festschrift in honor of Haddon W. Robinson.[386] Part 1 is entitled "Big Idea Preaching: Why a Single Idea Lands the Best Punch."[387] Haddon Robinson compared a sermon to a rifle bullet rather than buckshot. "A sermon should be a bullet and not buckshot."[388] Among American evangelicals in the 20th century, Robinson advocated the idea that an expository sermon should develop "a single sermon idea, proposition, or thesis."[389] He identified the theme of a passage as the sermon's "big idea."[390] Duane Litfin mentions a consensus among rhetoricians and homileticians of the importance of communicating just one big idea in a message.

> There exists a remarkable consensus among those who have studied and practiced public speaking over the last twenty-five hundred years that the most effective way to structure a speech is to build it around a single significant thought.

> From the ancient Greek and Roman rhetoricians to the latest communication theorists, from the preaching in the Bible to the sermons heard in pulpits today, from the political oratory of democracies long past to the persuasive message of our own times, the

---

[386] Keith Willhite and Scott M. Gibson, eds. The Big Idea of Biblical Preaching: Connecting the Bible to People 2nd Edition. (Grand Rapids, MI: Baker Books, 1999).
[387] Ibid., 11.
[388] Haddon W. Robinson, Biblical Preaching: The Development and Delivery of Expository Messages (Grand Rapids: Baker, 1980), 33.
[389] Keith Willhite and Scott M. Gibson, eds. The Big Idea of Biblical Preaching: Connecting the Bible to People 2nd Edition. (Grand Rapids, MI: Baker Books, 1999), 13.
[390] Haddon W. Robinson, Biblical Preaching: The Development and Delivery of Expository Messages (Grand Rapids: Baker, 1980), pp. 31-48.

history of public speaking and the lessons we have learned from that history unite to argue forcefully that *a speech, to be maximally effective, ought to attempt to develop more or less fully only one major proposition.*[391]

Litfin argues that a declarative sentence teaches one big idea. "The smallest unit of discourse is the simple, grammatically complete, declarative sentence. Such a sentence constitutes by definition a single idea; it consists of something being predicated about something else."[392] He writes that "some of history's most astute observers of human behavior" have noted "that effective communicators tend to organize their speeches around, not a random batch of ideas, but a single, significant, "central" idea."[393]

Litfin admits that it is difficult to narrow in on and develop just one big idea. It requires "clear and rigorous thought."[394]

Haddon Robinson said: "Thinking is hard work, and thinking about thinking is even harder work."[395]

James Daane's Emphasis on a Sermon saying "one thing"

James Daane defines expository preaching as "setting forth neither more nor less than the truth of the biblical text."[396] He taught that each sermon must "say one thing."

> There is at least one basic rule to which any type of sermon structure must yield tribute. *Ever sermon must say one thing, and one thing only; and this one thing must be capable of statement in a single sentence.* This rule governs what we shall here designate "the basic sermon." To the degree that a sermon of whatever structure fails to meet this requirement, it fails in its purpose. The more points a sermon tries to drive home, the les it drives home. A many-pointed sermon makes no point; it only conveys confusion. If after hearing a sermon an intelligent listener cannot state its point in a single sentence, the pulpit has largely failed him or her. It goes without saying that if the preacher cannot give the gist of the sermon in a single statement, neither will the persons who

---

[391] Duane Litfin, Public Speaking: A Handbook for Christians 2nd ed. (Grand Rapids: Baker, 1992), 80.
[392] Duane Litfin ,"New Testament Challenges to Big Idea Preaching" in The Big Idea of Biblical Preaching: Connecting the Bible to People 2nd Edition. Keith Willhite and Scott M. Gibson, eds. (Grand Rapids, MI: Baker Books, 1999), 54.
[393] Ibid., 55.
[394] Ibid., 57.
[395] Ibid., 57. Cited by Litfin.

hear it.[397]

Daane discusses the benefits of a minister preaching a "one-point sermon." This allows the uniqueness of each text to shine forth.

> A further advantage of the basic one-point sermon is that it enables a preacher to create sermons that are fresh and different every Sunday. Making sermons that present one specific point about one text prevents the preacher from preaching much the same sermon every Sunday. With rare exceptions every biblical text differs from all other biblical texts; even some which are verbally the same appear in differing contexts, and thus are not the same.[398]

Since the text finds its source in divine revelation, the preacher does not have to argue for every main point. Since the main point of the text comes from God, the saints must simply believe what God asserts. "The sermon proper is not an attempt to prove or even argue for the truth of the proposition. It rather explicates, exhibits, spells out what the proposition declares."[399]

The logic of the sermon should result from the logic of the text. Daane writes that "Thus the whole structure of the sermon outline is determined solely by the text. The Word articulated in a given text determines what the sermon asserts; and as such the sermon says what the Word says. It is thus an authentic *homiletical* effort."[400]

Daane's emphasis on the sermon saying "one thing" is good (as is his idea that the logic of the sermon outline should flow out of the logic of the text). But when he moves from theory to practice, we find him providing unhelpful homiletical outlines as examples. He provides this model outline for John 3:16:

> ***Proposition***: The Greatness of God's Love (God's love is great)
> I.   Its Costly Expression
> II. Its Unworthy Object
> III. Its Saving Purpose

Daane provides five more model outlines that all suffer from the same

---

[396] James Daane, Preaching with Confidence: A Theological Essay on the Power of the Pulpit (Grand Rapids, MI: Eerdmans, 1980), 50.
[397] James Daane, Preaching with Confidence: A Theological Essay on the Power of the Pulpit (Grand Rapids, MI: Eerdmans, 1980), 58-59.
[398] Ibid., 64.
[399] Ibid., 65.
[400] Ibid., 66.

deficiency as the one on John 3:16. Let me provide two more. The first is on Romans 1:16-17 and the second on Romans 9:1-3.

Proposition: The Power of the Gospel (the gospel is powerful.)
I.   Its Saving Character
II. Its Divine Source
III. Its Sequential Objects
IV. Its Pauline Consequence

Proposition: Paul's Anguish for His Brethren
I.   Its Sworn Verification
II. Its Amazing Nature
III. Its Un-Christian Object

In each example, Daane makes a fatal mistake that undermines the unity of each sermon. In the first example he provides a proposition that is the title or theme. But he has no logical place in his outline to develop it. The first point of the outline does not develop either the ideas of (1) love, (2) who the God is who loves, or (3) the greatness of this divine love. Rather it develops another idea, namely, the costly expression of this love. The main point (proposition) is not the main point of this sermon. Logically it goes undeveloped. There is no place in the outline to develop the massive concepts of (1) love, (2) the God who is love, or (3) the greatness of this love. The outline does not allow for the logical development or development of the central concepts in the title. Better to have simply developed the main point in the first point and then make the idea of its costly expression a subpoint that develops the idea of the greatness of God's love.

The second sample outline on Romans 1:16-17 makes the same mistake. Daane acts like the proposition or main point is the power of the gospel: "The Power of the Gospel." But he never even develops the two great concepts in this proposition in his outline. There is no logical place for it. The two main ideas that cry out for development are 1) what the gospel is and 2) the omnipotent power of the gospel. Astonishingly, Daane supposes it is logical and appropriate to jump into a first point that talks about the saving character of the gospel. This occurs without him providing a logical place to develop what this gospel is that saves and what is meant by the phrase that it is the "power of God unto salvation."

One can scarcely believe that leading homileticians in influential seminaries (Fuller Seminary in Daane's case) can teach such trite.

We expect the same confusion in the third sample outline on Romans 9:1-3 and are not disappointed. Daane identifies the proposition as "Paul's Anguish for his brethren" but he will not give us a first point where he develops the main ideas in this title which include 1) who Paul is, 2) who is brethren are, and 3) what is meant by Paul's anguish. Strangely Daane assumes that these massively important ideas do not need to be developed early in the sermon and he does not even provide a logical place in the outline to do this.

Daane is teaching the preacher to major in generalizations. This is in spite of the fact that he explicitly damns preaching in generalities as superficial preaching. When you just assume that the congregation understands the main theme of the passage and its massive concepts, you preach in generalities. Daane indicts his own homiletical approach when he wrote: "Superficial preaching on biblical generalities is profoundly detrimental to the preacher. The congregation gets little spiritual nourishment, and the preacher does not grow in an understanding of the word."[401]

It is one thing to state the unique idea in the text, as Daane exhorts the preacher to do in the title; but it is another thing to develop the concepts in it in a logical and orderly fashion. This Daane refuses to do.

Daane's approach to preaching majors in the minor issues, encourages generalities in the main point and leaves the congregation without a clear understanding of the unique idea in a text. It assumes that the congregation already understands the unique idea in the text and simply moves ahead to what normally should be in the second or third points of the sermon.

A Sermon that is a Unified, Organic Whole

Has anyone ever seriously argued that sermons should not be a unified, organic whole? Do homileticians ever argue that a sermon should be disunited and not fit together? I have never read a book on preaching that says that you should prepare three short, separate messages with three different main points and then paste them together to get a 40-minute sermon.

Yet the reality is that books on preaching do advocate by their example the preparation of sermons that are not unified, organic wholes. I see examples of homiletical outlines that involve four separate main ideas. The theme or title is given. But then the first point is a separate idea and the same is the case for the second and third points. The theme and division represent four separate topics or themes. When you have four separate

---

[401] Ibid., 64.

themes you have too many chiefs and not enough Indians. You need to have one chief, the theme or title. The second and third divisions need to serve the main point.

Did you ever read a book on preaching where the argument is made that a sermon should involve many separate, unrelated ideas? No one ever argues that a sermon should have three titles or three main points. Have you ever read a book that tells you to create three separate messages that all standalone by themselves and then simply preach them one after another?

Yet everywhere one is confronted by sermons that contain three divisions that might as well be three separate messages. It is true that the three messages all are given from the same text. It probably is a longer text. Because the minister has selected one text which he reads to the congregation and since he is preaching on it, he imagines that he will naturally be presenting a sermon that is a unified, organic whole. Actually, there are not just three sermonettes, the title is sometimes a separate idea from the three divisions, so you actually have four sermons. Somehow, somewhere the minister will need to try to fit in the idea that he makes the title of the sermon, although logically there is no place in the homiletical outline for him to do so.

Preparing a sermon that is a unified, organic whole takes work. It requires simplicity. And simplicity is more difficult to accomplish than complexity. It takes organization. Disorganization is easier than an orderly message. Simplicity requires logic; and by nature we are illogical.

It is easy to take three different ideas in the text and talk about the first one in the first point of the sermon, the second in the second point, and the third in the final point. But this does not mean that the sermon was a unified, organic whole. *If there is not a main point that is being developed and around which the various concepts are organized, you will not have a unified sermon.* You will have a disorganized message that is parading as a unified one. And you will trick people, just like you fooled yourself.

Your sermon should have one central idea, not four. I am afraid that if you look at your past sermons you will discover that you have prepared many sermons that do not have one main point that remains the central point of the sermon. You have often treated lesser, subsidiary ideas as if they are the main point. How do I know that this is the case with you? I know because I am guilty of the same errors. We make things too complex for the congregation.

Do you really imagine that you can send the congregation home with four big ideas and that they will remember them all? They will not. Your goal should be to preach the main point in the text and to hammer this home. You want the main point to sink into the hearts of the congregation. Yes, you will have an argument in your sermon. You will develop the central idea. You might talk about the way in which this central idea can occur. You might talk about the possibility of it being a reality. You might talk about God's goal in the central idea. But you want the main point to be the main point. You want them to remember the massive point. So, keep it simple.

You are preaching to children.

Will the children remember your main point? If they cannot remember your main point, who is at fault? Are they too stupid to understand the main point of a sermon? No, you are not doing the work necessary to impress the main point upon their minds. You need to work at this.

You probably can't say the main point of your sermon too many times. Use repetition so that your main point strikes home. Then use variety to say it from different directions. You can't connect the main point too often to your second and third points. I find that seminary students err by talking about their main point in the first point and thereafter seeming to forget what their main point was as they develop their second and third points. But this robs the sermon of unity. It makes the sermon unnecessarily complex.

Since when have professors of preaching exhorted their students to be unnecessarily complex? Have they ever told their students that when they come to the second and third points of their sermon that they should put out of mind the main point that they have already developed?

Remember the congregation does not have your outline.

They cannot see the logic of your sermon before their eyes.

They cannot see how you wrote it out to be an organic unity. They need to hear from your lips that it is a unity. You need to work at helping them to see what the main point is and how everything else serves and develops it.

Homer Hoeksema on Sermons as an Orderly, Concatenated Address

Homer Hoeksema defines a sermon as "an orderly, concatenated address, or discourse, proclaiming the whole counsel of God based on Holy Scripture from the viewpoint of a particular text or passage."[402] Since you are not William F. Buckley, what does Hoeksema mean by "an orderly, concatenated address"? The word "concatenated" refers to a logical chain. *The ideas in a sermon should be related to each other in a logical chain.* Hoeksema means that your message must be organized and linked together in a logical chain.

I appreciate how Hoeksema wants the sermon to be from "the viewpoint of a particular text or passage." It is vital that the sermon reflects the unique text. Away with sermons that apparently could be general

---

[402] Homer Hoeksema, Homiletics Syllabus, 11.

messages on a hundred texts. So develop the unique ideas in your text. Since the sermon should be "proclaiming the whole counsel of God" you need to add richness to the concepts in your text by developing them within the context of all of Scripture. You need to do systematic theology.

You need to have one main point. Your sermon needs to be a unified, harmonious whole. The way in which it will be a unified whole will be if your message is orderly and in a logical chain. In your homiletics you are developing a concatenated address. The logical chain will flow from the main point of the text as you take the congregation on a journey to the application of it to them. If your second and third points are not logically related to the main point, you will not have a concatenated address. You might have some lovely chain links, but they will not be linked together.

The title of the sermon or what is called the theme should express one main point. The theme merely reflects the sermon itself which must express one main point. The title should communicate the organic unity of the entire message. My fight for a theme or title that expresses one main point is intimately related to my requirement that the entire sermon possess an organic unity.

If a minister preached a sermon where the title did not express the main point of the sermon, but where the actual sermon was an organic unity; I would not complain. But I do not think that I have ever had the pleasure of hearing such a sermon. When the minister does not have a clear idea about the main point of the sermon, it will (practically speaking) be impossible for him to deliver a sermon that is an organic unity.

Preachers need to listen very carefully to Homer Hoeksema:

> But the sermon proper is, first of all, an *organic whole*, that is, an address in which the various points not only belong together, but also are developed from a common principle. This implies, in the second place, that a sermon develops *one main thought*, and not three or four chief thoughts which have little or nothing to do with one another, which are arbitrarily put together.
>
> Further, it implies, in the third place, that this one thought is presented and developed in logical order, so that the congregation can follow the sermon step by step to the very end. This implies also that there is progress of development in a sermon, so that in a properly arranged sermon there is a fitting introduction, an orderly arrayed body of the sermon, and a proper conclusion, or peroration.[403]

---

[403] Ibid., 14.

The sermon will not be an organic unity if the minister selects a text that is not unified. For example, if you select two widely different parables as a text for your sermon, it will be hard to have a sermon that is a unified and organic whole. Homer Hoeksema gives advice about text selection:

> It is important, of course, that the material in the sermon should be a unity, and that, therefore, the text on which the sermon is based is a unity. The text must present *one main thought* and so must the sermon. That does not mean, of course, that the sermon should be characterized by dead monotony, but rather that it should constitute one, organic whole, with all the elements subordinated under one main theme.[404]

Homer Hoeksema does not want the preacher to focus in so closely on the text of the sermon that he does not step back and compare Scripture with Scripture. Scripture must interpret Scripture. The rest of Scripture should shed light on the unique teaching in the text. Hoeksema states that "The content of the sermon must be the organic whole of the Word of God as it is conveyed by the vehicle of a particular text."[405] If it does not blow the preacher's mind that not only must the individual sermon be a concatenated whole, but Homer Hoeksema requires that the individual sermon must also reflect what the entirety of Scriptures harmoniously teaches on the topic. But Hoeksema does not stop here, he blows the ministers mind by requiring that a sermon series also be a concatenated whole!

Hoeksema requires that a sermon series also be an organic unity. He makes the surprising demand that if a minister is going to preach a series "It is necessary that the preacher work out the entire system of sermons in outline before he begins to preach."[406] He thinks that "the main lines of the exegesis must be completed, and the series of sermons as a whole must be worked out in outline form before a beginning is made without preaching that series."[407] One reason for this requirement, which might seem excessive to a minister always struggling to get his next two sermons completed for the following Sunday, is that

> A series of sermons is a unified group of sermons. There must be a main thought controlling the entire series. And in the series each particular sermon must be a part of the whole and must contribute to the development of that main thought."[408]

---

[404] Ibid., 22.
[405] Ibid., 23.
[406] Ibid., 25.
[407] Ibid., 25.
[408] Ibid., 25.

Hoeksema not only wants every sermon preached to be a unified, organic whole; *but he wants every sermon series to be a unified, organic whole!* Talk about high expectations!

One can perceive the value of understanding the canonical sense of Galatians before preaching a series on the book. When we search for the canonical significance of the book we will try to discern the main themes or the theme of the book and what unique contribution Galatians makes to the canon of Scripture. Notice an emphasis on the unique contribution of each book of the Bible. Each sermon on an individual text of Scripture should also communicate the unique contribution that the text makes to God's revelation in Christ.

As a pastor I learned that it is easy to write a complex sermon with many unrelated points. It is hard to write a simple, unified sermon that is logical and zeros in on one main idea.

If no one has ever argued that a sermon should involve two or three separate messages sewed together at the seams so that they appear as one message, why is this common practice? I think that the common approach to preaching today is one that involves a variety of messages thrown together.

The problem is that ministers are too befuddled. They cannot calm down and concentrate on communicating one main point. They need to be more like William Tyndale who is famous for his emphasis on simplicity, clarity, and the use of the shortest Anglo-Saxon word. Walt Whitman in his *Leaves of Grass"* modeled simplicity and clarity. But ministers do not produce simplicity, unity, and clarity. Why? They are not doing the hard work necessary to develop one main message and then seek that this message be developed so that it will have an intellectual and emotional impact.

It is possible that ministers are not being taught in seminary to produce a single, unified message. Or they are being taught and then are ignoring this advice.

The result is that the first point of the sermon is a standalone message. The second point is a second standalone message that bears no logical relation to the first point. In fact, everything discussed in the second point probably should have been discussed in the first point. And then comes the third point which is not a logical development of either the first or the second point.

But the minister acts like it is. And the congregation might be naïve to think that they have been on one journey when in fact they took three separate trips—all arriving at different destinations. Don't be surprised if they don't remember one trip that had one main point and that headed to one massive applicatory destination.

Chapter 23
Your Theme or Title: The Main Point

Your theme should be the main point of your sermon. I know that there is room for poetic license. Sometimes you might use a title that will be an attention grabber. But then make sure that the congregation knows what your main point is. You better verbalize it and make it clear. For example, one time I preached a sermon on the Lord's Day in the Heidelberg Catechism that deals with the question why the Son of God became a man. I gave it the title: "Cur Deus Homo?"

I used a question instead of a statement for my title. I also gave a Latin title because I knew that the oddity of this fact would catch their attention. I could explain that the title was: "Why did God become man?" But I also had to be about what the main point of my message was. God needed to become man, because man sinned and only a true man could pay for the sins of sinful men.

I hear too many sermons where the theme or title is not the main point of the sermon. Sometimes ministers hang a sermon or title on a text. They read the text, but never exegete it. They reference the text because it reminds them of what they really want to talk about. I find that ministers often provide an incomplete idea for their theme. This is evident when they do not even have a verb in their main point.

Lately I have noticed that ministers do not place their three points (divisions) in the bulletin or do not even announce them. Ministers are not giving a road map to the congregation. The saints do not know what kind of journey they are on. Ministers should engage in sign-posting.

A good theme is a complete statement, although it is not a complete sentence. It should reflect the main point of the text. But it certainly is different from a thesis statement which should reflect the main point and the entire argument of the sermon. A theme should have a verb, as a rule. Rarely this might be a form of the verb "to be." But since forms of the verb "to be" are weak, it is best to use a stronger verb. I was correctly taught in seminary than one good way to have a united sermon was to have a participle in the title. In other words, add an "ing" to the crucial verb in your theme. This will often allow you to develop second and third points that are closely and logically related to your main point.

Here are some examples of themes (titles) I have given to sermons along with the text they are based on. Notice how I use verbs with "ing" endings.

Acts 1:8: "Jesus Promising to Clothes His Disciples with Power"

Acts 16:13-15: "God Building the Church one Covenant Family at a Time"

Acts 17:16-34: "Proclaiming the Eternal Word to a Changing World"

Acts 19:1-20. Lord's Days 36 & 37: "Misusing God's Name"

Amos 5:21-27. Lord's Day 35: "Worshipping the Right God Rightly"

Daniel 1:8-21: "Rejecting Babylon's Food"

Deuteronomy 15:7-11: "Magnifying God with a Wide Open Hand"

Ephesians 4:30: "Grieving not the Holy Spirit"

Exodus 12: "Eating the Passover Lamb"

Galatians 2. Lord's Day 11: "Confessing Jesus as our All-Satisfying Savior"

Galatians 3:13-14. Lord's Day 15: "Christ's Curse-Bearing on the Tree"

Genesis 35: "Restoring the Family Altar"

I Peter 3:15-16: "Defending Your Hope"

Let's use the last example to demonstrate how using a participle in your theme can enable you to bind your theme and divisions together in a unity. A sermon on I Peter 3:15-16 had as the theme: "Defending Your Hope." The first point would be "The Meaning." Here I would develop the idea of what Peter means by the Christian "hope" and what it means to defend it. I might also talk about the necessity of defending our hope. The second point could be "The Manner." In this point I would discuss how we are to defend our hope, since the Apostle Peter has some things to say about this. For the last point, I could have "The Purpose." Here I could talk about what our goal is in defending our hope—namely, to win souls. Notice how the theme and divisions hang together. You should read the first point: "The Meaning *of* Defending Your Hope." The second point flows through: "The Manner of Defending Your Hope." The third point likewise flows into the theme: "The Purpose in Defending Your Hope."

Improper Use of Long Thesis Statements

There is a strange custom abroad. A minister will give a brief introduction and then announce his thesis statement. He will read a long sentence. A sentence that no one can remember. The sentence will be complex. Then only in an incidental way, the preacher will give the title for his sermon. It will not be clear what the relationship is between the thesis statement and the main point. Then as the minister goes ahead and delivers his message you never hear about the thesis statement again. You also might not hear much about the main point or the title again. What is going on?

Historically Reformed pastors did not mention a thesis statement in the introduction to their sermons. I can understand why. It provides too much information. It is giving away the entire argument of the sermon. Instead the minister would announce his theme and divisions. He would lay out the main point, which was a simple and memorable theme. He would give us an idea of where he was going with his divisions.

But I understand why some preachers might want to introduce a thesis statement. After all, this is what students of English are trained to do when writing an essay. Perhaps the giving of thesis statements is evidence that the minister is viewing his sermon more as an essay than an oral communication. Every sermon should have an argument that runs through it. Let us take an example from above. I just showed how logically connected a theme and division can be on I Peter 3:15-16. Here is the theme and division again:

Defending Your Hope
The Meaning
The Manner
The Purpose

It is easy to see how a thesis statement can be developed with respect to this message. But here is the important thing. The thesis statement should include the main point in the first point as well as the crucial arguments and development in the second and third points. Isn't that what a thesis statement is in a paper? It lays out the main argument and conclusion. Therefore, a thesis statement on this sermon would include three elements. First, the thesis statement would need to begin by talking about the importance of Christians defending their hope. The second part of the thesis statement would need to mention the crucial ways in which the Apostle Peter thinks that we should defend our hope. The last part of the thesis statement would explain what the purpose is in defending your hope.

The problem I find is that when seminary students introduce thesis statements it is not clear that they possess an argument that runs through the entire sermon. Once the seminarian has announced his thesis statement, he does not develop it consciously in the presence of the congregation. Sometimes the thesis statement only covers the content in the first point.

I am all for keeping the main point the main point. This can include keeping the basic logic of the sermon before the congregation. But then what you need to do is concisely summarize your main point in the first point before you start the second point. You can introduce your second point or conclude it by underlining the two main points made in this division. Once you come to the end of the sermon, it is fitting that you recap the entire argument. John Piper sometimes does an effective job of recapping his entire argument at the end of the sermon. He is imitating Jonathan Edwards who so effectively used argumentation in his sermons. When a minister has taken you from argument to argument and brought you logically to a conclusion, this impresses the mind. The congregation has been convinced. They have not gainsaid the presuppositions and arguments and, therefore, receive a strong impetus to believe the message and live in line with it. Reminding the congregation of your argument and the fact that you have demonstrated your conclusions to be valid has a strong psychological impact on the congregation.

Remember what the goal is in the sermon. You want to have a unified message. You want it to be a concatenated, harmonious whole. You want it to be logically unified. Having clarity about your theme, divisions, and thesis statement will go a long way towards having a message that is simple, clear, and concise. The more clearly you understand the central message and the logic of your message, the easier it will be to internalize and preach it.

Chapter 24
The Preaching Outline

How do you outline a sermon? This is how I do it in Microsoft Word:

I.   Introduction
    a. Subpoint
    b. Subpoint

Sermon Title

I.   1st Division
II. 2nd Division
III. 3rd Division

I.   First Main Point
    c. Subpoint
       i.   Sub-subpoint
       ii. Sub-subpoint
          1. Sub-sub-subpoint
          2. Sub-sub-subpoint
    d. Subpoint
II. Second Main Point
    a. Subpoint
    b. Subpoint
III. Third Main Point
    a. Subpoint
    b. Subpoint
    c.

The author of a leading textbook on communication argues that one should speak from an outline because

The clear visual framework of this outline immediately shows the relationships among the ideas of the speech. The most important ideas (main points) are farthest to the left. Less important ideas (subpoints, sub-subpoints, and so on) are progressively farther to the right. This pattern reveals the structure of your entire speech.[409]

Subpoints serve the develop the more important ideas. "Above all, remember that all points at the same level should immediately support the point that is just above and one notch to the left in your outline."[410] You do not want an outline that has incomplete sentences or that contains too little material. "In sum, a skimpy preparation outline is of little value. Stating your main points and subpoints in full sentences will ensure that you develop your ideas fully."[411]

Jay Adams explains the benefits of preaching from a full outline:

The method of using a full outline allows for the best of both worlds. It provides for the security, order, and precision of written sermons while at the same time allowing freedom to adapt to circumstances and to benefit from the "jelling factor." All in all, the full sentence outline, therefore, seems to be the best way to go.

What do I mean by a "full sentence outline"? Just that: an outline composed of complete sentences.[412]

Adams makes an important point that I am keen to emphasize. He writes that a benefit of an outline is that "at a *single glance* you can pick up each major point."[413]

However, the outline must be a preaching outline. Adams fears that preachers prepare outlines that serve as lecture outlines rather than preaching outlines.

Just as many (perhaps most) preachers lecture rather than preach, and they are concerned about central ideas, themes, and the like, rather than about purpose, so too do they develop outlines that are suited not to preaching but to lecturing. They don't know any better—that is how they were taught—and as a result find themselves cued by the outline for

---

[409] Stephen E. Lucas, The Art of Public Speaking 3rd Edition (New York: Random House, 1989), 191.
[410] Ibid., 192.
[411] Ibid., 193.
[412] Jay E. Adams, Preaching with Purpose (Phillipsburg, NJ: P & R Publishing, 1982), 49.
[413] Ibid., 50. Emphasis added.

lecturing, which they then proceed to do—on cue.[414]

What is different about a preaching outline? Adams writes that "If the basic purpose of an outline is to cue the preacher, then the outline should cue him to preach. Many men who want to preach, rather than to lecture, find themselves hindered by wrong signals emanating from their outlines, which cue them wrongly."[415] Adams contrasts the content of a lecture outline with that of a preaching outline:

Lecture Format
1. Then and there
2. Third person emphasis
3. Abstract
4. In terms of other
5. Informative

Preaching Format
1. Here and now
2. Second person emphasis
3. Concrete
4. In terms of the congregation
5. Persuasive or motivational[416]

"The preacher explains the text just as fully as does the lecturer; in fact, more fully. He explains the *telos* as well."[417]

Example of Sermon Outline on II Chronicles 33

Not many students today learn to read outlines or to write in outline form. I find that it is difficult for students to catch on to the idea that the main points in an outline function like thesis sentence statements. The subpoints serve and develop the idea in the main points above them. Here is an example of a sermon outline that I prepared for a sermon about King Manasseh from II Chronicles 33. It is unfortunate that we are printing it in this book form. We cannot fit much of the outline on each page in this

---

[414] Ibid., 51.
[415] Ibid., 51.
[416] Ibid., 51.
[417] Ibid., 54.

monograph. The outline is nine pages of computer paper with a font size of 12. In this format the outline takes up more pages. Therefore, it is also harder to follow the outline and see things at a glance as I emphasize.

II Chronicles 33 "The King Causing Judah to Sin"

I. Introduction
    a. Manasseh, was a king of Judah.
        i. He holds the record for the longest reign of any king in Israel or Judah, 55 years.
            1. 696-642 B.C.
                a. What is puzzling about Manasseh is his total lack of godliness.
                b. He is an exact opposite of his father Hezekiah.
            2. His was a deliberate, and total abandonment of the law of God.
        ii. And ye t this wicked king is by the end of his life a changed person!
    b. Manasseh belongs to the list of those who have greatly sinned, but who in the eleventh hour of their lives is amazingly converted by God.
        i. He fits well on the list with the Apostle Paul, who was guilty of persecuting the church.
            1. He confessed that he was the chief of sinners.
                a. We are reminded of the woman who was a harlot—who later is found washing the feet of the Savior with her tears and wiping them with the hairs of her head.
                b. Or we think of the elect thief on the cross, who in the last moments of his life was dramatically converted.
            2. These saints remind us that salvation is all of the free grace of God.
                a. No one deserves to be cleansed by the blood of Christ.
                b. But if God wants to save an elect sinner for the glory of His grace He is able to do that—and He does.
        ii. King Manasseh was a sinner and a saint!
            1. This story should lead us to be surprised that God saves sinners like Mannasseh and like we!
            2. For we Christians, like Manasseh, are sinner-saints!

The King Causing Judah to Sin
    I.   The Meaning
    II.   The Judgment
    III.   The Transformation

I.   The Meaning

    a.   King Manasseh is Judah's version of Jeroboam the son of Nebat.

        I.   Jeroboam was infamous for the title given to him by the holy men who wrote the history of Israel in the book of Kings and Chronicles.

            1.   The sacred historians record that the sin of Jeroboam is what caused Israel to sin.

                a.   It was the sin that led to the eventual destruction of the kingdom of Israel.

                    I.   It led to the quick end to the line of Jeroboam the son of Nebat.

                    II. Only his son reigned after him.

                b.   God sent the Assyrians after the kingdom of Israel because they would not turn away from the golden calf worship.

            2.   Manasseh, king of Judah, is the king who caused Judah to sin.

                a.   The sacred historian, inspired by God, tells us that Manasseh caused Judah to sin.

                    I.   II Chronicles 33:9: "So Manasseh made Judah and the inhabitants of Jerusalem to err, and to do worse than the heathen, whom the LORD had destroyed before the children of Israel."

                    II. II Kings 21:9: "But they hearkened not: and Manasseh seduced them to do more evil than did the nations whom the LORD destroyed before the children of Israel."

                    III. II Kings 21:16: "Moreover Manasseh shed innocent blood very much, til he had filled Jerusalem from one end to another; beside his sin wherewith he made Judah to sin, in doing that which was evil in the sight of the LORD."

                b.   The wicked reign of Manasseh becomes a capstone of the wall of sin that Judah had built between herself and God.

                    I.   Manasseh's personal example and leadership in sin were to have a permanent effect.

II. Manasseh enjoyed the legacy of a godly father, Hezekiah.

  1. He was the son of a God-fearing king of Judah.

    a. Hezekiah had led Judah in Reformation.

      I. We read of Hezekiah: "He did right in the sight of the Lord." (II Chronicles 29:2)

        1. He restored the true worship of Jehovah.

        2. He opened the doors of the house of God and repaired it.

        3. He brought in the priest and Levites and made them sanctify themselves for the true worship of Jehovah.

      II. He had re-established the temple worship--- and the celebration of the Passover Feast.

    b. Manasseh came to the throne at the age of 12.

      I. He was the son of his father's old age.

        1. Hezekiah had been sick unto death.

        2. But then God gave him 15 more years.

      II. For 12 years at least, Manasseh had received godly instruction.

        1. He had covenant training.

        2. That is no small matter.

        3. He was schooled in the

        4. law of Jehovah.

  2. Moreover, Manasseh was a royal son of David!

    a. He is in the line of the Messiah.

    b. With his father's death he soon plunged into apostasy.

b. Manasseh was the chief of sinners: He committed king-size sins.

  I. He engaged in star worship and child sacrifice.

    1. He plunged into every manner of spiritual wickedness.

      a. He introduced the Canaanite idols of Baal and Asherah.

        I. No matter how strange a god was presented, he had an offering for it.

        II. The Scriptures do not spare even the child of God when it comes to revealing his sins!

      b. He established and participated in a state astral cult.

    2. This was pure star-worship, based on the idea of the unchangeableness of the stars.

    a. Incense was offered to the stars.

        I. The sun was worshipped by the Persians.

        II. The signs of the zodiac had incense offered to them.

        III. Connected to this was astrology!

    b. He consulted sorcerers.

        I. He practiced divination.

        II. Anyone who pretended to have any sort of black art was welcome.

        III. He consulted witches who were purveyors of demonic activity.

3. Manasseh went so far as to involve his own son in the loathsome and detestable rites of infant sacrifice.

    a. Manasseh's Judah exceeded in spiritual degradation the original Canaanites whom God had driven out before Israel.

        I. When a person who grew up in the covenant does like the heathen, he does worse than they.

        II. An apostate Christian is more guilty than one who has never 'tasted the good word of God'.

    b. Manasseh's sins are so grave because he influences Judah to sin.

        I. The narrative lays stress on the fact that the king's inclination to idolatry was agreeable to the people.

II. Manasseh worshiped numerous idols in the temple of God.

1. So far did his spiritual prostitution take him that Manasseh introduced pagan altars in both the outer and the priest's courts.

    a. The hated Asherah pole was placed in the temple, the very abode of the sacred name.

2. Manasseh was smitten with a delirium of idolatry.

    a. He worships so many different gods.

    b. Notice that the idol gods of the pagans cannot satisfy!

        I. Why do you think Manasseh finds it necessary to worship Baal and Asherah and the son and the moon and the stars!

        II. It is because not one of these gods satisfies his soul!

III.   He does not feel safe with any one of them.

c. This is an unconscious confession of the insufficiency of each and all of them to fill the void in the heart, to satisfy the needs of a guilty man.

III. He showed long contempt for God's messengers and message.

1. A long reign.

a. 55 year reign.

b. Longest of all kings of Judah. 696-642 B.C.

2. Throughout Manasseh's wicked reign God warned of the grave consequences of the king's sin.

a. He sent repeated warnings through His prophets.

I. Yet the king did not pay attention.

II. Are you listening to the warnings of God?

b. What suicidal folly it is if you pay no more regard to God's voice than some husbands do to the words of their wives!

3. Instead Manasseh murdered prophets and faithful saints on a vast scale.

a. II Kings 21:16: "Moreover Manasseh shed innocent blood very much, till he had filled Jerusalem from one end to another;" (he had filled Jerusalem from mouth to mouth.)

b. The Jews had a myth that he had killed the prophet Isaiah.

I. According to the story Isaiah had been able to get inside a cedar tree that opened for him when he said the name of God.

II. But Manasseh had his men saw the oak tree in half—and in doing so cut Isaiah in half.

II. The Judgment

a. God ordains that Ashurbaniple, the Assyrian king, conquer Manassah and take him captive with a nose hook.

I. Someone has said that God is able to save from the "guttermost to the uttermost."

1. God now begins to save one of His elect.

2. God had revealed that the kingdom of Judah will be judged. (II Kings 21:11-14).

a. Ears shall tingle. (II Kings 21:12b)

I. God emphasizes the severity of the judgment.

        II.   It will be of such untold dimension that it will strike terror into the hearts of those who heard of its execution.

    b. God is going to stretch a plumb line over Jerusalem. (II Kings 21:13a)

        I.   The desolation of Jerusalem would be as complete as that of Samaria and of the house of Ahab.

        II.   God will raze Jerusalem to the ground so that the builder might stretch over it the measuring line and apply the plummet, as if not anything stands there.

    c. God will wipe Jerusalem like a man wipes a dish. (II Kings 21:13b)

        I.   Jerusalem will be emptied and cleansed, as a dish that is wiped, and then turned upside down.

        II.   None would remain.

  3.   God began to judge Judah by rendering her subject to Assyria.

    a. Manasseh and Judah became vassals to Assyria.

    b. This humiliation was not enough.

II. Then Manasseh rebelled against the Assyrian king, Ashurbanipal.

  1.   The historians tell us that there were widespread revolts during the reign of Ashurbanipal, which occurred from 652-648 B.C.

    a. This may have provided the occasion for Manasseh's rebellion.

        I.   Perhaps he stopped paying tribute.

           1. A number of Philistine and Sidonian cities had rebelled.

           2. Egypt, under a new dynasty, the 26th, had rebelled against Assyria.

        II.   This occasion was probably around 648—only 6 years before Manasseh's death.

           1. So Manasseh would be 49 plus 12—61 years of age at least.

           2. But Judah lacked Egypt's resourced---and more importantly God's help!

    b. As a result Ashurbanipal captured Manasseh and through him into a dungeon in Babylon.

I. We are told in II Chronicles 33:11: "Wherefore the LORD brought upon them the captains of the host of the king of Assyria, which took Manasseh among the thorns, and bound him with fetters, and carried him to Babylon."

II. The holy Scriptures tell us that Jehovah God played a role in this.

    1. This is a merciful chastisement!

    2. Note how emphatically God's hand is recognized behind the political complications that brought the Assyrians to Jerusalem.

    3. God brought the captains of Assyria to Jerusalem to capture Manasseh.

c. Higher Critics alleged that there was an error in the Bible because it claimed that Manasseh was imprisoned in Babylon.

I. You might know that Babylon was not the capital of Assyria.

    1. You children know that Ninevah was the capital.

    2. So higher critics have alleged that the Scriptures err in saying that Manasseh was imprisoned in the city of Babylon—the capital of the Babylonian kingdom that later destroyed conquered Assyria.

II. But now archeological discoveries have validated the Biblical text.

    1. It turns out that towards the end of Manasseh's reign, Ashurbanipal conquered Babylon.

    2. Ashurbanipal had a brother who had started a civil war from Babylon, where he was the viceroy—and had involved cities in Phoenicia and Palestine in this rebellion.

III. Ashurbanipal conquered Babylon.

    1. He temporarily lived there.

    2. We have monuments showing Ashurbanipal receiving ambassadors with tributary presents there.

        a. We also know that during the reign of his father, King Esarhaddon, that the name of Manasseh, is included among the subject kings of the Assyrians.

b. In the Assyrian the name reads: "Minasi sar mat (ir) Jaudi"—which clearly is Manasseh, king of Judah.

3. Therefore it is very possible that the king might have placed Manasseh in bonds in the city of Babylon which he was rebuilding.

2. The sacred text pictures Ashurbanipal's generals leading Manasseh to captivity with a nose hook.

a. Manasseh was taken into captivity in hooks and fetters, a most humiliating posture for one who was a king.

I. The word "thorns" is actually "hooks."

1. This word is used to describe a hook that was used to pull a large fish out of the water.

2. It is used for a ring that was passed through the noses of wild beasts to subdue and lead them.

b. The expression is figurative.

I. Manasseh is represented as an unmanageable beast, which the Assyrian generals took and subdued by a ring in the nose.

c. The fetters of brass were used to bind the feet of prisoners.

I. Picture an elderly king—in chains—in a dungeon.

3. Manasseh's exile is typical of that of Judah.

a. It points to being kicked out of God's land.

b. It is a picture of excommunication.

III. God's hand is behind the secondary causes of events.

1. God sends sorrows and misfortunes to us.

a. Sometimes they are meant to make us stop and repent.

b. Sometimes God is sending us a message to drop evil things from our lives.

c. God is sovereign over punishments and trials.

I. If you ignore this, you will not get the point!

         II.   Joseph knew that God was supreme over the evils that befell him: "But as for you, ye thought evil against me; but God meant it unto good, to bring to pass, as it is this day, to save much people alive" (Genesis 50:20).

         III.   Amos 3:6: "Shall a trumpet be blown in the city, and the pepole not be afraid? Shall there be evil in a city, and the LORD hath not done it?"

   2.   If we are God's children and remain stubborn, then God will take out the rod of reproof.

      a.   It is better that we should taste the rod of God's fatherly chastisements, than that He let us remain in our stubbornness.

      b.   *"The worst affliction is an affliction wasted, which does us no good."*

b.   In captivity, Manasseh humbles himself greatly before God.

   I.   II Kings 33:12: "And when he was in affliction, he besought the LORD his God, and humbled himself greatly before the God of his fathers,"

     1.   Manasseh had learned that his idol gods were unable to protect him!

       a.   They were worthless.

         I.   They could not be trusted.

         II.   The warnings of Jehovah's prophets came true!

       b.   Manasseh now humbled himself greatly before God.

         I.   God used his afflictions to bring him low.

           1.   God took away his self-confidence.

             a.   His arrogance is broken.

             b.   God kicked out from beneath him the possibility of trusting in idol gods.

           2.   God knows how to bring His beloved to despair in self, so that they cry out to Him!

II.   No chastisement has yielded its full blessing to us unless we also repent humbly like Manasseh.

   1.   Manasseh, the saint!

   2.   The mercy of God will reach down to every elect sinner to deliver him.

3. As we examine the account of the sins of Manasseh, we might conclude that the king was a reprobate of the worst sort.

    a. He turned His back on the God of His father, the covenant, and the laws of God.

        I. He embraced all of the abominations of the wicked.

        II. He was so bold in his wickedness.

    b. Yet, he is an elect child of God.

III. Manasseh prayed to God for mercy.

    1. II Kings 33:13: "And prayed unto him:"

        a. The prayer unto his God was recorded in "the book of the kings of Israel."

            I. This document is lost.

            II. Someone created a fictional prayer—that became an apocryphal book.

        b. Manasseh's praying led him to feel freer in his chains than he ever had felt on the throne.

    2. When God brings you low and convicts you of sin: Call upon God!

        a. The Apostle Paul writes: "For whosoever shall call upon the name of the Lord shall be saved" (Romans 10:13).

        b. God says in Isaiah 45:22: "Look unto me, and be ye saved, all the ends of the earth: for I am God, and there is none else."

            I. There is a look that saves!

            II. We are saved by grace alone through faith alone in Christ Jesus.

            III. There is a simplicity to salvation!!!

        c. This faith is a gift of God!

            I. About the children of God, the Apostle John writes: "Which were born, not of blood, nor of the will of the flesh, nor of the will of man, but of God" (John 1:13).

    3. Sometimes it takes a crisis for a sinful man to realize the folly of the idols he worships.

        a. He finds that his idols are bent reeds that break.

        b. They are unable to help!

III. The Transformation

a. God heard and forgave Manasseh and transformed him into a godly king.

    I. A God who shows mercy to repentant sinners.

        1. II Kings 33:13b: "and he was intreated of him, and heard his supplication,"

            a. The LORD does not treat us as our sins deserve.

                I. Psalm 103:10,14)

                II. God hears the prayers of elect backsliders.

                III. God's graciousness is remarkable by any human standards!

            b. God never fails to hear the cry of the humble!

                I. There is one voice that surely reaches God's ear and moves His heart—it is the voice of one of His chastened children!

                II. Cry to God out of the depth—and you can be sure that God will hear.

                III. Manasseh's experience may be repeated in us!!!

        2. God hears and forgives on the basis of the sacrifice of His Son.

            a. The King of the Jews who was to come would pay for the sins of King Manasseh—as He would pay for the sins of King David and King Solomon.

            b. Solely on the basis of the cross—where His justice was satisfied—and Christ paid for the sin and guilt of His people---God has mercy.

            c. The blood of Christ is able to cleanse great sinners—sinners as bad as King Manasseh---and sinners as evil as we!

            d. So there is hope for sinners—but the only hope is found in Jesus Christ and His righteousness!!!!

    II. God restored Manasseh to his throne.

        1. II Kings 33:13b: "and brought him again to Jerusalem into his kingdom."

b. God confirmed Manasseh's faith.

    I. "Then Manasseh knew that the Lord he was God." (II Chron. 33:13b)

        1. The *best part* is not that Manasseh was restored to his throne, *but that he knew that the Lord He was God.*

            a. The name had been but a name to him, but now it had become a reality.

      I. If we have cried to God, and been hard, then we have a profound conviction.

      II. We have experienced personally the wonder of a loving Father.

   b. The Apostle of love said: "We know that we are of God,...and we know that the Son of God is come, and hath given us an understanding, that we may know Him that is true."

  2. There was another king who had exalted himself *against* God, Nebuchadnezzar.

   a. He knew that God was God, but with a knowledge much different from that of Manasseh.

      I. A confession was forced out of Nebuchadnezzar.

   b. How different is the knowledge of the child of God!

      I. Manasseh knew that Jehovah was his God!

      II. He knows that God knows Him with a sovereign, elective, love.

II. King Manasseh was a model of repentance.

  1. He removed the idols.

   a. He knew that God alone must be worshipped in His temple at Jerusalem.

   b. II Chronicles 33:15: "And he took away the strange gods, and the idol out of the house of the LORD, and all the altars that he had built in the mount of the house of the LORD, and in Jerusalem, and cast them out of the city."

  2. He restored the true worship of Jehovah, which had been suspended.

   a. II Chronicles 33:16: "And he repaired the altar of the LORD, and sacrificed thereon peace offerings and thank offerings, and commanded Judah to serve the LORD God of Israel."

   b. He commanded the people to worship God in the temple.

   c. The altar of God was restored.

  3. He built up the walls of Jerusalem. (II Chronicles 33:14)

   a. A sign of God's protection.

   b. Manasseh fortified the walls of Jerusalem.

      I. He placed garrisons in fortified cities.

   c. Manasseh left a sad legacy.

III. A little too late.

   1. Manasseh in the last few years of his reign tried to reverse his many years of apostasy.

      a. But the people continued to sacrifice at the high places.

      b. Idolatry was not rooted out of the hearts of the men of Judah.

   2. Manasseh was forgiven and saved.

      a. The threatened judgment of Judah was deferred for 50 years.

      b. But Manasseh's sins made the punishment of Judah unavoidable, because Judah would not now thoroughly turn to the Lord, but will always fall back into the sins of Manasseh.

   3. The consequences of your sins can be lasting and life-long—and even beyond your death.

      a. Manasseh set a terrible example for his son Ahaz—and he who had sowed the wind in child-rearing, reaped the whirlwind.

      b. He had a wicked son—whose wicked reign was ended by God after 2 short years.

      c. Because of the sins of Manasseh and the sins of the people of Judah under his reign, God would send Judah into captivity in Babylon!

IV. But Manasseh was forgiven and saved.

   1. God would show mercy to him in his generations.

   2. His grandson, King Josiah, would be a reformer like no one else before him.

   3. So Christians, when you remember King Manasseh, you should remember him as a man who is like you and me--a sinner and yet a saint!!!!

   4. A saint—a holy one—a man who had a small beginning of the new obedience because of the remarkable grace of our Heavenly Father!

Chapter 25

The Weaknesses of John H. Broadus' Homiletics

Derek Thomas on Bad Homiletical Models

entitled this chapter "The Weaknesses of John H. Broadus' Homiletics" because I wanted to get your attention. I originally had as my working title: "The Strengths and Weaknesses of John H. Broadus' Homiletics." I think that what I have to say about the weaknesses of Broadus' homiletics is more important for you to hear. But before we look at the Homiletics of the Southern Baptist homiletician, let us listen to what Derek Thomas has to say about bad homiletical models.

Derek Thomas identifies a few bad homiletical models. First, some of the Puritans made the mistake of preaching too many consecutive sermons on books of the Bible. "To take an extreme example, we can safely say that Joseph Caryl, who took twenty-four years to expound the book of Job in 424 sermons (averaging ten sermons per chapter), was not a good model for preaching the book of Job or for expository preaching in general."[418]

Second, Dr. Martyn Lloyd-Jones' ambitious series of preaching through books of the Bible has been imitated by "practitioners that weren't up to the task."[419] Long series like Lloyd-Jones preached on Romans and Ephesians may not be fitting given "the make up of the congregation."[420]

Third, Charles H. Spurgeon's exegetical weakness mean that he should not be a model for the practitioner of expository preaching. Thomas expresses his dismay when he sees how Spurgeon exegetes his text. "His *intent* was always to be expository; in *practice*, he could sometimes introduce matters into the sermon that did not properly emerge from the text, and he

---

[418] Derek W. H. Thomas "Expository Preaching" in Feed My Sheep: A Passionate Plea for Preaching, R. Albert Mohler...[et al.], General editor, Don Kistler. (Sanford, Florida: Reformation Trust Publishing, 2008), 40.
[419] Ibid., 41.
[420] Ibid., 41.

never engaged in consecutive expository preaching."

Thomas identifies six benefits of preaching consecutive expository sermons from a book of the Bible. First, the *lectio continua* approach helps the church learn the whole Bible.[421] Second, preaching consecutive sermons from a book lead to the preaching of passages that would otherwise be infrequently chosen as texts.[422] Third, as the minister preaches on sometimes difficult passages, the congregation learns how to read and interpret their Bible as they observe their pastor at work.[423] Fourth, it introduces Christians to the full counsel of God.[424] Fifth, it ensures variety. If the minister selects different texts, he might begin to select the kind of texts that appeal to him.[425] Sixth, the preacher does not need to worry about what text to pick for the next week. Spurgeon needed to select two new texts for each Sunday. "It frees preachers from the tyranny of having to choose a text" each week.[426] He will simply select his text from the next section in the book that he is reading. It also "enables him to think well ahead."[427]

In this chapter we want to look at the homiletics of a leading homiletician, John Broadus. He has had a long influence on American approaches to homiletics through an influential textbook on preaching. We first look at what Broadus has to say about an important homiletical issue, the reason for and value of three divisions (or points) in a sermon.

John Broadus on the Use and Nature of Divisions (the 3 points)

John Broadus discusses the question of divisions. He notes that the ancient Greek and Roman orators rarely set out clear divisions. "Yet, in all cases they followed a definite plan and advanced in an orderly manner."[428] The church fathers imitated the Roman orators and did not announce their divisions.[429]

Unfortunately, in the 1700s and 1800s there was an "excessive multiplication of formal divisions and equally formal subdivisions."[430] Phillips Brooks criticized American preachers because "In the desire to make a sermon seem free and spontaneous, there is a prevalent dislike to giving it

---

[421] Ibid., 44.
[422] Ibid., 45.
[423] Ibid., 45.
[424] Ibid., 46.
[425] Ibid., 46-47.
[426] Ibid., 47.
[427] Ibid., 47.
[428] John A. Broadus, On the Preparation and Delivery of Sermons. (New York: Harper & Row, 1944), 111.
[429] Ibid., 111.
[430] Ibid., 111.

its necessary formal structure and organism."[431] Brooks mentions that people would joke about three-point sermons. Broadus concludes that

While not necessary, distinctly marked divisions will usually be of service, not only making the train of thought plain to the hearers, but also in serving to the preacher himself, both as compelling to logical correctness and completeness of preparation and in helping him to remember in an extemporaneous delivery.[432]

Broadus discusses how many divisions that there should be in a sermon and states that "we must consult simplicity and, at the same time, vividness and variety."[433]

Why Sermons Have Three Points

Broadus explains why sermons naturally have three points.

But the custom itself must have had some natural origin. Now a principal reason for it is seen from the consideration stated above; three divisions will give a goodly variety without distracting attention or bordering the burden in the memory.[434]

The logic in syllogisms comes out in three-point sermons:

A syllogism, when fully stated, furnishes three propositions. There cannot be a climax without at least three steps. Three gives the idea of completeness,--beginning, middle, and end.[435]

Broadus believes that "these considerations go to show that it is not accidental, not strange that elaborate discourses so often have three divisions."[436] I agree.

The First Point

Given the confusions surrounding Broadus' conception of what the title and proposition are, we shouldn't be surprised that the great homiletician also makes mistakes when it comes to his conception of the first division in a sermon.

---

[431] Ibid., 112.
[432] Ibid., 112.
[433] Ibid., 113.
[434] Ibid., 114.
[435] Ibid., 114.
[436] Ibid., 114.

What should your first point (or division) be like? Broadus tells us what should characterize the divisions:

> The character of the divisions must be determined by their relation to the subject proposed and to each other. (1) As to the former, it is obvious that no one division should be coextensive with the subject; and yet inexperienced sermonizers sometimes unconsciously have it so.[437]

When Broadus tells us that "no one division should be coextensive with the subject" he seems to be saying that no division should express the main point (theme) of the text. This is a serious error. The influence of homileticians like Broadus explain the lack of development of the main point of sermons in the first (and main!) point.

But if it is the case, as I am arguing, that you should have a simple theme which expresses the main point of the text as your title and if this expresses the main point of the text, then certainly the first point of the sermon will explain and develop this theme.

Preachers apparently do not perceive that they cannot develop the main point of a text, if they do not first explain what the main point is! One of the devastating problems with preaching is that ministers assume that everybody knows what their main point means. Therefore, they do not develop the theme. Instead they jump to secondary considerations. They jump from the what to the how.

In proper homiletics the second and third divisions will bring out other aspects of the theme and develop it further. In other words, I am arguing for the fact that the first point of the sermon always should express the main point of the text.

Logic is on my side. How can you talk about something if you do not know what it is? How can you develop implications of a theme, if you have not looked at what the theme itself means?

Let's say that you have a legitimate thesis statement that expresses the entire argument of your sermon. But what do you have to deal with first when you are writing a paper and, therefore, elaborating upon and defending your thesis statement. You need to explain and defend the central thesis. Only then can you talk about a variety of other matters. There is logic in a sermon when you first explain the meaning of your theme in your first point and then move on to other important, subsidiary points that move the argument forward.

---

[437] Ibid., 114.

Do not be surprised if a sermon should progress like this:
    What?
    How?
    Why?

This is parallel with:

    I.   The Meaning
    II. The Manner
    III. The Purpose

I get the sense that ministers do not think that it is cool to have a first point entitled "The Meaning" or "What?" Not flashy enough. But the main problem with their antipathy to having a first point that is "The Meaning" is that they were taught bad homiletics. They do not expect to develop the big idea in the first point. From a logical perspective, if one examines their written essay or outline, it will appear that the theme is being developed in the first two points or in all three! But when you are developing your theme in all three points, I can guarantee that you are not really grasping the need to develop the theme at all. It is the subsidiary points that will be emphasized.

If you want the central point of the passage to be the main thing in the sermon, then you need to deal with it first. You need to explain and develop the central concept in the text. Only then can you logically proceed to talk about the subsidiary ideas that are covered in the second and third points. It is not that these subsidiary points are unimportant. Application is not unimportant. But the application will flow out of the main point of the text. How can you know what the proper application is, if you have not considered what the big idea really is?

Broadus does have a proper concern for the fact that each one of the divisions needs to stand in a distinct and symmetrical relationship with each other. He writes,

> As regards the relation of the divisions to each other, they must be distinct and symmetrical. It is not uncommon for unpracticed speakers to have one division that really includes another, and very common to see one that includes some part of what also comes under another.[438]

Broadus addresses a serious problem in sermon structures. He is correct in perceiving that each division should contain what is properly and logically

---

[438] Ibid., 115.

included in that section. But he doesn't see a more serious problem which is the fact that he talks about the various points being symmetrical without making the point that it is the first point that communicates the main point of the text. In some sense the three divisions will not be symmetrical. After all, the big idea of the text is the big idea. If the three divisions are symmetrical from the perspective of logic and importance, then there will be three big ideas in the sermon. This evil is wide-spread.

Broadus also discusses whether the minister should announce his divisions. He thinks that the minister should not announce his divisions in the introduction of the sermon unless three conditions exist. First, he thinks that it is okay to announce the divisions if the argument is challenging. Second, he thinks that the divisions can be announced. If it is important for the congregation to follow and be aware of the various steps in the argument. Third, he thinks that the divisions can be mentioned when they will awake interest.[439]

I disagree.

If the whole point of preaching is to communicate the message with simplicity and clarity so that the congregation above all understands the message, then ordinarily, the minister should let the congregation know where he is going with the message. It is easier to understand the message if you have a roadmap.

I know that research shows that a more educated congregation would rather be surprised than to know things ahead of time. But in giving the three divisions of the sermon you are not giving away the farm. You are providing a general sense of the direction of the argument so that the congregation knows that you are heading on a journey to a sure destination.

When ministers do not announce their divisions, it probably is a sign that they will wander sideways rather than make progress towards a goal. I think that the announcing of concise, clear, and simple divisions does not overtax the minds of the hearers and allows them to get a sense of direction.

If you have long divisions (which you probably shouldn't have), then you better make sure that when you come to each point that you work on explaining the long name (title of the division). You will need to work to get it into the memory of the congregation. Too many sermons have a title along with three additional divisions that each contain a longish phrase. If this is the case with your message, you are in danger of delivering four messages that are patched together to counterfeit a unified sermon.

Broadus valued the use of argument in the sermon. He thinks that the minister "Must sometimes follow a line of reasoning, i.e., make an argument,

---

[439] Ibid., 118.

to sustain his judgment and so establish the truth and justify the application he would make of it."[440] He admits that "There are preachers, it is true, who seem to consider that they have no occasion for reasoning, that everything is to be accomplished by authoritative assertion and impassioned appeal."[441]

One merely needs to read sermons by Jonathan Edwards or John Piper to see the power of careful argumentation in sermons. On the other hand, Broadus warns against argumentative preaching.

> Yet in preaching we need not act as if everything had to be proved, and every proof to be a formal argument. Some things cannot be proved, some do not need to be, and others have been sufficiently proved before and should now be taken for granted. Elaborate argument which is not called for will only awaken doubt or lead to weariness and disgust.[442]

I think that an over reliance on argument as a rhetorical technique undermines the authority of God's Word. As Christians we do not need to be argued into everything. We simply need to submit ourselves to God's revelation in Scripture.

Passionate Persuasion

Broadus thinks that the minister should engage in passionate persuasion. He has a section entitled "Persuasion unto vital response."[443] The Calvinistic Baptist theologian thinks that we should try to "persuade men" just like the Apostle Paul did. Persuasion involves passion and emotion. Broadus states that the preachers "Task is not merely the calm exhibition of motives, that men may coolly act according to them. Many truths of religion are imminently adapted to stir the feelings, and to speak of such truths without feeling and awakening emotion is unnatural and wrong."[444]

> It is matter of universal observation that a speaker who would excite deep feeling must feel deeply himself. Demosthenes sometimes spoke with such passionate earnestness that his enemies said he was deranged. Cicero remarks that it is only passion that makes the orator a king; that, though he himself had tried every means of moving men, yet his successes were due, not to talent or skill, but to a mighty fire in his soul so that he could not contain himself; and that the hearer would

---

[440] Ibid., 167.
[441] Ibid., 167.
[442] Ibid., 169.
[443] Ibid., 215.
[444] Ibid., 217.

never be kindled unless the speech came to him burning.[445]

Broadus laments:

> Alas! It is often our chief difficulty in preaching to feel ourselves as we ought to feel. And a genuine fervor cannot be produced to order by a direct effort of will. Nor is it possible to conceal from the audience the deficiency of real emotion by high and loud or tremulous tones of voice, wild gesticulations, etc. We must cultivate our religious sensibilities, must keep our souls habitually in contact with gospel truth, and maintain, by the union of abundant prayer and self-denying activity, that ardent love to God and that tender love to man which will give us, without an effort, true pathos and passion.[446]

Broadus states that

> When the preacher does feel very deeply, his mere exhortation will have some power to move, especially where he has personal influence as a devout man, or for any reason has the sympathies of his audience.[447]

Among the various emotions that should affect the people of God are "fear, disgust, wonder, anger, subjection, elation, and tender emotion."[448] Broadus warns that the preacher cannot remained impassioned throughout his entire discourse. There are appropriate times to express feeling, especially in the third point as the preacher applies the message to the hearts and lives of his hearers. That is the time to preach with passion and "full vigor."[449]

Energy the Characteristic Property of an Eloquent Style

What is characteristic of an eloquent style? Broadus believes that it is energy. He defines an energetic style to include "all that we mean by such separate terms as animation, force, and passion."[450] What is the relation between energy and passion?

---

[445] Ibid., 218-19.
[446] Ibid., 219.
[447] Ibid., 219.
[448] Ibid., 221.
[449] Ibid., 221.
[450] Ibid., 252.

Passion—which in its milder and more tender forms we call "pathos" and in its highest form the "sublime"—has its effect upon the feelings, often by means of the imagination; and both force and passion aim at last to influence the will. It is thus plain that the characteristic property of an eloquent style is energy."[451]

How will there be passion in a sermon?

The chief requisite to energetic style is an energetic nature. There must be vigorous thinking, earnest, if not passionate feeling, and the determined purpose to accomplish some object, or the man's style will have no true, exalted energy. It is in this sense emphatically true that an orator is born, not made.[452]

Broadus is convinced that "if a man has not force of character, a passionate soul, he will never be really eloquent."[453] For there to be passion there must be an appeal to the imagination. Concrete ideas must be brought before the imagination of the audience. "In order to give animation and passion to style, there must be an appeal to the imagination."[454]

In oral communication, short sentences are preferred. "In fact, very long periodic sentences are, in speaking, to be avoided."[455]

Given Broadus's emphasis on both imagination and passion, it is not surprising that he says that

Perhaps the chief element of energy in style is the use of figures of speech. Passionate feeling, whether anger, fear, love, or the emotion of the sublime, naturally express itself by means of bold imagery,-- bold, though never elaborate or far-fetched.[456]

All one needs to do is to read Spurgeon's work to see that the power of his sermons was found in his use of figures of speech. Broadus is correct in saying that "metaphor is more conducive to energy than comparison."[457] He discusses how synecdoche, hyperbole, and personification all contribute to an energetic style.

---

[451] Ibid,. 252.
[452] Ibid., 252.
[453] Ibid., 252.
[454] Ibid., 254.
[455] Ibid., 257.
[456] Ibid., 263.
[457] Ibid., 263.

There will be effective communication when there is a variety of energy demonstrated in a discourse. Broadus states that "in highly passionate speaking, there must be variety, alternation."[458] Just like in physical exercise where there is variety between intense exercise and times of rest, so one needs variety of emotion in a sermon. If the minister tries to stir up mental excitement during the entire sermon, he will over stimulate the congregation.

---

[458] Ibid., 267.

Chapter 26

Nonsense about Propositions from the Celebrated Broadus

Reject Attention Grabbing Titles

John A. Broadus is partially responsible for a great evil found in the homiletical structures of sermons today. In his influential work, *On the Preparation and Delivery of Sermons*, he introduces confusion and complexity into the basic structure of a sermon.[459] John Broadus was on the founding faculty of Southern Baptist Theological Seminary in the 19th century. He taught homiletics and later was the second president of the seminary.

The first evil Broadus introduces is exhorting the minister to have a title or theme that is an attention-getter rather than one that expresses the main point of the text. He gives this poor advice: "The principal function of the title is to attract and interest the public."[460] He quotes Ozora Davis with approval. This writer compared a sermon title to the title of a book: "so the attractiveness of a sermon is conditioned largely by the choice of the title."[461]

William Zinsser schooled a couple of generation of American non-fiction writers on the importance of brevity, simplicity, and clarity in communication. I am convinced that, as a rule, the title of the sermon should be the main point of the text. It should communicate the central, simple idea of the text.

The problem with having an attention-getting title is that it confuses the auditor. One imagines that the title will express the main point of the sermon, but when it is merely expressing an attention-getting idea, by definition it will not express the main point of the text.

---

[459] John A. Broadus, On the Preparation and Delivery of Sermons. (New York: Harper & Row, 1944).
[460] Ibid., 54.
[461] Ibid., 54. Cited from Principles of Preaching, p. 199.

The congregation will immediately be faced with two themes, the title and the actual central theme of the text.

This is confusing.

The congregation will be dealing with two realities, a title and then the actual main point. The actual theme of the sermon probably should express the unique language of the text if it is going to communicate what God's unique revelation is in this specific text. This protects freshness in preaching and keeps the minister from laziness.

Confusion is introduced when the congregation really has two titles or themes before them. The title at the very least distracts the congregation from what the actual main point of the text is. While the catchy title was supposed to attract the attention of the congregation, it distracts the congregation from the central idea of the text.

The central idea of a text ought to, by its very nature, be of interest to the children of God. We do not need to play dress-up with the ideas and rhetoric in God's Word to make them interesting to Christians. I am not against poetry and rhetoric in the pulpit. But I am against showy rhetoric that is a mere attention-getting device. This is sophistry.

The Wretched "Proposition" of Broadus

John H. Broadus has negatively impacted American preaching with his idea that the title should not communicate the main idea of the text. The announced title is one thing and the actual main point of the text is another thing. Broadus adds to his homiletical errors. It is easy to grasp why he makes this next mistake. He has not given us a sermon title/theme that with simplicity, brevity, and clarity communicates the main point of the text. Yet he knows in the back of his mind that he should communicate the main point of the text.

So he goes to the opposite extreme. He realizes that in his introduction he cannot express the main point with simplicity and brevity in a theme because he selected a catchy title. Yet he sees the need for communicating the central idea of the text to the congregation. Broadus invents what he calls "the Proposition" to rectify this error. He hurls a great mass of information at the congregation in his proposition. He provides a complete thesis statement in his introduction.

He gives a complex thesis statement that not a single member in the congregation will be able to remember, process, digest, or internalize.

Martin Luther tells us that he tried to preach to the children in the congregation at Wittenberg, because he was convinced that if the children could understand him, the adults would too. Not even professors of theology in the congregation can remember the complex proposition that is just read one time at the beginning of the sermon. The minister theoretically lays out the whole argument of the sermon in this proposition.

I believe that complex thesis statements are for term papers, essays, and dissertations. They are an offense to the children in the congregation. Following Luther's maxim they are, therefore, also an offense to the whole congregation. The minister throws everything at them at once. Instead of providing them with a simple, concise, clear theme that communicates the main point of the text; the preacher commits the error of complexity.

Broadus' Dastardly Definition of a "Proposition"

Broadus defines his dastardly "proposition":

> The Proposition deserves more attention than is given by many preachers. It is a statement of the subject as the preacher proposes to develop it. It is subject (idea) and predicate. The subject answers the question, What is the sermon about? The proposition answers the question, What is the sermon? Phelps likens the proposition to the trunk from which the body of the sermon expands, the root being the idea in the text..."the discourse is the proposition unfolded, and the proposition is the discourse condensed" (Fenelon). Its form should be one complete declarative sentence, simple, clear, and cogent. It should contain no unnecessary or ambiguous words. "It should contain all that is essential to the sermon, no less and no more, and no other than the truth of the subject, stated in cumulative order." It is important to distinguish between the proposition and the objective. The latter has to do with the desired ends of the sermon in the character and conduct of the hearers; the former, with the form and substance of the message.[462]

I must confess my amazement at such nonsense coming from the celebrated Broadus. He acts like the proposition is a thesis statement for a sermon, just like one has a thesis statement in a doctoral dissertation. But then he claims that the proposition is distinct from the objective. Practically speaking this means that Broadus' imagined proposition is only a thesis statement for the first point of the sermon—but not the third point that probably will move

---

[462] Ibid., 54-55.

towards application and ramming home the message to the hearts and lives of God's people. Therefore, we have a thesis statement that leaves out "the desired ends of the sermon in the character and conduct of the hearers." As if the third point of the sermon does not also contain an important idea and argument?

It is a damning indictment of Broadus' approach that the main idea in this proposition is not expressed in the title. It is not expressed in a simple theme at all!

In fact, the central theme is almost hidden from the congregation. Only an attentive hearer will by random chance figure out what the proposition is or what the central theme of the sermon is. Broadus even states that this proposition will not even be "formally stated with any such introductory words."[463] In fact, it can be "incidental; and sometimes it does not appear at all in the sermon."[464] How then will the congregation know what the complex proposition is or what the central idea of the sermon is? Broadus tells us. What he says does not lend itself to optimism about covenant children perceiving the main point: "But usually the reader, or hearer, is more interested if in the introduction or early in the sermon there is a revealing statement of the heart of the message."[465] What are the chances of the ordinary listener catching on that this "revealing statement" reveals the simple, clear meaning of the text? Nil. Maybe a homiletics professor or fellow preacher will grasp that the main point was just mentioned. I dare you to poll a congregation that sits under such preaching to discover how many people understood that the "revealing statement" was revealing.

Don't get me wrong. Broadus is correct in wanting a main idea to be developed. He is right in wanting order, logic, and development in the sermon. I have no problem with full-fledged thesis statements and a right way of handling them within the context of a sermon. Broadus wants the preacher to clarify and develop one main argument: "To write out a proposition as one begins to compose the sermon, even though it may have to be revised more than once as one proceeds, is to give point and direction to the writing. It will serve as a sort of magnet to keep one on the main track."[466] Amen to this.

---

[463] Ibid., 56.
[464] Ibid., 56.
[465] Ibid., 56.
[466] Ibid., 57.

Wretched Examples Commended by John H. Broadus

It is also astonishing that Broadus would set forth such wretched examples of propositions as exemplars. Check out this proposition that he commends from Horace Bushnell:

> The truth I propose then for your consideration is this: That God has a definite life-plan for every human person, girding him, visibly or invisibly, for some exact thing which it will be the true significance and glory of his life to have accomplished.[467]

You have read through this proposition once. Lay this book down immediately and go explain this proposition to a child in another room. Find your 12-year-old child and tell him or her what this proposition is and what biblical text you think that Horace Bushnell is trying to preach on. Good luck!

Broadus then selects another exemplary proposition from a Bushnell sermon. This sermon contains the strange, but apparently catchy title (that lacks a verb) "Unconscious Influence":

> Thus it is that men are ever teaching unconsciously the springs of motion in each other, (so that) one man without thought or intention or even a consciousness of the fact is ever leading some other after him.[468]

Too much information! Too many words! Bushnell violates the laws of simplicity, clarity, and brevity. I am struck by the abstractness of the marvelous propositions that Broadus holds up for our admiration. Bushnell is gifted at making Scripture truth abstract and hiding the actual rhetoric of the Bible.

Broadus then gives us another magnificent specimen of a proposition, this time from a sermon entitled "Light of the World" by Phillips Brooks. Broadus provides us with two specimens that come from the same sermon:

> [1] That the soul of man carries the highest possibilities within itself, and that what Christ does for it is to kindle and call forth these possibilities to actual existence.

---

[467] Ibid., 55. Cited from Sermons for the New Life, p. 10.
[468] Ibid., 55. Cited from Davis, Principles of Preaching, p. 21.

[2] Christ when he comes finds the soul or the world really existent, really having within itself its holiest capabilities, really moving, though dimly and darkly, in spite of tis hindrances, in its true directions; and what he does for it is to quicken it through and through, to sound the bugle of its true life in its ears, to make it feel the nobleness of movements which have seemed to it ignoble, the hopefulness of impulses which have seemed hopeless, to bid it be itself.[469]

We discover to our delight that Broadus does have some discretion! He tells us that "The student will readily see that the briefer is the better statement."[470] But the esteemed professor does not readily see that both are garbage. The content of the propositions appears (on the face of them) to be Pelagian garbage. But both are stellar examples of obfuscation and abstraction.

J. Daniel Boumann Imitates Broadus' Errors

J. Daniel Baumann imitates the errors of Broadus in his influential textbook on preaching that has reached multiple editions. Instead of teaching the preacher how to identify a theme that will be the main point (big idea) of the text, he writes about three things: the subject, the proposition, and the title. He identifies these latter three things as the important elements in homiletics.

> Early in the development of any sermon satisfactory answers must be found for three questions: What will I talk about? What will I say about it? How will I advertise it? Response to the first is the "subject"; to the second is the "proposition"; to the third is the "title." We will deal with these sermonic ingredients in order.[471]

If you have the wrong ingredients, you will not make good cookies. Baumann's recipe lacks a key ingredient. As a teenager I baked at my uncle's Dutch bakery. I was supposed to add 1 ½ oz. of salt and baking soda to a large cookie recipe. Instead I added 1 pound and ½ oz. of both. Fortunate for me, a little boy walked by my table and snitched some of the raw cookie dough. He thought he was in for a treat. He began spitting and sputtering and emptied his mouth in the metal sink. We investigated the problem and discovered my ingredient error. Baumann's recipe for homiletics will leave a similar bad taste in the mouths of parishioners.

---

[469] Ibid., 55. Cited from Davis, Principles of Preaching, pp. 43ff.
[470] Ibid., 55.
[471] J. Daniel Baumann An Introduction to Contemporary Preaching 5th Edition (Grand Rapids: Baker Book House, 1984), 123

Baumann defines the subject as something that "states what the sermon is about. It is one word or phrase which defines the limits of sermonic consideration."[472] He talks about the necessity of identifying a narrow and specific subject. The example he provides of subjects are not like the themes I am proposing. Examples are:

> "Prayer as Adoration"
> "The Purpose of Prayer"
> "The Way of salvation"

Baumann admits that they are general subjects, which they are, but they are not stand-alone themes with a subject and verb as I propose. How can you express the main idea of a text without a verb?

Baumann describes the proposition much the same as Broadus: "It is a succinct statement of the subject in sentence form."[473] He even follows the same folly of Broadus in claiming that this critical proposition need not be stated in the sermon. That is funny. The title will not state it. The divisions will not state it. The minster may even choose not to divulge it. Yet wonder of wonders, Baumann imagines that the congregation will know what it is. Apparently he thinks that congregants can read their minister's mind. Answering his own question about whether the proposition should be stated, Bauman answers:

> Generally yes. It need not be, however. A carefully worded proposition is necessary for guidance in the preparation and delivery of the sermon, but the preacher may choose not to divulge it in so many words. If it is clearly in his mind and in the minds of his listeners, that is all that matters.[474]

He argues that "The proposition, latent or manifest, at the outset, middle, or conclusion of the sermon, is the best guarantee that a single truth will emerge in clarity."[475]

Why would a preacher withhold the main point of his message from the congregants? Why hide the proposition? One reason that I can think of us that the preacher knows that his proposition is too complex. He knows that it violates the laws of simplicity and clarity.

---

[472] Ibid., 123.
[473] Ibid., 126.

[474] Ibid., 128.
[475] Ibid., 128.

If the concern of the ministers is to convey the main point of the text to his hearers, there is no excuse for withholding the clearest and simplest statement of this big idea from the congregation. If the proposition helped the minister wrap his mind around the text, why will he not share it with the congregation so that they can wrap their mind around the text as well? If the minister who studied the text all week long needs the guidance of the proposition, how much more the congregation that is introduced to the text in 45 brief minutes! If there is a single truth that should emerge in simplicity and clarity, then the minister ought to make this his title or theme.

The idea of presenting a proposition (a sentence-long thesis statement) at the beginning of the sermon is too much information, too soon. According to me, the preacher should present the main idea of the text in a simple theme. This theme will become the title of the sermon. It is the one big idea that he wants to imprint on the minds of the congregation.

Baumann plays the same game as Broadus in defining the nature of the sermon title. It "is an imaginative, suggestive word or phrase used in the advertising of the sermon."[476] It "is used solely for public purposes. It is not a guide for the preacher in his preparation nor his selection of materials per se."[477] In his infinite wisdom, Baumann dares attack a few homileticians who want the title to express the substance of the text. He takes "issue" with Brown, Clinard, and Northcutt who argue the following:

> An effective title furnishes the preacher a divisible whole from which he can develop the framework of the sermon body. Even a general idea of the title helps the preacher in collecting, selecting, and condensing materials. A precise title is an invaluable tool in limiting and unifying each and every item in the structural development of the sermon.[478]

Brown, Clinard, and Northcutt are on the side of the angels.

Baumann himself recommends such baubles and tom-foolery as the following for sermon titles:

"The Wages of Sin is Aaaughh!"

"Siamese Twins: Pulpit and Pew"

"Those Four-Letter Words"

"Freeway Faith"

"A Pastor Ponders Vietnam"

"Morticians of the Mind"

"The Roar of a Lion, the Heart of a Rabbit"[479]

---

476 Ibid., 128.
477 Ibid., 128.
478 Ibid., 128. Cited by Baumann.
479 Ibid., 129.

Titles are for advertising purposes. They should be "contemporary", "succinct", and "stimulate interest."[480]

I get the feeling that Baumann thinks that he needs to dress up the main idea in the text for church. He has to make it appear sexy with a catchy, relevant, and cool title. Why Baumann thinks that the actual main point of the text isn't contemporary or able to stimulate interest is beyond me. With textbooks on preaching like Baumann's, it is no wonder that preachers have not learned to prepare unified and organized messages that find their unity and organization in a simple, concise, clear theme that expresses the main point of the text.

When was the last time a child or teenager left church and could tell his parents what the proposition of a sermon was? It is one thing for a child to be able to express the main point (theme) of the sermon. A child might say, "The sermon was about 'Putting on the Lord Jesus Christ.'"

I am convinced that preaching should attempt to communicate the main point of the text in the simplest way so as to get it to stick in the mind of the saints.

Donald G. McDougall on the Central Idea

The minister needs to identify the central idea in the text. Donald G. McDougall defines the central idea in a text: "The central idea of a true expository message reflects the central idea intended by the Bible author himself."[481] The preacher may not invent the theme of the text. He is a servant of the Word of God. The minister needs to get his own private opinions out of the way and let the unique revelation of God in the text shine forth. McDougall emphasizes that the exegete must determine the central idea of the text.

Our task is NOT to create our own message;
  It is rather to communicate the author's message.
  Our task is NOT to create a central theme;
  It is rather to
    1. find the author's central theme
    2. build a message around that theme, and
    3. make that theme the central part of all we have to say.[482]

---

[480] Ibid., 130.
[481] Donald G. McDougall "Central Ideas, Outlines, and Titles" in Rediscovering Expository Preaching: John MacArthur, Jr. and the Master's Seminary Faculty Ed. Richard L. Mayhue (Dallas: Word Publishing, 1992), 229.
[482] Ibid., 229.

McDougall provides advice on how to identify the central idea in a text. Sometimes the central idea is "found at a single point in the text."[483] He provides an example:

> 1 Tim. 4:6-16. The main thought of 1 Tim. 4:6-16 is in verse 16, where Paul states, "Pay close attention to yourself and to your teaching." This is central to the entire passage. It helps if the expositor and his audience are aware of this principal thought from the very beginning of a message. It helps them piece the rest of the passage together.[484]

A second way to identify the central idea in a passage is to find it in the wider context. A third way to identify the central idea is to notice a recurring theme in the context. "As one reads and repeatedly rereads certain passages, an outstanding idea (or group of ideas) comes to the fore."[485] McDougall challenges the Broadus/Baumann tradition concerning titles. "Devising catchy titles for messages has become a highly developed skill for many preachers."[486] For preachers who are naïve and foolishly optimistic about the importance of a catchy title, McDougal warns: "It is possible to labor hard and long to come up with that special wording to attract the attention of many, only to find that very few people pay attention to it or *even care*."[487] I also think that if you think that you need to dance on your head with a catchy title to catch the congregation's attention, won't you have to continue to dance on your head to maintain their attention?McDougall, being on the side of the angels, argues that the title should reflect the central idea of the text. "Make the title reflect what the sermon will say."[488] I can only say "Amen" to this following statement: "The title should reflect the sermon content and should in no way transcend or obscure it."[489] The title should communicate the big idea of the text. "Make the title complement the message in its thoughtfulness and pattern."[490] The title, central idea, and outline "must accurately reflect, and none should obscure or take precedence over, the message of both the human and divine authors of Scripture."[491]

---

[483] Ibid., 229.
[484] Ibid., 229.
[485] Ibid., 232.
[486] Ibid., 239.
[487] Ibid., 239. Emphasis added.
[488] Ibid., 239.
[489] Ibid., 239.
[490] Ibid., 241.
[491] Ibid., 241.

Just as the central idea needs to be extracted from the text, the outline of the sermon should reflect the logic of the text. "There is a need to determine not only the central idea of a passage but also the outline that reflects the thinking of the author."[492]

McDougall exhorts: "**Find the outline; don't create it.**"[493] He writes: "**Let the passage dictate to you; don't dictate to it.** A major danger for those who prefer neat, three- or-four-point outlines with parallel points is that the passage may not lend itself to that luxury. When it does not, you dare not force it."[494]

There is something to what McDougall says here. At the same time, there is a logic to a message with three points. I often find that the logic in a text points to two clear points. But they often are the first and second points and the third point might very well turn out to be one that focuses on the significance, application, or lesson for believers of the main point of the text. The third point will involve putting together what you learned in the first and second points and driving it home to the life of the believer

When you have a good outline with good transitions, the sermon will flow. When there is good logic in the sermon, the sermon will flow forward. The naïve ear will not realize that the minister's sermon flows so smoothly because he has such a good skeletal outline. It is difficult to have smooth flow and logic in a sermon. It is a result of hard work. The outline should reflect the logic of the text. It should emerge from the "thought pattern of the author."[495]

Even though McDougall has a lot of good things to say about titles, central ideas, and outlines; one is let down by how he translates these insights into actual sermons. He manifests confusion in identifying the central idea of a text and then translating this into a logical outline.[496] The big thing does not remain the central idea in the sermon outline.

---

492 Ibid., 233.
493 Ibid., 233.
494 Ibid., 234.
495 Ibid., 234.
496 Ibid., 235ff.

Chapter 27
Legitimate Thesis Statements and Their Use

e have observed Broadus' attempt to convince us that we should either state or use a proposition. This proposition is like a thesis statement. It expresses the main argument of the first point of the sermon. We have no evidence of how it might logically include or lead to a second point in the sermon. The proposition is said not to include the objective—or the applicatory goal of the sermon (which is logically found in the third point of the sermon). It is an odd thesis statement that does not reflect the implications of what the thesis statement allegedly discovers. In an essay a thesis statement needs to contain not only the argument, but the conclusion. Yet Broadus does not want the proposition to include the significance, implications, or practical lessons for Christian life and belief that flow from his limited thesis statement.

Let's talk about what a legitimate thesis statement for a sermon can be like and how it can function in the act of preaching.

An Accurate Thesis Statement

First, an accurate thesis statement would express the argument that works its way through the first, second, and third points of the sermon. The value of expressing the main argument and logic of the sermon is that it will help the preacher to internalize the message. If you come up with a wordy, abstract thesis statement for each point in your sermon, your eyeballs will roll back in your head as you try to remember your foolish thesis statement. If you have a simple, brief, clear thesis statement you can remember it and comprehend the logic of your sermon. Then as you preach you will know where you are and where you are going.

An authentic thesis statement would lay out the central argument of the sermon as it moves from the first point (and the two central subpoints under it) to the second point (and the two central subpoints under it) to the third point (and the two central subpoints under it). It might be the case that the preacher has three central subpoints for his first point. If a minister regularly has more than two subpoints under his divisions, he needs to start synthesizing his material better. He probably is not organizing and synthesizing his material. But the number of subpoints will flow out of the text.

If a minister has three main subpoints under his first point, three more under his second point, and then three more under his third point, he will have 9 important ideas that he is trying to present. Too much information. Simplicity is lacking exactly where it is needed.

Let us assume that our preacher does have two major subpoints (a & b) under each one of his divisions (main points). If he has done his job well, he should be able to look at his outline and simply lay out the extended argument by reading out loud the main point, the two subpoints under it, the second point, the two subpoints under it, and the third point with its two subpoints. He will have read out the actual argument of his sermon.

I can imagine the minister or seminary student being shocked. They might say that this is too much information to share with the congregation. Every one of their subpoints is probably a nicely crafted sentence. They intended it as a thesis sentence. When you start adding six sentences to the brief name given to each one of the three points, things start adding up. The point I am getting at is that the thesis statement in a solid sermon will not be such a short thing, because it will a brief and concise statement (one short sentence) of the six thesis sentence statements that are made at the beginning of each one of your main subpoints.

If a minister wants to understand the thesis of his sermon, he needs to look at these thesis sentence statements in the subpoints. It is true that he can then try to state the thesis of the entire sermon in ever briefer ways. Let him try. This will be beneficial. But let the minister make sure that he is including something from every one of his points. Don't leave out the third point.

Should the preacher tell the congregation at the beginning of his sermon what his extended argument is? Probably not. Too much information. What I observe are preachers and seminary students who do not clearly introduce a theme that is the central idea of the sermon to the congregation. Instead they introduce a long thesis statement that they rattle off. They don't have it memorized. They read it off the page. It is too long to memorize (or internalize). If the minister is unable to memorize and internalize his thesis statement, neither will the congregation.

Let us suppose that our preacher does introduce a concise and clear theme in his introduction. It expresses the main point of the text. He sets the table for a sermon that will hammer home the central point of the text. He begins to introduce the ideas in the text to gain interest and let the congregation know where he is going. He provides the context. He uses a hook to draw the congregation in to the importance of the subject before them. Should he share his entire thesis statement with the congregation?

Not usually.

This is because the great principle of oral communication is: one idea at a time.

There might be rare exceptions where you want to get the congregation to see the outline bones of your sermon or the extended argument. You might want to communicate the thesis statement for rhetorical reasons. Jonathan Edwards and John Piper have shown the rhetorical power of providing an argument that is convincing for Christians. But you better be prepared to work if you are going to share your thesis statement in the introduction.

You will need to work hard. You will need to explain the thesis statement. You will need to repeat it. You will have to communicate where you are in the extended argument that you are producing.

But most of the time the saints can only handle one idea at a time.

A crucial element in all good preaching is to communicate one concept or idea at a time.

Not three ideas. That is complexity and confusion.

It is one thing to have elaborate thesis statements in a doctoral dissertation. The reader can reread the statement. The parishioner cannot hit reverse and listen to the thesis statement repeatedly. In the oral event of preaching, the congregation gets to hear a thesis statement once—unless the preacher repeats it.

But the reality is that the use of an extended thesis statement violates the laws of brevity, clarity, and simplicity.

A better idea is simply to develop the theme and main points (with their subpoints) one idea at a time. I have no problem with giving the congregation an idea of where the sermon (and the argument) are going. It is good to make transitions where you clarify the logic of the sermon. Preachers do not often enough clarify what they have proved and what they want to demonstrate next.

As you preach you are verbally communicating the logic and argument of the sermon. You need to advance the argument in ways that teenagers can understand. *Broadus and Bushnell act as if a sermon is for sophisticated adult intellectuals.* Adult intellectuals will comprehend a sermon better when you demonstrate the virtues of simplicity, clarity, and brevity. Your sermons and its points will have clarity as you develop one simple idea at a time.

Too often preacher run ideas into each other. They mash them. They squash them. They will not focus attention on one idea. They will not limit themselves. This is because their minds are confused. Complexity is the sign of a confused and lazy mind.

You need to tell yourself that you will be dealing with one main idea in each section of your sermon—and each of these *must* serve the communication of the main theme of the sermon. You need to develop, argue for, and communicate one idea. Then stop. Transition. Then develop, argue for, and communicate a new idea. Show the relationship between the new idea and the earlier one.

One of the greatest problems with preaching is that preachers do not develop their concepts in a rounded, distinct, and complete way. Everything is mushy, vague, and unfinished. The preacher needs to clarify each one of his main subpoints so that he is limiting himself to one idea in each of them and then sticking to that one concept in that section.

So what should we think of thesis statements? The benefit of thesis statements is that they clarify the argument and logic of an essay or a sermon. But Reformed preachers have not historically given out long thesis statements early in their sermons. This is not because their sermons lacked argument or logic. But they simplified matters by having each point (or division) advance the argument and logic of the sermon one step at a time. They did not feel the need to give away too much information early on in the sermon or to give away the farm. It was rather the theme or division that played the central role in the sermon—and this theme was developed in a simple way in the first point and then further developed in the second and third points. The sermon centered around the simple theme rather than around a more complex thesis statement. That is what I recommend.

Chapter 28
Dirk Miedema on Creating a Moving Message

irk Miedema argues for creating a *main movement* rather than a theme in *The Moving Message: A Systematic Approach to Sermon Preparation.*[497] Miedema entitles chapter 1 "A Moving Message Needs a Simple Structure."[498] Amen to that. He argues that good structure is needed for there to be appropriate movement in the sermon. He argues for the use of a simple structure. He thinks that a simple structure benefits the preacher because it improves his ability to deliver the message. He can remember the message and better communicate it. Simple structure makes the message intelligible to the listener. The congregation can remember the message. A sermon with good structure "gives the message in chunks that the listener can chew."[499]

I have been arguing for the necessity of presenting one concept or one idea at a time to the congregation. Miedema quotes Sweazy who states "An audience needs definite segments, like innings in a baseball game, the pieces in the concert, or the acts in a play. It's a weary road that has no mileposts. There is a rhythm in listening."[500]

Miedema argues that a structured outline "sets out thought units between which the audience can momentarily relax."[501] Finally, good sermon structure benefits the congregation because they can have "the confidence that your sermons are going somewhere" which inspires them to listen.[502] He even argues that a structured sermon benefits God because "a disorganized

---

[497] Dirk Miedema, The Moving Message: A Systematic Approach to Sermon Preparation (Lima, Ohio: Fairway Press, 1991).
[498] Ibid., 11.
[499] Ibid., 15.
[500] Ibid., 15.
[501] Ibid., 15.
[502] Ibid., 15.

message makes God look "stupid.""

Since a sermon should have structure, Miedema argues that it should have one main movement. He challenges the approach to preaching where one simply goes through a text and "explains it word for word."[503] He also challenges the idea that the sermon simply follows the narration in the story.

Both approaches have a "staccato – like" effect and do not communicate the main message of the text. He agrees with Klaas Dijk that the proper approach to preaching begins with the major thought of the text which is developed through the material provided in the passage. Sermons are not simple word studies or bits of insight that are flowing messages that communicate the major thrust of the text.[504]

Miedema agrees with Klaas Dijk's approach to developing a theme and then developing it from the text in the sermon:

> Dijk espouses the thematic approach to preaching in which the preacher assesses the major thought of the text and expounds on that theme according to the information given in the text. In this book, the approach to preaching is basically the same--with modifications.[505]

What is unique to Dirk Miedema's approach to homiletics is that he does not want the preacher to begin with a theme or central idea but with what he calls a "main movement."

> A main movement is a full sentence statement (complete with subject, verb and object) that differs from a theme in a number of ways. First, themes and concepts appeal to the mind and are often written in passive language. Main movement seek to produce a response or movement in the heart and hands of the listener through active language. Second, a theme expresses itself in thoughts and ideas, but the main movement expresses itself in terms of a purpose. It accomplishes a specific task. Third, a theme or concept tends to be impersonal. A main movement either explicitly expresses God as the main actor who wants a personal response from his children, or expresses God as the personal recipient of his children's activity.[506]

---

[503] Ibid., 19.
[504] Ibid., 19.
[505] Ibid., 19.
[506] Ibid., 19-20.

He connects his concept of a main movement with the traditional idea of a theme: "The main movement is the theme or concept of the text activated, functionalized, and personalized."[507] Miedema explains what this activating, functionalizing, and personalizing involves:

> A truly moving message has movement. Therefore, it requires active language; it must be **activated**. But, activity without direction and purpose wastes time and energy. Therefore, a moving message needs purpose and direction. It must go somewhere; it must be **functionalized**. But, at this point the message is still technical and abstract, if the preacher fails to apply this truth to the listener's hearts and hands. Therefore, the main thrust of the text must also be **personalized**.[508]

He argues that a theme must be activated, functionalized, and personalized for it to be transmogrified (to use a word from the Calvin and Hobbes cartoon) from a mere theme into a main movement.[509]

Miedema's formulation of a main movement is done as a corrective to what he perceives as a weakness in Haddon Robinson's approach. While Haddon Robinson talks about the necessity of a minister figuring out what the purpose is of his text and the goal of the sermon, Miedema says that he doesn't

> read anywhere about the integration of the purpose into the homiletic idea. To my understanding, he does not suggest a rewriting of the homiletic idea in light of the purpose. Rather, the purpose remains something that plays a role somewhere in the back of the preacher's mind.[510]

Robinson doesn't include the purpose in his main point. Miedema thinks that the benefit of his own approach is that

> The main movement incorporates all aspects into one simple statement, so that the thesis, the purpose, and the desired outcome are all expressed as one. If the rest of the sermon is true to its main movement, all of these aspects will unfold naturally in the body of the sermon.[511]

---

[507] Ibid., 20.
[508] Ibid., 20.
[509] Ibid., 20.
[510] Ibid., 21.
[511] Ibid., 21.

Miedema provides us with an example of him transforming a theme into a main movement. For this example, he uses the text of the Magi arriving in Jerusalem to worship the newborn King of the Jews. He thinks that the theme or idea of the text might be "The Jews were being put to shame."

The first step of turning a theme into a main movement is to activate it. In this step Miedema wants the preacher to identify a predicate for the main verb of the theme or the main movement. He states that "The main movement must be a sentence, complete with a verb."[512] He is correct that often homileticians make a mistake when they do not tell preachers to include verbs (and strong ones) in their themes. He gives some examples of weak themes that are simply made up of nouns. He is right that themes or sentences without verbs "deaden the heart of" a sermon.[513]

You do want to use "lively" verbs in your theme.[514] He recommends that the verb be in the active voice, which is the advice that any good writer would give to a preacher. He warns against the use of the verb "to be" which is a weak verb. He also encourages that the minister to use present tense verbs. H. Grady Davis said: "Great preaching is always in the present tense and thus always speak to the concerns of the day and the thought forms and language of the day."[515] Miedema activates the verb so that he has a new theme: "The Jews are put to shame."

The second step in moving a theme into a main movement is to personalize it. Miedema argues that a good way to personalize this theme is to have God become the subject of the verb so that the title becomes "God puts you to shame." The direct object is no longer the Jews, but it is personalized to refer to the church today. The third step is to functionalize the theme. This involves writing the thematic sentence while including the purpose of the passage in it. Miedema thinks that the purpose of a text will answer the question, how, what, why, when, where, or who. Properly functionalized, the thesis statement becomes: "God put you to shame by contrasting you with the Wiseman."[516]

---

[512] Ibid., 24.
[513] Ibid., 24.
[514] Ibid., 24.
[515] Ibid., 25.
[516] Ibid., 28.

Problems with Miedema's Approach

The initial problem I have with what Miedema has done is that he has not actually developed a thesis statement that can function as the entire argument of the sermon. He probably has developed the first point of the sermon which would be that God puts His people to shame. Logically the next step will examine how God does this. Therefore, we can assume that the second point would be "The Manner" in which God puts His people to shame by contrasting them with the wisemen. How can we talk about the "how" if we have not yet understand the what. If we have not examined what it means that God puts people to shame and what it means that God contrasts us with the wisemen, it is hard to see how we could further develop how God actually does this.

This is the point of weakness in much current preaching.

At this stage Miedema only has his first point. He has not shown us what a second or third points should be. He naively seems to imagine that his second and third points are contained within this main movement.

It is logical to look at the ultimate purpose and goal of the message in the third point. Miedema is wrong to imagine that he has placed the purpose or goal in his main movement. It is not there. The main movement simply states that God puts His people to shame by contrasting them with the Wisemen. What is God's purpose in communicating this to us? Why is it relevant for us to know this? Miedema does not consider this in his main movement and yet he imagines that he has covered the purpose of the message!

It seems logical that you would find the ultimate purpose or goal of God doing this in the third point. In the third point you are going to look at the implications of the passage for the lives of God's people. Without that third point and the application, the sermon really isn't applying God's word to the life of God's people.

To use an example, it seems like Miedema needs to move from God putting us to shame to talking about how He does that by contrasting us with the Wiseman and then moving to the third point where the minister talks about what God's goal is in all of this. What does He want from us? How do we need to change so that we are not put to shame? The "Lesson for Us" in a third point would need to lay out the changed attitudes and actions that God requires.

A crucial part of selecting the theme is limiting what is covered in the theme so that one can work out a logical sermon. If one packs too much into a theme, everything that would logically fit into the second point will from a logical perspective need to be included in the first point. For homiletical reasons the preacher needs to limit the extent of his theme so that he can save the second critical idea for the second point and the next central idea for the third and final point. I hear preachers including far too much in their theme with the result that their sermon turns into just a sermon with one main point and then a bunch of stuff in the middle and then some application at the end.

It is not clear to me how Miedema is going to deal with this new movement because it really has two main ideas in it. The first is that God puts us to shame. The second is the way in which God puts us to shame, namely, by contrasting us with the wisemen. Therefore, his main movement has two central ideas in it. It contains the what and the how. But this "how" is different from the actual ways in which God contrasts us with the wisemen.

His main movement certainly does not have the wholeness of what we would need in a thesis statement for a message to begin somewhere and then smoothly transition to a second point.

The Moves

When we come to chapter 4, entitled "The Moves", we discover that Dirk Miedema does not know how to develop a sermon. We might have become concerned when we saw how he was developing his limited type of thesis statement.

Miedema talks about how he is using the word "move" instead of a "point" and, therefore, he uses the idea of a "main movement" instead of "theme" and then "move" instead of a "division." He states that

> Moves are usually known as the main points of the sermon. As a main movement differs from a theme, so also moves differ from sermon points in a number of ways. Moves, like the main movement in which they have their origin, must be activated, personalized and functionalized.[517]

Miedema makes the mistake of having the preacher look at the text to find three or four main ideas that can be connected to the main movement. He tells the preacher

> By the time you have composed your main movement, the major thoughts of your scripture passage should be in sight. Scribble what you believe to be the main concerns of your text on a piece of paper. Think

---

[517] Ibid., 51.

about how they relate to the main movement. Then select only three to four of these thought units to become the basis for your moves. If you begin with more than three or four thought units, you may be able to subordinate them to one of the major thoughts you have selected.[518]

But what does Miedema do with the homiletics? The devastating accuracy of my criticisms are confirmed when we look at his moves (points). He presents the following four moves (which are equivalent to old-fashioned divisions):

I.   God pokes you in the ribs by pointing to your lack of expectation.
II. God pokes you in the ribs by pointing to your worldly accommodations.
III. God pokes you in the ribs by pointing to your immobility.
IV. God pokes you in the ribs by pointing to your narrowness.[519]

After more work on his "moves" he concludes with the following:

I.   God pokes you in the ribs for your lack of expectation.
II.   Also for your "chumminess" with the world.
III. And on top of this for your "stuck in the mud religion,"
IV.   And your narrow religious perspective.

Notice the devastating problem with Miedema's homiletics. He keeps repeating the words "God pokes you in the ribs by pointing to."

For every single one of these four points.

This logically means that he will develop the concept of "God poking you in the ribs" in every single one of these four points.

Without having a first point where he explains the idea of God putting His people to shame by comparing them with the wisemen, he simply jumps into the four ways that God puts us to shame.

All four "moves" are what should be contained in the second point of a sermon with a name like "The Manner" or "How?"

He neglects the heart of his text. He does not even explain the main movement. In fact, what he is doing is simply providing us with what all should be under the second point. He is simply answering the question how it is that God puts us to shame and the answer is that God puts us to shame by doing four things: pointing to our lack of expectation, pointing to our worldly accommodations, pointing to our immobility, and pointing to our

---

[518] Ibid., 51.
[519] Ibid., 52.

narrowness.

This is not a sermon that moves from a main point to a second point and then to a third. The four points are all logically equivalent. Both a proper first and third point are lacking.

The oddness and strangeness of his formulation is that you have four points that are all parallel logically and in importance with each other. There is an absolute lack of development. This is the error of so much preaching today.

Yet Miedema does defend the use of three-point sermons. Not sure why. The idea of a three point sermon is to provide logical movement. His examples of "moves" just show sideways movement as he is stuck on the "how" for four points.

A logical theme and division would be:

God Poking You in the Ribs
I.   The Meaning
II. The Manner
III. The Implications

The concept that God puts us to shame is very, very deep sort of concept. What does it mean that God puts the Jews to shame? The idea that God shames us by contrasting us with the wisemen is also an idea that needs to be explained and developed. But in Miedema's homiletics, he does not provide us with an opportunity to do so.

Chapter 29
Reformed Homiletics

he study of preaching is called "homiletics". This English word comes from a Greek word "homileia". This Greek word comes from two other words, the first being the word that means "at one" or "to gather" while the other word means "a company" or "a crowd". The Greeks used "homileia" to refer to a company of people who were at one in fellowship. We find the Greek word "homileia" used in Luke 24:14-15, Acts 24:26, and in I Corinthians 15:33.

The early church began to use the word "homily" to refer to the church as a congregation that gathered together as one to worship Christ. The early church understood the importance of communal worship. In the synagogues it was the custom for there to be an explanation of Scripture. For example, when Jesus visited his hometown synagogue in Nazareth he read a specific passage from the Old Testament and then commented on it. In the early church the saints read the Scriptures (including Paul's letters) and someone would give what we would today call a sermon.

Justin Martyr, writing about the year 150 A.D., famously wrote:

> On the day called Sunday all who live in the cities or in the country gather together in one place, and the memoirs of the apostles are the writings of the prophets are read, as long as time permits; then, when the reader has ceased, the president verbally instructs and exhorts to the imitation of these good things.

In the early church the addresses given in the gathered congregations became more unified and developed discourses. Since the sermons were delivered in the context of the communal worship of the church, the talks were called "homiliai". This is where we get our word for the study of preaching. The Apostle Paul's sermon to the believers in Troy was called a "homiliai". (Acts 20:11)

The use of the word "homiliai" for a sermon has a long history in the Christian church. For example, sermons by the church father Origen were published with the title of "homiliai". In the Middle Ages, it was defended as appropriate to use the word "homily" to refer to the sermons of Chrysostom.

Augustine introduced the Latin West to "homiliai" but used it mainly for the form of his message. The bishop of Hippo used the Latin word "sermo" for the actual message he preached.

In the 17th century the Orthodox Reformed used the term "homiletics" to describe the study of the principles of preaching. Therefore, homiletics is the study of the principles of sermon making and delivery. While homiletics is concerned with the missionary proclamation of the gospel and the principles involved in delivering exegetical and Christ-centered sermons on the mission field to unbelievers, the study of homiletics especially focuses on preparation and nature of the sermons that are delivered within the context of the covenant community.

The study of the nature and principles behind preaching involve both science and art. When I was in seminary, one of my professors would often state, "Preachers are not made; they are born." God gives some men the gift of communicative abilities. God uses all of the gifts and the life preparation of a minister to empower him to preach. We could say that preachers are born, but they are also providentially prepared all of their life long. I recently met a young minister whom I catechized. He reminded me that when he was a senior in high school he had been the only student in his catechism class. Since he was more mature than many of his peers, I had him read with me through a'Brakel's dogmatics. The young minister looked back on this as providential preparation for the ministry.

Augustine as a classical rhetorician understood in an almost innate way how to communicate a sermon with clarity, simplicity, and the fervor that would affect the minds and emotions of his hearers. He had learned how to communicate as a pagan.

The Possibility of Growing as a Homiletician

Pentecostals have supposed that there is no room for the study of homiletics. Some of claimed that the Holy Spirit simply inspires and enables men to preach and, therefore, there is no need to study the principles of homiletics or the best way to put together a sermon. The reality is that the Holy Spirit uses the minds, logic, and regenerated hearts of preachers to present the message in a way that is spiritual, meaningful, and logical. Although it is true that the Apostle Paul emphasizes that he did not come preaching with pagan rhetoric, he did communicate in such a way that the method fit the message.

The wise man says in Proverbs 25:11 that a "word fitly spoken is like apples of gold in pictures of silver" (KJV). There is marvelous dignity and force in the writings of the Prophet Isaiah and the Apostle Paul. Jesus told marvelous parables in such a way to impact the emotions and hearts of Christ's disciples.

While God does give to his ministers a diversity of linguistic gifts and emotional expression, the reality is that ministers can grow in their ability to express themselves in good English. It is also naïve to suppose that ministers will be able to interpret the text of Scripture in a way that glorifies God and communicates the message to God's people if they do not learn how to interpret Scripture. The study of hermeneutics and exegesis is crucial for a minister. The study of the original languages can serve the proclamation of the gospel. Martin Luther said that the biblical languages were the sheath in which the sword of the Word was placed. The student of Greek and Hebrew can more carefully ascertain the sense of sacred Scripture.

While it is true that the Holy Spirit empowers preachers, it is naïve to suppose that the Holy Spirit will use lazy ministers to convey the truth of the gospel. The Holy Spirit empowers ministers to meditate on the Law day and night and uses their meditation to equip them to preach.

Some suppose that there is no need for ministers to attend seminary or to have studies that prepare them for the ministry of the Word. The argument is made that Peter, James, and John were all mere fishermen and yet they became apostles of Jesus Christ. But this doesn't recognize the reality that the Lord Jesus Christ Himself taught His disciples in word and deed for three and one-half years. I would agree that if a man today had spent 3 ½ years with Jesus, that he would not need to attend seminary.

How can a seminary student benefit from the study of theories of preaching or theories about how to put an effective sermon together? On the one hand, a student can expect too much from a book on homiletics. He might suppose that if he simply reads the book he will then be able to put its' insights into action. But this expects too much. What goes into the preparation of a sermon involves far more than just following certain homiletical principles. The work is from beginning to end spiritual and emotional. The minister needs to reflect first on the sacred Scriptures and begin to plumb the depths of the text so that he can see what the Scriptures are teaching. Then he needs to have an understanding of the congregation so that he can wisely apply the text to the living congregation within their unique context.

Charles Spurgeon talked about the need not only to depend upon the Holy Spirit, but also to be a worker who rightly divides the word:

The Holy Spirit has made no promise to supply spiritual food to the saints by an impromptu ministry. He will never do for us what we can do for ourselves. If we can study and do not, if we can have a studious ministry and will not, we have no right to call in a divine agent to make up the deficits of our idleness or eccentricity.

There are some ministers who do not love the word. There are others who never learned how to interpret Scripture. They simply do not know how to approach the text and develop the concepts within it and present the message in a logical way. Instead, every sermon is a vague general presentation of some gospel truth that the minister knew before he approached the specific text. God can use such vagueness and generality; He often does. But that does not give ministers of the Word a license to be lazy or to be content with their weak exegetical skills.

Because the preaching of the word of God addresses itself not only to the intellect, but also to one's emotions and will; preparation for preaching involves developing a sermon that does all three of these things. The preacher needs to respond to the text with his own intellect, heart, and will so that he can help the congregation see how this applies to them as whole persons.

If preaching is to be doctrinal, the minister must understand what the Scriptures teach about the truth. In other words, the minister needs to have both a biblical theology and a systematic theology. He needs to be a confessional Christian. He needs to understand what the ancient church confessed, what the churches of the Reformation confessed, and how the contemporary church needs to be a confessing church.

With the coming of the Protestant Reformation, there was a new emphasis on the proclamation of the gospel of Jesus Christ in the public worship of the church. Both Martin Luther and John Calvin by their life and example emphasized the necessity of the minister preaching in a lively way.

Philip Melanchthon, following the influence of Erasmus, focused too much on proper rhetoric in preaching. Melanchthon has been faulted with negatively impacting the preaching of Lutheran orthodoxy. Lutheran theologians did talk about the importance of explicating the biblical text, but sometimes they did not emphasize the importance of application like they ought to have.

In the post-Reformation era under Lutheran orthodoxy too much preaching that was abstract, dogmatic, and polemical. In response to a perceived dead orthodoxy, the Lutheran Pietists responded to this abstract intellectualizing of the message by focusing on the signs of spiritual life and genuine conversion. Among the pietists there was the danger the sermon moved away from proclaiming Christ to examining what the signs of a genuine Christian faith is like in the auditors.

Schleiermacher emphasized that Christianity involved a feeling of dependency. Through Schleiermacher's influence Lutherans viewed preaching as an opportunity for the minister to express his own religious feelings of dependency with the hope of kindling the same experience in members of the congregation.

John Calvin and other leading reformed preachers emphasized the preaching of the word of God as the chief means of grace by which Christ spoke to His sheep.

The most important early Reformed theologian to develop the science of homiletics was Andreas. He was professor at Marburg from 1511 to 1564. His writings on homiletics influenced Reformed universities and ministerial training. He emphasized that the minister of Jesus Christ is an official ambassador of Christ. He properly emphasized the office of the minister of the word. He rightly took issue with the idea that a sermon was a religious lecture and he emphasized that the sermon needs to be communicated in a way that could be understood by the gathered congregation.

He argued that sermons were to be popular and understood by ordinary Christians and their covenant children. He also understood the important role that the emotions and the will play in responding to the Word preached. He had a proper psychological understanding of what occurs as the believer hears the Word preached, responds to the message, and remembers what he learned. He taught that the sermon was meant to lead to emotional responses like joy, sorrow, or fear.

Gijsbert Voetius (d. 1676) also emphasized the importance of the preaching of the Word as the official proclamation of God's ordained ministers who are ambassadors of Christ. He warned that ministers must not get caught up in minutiae and should preach in a way that is simple and easily understood. Even though Voetius was an intellectual, he did not want the minister to show off his learning in the pulpit.

Unfortunately, Cocceius (d. 1669) developed an analytical method of homiletics that involved dividing the sermon up into so many points and subpoints that the congregants could not follow the details. Some of the Orthodox Reformed (and even some of the Pietists) were influenced by this almost scholastic way of presenting the sermon to the congregation. While this scholastic approach might have served theological students during lectures at the university, it was not a method that fostered communication to the ordinary Christian and his covenant children. Ministers eclipsed the main point with a plethora of minor subpoints.

William Perkins (d. 1602) emphasized that good sermons involve both exposition of the biblical text and application for the lives of the hearers. The Puritans focused on first of all discovering the meaning of the text and, then, applying it to the lives of the hearers. Some of the Puritans were so preoccupied with the state of the souls of their hearers that they were tempted to preach about soteriology (the way in which God applies the blessings of salvation to elect sinners) than proclaiming Christ and Him crucified. They majored in the genuine evidences of true conversion rather than in the person and work of Christ. Their preaching led people to look at themselves (and their spiritual condition) rather than Christ.

Chapter 30
Pray to Preach

have never felt equal to the task of preaching. Phillips Brooks warned: "Never allow yourself to feel equal to your work. If you ever find that spirit growing on you, be afraid."[520] John Piper's experience is my own:

> How utterly dependent we are on the Holy Spirit in the work of preaching! All genuine preaching is rooted in a feeling of desperation. You wake up on Sunday morning and you can smell the smoke of hell on one side and feel the crisp breezes of heaven on the other. You go to your study and look down at your pitiful manuscript, and you kneel down and cry, "God, this is so weak! Who do I think I am?[521]

Preaching is very healthy for my prayer life. I have found that when I need to preach on Sunday, I am fervent in prayer on Fridays and Saturdays and Sundays.

The best word to describe my prayer life is "desperate."

As the time comes closer for me to preach, I have a deeper sense of my need for the Holy Spirit to equip me.

I am desperate in prayer because of fear. Fear of failure. Fear of not getting to the heart of the text. Fear of not getting the right and relevant application. Fear that the people of God will be bored, not fed. Fear that I will not present a fresh perspective on Christ and Him crucified. Fear that I will not finish preparing the sermon on time.

In fear I cry out to God for help.

There is a paradox in the minister's prayer life. As the time comes for him to preach, he is desperate for help from God. He senses his weakness and need.

---

[520] Phillips Brooks, Lectures on Preaching (Grand Rapids: Baker Books, 1969), 106.
[521] John Piper, The Supremacy of God in Preaching (Grand Rapids: Baker Books, 1990), 37-38.

But earlier in the week, as I work on my sermons, I am not as quick to pray. I am focused on studying the text and doing research. And I am distracted by a thousand things.

I am too distracted to pray.

Here is the paradox. At times the preacher is too distracted to pray while at other times he is desperate in prayer—pouring out his heart to God.

I suppose that if the preacher would pray without ceasing early on in the week, he would be less desperate as Sunday approached.

I have found that prayer is especially necessary for the preacher who internalizes his message and tries to preach from the heart.

I do not think that ministers who write out an entire sermon in essay form and then read it from the pulpit feel much of a desperate need for prayer on Saturday and Sunday. Their work is done. Their sermon is written. I am amazed at the ho-hum approach of such preachers towards the act of preaching. They do not treat the preaching event as an oral event. They do not try to internalize the message in their hearts so that they can speak without paper. Reading an essay is easy. It involves no stress. But preaching without notes involves hard work. If you are simply reading an essay and saying the rhetorical words that you wrote on Thursday morning, there is no stress. But if you are trying to put things in your own words in the act of preaching, that is hard work. It requires that you bring all of your linguistic gifts, biblical and theological knowledge, and spirituality to bear on the topic. It requires that you engage with the topic such that in the act of preaching your emotions are properly firing and affecting what you are saying and how you say it.

This is spiritually difficult work.

It is difficult to preach in faith. We need to struggle to believe the verities of the gospel as strongly as we should.

It is a struggle to love Christ and the congregation as we ought.

Preaching is one of the most difficult things known to man.

Of this I have no doubt.

So it is no wonder that the minister who is trying to internalize the message and attempting to glorify God in the act of preaching is desperate for help.

The preacher cries out to God for grace in the act of preaching. Perhaps he feels that there are weaknesses in certain transitions or in the development of certain ideas. Maybe he did not have enough time to develop how the text speaks about Christ and His work. So the preacher needs to depend upon the Holy Spirit to give him fresh insights even as he preaches. Perhaps the applications that he has reflected on does not seem to hit the target. In the act of preaching, as the minister faces the congregation, reading their faces and looking at the people to whom he needs to apply the message; he suddenly grasps what the relevant application is. He cannot depend on what he wrote down for this moment. He needs to trust that the Holy Spirit will use all that God has taught him about the matter to bring relevant application that impacts the congregation.

The goal of preaching is to impact the congregation. The old Romans valued eloquence because of its ability to move the hearts and minds of hearers. The idea of preaching is not merely to read an essay that the congregation can enjoy because it makes some nice biblical points. The minister is not a Bible teacher. If one wants a Bible teacher you can go to junior high and listen to a junior high teacher teach the Bible. You can listen to Nancy Leigh DeMoss on Moody radio if you want to listen to a good Bible teacher. You can attend Sunday School classes to receive biblical teaching. But a minister is doing more than teaching the Bible, he is proclaiming God's Word with divine authority. He speaks as an ambassador of King Jesus.

It is true that in the United Nations that ambassadors read speeches. But have you ever listened to a speech read by an ambassador and been impressed? I hardly ever am impressed by a speech delivered by an American president when he reads out his speech from a teleprompter. I get the feeling that the speech is far too artificial. It is. Worse yet, I know that the speech was not written by the president. Speech writers with their fingers raised to the political winds carefully craft a non-controversial speech. President Donald Trump must drive his speech writers crazy because he is known to ditch the prepared speech in a moment of spontaneity. But this is not the usual approach to political speech. Most of the time our presidents, governors, and senators are not themselves. Instead they read political speeches that are compromise documents.

Abraham Lincoln was different. He wrote his own speeches. You can tell. They have the stamp of his unique personality on them. His Gettysburg Address is strong because it is the unique work of a unique personality. He did read it. But it was short. The application is that if ministers are going to read something, let it be something brief—like a highly relevant, longer quote. If a minister is going to read his entire sermon, it should be no longer than the Gettysburg Address. Lincoln crafted an address with 300 words. It took President Lincoln two minutes to read the Gettysburg Address. Or let the minister read a part of his sermon if he is dealing with a sensitive subject where careful distinctions must be made or he is fearful of making a misstatement about something important.

It is true that ministers can read their sermons and yet have the sermons express their unique personality. But our personality comes out best in free and spontaneous discourse.

If you are going to internalize your message and be able to exercise freedom in the pulpit that allows your unique personality to communicate the gospel, you will have a desperate need for prayer. You will cry out to God, even in the act of preaching.

If you are simply going to read your sermon, while adding a little emphasis; you will feel no such desperate need for prayer. You will feel competent and will depend on your paper for what you need.

I think that meditation on the Word and then responsive prayer is a lost art. It was lost about 100 years ago when a slower pace of disappeared. With electric lighting came the possibility of doing more things before sunrise and after sunset. With the arrival of the automobile people became mobile and could leave home far more often. With the advent of the telephone came the possibility of communicating across great distances. Then came radio and television which encroached into the homes of Christians. Worse yet came the internet and the smart phone. Distractions multiply. Time for concentration and prayer disappears.

We need to be on our faces before the sacred Scriptures. We need to memorize our text so that we can reflect on it and pray over it. We need to bring the ideas of the text and problems in understanding it before the face of God.

One reason we do not pray is because our minds are so distracted. Let us turn to this problem. And turn off your smart phone. Click out of the email program that you keep open on your computer screen.

Chapter 31
Am I ADHD? The Necessity of Concentration

ave you ever asked yourself: Am I ADHD? Do I have Attention Deficit Hyperactivity Disorder?

I have asked myself this question. Don't tell me that you haven't!

I have an adopted son who showed symptoms of ADHD. He couldn't concentrate while reading a book. He can concentrate if he is involved with working on a computer screen. On the internet he can flit from one screen to another. He can concentrate on computer screens as there are rapid transitions from one image to another. But he cannot concentrate on a written text for long.

You sit in your study. A new day has begun. What do you have flitting across your brain? I despise administrative duties. Why? I always feel like they are taking me away from something more important. As a preacher you probably feel the same way. You feel that Christ has called you to preach the gospel and instead of having abundant time to concentrate on your Scripture texts you are

1) preparing and printing the bulletin,
2) answering the church door and then listening to an appeal from a Christian organization,
3) responding to e-mails connected to activity in your classis,
4) checking whether the leak in the furnace room has stopped,
5) trying to figure out what study guide to use for Youth Group,
6) calling to make plans for a hospital visit,
7) sending in your application to attend a golf outing for pastors,
8) calling the chiropractor for an appointment,
9) ordering a book from Amazon,
10) e-mailing your extended family,
11) cleaning your desk so you can have a space where you are mentally at rest,

12) running to the microwave for a hot cup of coffee,

13) finishing an article for a Christian magazine,

14) calling the internet company about how slow your internet is,

15) installing a necessary program on your computer,

16) preparing the agenda for the consistory meeting, and

17) quickly getting ready to teach catechism.

And this is just the start of your administrative duties.

I arrive in my study and already have a list of administrative duties. This person needs to be called. That person needs a response to an e-mail. There is nothing more satisfactory than crossing some of these wretched administrative duties off your list. But the list grows. How do you stay ahead of it? You choose to do only those thing that absolutely need to be done today. But then other duties hang over your head.

How can you concentrate on your studies? How can you wrap your mind around your text?

And then you have a computer. And it is connected to the internet. You have a smart phone. You spend more time on your smart phone checking the news or responding to e-mails than you do talking to people. People text you rather than call. There is a lot of communication, but little personal interaction. You sit alone in your study, yet you are besieged by distractions. What can you do?

William Zinsser would advise you to write in a place where you do not have a phone or the internet.

Zinsser wrote his book, *On Writing*, in a little shed with a chair, a table, a pile of paper, a wastebasket, and a typewriter.

That's all.

A chair, a table, paper, a typewriter, and a wastebasket for the wretched first drafts.

Nothing else.

No computer.

No smart phone.

No iPad.

No land-line.

No cushy chair.

I could wish that every preacher had a little shed in his backyard where he could work on his sermons.

The church should buy him one.

Instead some churches want ministers to study in their study in the church building. This ensures that the minister will have contact with people who are in and out of the church building. It means that people will be able to contact him by phone when they call the church number or his office number. It will mean that he remains in contact via text messaging and e-mail. People who stop by the church will knock on the church door and the minister will need to leave his study to answer the summons.

Instead of asking the minister to study in church with these potential distractions crowding out his concentration, each church should purchase a 10 X 20 foot shed or cabin to plant in the pastor's backyard.

You will need to run electricity to it so that you can install lights, an electric heater, and an air conditioner. But no phones are allowed in the hut. I know that this will hurt your feelings—but absolutely no internet.

Maybe the church should provide legal pads and an old typewriter. Typewriters are now a dime a dozen and are either being thrown away or being placed in museums. So you could get your minister a fancy typewriter. One of the kinds that I used as a sophomore in high school in 1986. My junior year we got basic computers for the first time in the school. But the computers came too late for us to learn how to type on them. That happened our sophomore year. We plucked away on typewriters. Our fancy typewriters had a button where you could hit backspace and it would erase any mistakes you made. Good luck finding the ribbons or erasing ribbons for typewriters today. You will have to haunt second-hand stores.

If you can't find a good typewriter, just use your hand. Be old-fashioned. There is something to writing things out by hand. You feel more artistic and original. You feel that you are shaping words a little more than when you quickly type them on the computer. When you need to write things out by hand, you have more time to reflect on what you are communicating. I can type around 100 words a minute—so I can type a lot faster than I can write. Writing by hand is such a lost art that public schools have stopped teaching children how to write in cursive. But most ministers still know how to write in cursive, so try the ancient art of writing by hand.

You will need to buy a comfortable chair. But it can't be too comfortable. Perhaps you should attach a rope to it. When my brother was in seminary he tied a rope around his waist as he sat in his chair at his desk. The rope reminded him not to jump up and run off from his desk at the slightest provocation. Buy a rope. Tie yourself to your chair.

Writers have been known to have a couch or twin bed placed in their writing studio. All the best experts advise against this. If you need to take a nap, you will need to do it sitting at your desk. The chair must be rather simple. It certainly cannot be one of those big leather comfy chairs that leans back such that you can prop your feet up on the desk and snooze. The idea is to think and write while you are in your study cabin. If you get sleepy, run into the house to get a cup of coffee. Maybe not. You will get distracted. You will pet your dog. You will chat with your children. Your wife will hand you a honey do list. So buy a hot pot (if you like tea) or a coffee pot to use in your study cabin.

Have your caffeine readily available.

Your desk can be plain. I always go for big desks just because there is more room available to lay out papers. I never had a desk top that was too big. A large table will do.

If you need to have your computer and think that you will be able to be more productive with Microsoft Word, then install a computer. But no internet. If you can detect the internet from the house, you might need to smash the modem in your computer. I need to be firm on this point.

You can keep a hammer in your study cabin. The hammer is for you to use in case you sneak your smart phone into the building. If you have an iPad, the hammer will perform the same function and you will not have to worry about wasting any time on your tablet ever again.

You complain: "But I use LOGOS, so I need my internet connection." I know that you as a twenty-first century preacher use LOGOS or Bible Works. Thankfully with these programs you can download your favorite commentaries onto your computer. So do this. Then you will be able to avail yourself of your best commentaries out in your study.

But remember that I did not tell you to destroy your study in the house or at church. It is fine to have two studies. In the study in your home you will have a computer connected to the internet. You can search your LOGOS program there for anything you need to print—and print out the commentaries on paper. I usually print out my commentaries from LOGOS so that I can work from the hard copy. You can do this when the commentaries you are dealing with have long passages or cover more difficult subjects. Print these out inside and take them to your study. In the peace and quiet of your cabin study you can read and reflect on the insights of the commentators.

Prominent writers are pro and con on the subject of whether or not you should have a nice view from your study. Should you arrange your cabin study so that you have a beautiful view of a distant mountain or backyard woods? Should you even have windows in your cabin study? Philip Yancey writes about the inspiration he derives from looking out the window of his study which is located in a large home up in the Rocky Mountains in Colorado. He can look out his window and see majestic vistas.

Other experts argue just as strongly against having a nice view out of your window. Anne Dillard recommended that you not have a window. If you happen to have a window in your study cabin, install the air conditioner in it. This will do away with the view. The air conditioner will also make your hut livable in the summer time. If it is too hot in there you will make excuses for getting out of the cabin and working on your yard, fishing, or meeting your pastoral buddy at the golf course.

You will need to make up for the lack of a window. I remember one author who placed a painting on the wall of his study in the place of a window. You might have your child draw you a large picture and you can hang that on the wall. Do not use the picture of a famous artist or the high quality of the painting might attract your attention too much. For example, don't hang up a reproduction of Rembrandt's "The Prodigal Son." Far too interesting and profound. You want a picture drawn by one of your children since the whole idea is to avoid distraction. Do remember to praise your child for the painting—although what you are actually praising the child for is producing a drawing or painting that is totally forgettable and uninteresting. Perhaps you can create a competition among your many children for who can produce the painting that dad will hang in his study. I am pretty sure that your youngest child will produce the worst painting and this will provide you with an opportunity to improve this child's self-esteem. It is hard to be the youngest.

Chapter 32
Why do the Saints eat Roast Minister

The honeymoon is over.

he minister has been preaching for three years.

At first there was excitement. Little criticism. No negative feedback. Just encouraging words for the recent seminary graduate.

Now the criticism has begun.

The minister, who is throwing his heart into the ministry, is hurt. Most of the criticism is either ignorant or improper. Nathan Langerak comments on what the Apostle Paul writes in I Corinthians 4:1-5:

> There is an improper judgment of ministers by incompetent judges. This is the improper judgment of ministers that the apostle refers to in verse 3 as a judgment "of you, or of man's judgment." "Of you" means a judgment by the Corinthian congregation. The apostle calls it "man's judgment" because it is a judgment according to a human standard, by humans, for human interests.[522]

Langerak adds that "Man's judgments are so low in Paul's estimation that they never get on the list of what is important in his ministry, and he labors in the conviction that what men say of him and his labors is a very small thing."[523] The minister must ignore improper judgments by carnal members of the church. "He must also ignore it because man—the carnal man who issues such a judgment—is an incompetent judge. Man is incompetent because he cannot see the heart."[524] Since the minister is a servant of Christ, only the Master has a right to judge him. "Besides, man also has no authority

---

[522] Nathan J. Langerak. Walking in the Way of Love: A practical Commentary on 1 Corinthians for the Believer. Volume 1. (Jenison, Michigan: Reformed Free Publishing, 2017), 180.
[523] Ibid., 181.
[524] Ibid., 182.

to judge the minister by man's standards and for his purposes."[525]

Not everyone can evaluate whether a sermon is biblical and Reformed. If the saints are a nation of priests and prophets, why can they be so incompetent at evaluating sermons? If a man is elected to the office of elder, how can his analyses of sermons be so wrong-headed?

Not everyone is competent for everything else. Yet many church members act like they are competent to judge sermons.

If one does not understand the mechanics of car engines, he is not capable of judging the work of a mechanic—other than noticing that an engine doesn't run or is making loud noises. A farmer is not capable of judging the work of a heart surgeon. It is true that he can tell whether a heart surgery is leading to recovery; but if he watched the surgery live, he would not be an able critic of the surgeon.

Why do ministerial students learn about hermeneutics, exegesis, and homiletics? The assumption is that they need to learn principles of interpretation, how to exegete Scripture, and how to put together a unified, orderly message that proclaims Christ. The seminary student needs to learn these things.

An elder in the congregation is perceived as having *gravitas*. He is good with the teens. He doesn't like the minister's sermons because they are not like those of his favorite radio minister, John MacArthur. The elder talks about how he listens to MacArthur as he drives in his work truck. The elder's pastor senses an antinomian vein in the elder's thinking. Later this antinomianism comes into full flower in public, gross sins. Yet the former elder thought that he was a good sermon critic.

Another elder is anti-intellectual. Translated into the church context this means that he is not interested in reading Christian theology. He pushes for practical sermons—being naïve about the vital role that right doctrine plays in right living.

A deacon is critical of the preaching because he wants to hear more sermons that 1) vindicate the denomination, 2) express a 200 percenter approach to doctrine and life, 3) wants to hear sermons that are "distinctively Reformed" by which he means sectarian, and 4) that praises the people in the congregation for standing for truth in contrast to people in less faithful denominations.

Another elder doesn't want to hear sermons that distinctively teach the covenant of grace and infant baptism because he is considering a transfer to a Reformed Baptist church (something he is keeping secret).

---

[525] Ibid., 182.

The preacher soon discovers that among the elders in the congregation there are diverse judgments of what is a good sermon. Each elder appears to have a different idea of the ideal sermon. Some want passion. Others want strong exhortation. Others do not want a strong presentation and do not feel the need to be challenged.

One overweight member of the congregation is offended by a sermon on the sin of gluttony. Another is offended by a sermon that teaches about the intimacy that the children of God can enjoy with their Abba Father.

Yet a third wants to hear optimistic sermons that inspire and encourage.

One congregant likes sermons that waver on the edge of allegorical exegesis in trying to preach Christ from the Old Testament.

Another doesn't want to hear so much about sin and the law and wants to hear more grace.

A woman in the congregation wants to be convicted about her sins and begs for sermons that clearly and forcefully confront Christians about their sins.

Some Christians want sermons that are clear and forceful. Others are content with sermons that do not rock the *status quo*. They do not want to be bothered by fresh challenges.

One person thinks that the minister preaches too long. Another Christian thinks that he is being ripped off and not getting his money's worth because the sermon was too short.

An elder believes that it is boring for the minister to have three points to his sermon. Another is okay with three-point-preaching but wants each of the points to be more sexy and catchy.

One person wants more sermons about missions and evangelism. Another would rather not hear sermons about evangelism, but does want to hear more sermons on divorce and remarriage. Others want messages about Christian schooling and the covenant.

The Minister's Broader Set of Pastoral Concerns

The preacher is aware of a broad set of pastoral concerns that he needs to address in his preaching. The church has doctrinal and practical needs. The saints need to learn about justification by faith alone and need to hear about their calling as covenant fathers and mothers in the education of their children. The preacher needs to call the congregation to obedience to the Great Commission while promoting the catechetical education of covenant children. The preacher needs to address the issue of resolving conflict in a

Christian manner and how to fight against addictions (like the sin of drunkenness).

The preacher needs to teach the confessions of the church so that the church will be a confessing church while he also needs to engage in exegesis and the development of a biblical theology. He needs to grow theologically for the good of the church. He needs sermons that find a point of contact both with new converts and mature Christians. He needs to address contemporary issues in a prophetic way as a student of the culture, while calling the saints to follow the old paths.

The minister wants to preach in such a way to edify and comfort widows, single young women, and teenagers.

The members of the congregation have their own felt needs. They also have a vision for how those felt needs should be met by the preaching.

Then there is the vision that people have for their church. In an older church one way of doing church has won out. There might be a disgruntled minority. When a new daughter church is planted, guess who will join the new work? You guessed it. The disgruntled minority.

In every local congregation there are members with diverse visions for the life of the church. Have you ever noticed how after three to five years, a good number of the founding members of a church will leave? Why did they leave? At the beginning they imagined what the church could be like. Over time their vision did not materialize. They felt betrayed and left.

People have visions for the preaching and what the preaching will promote. They have a vision for the preacher as their personal friend. Some want a more evangelical church where the members are being inspired and equipped to bring the gospel to their lost neighbors. Others want an active church, the kind of church campus where the parking lot has many cars parked in it every day, with saints engaging in all kinds of good deeds.

Another person wants church to be like the church in which he grew up. This person doesn't so much seem to have a positive vision of which he is aware. He will put a veto on anything that challenges the *status quo* because it is different from how he learned to do church.

If a person has a vision for a church that promotes Christian day schools, he will not like homeschoolers. If another member wants a church that supports homeschoolers, he will be upset with a culture and institution that is not set up to support homeschool families.

The members of the congregation need to try to grasp the big picture. Elders who are anti-theological need to be challenged. Elders who act lacksadaical about the Reformed tradition need to be challenged to become excited once again about the Reformed faith. The minister needs to communicate to the congregation what some of the felt needs are among the congregants so that people will see that their concerns (felt needs) are not the only ones in the life of the church.

How can new elders evaluate sermons? Ministers need to share books on preaching with their elders. If an elder has never read a book on the subject of preaching, how can he understand the goal for which the preacher strives in his sermons?

While it is true that individual members of the congregation can be critical of the preaching because it does not meet some of their felt needs, on the other hand, there are pious members of the church who can recognize a lack in the preaching.

The minister needs to be willing to listen to pious Christians who bring up a topic, issue, or Scripture text about which the congregation needs to hear. It is good for the minister to keep an open line of communication with the saints so that he can be aware of Bible passages, doctrinal issues, or ethical matters that are timely topics for sermons.

If a minister is neglecting sermons on the mission of the church, let the rebuke of the least of the children of God encourage the minister to rectify this weakness. If a saint points out that the minister is not developing and defending a Reformed spirituality in the face of Pentecostalism, let the minister do this. If a saint brings to the attention of the pastor that members of the congregation are functional Arminians, let the preacher present a series on the Five Points of Calvinism. If members of the church are tempted to legalism or sectarianism, let a saint bring this to the attention of the minister.

A preacher must not take it too personally when an immature member of the congregation sits in judgment of his preaching. But I am more concerned about elders who are incompetent to judge the preaching of their pastor. We turn to this subject in our next chapter.

Chapter 33
Elders, Wisely Oversee the Preaching

It is the calling of the elders to oversee the preaching of the Word. It is also the calling of the minister of the Word to challenge elders who have a wrong philosophy of preaching. Ron Cammenga discusses the calling of the ruling elders to supervise the preaching of the word:

> I am fully aware that this is a very sensitive subject. It is a sensitive matter for the minister whose preaching. The elders are called to scrutinize. From his point of view, his sermons are very personal. Perhaps only minister can fully understand the fact that the minister pours himself into the sermons that he makes. To have his sermons critiqued, though necessary, can be a very painful thing. The elders need to remember that, too, in their criticism of the ministers preaching. They must be sure that there criticism in the way in which they critique their minister sermons reflects an awareness of this reality.[526]

I sometimes think that more must be done to train elders to provide constructive criticism of the preaching of the word. I know of some churches where, for example, they have called in professors to help them understand better how to evaluate preaching and yet at times this has led to imbalance. The visiting professor becomes a sort of seer or guru on the topic of preaching. The elders might take certain of his insights and try in an artificial way to get the minister with his gifts and abilities to fit into some mold.

I have seen situations where elders have come up with funny, almost legalistic rules that they wanted their minister to follow in his preaching so that various criticisms of his preaching could be addressed. I think of a case where the minister was critiqued for not being theological enough. The real problem is that the minister was not doing fresh exegesis and, therefore, was not presenting doctrine in a fresh way. The elders also had a more sectarian

---

[526] Protestant Reformed Theological Journal. Volume 48. April 2015. Number 2., 19.

vision for the preaching. They wanted the sermons to promote the distinctives of a denomination. The elders thought that the minister should teach more theology. The result is that minister gave abstract systematic theology lectures from the pulpit rather than exegeting a text and teaching the theology in the text. The congregation heard theological preaching, but it was at the expense of truly expositional preaching. This is one example of how either sectarianism or a wrong desire for a type of abstractness in preaching came from the eldership in an attempt to get the minister to change. The solution was as bad as the problem.

John Calvin famously said that in his commentaries he didn't feel the need to go into elaborate detail on various doctrines because his listeners could go to his *Institutes of the Christian Religion* if they wanted a more systematic development of the idea. This allowed Calvin to remain simple and concise in his commentaries.

Elders need to exercise wisdom in their evaluation of the ministry of the Word. They need to read good books on preaching. Elders and ministers should read good books on this topic and discuss them together. This will help liberate elders from their narrow or imperfect understandings of what preaching ought to be. If there elders who say that they do not have the time to read books on preaching, they are expressing an unwillingness to equip themselves properly to supervise the preaching. We must not give weight to sermon evaluations by elders who lack competence in the proper evaluation of sermons.

There can be a wrong type of exaltation of elders. In the Reformed churches there can be a tension between legitimate pastoral leadership on the part of the minister of the Word and the calling of the ruling elders to exercise wise and godly leadership in the congregation. Sometimes ruling elders as a body will try to show leadership in areas where they do not have competency. This is folly. On the other hand, there are areas where the minister of the Word does not have competency because of his youth or ignorance of the local context.

I think of an elder who was critical of my preaching because it wasn't like that of a favorite radio preacher. He even left the congregation partially because of a supposed lack in my preaching. Later I needed to visit him in jail. He was a drunk. He abused his wife. He used drugs. He contacted other women in inappropriate ways. He defended antinomianism. But the man thought that he was in a spiritual and theological position to critique my preaching. And others listened to his opinion as if it carried weight.

One of my seminary professors told me that in every congregation where he had served there has been a Billy-goat. God in his sovereign providence did this. God uses Bill-goats as part of His plan to strengthen His ministers and provide them with an opportunity to suffer for the sake of the gospel.

Abuse Perpetrated by Elders

Ron Cammenga talks about elders who do not help ministers of the word grow in their preaching or who do not encourage them in this holy task.

> But there is also the abuse perpetrated by elders who intend not to help the minister, but to break the minister. They're not motivated, not really, by love for Christ's representative in their congregation. They do not have the proper regard for the office, the high and holy office of the ministry of the gospel. They often have an agenda; they want to control the minister so that he promotes their agenda, sometimes even the countenancing of a false doctrine, like the conditional covenant view or antinomianism. They fancy themselves to be expert sermon critics and have a preconceived mold into which they insist every sermon must fit there looking for the minister to say certain things in nearly every sermon.[527]

Cammenga calls this "ugly and shameful and an abuse of the rightful calling that the elders have."[528]

What Elders Can Try to Evaluate

What should godly elders look for in the sermons of their pastor? The first thing that the elders need to look for is for content that arises out of the text. Cammenga writes:

> But the main focus of the elders ought to be on the content, the substance of the messages. In the case of a sermon based on a Texas trip Scripture, is the sermon expository, that is, does it faithfully set forth the text? Does the minister really say the same thing as the text, expanded, developed, and applied? But as he nevertheless say basically the same thing as the text? Does what he say arise out of the text, as the fruit of faithful exegesis, that is, interpretation of the text? Are all the main parts of the sermon (certainly the main divisions--what are often referred to as the "the three points") part of the text? Are the main parts of the text, the main "concepts" within the text, developed in the sermon?[529]

---

[527] Ibid., 28.
[528] Ibid., 28.
[529] Ibid., 29

Cammenga also emphasizes the importance of identifying the main point in the text.

> In the second place, the elders ought to ask themselves whether the sermons develop a main theme, the main theme of the text. The goal of the sermon ought to be to present the one word of God that is unique to the sermons text. The sermon must come down to one main thought; a single message. This is the importance of in our tradition[530] of the sermon theme, a theme that encapsulates the theme of the text. Our reformed fathers recognize the importance of this. The sermon must present a unified message, not merely a collection of ideas. The individual points of the sermon must develop the italicized point of the sermon. The people of God to go home with one word of God ringing in their ears and they should be able to identify what that one word of God is.[531]

Cammenga believes that the sermon needs to present what is unique in the text. The Scriptures are so multifaceted that there are such depths to plum that the minister does need to explore what is unique in the specific passage. This will lead to originality in preaching.

Cammenga also makes an important point about how to evaluate the application found in a sermon: "The applications ought to be natural and arise out of the text, and not be forced."[532] The application "ought to be personal, warmly personal."[533] I could wish that ministers would focus on giving applications that rise out of the text.

Elders need to evaluate whether the sermons are easy to follow. When a minister uses good order and logic in his message, it will be easy to follow and understand. A message that does not include order and logic will confuse the hearers. Cammenga writes that

> The elders ought also to ask themselves whether the sermons are generally easy to follow, and therefore also generally easy to recall. A sermon may be the truth; may even be the truth, arising out of the specific text. But if it is presented in a convoluted and confusing way, the people are going to be lost, and are going to stop listening. Those who take notes are going to begin to doodle and eventually close their notebooks. The children and the young people are going to become

---

[530] The tradition he is referring to is the Reformed tradition as it is manifested in the Protestant Reformed Churches of North America.
[531] Protestant Reformed Theological Journal. Volume 48. April 2015. Number 2., 30.
[532] Ibid., 31.
[533] Ibid., 31.

restless. The minister must present the work clearly and logically. He must make things clear, which is necessary for the edification of elect believers, but it is also necessary for the hardening of the reprobate wicked. If the people cannot see the logic and follow the logical flow of the sermon, the sermon is seriously flawed.[534]

I think hypocrites and unbelievers can put up with ministers in mainline congregations because the ministers are never clear about what the Bible teaches. They do not communicate clearly and with authority the warnings in Scripture. Clarity and logic are important in preaching because God uses His Word clearly preached to convict elect sinners and to harden the hearts of the reprobate wicked. Stark clarity should characterize the sermons of orthodox ministers.

Cammenga thinks that elders need to evaluate how the minister preaches the cross. He thinks that a warning is in order. He realizes that elders can have a narrow understanding of what it means to preach Christ and Him crucified.

Arminian preachers often use a boiler plate presentation of the gospel and the cross and a similarly boring and repetitive altar call at the end of a service.

Reformed preachers need to proclaim Christ and the gospel from the text. The cross must be preached from the viewpoint of the specific text in which the sermon is based. The nature of the text must always be taken into consideration. The prominence of the cross in the text is going to determine its prominence in the sermon. The cross is prominent in some passages—it might be mentioned explicitly. If the text is an exhortation or warning, the cross will not be as prominent. Even then, the people of God must learn that exhortation, warning, or rebuke arise out of the cross and are grounded in the cross. The cross will inspire the gratitude that leads to submission to God's preceptive will.[535]

Warnings to Elders

Cammenga gives a final warning to elders. He takes issue with elders who talk behind the back of their minister. He does not want elders having private meetings for coffee where they roast the minister. The danger is that the elders have known each other for a long time and, therefore, are friends. The minister has moved to town and is outside of the "old boys" connections. Cammenga writes:

---

[534] Ibid., 31-32.
[535] Ibid., 32-33.

Let it be emphasized that the place for sermon evaluation is in the *official meetings* of the consistory. Let this be underscored. There must not be secret meetings of a couple of elders in the coffee shop. It must not be meetings of the elders unofficially and behind the ministers back. Occasionally it may be wise and necessary for the elders to meet apart from the minister so that they may have greater freedom in expressing themselves. But these are not secret meetings of which the minister has no knowledge. These are planned, official meetings.[536]

The work of the elders must be constructive—to help the minister mature and prosper. Cammenga talks about how elders need to be patient and they also need to give their minister "The confidence that you trust him to do his work and to do it well."

Elders need to look for slow, gradual improvement in new ministers.

I think that elders ought to encourage their minister to get together with other ministers for mutual encouragement. I think that they should even be encouraged to do exegetical and homiletical work together. If there is anyone who needs encouragement, it is the minister in the difficult work of sermon preparation. There is a need for ongoing education. One of the best ways for this to occur is by mutual instruction by ministers from the local area.

---

[536] Ibid., 37.

Chapter 34
Preach Christ and Him Crucified

n I Corinthians 2:1-5 the Apostle Paul tells the Corinthian church about how as a missionary preacher he was "determined not to know anything among" them except "Jesus Christ, and him crucified."

And I, brethren, when I came to you, came not with excellency of speech or of wisdom, declaring unto you the testimony of God. For I determined not to know any thing among you, save Jesus Christ, and him crucified. And I was with you in weakness, and in fear, and in much trembling. And my speech and my preaching was not with enticing words of man's wisdom, but in demonstration of the Spirit and of power: That your faith should not stand in the wisdom of men, but in the power of God.[537]

The Main Subject of Your Study and Reflection

The study of Christ crucified should be the main subject of your study and reflection. There is something that the Apostle Paul resolved to know. He wanted to know what the great Bride-groom did to purchase His beloved church.

There are many benefits to meditating on Christ crucified. What is faith: it is a looking to Jesus and perceiving who He is and what He accomplished on Calvary. If the minister will inspire the members of the congregation to study Jesus, he must first himself look to Jesus, the author and finisher of our faith.

Why should you determine to know Christ and Him crucified.

First, it will inspire your faith when you see Christ's blood confirming the everlasting covenant, in which God promises to be gracious. All the promises center in the cross. At the cross you find great assurance that God will spare nothing for you, since He has not spared His Son.

---

[537] I Corinthians 2:1-5. KJV.

Second, as you are determined to know Christ and Him crucified, you will cry out to God in prayer. You will come with boldness and confidence when you consider that by his blood Christ has made you a priest to God. Through the cross the throne of grace was opened to you. Knowing Christ as crucified chases away the fear that God will not accept you.

Third, meditating on Christ crucified will help you to grow in holiness. A love for sin is inconsistent with a sound knowledge and serious study of a crucified Savior.

A Missionary who Preached Christ

As a missionary in Corinth, Paul determined to know nothing except Christ crucified. This does not mean that he avoided the whole counsel of God. Paul is not saying that he only wanted to preach Christology—the doctrine of Christ. He did not limit his message to the death of Christ in the narrow sense.

Paul did not only mention the cross during his 18 months in Corinth. We know this because in his letter he scolds them for not understanding other doctrines. He taught the doctrine of the church—see I Corinthians 12. He taught about the end times—see I Corinthians 15. He writes about the whole counsel of God. Paul is not saying that Christians should stop at Christology. But Paul is making a very important point about what is at the heart of the Christian faith and Christian doctrine: the crucified Jesus.

The cross is the *only ground of our justification!*

When the apostle Paul says that he wanted to preach only Christ and him crucified, he uses a figure of speech called synecdoche. A synecdoche is a figure of speech in which a part is used for the whole. Paul uses the most significant element in Jesus saving work (his crucifixion) to stand for the whole of it. He uses the most significant part of God's saving work in Jesus Christ to stand for the whole of that work as it is carried out by the triune God in human history, whether in the eternal decree of the Father, the redemptive work of Jesus in time, and the application of the benefits of the covenant to God's elect throughout history by the Holy Spirit.

Whatever you know—know it in relation to Christ crucified.

Paul teaches the law of Christ in the shadow of the cross: a path for grateful living.

As a missionary, preaching Christ and Him crucified did not signal a change in his methodology. He did not change his approach based on a supposed failure in Athens. He didn't alter his method and message to reach the philosophers. Paul was invited to speak in the Areopogus because he was speaking about the resurrection: this implies a death (Paul has the crucified

Jesus in mind). A wise minister or missionary addresses the message of Christ crucified in a way that communicates to people in a unique time and culture. This method retains the uniqueness and natural offensiveness of the cross. Paul simply uses the altar to the unknown God as a point of contact to testify to the Athenians of sin, righteousness, and judgment.

He is the unchanged Paul.

There was real fruit from preaching Christ crucified and resurrected in Athens. "A few men became followers of Paul and believed. Among them was Dionysius, a member of the Areopagus, also a woman named Damaris, and a number of others" (Acts 17:34). In Corinth, where Paul began teaching in the synagogue—he did not shy away from preaching a crucified Messiah.

Preaching Jesus Christ

The message that Paul preached was "Jesus Christ and him crucified." Let us examine the first part of this: He preached "Jesus Christ". He proclaims the messianic king—the Christ, the King of the Jews. He presents the Messiah as the King of kings, the Great High Priest, and the Prophet greater than Moses. He is "Jesus"—"Jehovah salvation". He preaches the One who said: "Before Abraham was, I am." Pharisees thought that the stars would fall from the sky when a man dared to call Himself "Jehovah"—the "I am who I am."

Christ Crucified

The second part of what Paul preached was Jesus Christ "AND HIM CRUCIFIED". He preached that the High Priest greater than Aaron sacrificed Himself on a tree. In the Old Testament, wicked men were stoned to death and then hung on a tree. This was a sign of rejection by Heaven's God and earth's population. The message of the gospel is about the shameful death of the Messiah on a cross. Slave rebellions ended in crucifixions. The Roman overlords had crucified thousands of rebellious Pharisees. This instrument of torture also pictured the curse.

It is a paradox that the Messianic Savior is killed! It seemed bizarre to the Jews and to the Greeks, and it seems bizarre to Americans. It is a paradox that the Lord of glory was crucified (I Corinthians 2:8).

The Accursed Tree

It is significant that Jesus was crucified on a "tree." The Apostle Paul quotes the Old Testament when he writes: "Christ redeemed us from the curse of the law by becoming a curse for us, for it is written: "Cursed is everyone who is hung on a tree" (Galatians 3:13).

Dr. Luke quotes the Apostle Paul as preaching: "When they had carried out all that was written about him, they took him down from the tree and laid him in a tomb" (Acts 13:29). The reason why the Apostle Paul twice refers to the cross as a "tree" is because he understands the cross in terms of Deuteronomy 21:23. God tells His people that they must not allow a body to hang on a tree all night long. When a rebellious son was stoned to death, his body must not hang all night on a tree. The mode of capital punishment in the case of a rebellious son was stoning. Apparently, there was a custom of hanging dead bodies. This pictured that the sinner was excommunicated from the church and rejected by Heaven's God.

We can only understand Christ crucified in terms of this teaching in the Law. When God gave this commandment about hanging in the Old Testament, He knew how Jesus would die. He ordained that hanging on a tree would picture the curse of God. The Law said: "Cursed is everyone who is hung on a tree." The curse is an imprecation of God. God's wishes punishment on the sinner. God's curse is powerful and EFFICACIOUS. The curse that God speaks over the sinner is: "You shall surely die!" These words spell certain doom for the sinner.

The Crucifixion Reveals Four Truths the Wicked Hate

The crucifixion of Jesus Christ reveals four truths that fallen sinners hate. First, because of the Fall and our sins, the curse is universal in scope. The curse rests upon every one of the seed of Adam, by nature.

Second, God would be just to place His curse upon us. This is the great truth that fallen man does not want to face. It is with strictest justice that God curses the sinner. We stand before God's bar, like poor condemned criminals before the judge.

Third, we deserve a terrible punishment. If we understand the fearful consequences of the curse, we would shudder in terror. Every individual hair on your head would stand on end. The curse demands that the sinner be banished from God's presence. Jesus knew ahead of time the terrible nature of the curse and so sweated a bloody sweat in the Garden of Gethsemane.

Fourth, the gravity of being under the curse of God is that we deserve temporal and eternal punishment. The curse follows everyone who is apart from Christ throughout all his earthly existence and then banishes him to everlasting destruction.

Boasting in the Cross?

Paul wanted to boast of Him whom others despised because He is the Curse-bearer for the elect of God. Even though death by crucifixion was often the penalty for slaves, malefactors, and rebels; Paul glories in the crucifixion of Jesus. Even though this torture was devised for the lowliest of humans—slaves—and for criminals whose crimes had made them abominable, Paul was not ashamed of the death of the Son of God.

Everything Paul preached had Jesus' death as its point of reference.

Paul wanted to preach Christ crucified because it was the message that lost sinners need to hear. Because of the preaching of the Apostle Paul—and his disciples—many Jews and Gentiles would accuse Christians of worshiping a dead man!

The Method Must Fit the Message

The method of proclaiming Christ crucified must fit the message! Because the Holy Spirit uses the testimony of the cross brought in a way that fits the message, Paul made a deliberate decision. Paul testifies that the manner of his preaching wholly agreed with the content of the gospel of Christ.

Paul states what two methods he did not use. First, he did not come "eloquence": "When I came to you, brothers, I did not come with eloquence" (I Corinthians 2:1).

Paul could use language powerfully—as his letters demonstrate. He did not present the gospel with flourishes of eloquence so that he might win a following of people who just admire oratory. Paul avoided the rhetorical flourishes that could win supporters, but not converts. Paul had great natural abilities, but he did not rely on them. He died to proud, show off performances.

Second, he did not come preaching with "wise and persuasive words": "My message and my preaching were not with wise and persuasive words" (I Corinthians 2:4).

Paul avoids popular and faddish views of God in Greek philosophy. Paul died to intellectual braggadocio. The Jews had their traditions that they deemed wise. All human wisdom must be denied when it comes in competition with the doctrine of Christ.

The Corinthian Christian wanted a respectable faith.

They wanted one that was respectable to their fellow Jews and the Greeks. They had a bias towards dressing up the gospel to make it more palatable. Both approaches denied Christ crucified.

Charles Spurgeon said:

> The power that is the Gospel does not lie in the eloquence of the preacher, otherwise men would be the converters of souls, nor does it lie in the preacher's learning, otherwise it would consist in the wisdom of men. We might preach until our tongues rotted, till we would exhaust our lungs and die, but never a soul would be converted unless the Holy Spirit be with the Word of God to give it the power to convert the soul.

Paul's Methods

Paul states what methods he did use. First, he simply came with the testimony of God. He did not bring his own opinions or own testimony—but the testimony of God about His Son. He humbly transmitted the testimony of God Himself. He is just a messenger. Why is Paul so stubborn about not embellishing the gospel? He is convinced that the gospel was God's own testimony and exactly what sinners needed to hear.

Second, he came preaching with weakness. "I came to you in weakness and fear, and with much trembling" (I Corinthians 2:3). What was Paul's weakness? His opponents were saying: "For some say, "His letters are weighty and forceful, but in person he is unimpressive and his speaking amounts to nothing." (II Corinthians 10:10) Paul did not have an impressive presence. He seems to have been chronically weak. He did not look like a Julius Caesar or possess the stage presence of his colleague Apollos.

Paul has crucified his old man with its pride in his own abilities, strength, and sufficiency. Besides weakness, Paul came with "fear" and "much trembling." He did not come to Corinth with a cocky air. Instead there was meekness and trembling because his sense of inadequacy was so great, the dangers so real, and the stakes so high.

Third, he preached the simple gospel of Christ crucified that demonstrated the power of the Holy Spirit to save elect sinners: "But with a demonstration of the Spirit's power" (I Corinthians 2:4b). Saving power is not found in the preacher any more than in the hearer of the Word. So exalting one preacher over another constitutes a complete misunderstanding of what preaching is all about. Paul wanted to communicate the gospel as a weak sinner so that it might be clear that new converts had been transformed by God the Holy Spirit.

If God's power resides in the message of Christ crucified, so should our confidence. Paul wanted to placard Christ crucified since the message of the cross is what the Holy Spirit uses to convert sinners. These three methods are in harmony with the message of the cross. John Stott states, "It seems that the only preaching God honors through which His wisdom and power are expressed is the preaching of a man who is willing in himself to be both the weakling and the fool."

So Paul would not compromise with the people who cried for a golden calf, otherwise the cross would lose its cutting edge. "For Christ did not send me to baptize, but to preach the gospel—not with words of human wisdom, lest the cross of Christ be emptied of its power" (I Corinthians 1:17).

Russ Dykstra on Preaching Christ Crucified

In the Protestant Reformed Theological Journal, Russ Dykstra discusses the importance of preaching Christ and Him crucified. He states that there are two reasons why ministers must preach Christ crucified and resurrected.

First, Dykstra writes that "Biblical preaching sets forth Christ crucified and risen. This is required of all biblical (and that is Reformed) preaching because that is the nature of the Bible itself. God has determined to reveal himself in and through Jesus."[538]

The second reason why Reformed pastors must proclaim Christ "is that only in Christ is there salvation."[539] Dykstra states that exegesis involves searching for the main idea in a passage: "That includes searching for how this text reveals God in the face of Jesus Christ."[540]

Scripture passages can point to Christ's person and work in different ways. Sometimes texts explicitly mention the cross. In the Old Testament the cross is quite clearly pictured in the animal sacrifices. At other times passages communicate what "the fruits of the cross" are in the lives of elect believers. Dykstra writes that "Sometimes the text sets forth the power of the cross in the daily lives of the believers."[541] At other times a passage "reveals the culmination of the cross--the judgment of the wicked, the return of Christ, and eternal glory."[542]

---

[538] Russell Dykstra, "Developing God-Honoring, Faithful, and Effective Preaching." Protestant Reformed Theological Journal. Volume 48. April 2015. Number 2., p. 42.
[539] Ibid., 42.
[540] Ibid., 43.
[541] Ibid., 43.
[542] Ibid., 43.

What is Paul's Reason?

What is Paul's reason for being determined to preach Christ and Him crucified?

First, the preaching of Christ crucified is the good news that sinners need to hear. In Galatians Paul would write that Christ became "a curse for us" (Galatians 3:13). It is not merely that Christ became accursed, but he "was made a curse for us." Our whole curse was on Him, so that He was all curse. Christ became the embodiment of our curse.

This cannot mean that God cursed Jesus personally, as a person. Jesus personally did not experience the hatred of God.

Jesus experienced the consequences of the curse we deserved. God's curse results in the burden of divine wrath that Christ suffered in His body and soul. Christ redeemed us by bearing the curse in our stead.

Christ was made a curse "for us." Jesus' suffering was vicarious. He suffered the self-same pains that we ought to have endured. How important the doctrine of substitution is! I am fully persuaded that the gospel of Jesus is not preached where the doctrine of penal substitution is omitted. Unless sinners hear plainly that Christ stood in the room of elect sinners, there is no good news. Jesus suffered in our stead. He bore our curse and carried it away.

The message of the cross makes clear that no sinner can be justified by his own good works, but only through faith in Christ. And the only ground or basis of our justification is the cross of Christ (his active and passive righteousness). The Apostle Paul makes clear in Galatians 3 that we appropriate the benefits of the crucifixion by faith alone. Paul speaks of church members throughout Galatia who, he said, kept the "works of the law." They were Judaizers—outwardly pious people who were trying to mix Pharisaical works-salvation doctrine with Christianity. Paul writes: "All who rely on observing the law are under a curse, for it is written: 'Cursed is everyone who does not continue to do everything written in the Book of the Law'" (Galatians 3:10). The key word is "everything." If you do not keep the law perfectly, you are under the curse. The "works of the law" are actions by which one tries to be justified by law keeping. Paul writes: "Clearly no one is justified before God by the law, because, "The righteous will live by faith" (Gal. 3:11). So the phrase "the works of the law" has a negative, legalistic meaning. These Judaizers imagine that they are involved in self-reliant efforts at obedience. So Paul disputes with opponents in the shadow of the cross: Any doctrine that denies the perfection of the atoning work of Christ on the cross is heresy.

The second reason why the Apostle Paul is determined to preach Christ and Him crucified is that God uses the preaching of Christ crucified as "the power of God for the salvation of everyone who believes" (Romans 1:16).

God uses the preaching of Christ crucified to work faith in the hearts of believers.

What happens when God uses the message of a crucified God to convert a sinner? When we embrace Christ as our Curse-Bearer, there is the instantaneous removal of the curse through faith in Jesus. One moment a sinner stands under the curse, but when the clock has ticked and the Holy Spirit has given an elect sinner faith in Christ, he stands forgiven. Justification is instantaneous. The moment we embrace Christ by faith, God declares us innocent. Through faith in Christ we enjoy the entire removal of the curse. It is not a part of the curse that is taken away. When Christ pardons, He pardons all sin. All the guilt for Adam's sin as well as your own are immediately pardoned. The sentence of judgment is entirely reversed. This removal of the guilt is an irreversible removal. Once you are acquitted, no one can condemn you.

There are people who imply that God can justify a person and then later condemn him. It is true that a Christian who has been justified can lose the experience of that comfort for a time, but not even Satan can rob a Christian of his pardon. The original pardon is filed away in Heaven.

Third, the Apostle Paul is determined to preach Christ and Him crucified because this message should stop all party-strife in its tracks. The Corinthian Christians were entangled in the nasty business of exalting one preacher over another. To counter this, Paul says that the nature of preaching is such that there is nothing for man to glory in. There is no reason to glory in preachers.

Paul is waging battle against the sin of schism and party-strife in the church. Paul tells the Christians how his preaching and conduct were in harmony with the work of Christ on the cross. There should be no following of a certain preacher because of his manner of presenting Christ crucified or a secondary doctrine.

Fourth, Paul is determined to preach Christ and Him crucified because he knows that pride is a constant threat to us. The pride of natural man (an unsaved person) leads him to reject the message of Christ crucified. The problem (which is natural man's fault and his problem) is that the death of the Son of God implies that man's sin and guilt is so great that God needed to sacrifice His Son. But natural man does not want to admit his sin or that he is under the curse of God.

We need to determine to know nothing except Christ crucified because naturally this is the one message that we do not want to know.

What is it that is so hateful about the message of Christ crucified?

The root and core of the wisdom of men is pride. The wisdom of men is a philosophy or religion that protects human pride.

False religions are navy destroyers used to protect man's right to boast before God and man. Heresy always serves and upholds pride.

Jesus' cross is such a powerful indictment of our wickedness that human religious systems and vain philosophies try to launch ballistic nuclear missiles to silence the message of the cross. Rebellious man does not want to lose his ground for boasting. Human wisdom is developed to protect our self-sufficiency and pride. It hates the God of glory.

When we trust in Christ crucified, we die to human wisdom and we give up every ground for boasting. In the cross, God eliminated human boasting. The only boast that is left is in the crucified Lord. The cross strips us of self-reliance, self-righteousness, and self-glorify.

The Goal of Preaching Christ and Him Crucified

The goal of preaching the cross without human words of wisdom is so that believers should stand wholly in the power of God. Paul thunders out His purpose: "So that your faith might not rest on men's wisdom, but on God's power" (I Corinthians 2:5). Believers should know experientially that they are Christians not because of the preacher but because of the power of the Holy Spirit.

A faith that is dependent on an eloquent and encouraging preacher will be at the mercy of an even more eloquent and encouraging personality. A faith that is dependent upon the false promises of a health/wealth gospel preacher will be at the mercy of a shyster with even greater promises of human well-being in the here and now.

The power and influence of men readily impresses us instead of the "weakness of God." The natural man is impressed with the power of men—whether their power to move others by their charisma as a preacher or to fund expensive "Christian" projects. The wisdom of God involves the message of "weakness of God". Paul states: "For the foolishness of God is wiser than man's wisdom, and the weakness of God is stronger than man's strength" (I Corinthians 1:25).

The weakness of Paul as a preacher tended to shed light on the power of God. It demonstrated that the message of the cross was of divine origin. No other message has been ordained by God as the powerful means to save sinners. In America the demand for preaching other than Christ crucified creates the supply.

When Israel wanted a golden calf, it was not difficult for them to find a calf-maker. Aaron readily volunteered. John MacArthur states: "Today when people desire a calf to worship, a ministerial calf-maker is readily found." Unfortunately, the calf is not sound biblical exposition, but interesting observations and stories based on the preacher's personal philosophy. Perhaps the preacher is interested in sharing his political philosophy.

On the Sunday before Super Tuesday the golden calf might be politics.

Other Sundays the Golden Calf might be tips about how to achieve financial success.

The purpose of the message of the cross is to disarm men, especially if they are wise and powerful, so that they learn why they must trust God alone and completely for salvation.

Living in Sync with the Cross

Paul wanted Christians to live in sync with the cross. The message of Christ crucified points us to how we must live in this fallen world. As we are determined to know nothing but Christ crucified, we learn that we are called to take up our own crosses.

We tend to want to carry scepters now—not crosses. We want thrones, not stakes with flames beginning to lick up them.

Christians who believe in a Crucified Savior are best witnesses as they carry their own crosses. The Corinthians were kings in their own eyes. By nature, we do not want the humiliation and suffering of cross-bearing. We want affirmation.

So Paul uses rich irony in I Corinthians 4:8-11. The Paul who is daily carrying his cross outside the gates is held in disrepute. The Corinthians were not carrying a cross, but a scepter. They were trying to bring into the present what belonged to the future!

In the future we will reign with great authority. We will judge the angels.

The Corinthian Christians wrongly think that Jesus died on the cross so that NOW Christians might have wealth, kingly dignity, worldly wisdom, respect, and strength.

We need to join Jesus outside the camp—where we suffer death to self.

Christ died to save us from Hell, but not to deliver us from taking up our crosses and following Him as faithful disciples!

Jesus died to earn us all of the pleasures that are found at God's right hand, but not to keep us from having the honor of being persecuted for His sake.

William Tyndale was burned at the stake. He first had to flee persecution in his homeland. He lived as an exile in Germany. The first English New Testament was published in Worms, Germany. Tyndale was hunted down on the continent. Why was he incarcerated and burned at the stake? He was murdered because he loved God's Word and wanted to translate it into colloquial English so that every Christian could read God's Word. Tyndale willingly took up his cross. He did not fear King Henry VIII. He denounced the wicked prelates of England.

Jesus said: "If anyone would come after me, he must deny himself and take up his cross daily and follow me" (Luke 9:23). Christ was crucified to purchase disciples—who would willingly deny themselves and suffer for the cause of God.

Twenty centuries ago Christ died on Calvary for us.

Today Christ calls us to suffer for His name.

The great tragedy for many confessing Christians today is that the only cross that they think of is one on Golgotha.

Christ has purchased for us many pleasures. We experience the pleasure of the forgiveness of sins now, a small beginning of our future holiness, and fellowship with God. But most of our pleasures lie in the future! Most of the joy that we will experience is over the horizon. If we imagine that we should be treated by kings and accepted by the world, we deny the cross.

We need to take up our crosses and suffer.

Daily our pride needs to be executed.

Our boasting in self needs to be crucified.

Die to self-reliance.

Mortify your love of money and status.

We who have been saved by the crucified Christ need to live a life of thankful self-denial. We are motivated by astonishing grace to fill up the sufferings of Christ—since we are His body.

As preachers we need to preach Christ and Him crucified. Since God has ordained that He would gather His elect through the proclamation of the message of the cross, we must take up our crosses and preach the cross.

Chapter 35

Greidanus on Preaching Christ from the Old Testament

ne of the most influential books on preaching Christ from the Old Testament is by former Calvin Seminary professor Sidney Greidanus: *Preaching Christ from the Old Testament: A Contemporary Hermeneutical Method.*[543] In this chapter we want to look at some of the chief insights that can be gleaned from this popular book.

Greidanus realizes that one must first define what it means to preach Christ and defend the necessity of doing so, before arguing that Christian preachers should preach Christ from the Old Testament. Greidanus writes that "Our voyage will take us from the necessity of preaching Christ to the necessity of preaching from the Old Testament (Chapter 1), to the necessity of preaching Christ from the Old Testament (Chapter 2), to the struggles in church history to attain this requirement (Chapters 3 and 4)."[544]

Homileticians might emphasize preaching Christ. But what exactly does this mean? Greidanus explores the answer to this question. He finds confusion among preachers about what is meant by preaching Christ and Him crucified. "To some, the notion of "preaching Christ" also seems rather narrow and confining, removed from that other ideal of Christian preachers, namely, preaching "the whole counsel of God" (Acts 20:27)."[545] He explores what the apostles, who "first coined the phrase" meant by preaching Christ.[546] There is a "tremendous breadth" to preaching Christ.[547]

The New Testament church preached the birth, ministry, death, resurrection, and exaltation of Jesus of Nazareth as the fulfillment of God's

---

[543] Sidney Greidanus Preaching Christ from the Old Testament: A Contemporary Hermeneutical Method (Grand Rapids: Eerdmans, 1999).
[544] Ibid., xiii.
[545] Ibid., 2.
[546] Ibid., 3.
[547] Ibid., 5.

old covenant promises, his presence today in the Spirit, and his imminent return. In short, "preaching Christ" meant preaching Christ incarnate in the context of the full sweep of redemptive history.[548]

Preaching Christ means that you proclaim the coming of the kingdom of God.

The cross cannot be understood in isolation from Jesus' miracles and preaching. It ought not to be preached in grand isolation from the attributes of God. It reveals the justice and love of God.[549] While "the cross is but a point in the sweep of redemptive history..., the cross is such a pivotal point that its impact echoes all the way back to the fall of humanity...even while it thrusts kingdom history forward to its full perfection."[550]

That the minister preaches Christ crucified does not mean that he avoids the Easter Triumph. "We ought not to play the crucifixion and the resurrection off against each other."[551]

Greidanus defines preaching Christ as proclaiming "some facet of the *person, work,* or *teaching* of Jesus of Nazareth so that people may believe him, trust him, love him, and obey him."[552] After explaining what it means to preach the person, work, and teachings of Jesus; Greidanus provides a formal definition of what it is to preach Christ: It is "*preaching sermons which authentically integrate the message of the text with the climax of God's revelation in the person, work, and/or teaching of Jesus Christ as revealed in the New Testament.*"[553]

Having identified what preaching Christ involves, Greidanus asks whether preachers today should preach Christ. And if so, why?

The first and often overlooked reason is the Great Commission. A second reason is that the arrival of the promised Messianic king is a "newsworthy event."[554] Third, Christ needs to be preached because of "the life-saving character of the message."[555] Fourth, since salvation is only found through faith in Christ, His name must be preached. Finally, Christians are built up in the faith as Christ is preached.[556]

---

[548] Ibid., 4.
[549] Ibid., 5.
[550] Ibid., 5-6.
[551] Ibid., 7.
[552] Ibid., 8.
[553] Ibid., 10.
[554] Ibid., 11.
[555] Ibid., 12.
[556] Ibid., 13-14.

Having demonstrated that New Testament preachers must proclaim Christ, Greidanus next argues that they ought to preach Christ from the Old Testament.

Greidanus provides six reasons for preaching Christ in the Old Testament.

    (1)   the Old Testament is part of the Christian canon,
    (2)   it discloses the history of redemption leading to Christ,
    (3)   it proclaims truths not found in the New Testament,
    (4)   it helps us understand the New Testament,
    (5)   it prevents misunderstanding the New Testament, and
    (6)   it provides a fuller understanding of Christ.[557]

The Relation of the Old to the New Testament

A wrong understanding of the relationship of the old covenant to the new covenant will lead to misinterpretations. A correct understanding of their relationship will provide the preacher with a solid hermeneutic.

Greidanus provides five theses about the relationship between the Old and New Testaments. First, "The Old Testament is Open to the Future." It is incomplete. Prophecies remain unfulfilled. "We can liken the Old Testament to a painting which God is sketching on the canvas of history....when the painting has received its definitive shape and hues with New Testament teaching about a first and second coming of Christ, the ambiguity inherent in the Old Testament is resolved."[558]

Greidanus' second thesis is that both the Old and New Testaments are witnesses to the unfolding of the one covenant of grace.

Third, Christ is the bond who links together the Old and New Testaments.

Fourth, the apostles "deliberately connected their work to the Old Testament."[559] "Clearly they saw the Old Testament as the book of God's promises, which find their fulfillment in Jesus Christ."[560]

Greidanus' fifth thesis about the relationship between the Old and New Testaments is: "*The Old Testament must be interpreted not only in its own context but also in the context of the New Testament.*"[561] "The two Testaments are not two books but one."[562]

---

[557] Ibid., 25.
[558] Ibid., 47.
[559] Ibid., 50.
[560] Ibid., 51.
[561] Ibid., 51.
[562] Ibid., 51.

Jesus' Exegesis of Himself in the Old Testament

Both Greidanus and Edmund Clowney emphasize that the apostles preached Christ from the Old Testament. Clowney makes the point that we are not left in the dark about how Christ saw Himself in the Old Testament. After His resurrection, Jesus exegeted the Old Testament, showing how it pointed to Him. The risen Christ explained to Cleopas and the other disciple how the Old Testament testified about Him. Clowney writes that we are not ignorant of Jesus' exegesis of the Old Testament.

> In all the preaching recorded in the Book of Acts we find the same themes appearing. Plainly Luke did not think that we left in the dark about Jesus' interpretation of the Old Testament. What the Lord taught the disciples, they declared to the church.[563]

On Easter Sunday night the resurrected Jesus joined two disciples who glumly walked away from Jerusalem toward the little town of Emmaus. We know the name of one: Cleopas. Jesus kept their eyes from recognizing Him.

The mysterious stranger authoritatively rebukes the two travelers for their ignorance of the Old Testament.

He calls them foolish and slow of heart for not believing what the prophets spoke. Jesus asks them: "Ought not the Christ to have suffered these things and to enter into His glory?"[564] It was necessary for the Messiah to suffer the accursed death. The mysterious stranger teaches the necessity of the passion and crucifixion of Jesus.

The stranger then expounds Christ from the Old Testament to Cleopas and his friend. "And beginning at Moses and all the Prophets, He expounded to them in all the Scripture the things concerning Himself."[565] The root word of "expounded" is where we get the word "hermeneutics" which refers to the science of interpretation. During His ministry, Jesus taught that He was central to the Old Testament. He told His opponents: "You search the Scriptures, for in them you think you have eternal life; and these are they which testify of Me. But you are not willing to come to Me that you may have life."[566] On Easter Sunday night, Jesus surprises the disciples in the upper room. Once again, Jesus exegetes Himself in the Old Testament.

---

[563] Edmund P. Clowney "Preaching Christ from All the Scriptures" in The Preacher and Preaching: Reviving the Art in the Twentieth Century ed. Samuel T. Logan, Jr. (Phillipsburg, N.J.: P & R Publishing, 1986), 165-66.
[564] Luke 24:26. NKJV.
[565] Luke 24:27. NKJV.
[566] John 5:39-40. NKJV.

> Then He said to them, "These are the words which I spoke to you while I was still with you, that all things must be fulfilled which were written in the Law of Moses and the Prophets and the Psalms concerning Me." And He opened their understanding that they might comprehend the Scriptures. Then He said to them, "Thus it is written, and thus it is necessary for the Christ to suffer and to rise from the dead the third day."[567]

The disciples had the same treat as the travelers to Emmaus. Even the Old Testament prophets knew that they were preaching Christ.

The Apostle Peter writes that "Of this salvation the prophets have inquired and searched carefully, who prophesied of the grace that would come to you, searching what, or what manner of time, the Spirit of Christ who was in them was indicating when He testified beforehand the sufferings of Christ and the glory that would follow."[568]

As the mysterious stranger explained what the Old Testament said about the Messiah's suffering and death on the way to Emmaus, the hearts of Cleopas and his friend burned with a strange sensation. Their pulses raced! They sensed the truthfulness of what He was saying. Hope began to be revived in their hearts. They sensed that the mysterious stranger was correctly exegeting what the Old Testament said about the Messiah.

Jesus wanted the faith of His disciples to be built on the sure Word of God and not solely on their personal experience of His resurrection. He wanted their faith to be grounded in the massive testimony of Scripture. Jesus made the point in the Parable of the Rich Man and Lazarus that if men reject Moses and the prophets, they will not believe even if a man came back from the dead to warn them about the flames of Hell. In the parable Jesus has Father Abraham tell the rich man: "If they do not hear Moses and the prophets, neither will they be persuaded though one rise from the dead."[569] Jesus wants His disciples to know that His death and resurrection were part of God's ancient plan. He is the Christ of the covenants. He is the fulfillment of the Old Testament types and shadows. Christ wants His preachers to witness about Him as the Christ of the covenants who was predicted in the Old Testament so that we might see that in Him God has fulfilled and kept all His covenant promises. All of God's promises are "Yes" and "Amen" in Jesus Christ.[570] Jesus did not appear at the pivotal point in human history unpredicted and unforetold.

---

[567] Luke 24:44-46. NKJV.
[568] I Peter 1:10-11. NKJV.
[569] Luke 16:31. NKJV.
[570] II Corinthians 1:20.

Paul told King Agrippa: "I stand, witnessing both to small and great, saying no other things than those which the prophets and Moses said would come—that the Christ would suffer, that He would be the first to rise from the dead, and would proclaim light to the Jewish people and to the Gentiles."[571]

---

[571] Acts 26:22-23. NKJV.

Chapter 36
Edmund Clowney Finds Christ in the Old Testament

dmund P. Clowney shows the preacher how to discover Christ in the Old Testament by his own example. In *The Unfolding Mystery: Discovering Christ in the Old Testament*, Clowney takes the reader on a journey through redemptive history.[572] He presents a biblical theology as he traces Christ and his centrality in the Old Testament. Clowney takes the reader on a tour of the unfolding covenant of grace and God's gradual fulfillment of His covenant promises. What interests us is how Clowney discovers Christ in the Old Testament. We will focus in on the key passages in this book where the author specifically discovers Christ in promises, prophecies, and types. I want to point out the key places in this book where he finds Christ in the Old Testament. This will provide a model for how the preacher can discover Christ in the older testament.

In a widely read book on preaching[573], Clowney contributed a chapter in which he discusses three ways in which the Old Testament reveals Christ.

First, explicit messianic promises predict the coming of the Messiah. But there is more. The Westminster professor writes that a second way in which the Old Testament reveals Christ is in the unfolding covenant of grace that points to redemption in Jesus Christ.

"It is rather the history, the history of His great work of salvation as He prepares for His own coming in the person of His Son."[574] A third way in which Christ is revealed is in types.

---

[572] Edmund P. Clowney, The Unfolding Mystery: Discovering Christ in the Old Testament 2nd Edition. (Phillipsburg, NJ: P & R Publishing, 2013).

[573] The Preacher and Preaching: Reviving the Art in the Twentieth Century ed. Samuel T. Logan, Jr. (Phillipsburg, N.J.: P & R Publishing, 1986),

[574] Edmund P. Clowney "Preaching Christ from All the Scriptures" in The Preacher and Preaching: Reviving the Art in the Twentieth Century ed. Samuel T. Logan, Jr. (Phillipsburg, N.J.: P & R Publishing, 1986), 173.

The use of models, images, or symbols is part of God's design to anticipate the fullness of meaning that cannot yet be revealed. The blood of bulls and goats cannot make atonement for sin (Heb. 10:4). But the blood of sacrificial animals may convey *significance.* It may serve as a sign, a symbol that points beyond itself to the reality of Christ's atoning sacrifice.[575]

The unfolding covenant of grace points to the coming of the Messiah: "Rather, the whole history of redemption before the coming of Christ has a symbolic dimension."[576]

Clowney's Biblical Theology: Finding Christ in the O.T.

We now turn to Clowney's book on preaching to see how he discovers Christ in the Old Testament.

Clowney begins to discover Christ in the Old Testament in the mother-promise in Genesis 3:15.

"Specifically, it was the woman and the offspring of the woman who were made the enemy of Satan through the generations of conflict that were to follow. Not Adam but the future offspring of Adam would be the Enemy of Satan."[577]

Clowney identifies Isaac as a type of Christ. "Without the typology of Abraham's sacrifice, we could not understand the depth of meaning in the New Testament teaching about God's love in giving His Beloved."[578]

Clowney identifies the stairway in Jacob's dream as a type of Christ. "The stairway of Jacob's dream was a symbol of the communication that God provides between heaven and earth. By that stairway angels can go up to heaven from God's presence on earth and come down to earth from God's dwelling in heaven."[579] Jesus told Nathaniel that this stairway was a type of the son of man. "But what the dream promised became a reality in Christ's incarnation. God came down in the person of His Son to dwell on earth. Christ is the link between earth and heaven. He is the true Bethel, the House of God, Immanuel, God with us."[580]

---

[575] Ibid., 175.
[576] Ibid., 178.
[577] Ibid., Location on Kindle, 543.
[578] Ibid., Location on Kindle, 884.
[579] Ibid., Location on Kindle, 1007.
[580] Ibid., Location on Kindle, 1010.

Clowney identifies the Angel of the LORD who wrestled with Jacob as the pre-incarnate Son of God. "The prize was the blessing that he sought; the One who struggled with him was the very Angel of the Lord—God Himself appearing as a man."[581] "The theophany of God's presence anticipates the coming of Christ as the Lord."[582]

He also affirms other theophonies like the appearance of the three visitors to Abraham. "One remains with Abraham, and He is identified as the Lord (Gen. 18:17,22)."[583] We have another theophany in the appearance of the Lord to Joshua. "So, too, it is the Lord Himself, who appears in order to challenge Joshua; He identifies Himself as the Captain of His armies."[584]

Clowney writes that "In the rich symbolism of Joshua's meeting with the Commander, we have an anticipation of the whole history of redemption seen in the format of holy war. Jesus comes as the Prince and Commander, the Lord of Hosts who will conquer and reign."[585]

The lifting of the brass serpent in the wilderness symbolized Christ's crucifixion. "The brass serpent, the image of the curse upon Israel, was lifted up as a sign of God's power over the curse and His deliverance from it."[586] Clowney identifies the rock in the wilderness as a type of Christ. "In His own Son, God came to bear our condemnation. What amazement, what awe Moses must have felt as he struck the rock of God! In God's due time that symbol was made a reality. God "did not spare his own Son, but gave him up for us all" (Rom. 8:32)."[587] Clowney connects the blood and water that poured from Jesus' side with the idea of "living water." He also tells us why he thinks that Moses got in trouble for striking a rock a second time (when God told him to speak to the rock): "Only once, at His appointed time, does God bear the stroke of our doom."[588]

When looking at the history of the judges, Clowney identifies Samson as a type of Jesus. Jesus "is a spiritual Nazirite, called by the Father from His mother's womb. His distinctiveness is shown by His perfect obedience, obedience acknowledged by His Father's voice from heaven."[589]

---

[581] Ibid., Location on Kindle, 1080.
[582] Ibid., Location on Kindle, 1136.
[583] Ibid., Location on Kindle, 1117.
[584] Ibid., Location on Kindle, 1119.
[585] Ibid., Location on Kindle, 2053.
[586] Ibid., Location on Kindle, 1789.
[587] Ibid., Location on Kindle, 1896.
[588] Ibid., Location on Kindle, 1907.
[589] Ibid., Location on Kindle, 2152.

The book of Ruth reveals Christ as our Kinsman-Redeemer. "Further, in the figure of Boaz, the redeeming grace of God is portrayed....Isaiah uses the terms for kinsman-redeemer to describe the coming salvation of the Lord."[590]

In his biblical theology, Clowney next turns to David as a type of Christ. He tells us that King David fell short as a type of Christ. "But because David himself did not measure up to the ideal of God's anointed, God's promise was directed to a future Son of David (2 Sam. 7:12-13)."[591]

Clowney finds Christ in David's Psalms. "David's psalms and the other inspired songs of Israel carry forward the story of Jesus."[592] For example, Psalm 22 "describes in graphic detail the agony of the Crucified."[593]

Continuing to follow sacred history, Clowney explores how King Solomon was a type of Christ. "While Solomon is not the Son of David in whom all the promises are fulfilled, he does stand as a type of Christ, the Prince of Peace."[594] The wisdom of Solomon points to Christ. "In the proverbs of Solomon no less than in the psalms of David, we are pointed toward Jesus Christ."[595]

"God is the Possessor of wisdom (Prov. 3:19). Indeed, in a remarkable figure, God's wisdom is personified as His companion, present with Him in the creation of the world (Prov. 8:22)."[596] "The personification of wisdom in Proverbs 8 foreshadowed the revelation of a deeper reality. Wisdom is not just an attribute of God that may be pictured poetically as serving God in His work of creation. Wisdom is personal in the being of the Son of God."[597]

Following the death of Solomon, the split between the kingdoms of Judah and Israel occurred.

Clowney describes this subsequent history as one of spiritual decline.

"From Elijah to John the Baptist, all the prophets were preparing for the One who was to come. Moses himself foretold the coming of a great Prophet whom the people must heed (Deut. 18:18)."[598]

Although God would send His people into exile because of their sins, God would come as a warrior to fight for Israel and as a shepherd to shepherd her. At the end of the Old Testament, we find that while

---

[590] Ibid., Location on Kindle, 2388.
[591] Ibid., Location on Kindle, 2419.
[592] Ibid., Location on Kindle, 2431.
[593] Ibid., Location on Kindle, 2431.
[594] Ibid., Location on Kindle, 2577.
[595] Ibid., Location on Kindle, 2626.
[596] Ibid., Location on Kindle, 2639.
[597] Ibid., Location on Kindle, 2700.
[598] Ibid., Location on Kindle, 2853.

"God had kept His covenant; His people were the covenant-breakers."[599] God would send the Savior. "

That Savior, too, would come. Keeping pace with the promise that the Lord would come is the promise that the Servant would come: a Prophet like Moses, but a better Mediator; a Priest like Aaron, but One of the royal order of Melchizedek; a King like David, but given an eternal throne."[600]

"God's elect Servant was to be His delight, yet He would be called to humiliation and suffering."[601] "He would suffer as the substitute for those to whom the stroke was due."[602]

Clowney discovers Christ in messianic prophecies. He mentions the explicitly messianic prophecies in Isaiah where Jesus is identified as "Mighty God" and "Immanuel."

He concludes with a brief discussion of how Jesus birth and ministry are a fulfillment of Old Testament prophecy. "

The story of Jesus in the Old Testament becomes the gospel story in the New."[603]

I have traced some of the highlights in Clowney's biblical theology.

He shows the preacher (by his own example) how to identify Christ in the Old Testament.

---

[599] Ibid., Location on Kindle, 3053.
[600] Ibid., Location on Kindle, 3067.
[601] Ibid., Location on Kindle, 3086.
[602] Ibid., Location on Kindle, 3097.
[603] Ibid., Location on Kindle, 3121.

Chapter 37
Redemptive Historical Preaching
The Dangers of a Redemptive-Historical Preaching that Avoids the Ethical Commands in Scripture

here is a type of preaching that undercuts ethical application. Peter Y. De Jong warned about abuses connected to the "redemptive-historical" school of preaching. De Jong criticizes even Reformed scholars and preachers in the Netherlands who emphasized seeing Christ in the Old Testament to such an extent that they played down the ethical requirements in the Old Testament texts.

> At times the "ethical," the "practical," the "devotional" materials in which the Bible abounds were neglected. Some asserted that the congregation should be able to "make the practical application" for themselves....Simply proclaiming the mighty works of God unto salvation, so the argument ran, should be sufficient stimulus to walk well-pleasing to Him.[604]

Derek Thomas identifies as a bad homiletical model a kind of "Redemptive-historical preaching" that wearies the hearers by a constant repetition of the history of salvation. "But what often results from this hermeneutic is a certain predictability (a rehearsal of the history of redemption) that those who repeatedly hear it regard as "boring" and "irrelevant."[605] But a greater weakness of this wrong-headed "redemptive-historical preaching" is its antinomianism. "Indeed, in its fear of moralistic exegesis (*biographical* preaching is particularly criticized), application is noticeably absent from these sermons."[606]

---

[604] Ibid., 183.
[605] Ibid., 42.
[606] Derek W. H. Thomas "Expository Preaching" in Feed My Sheep: A Passionate Plea for Preaching, R. Albert Mohler...[et al.], General editor, Don Kistler. (Sanford, Florida: Reformation Trust Publishing, 2008), 42.

The preacher must not fall into a wrong type of redemptive-historical preaching where the minister ignores the main point of the text if it is ethical and instead emphasizes only what is in a narrow sense connected to Jesus' active and passive righteousness. For example, if a passage is talking about the need to pray for wisdom, this needs to be the main point of the sermon. Yes, it is true that the minister will talk about how Christ is the wisdom of God. He will need to connect our prayer for wisdom to Christ's person and work. If the central idea of the text is an exhortation, the preacher should develop this ethical requirement and then exhort the congregation. This may not be done within a legalistic context, but the main point of the text needs to be the main point of the sermon.

I have also observed the strengths and weaknesses of those who have identified with a "redemptive-historical" school. Sometimes they do a wonderful job of expositing Christ in the Old Testament. They show Christ in the types and shadows of the old covenant. But there is a clear danger of elevating Christ as our Justification over Christ as our Sanctification. What Christ has done *for us* is emphasized at the expense of what Christ does *within us*. But the Old Testament not only reveals the saving work of God in Jesus Christ, but it reveals how we ought to live as God's covenant people.

The Bible is filled with stories. These stories reveal both God's preceptive will for His people, but also His saving work.

It is wrong for proponents of an imbalanced "redemptive-historical preaching" to attack preaching that communicates God's preceptive will as "moralistic." God's Law functions in at least three ways: 1) to show our sin, 2) provide a basis for civil law, and 3) provide a path for grateful living. We find God's preceptive will in the Old Testament as well.

It is true that if we ignore God's saving work in the Old Testament and do not see God's grace in Christ Jesus in the Old Testament (and New) our preaching will be moralistic in a wrong way. We need to preach both law and gospel. And we need to preach the law both to convict people of their sin and show them how now to live as God's thankful people.

The big issues becomes: what is the text teaching? If one is preaching on a text where the necessity of obedience to one of the Ten Commandments is being emphasized, the minister will not faithfully teach the text if he ignores the ethical teaching in the text.

It is true that preachers like Chuck Swindoll have fallen into a "moral example" approach to preaching where the ethical or character issue in the text trumps redemptive history, the unfolding covenant of grace, and the message of salvation that is found in the Messiah. But Reformed preaching that avoids teaching how God's moral will is revealed in a text will produce the bitter fruit of an antinomian ministry.

And the Bible clearly tells us that the Scriptures recorded the lives of Old Testament saints for our admonition. We need to learn from their bad and good examples. And the minister's calling is certainly to exposit what the text teaches about this.

Another problem with some advocates of "redemptive-historical" preaching is that they engage in allegory. Such preachers are so keen on identifying Christ and His work in a text that they read it into the passage. They produce fanciful interpretations that are not found in the text. The danger is that the congregation is impressed by the exegetical gymnastics of their preacher and naively support allegorical preaching.

Chapter 38
Be a Doctrinal Preacher

he New Testament word that is translated "doctrine" literally means "teaching." "It goes without saying that Scripture is replete with "teaching."[607] De Jong writes: "Let it be observed, then, that every congregation is always in need of sound doctrine."[608]

Yet Americans view doctrine as irrelevant.

Doctrine "is thought of as too deep, too irrelevant and impractical for the exigencies of daily living."[609]

In the 21st century we have churches that are filled with people ignorant of both Bible history and biblical truth.

De Jong gives a few warnings about doctrinal preaching:

Indeed, he [the Reformed preacher] must guard against reading into the text more than it actually contains. Nor may he allow his exegesis to be pre-determined by the doctrinal definitions which he has learned.[610]

Doctrinal preaching may not be done at 30,000 feet over the Biblical text. Legitimate doctrine preaching occurs when the teaching in the sacred text is discovered and proclaimed. "Doctrine, therefore, is never to be proclaimed abstractly."[611]

Doctrinal preaching is intensely practical. Preaching the truth about the holy Trinity has practical implications. If the three-personed God is a personal God, then we need to pray to Him. Your teaching on ecclesiology will have many practical implications for the life of the church.

Preaching the doctrine of election has practical implications. The believer can enjoy the assurance of His salvation.

---

[607] Peter Y. De Jong, Homiletics, 178.
[608] Ibid., 179.
[609] Ibid., 179.
[610] Ibid., 180.
[611] Ibid., 181.

The preacher must preach sermons that are orthodox. He needs to teach orthodox doctrine—in line with Scripture, the ecumenical creeds, and the Reformed confessions.

Doctrinal preaching requires precision. Careful distinctions must be made. De Jong writes:

> Requisite here is first of all precision. When the text speaks about faith or sanctification or the Holy Spirit or providence or sin or judgment or deliverance, not only do the terms demand clear and simple definition; the aspect from which the subject is presented in the passage must be clarified. Also the intent of the writer in speaking about the subject is to be set forth clearly.[612]

The last thing that Peter Y. De Jong states about doctrinal preaching is that "Above all, doctrinal sermons are to be doxological."[613] When the preacher praises God as He is revealed in Scripture, then the sermons will be alive and exciting. Doxological sermons spare doctrinal "preaching from ever being dull, abstruse or impractical."[614]

---

[612] Ibid., 181.
[613] Ibid., 182.
[614] Ibid., 182.

Chapter 39
Experiential Preaching

inisters in the Free Reformed Churches, the Netherlands Reformed Congregations, and the Heritage Reformed Congregations write about "Experiential Preaching." They tend to think that their traditions have a patent on whatever this experiential preaching might be. They understand "Experiential Preaching" within the framework of the Dutch Further Reformation. The Dutch Further Reformation was a pietistic movement that was influenced by German Pietism and English Puritanism. In response to dead orthodoxy and heresy in the Dutch Reformed Church, individual believers as well as Dutch pastors emphasized the interior life and the experience of right doctrine.

There were strengths and weaknesses to this movement. The strength was that Reformed believers who did not hear the preaching of evangelical (Reformed) doctrine from the pulpits could get together to study the orthodox writings of a previous generation. Pious saints recognized that membership in the Dutch Reformed state church was not sufficient for salvation. One needed to be born again and to live a life of repentance and trust in Christ.

The weakness of this movement was an over emphasis on the interior life. Ministers in this tradition came up with elaborate descriptions of the stages by which one would actually come to the experience of the assurance of one's salvation. A major concern in this movement was to identify hypocrites.

When I hear people talk about "Experiential Preaching" I think of preaching that does at least two things. First, it is concerned to identify hypocrites in the congregation and call them to repentance. Second, it has an elaborate emphasis on the type of experiences that a genuine Christian needs to have in order to enjoy the assurance of his salvation.

This type of experiential preaching is not to be praised. It is wrongheaded and spiritually destructive to covenant congregations.

Behind every error, they say, is a grain of truth. The grain of truth behind "Experiential Preaching" is that faithful Reformed preaching will involve the proclamation of sin and grace in such a way that the emotions of the preacher and congregation will be fired.

I suppose the reason why I am disgusted by how people from the tradition of the Dutch Further Reformation use the language of "experiential preaching" is that they imply that historic, confessional Dutch Reformed preaching was non-experiential. The impression that is left behind is that the preaching by an Abraham Kuyper in the GKN or a Henry J. Kuiper in the CRC or a George Ophoff in the PRC were somehow non-experiential.

All good Reformed preaching is of necessity experiential.

But good Reformed preaching does not major on the sin of hypocrisy. And it does not use forced "discriminatory" methods of preaching to identify and classify all of the different kinds of members sitting in the covenant congregation. And it does not create a legalistic list of emotional experiences necessary for a conversion to be acknowledged as legitimate.

Chapter 40
The Indispensability of Application
Application: The Heart of the Sermon

eter Y. De Jong makes a strong claim about the importance of application: "Important and indispensable as is the exposition of the text, it is not the heart of the sermon."[615] The heart of the sermon "is found in its application."[616]

Spurgeon once said: "Where the application begins, there the sermon begins."

Broadus stated: "The application in a sermon is not merely an appendage to the discussion, or a subordinate part of it, but it is the main thing to be done."

Providing application is not an inappropriate attempt to make the truth relevant. God's Word is relevant for every age. De Jong writes:

> But having learned what the text means to its first hearers or readers, we must now come to grips with the issue what it is to mean, by God's appointment, to people today. This is the application of the text to the hearts and minds and lives of believers gathered together to hear what the Lord is saying to them now.[617]

---

[615] Peter Y. De Jong, Homiletics, 147.
[616] Ibid., 147.
[617] Ibid., 148.

Iain Campbell on Application

Iain D. Campbell writes about the relevance of expository preaching for the lives of the saints:

> That is not to say that preaching is escapism; preaching that is the most biblical, Christ-exalting and other-worldly will also be the most contemporaneous and relevant. By raising the sights of our hearers to what is unseen and eternal, we will enable them to endure as those who see the invisible (Heb. 11:27), and to contextualize their everyday experiences, concerns and anxieties in the plan of God for them.[618]

He adds:

> This is both the irony and the grandeur of preaching. The more Bible-based, Christ-centred, glory-focused and otherworldly our preaching is, the more relevant, earthy, appealing and engaging it will be. But the more entertaining and contemporaneous we attempt to make it, the more often it will lose its very soul—not to speak of the souls of those who are listening.[619]

Iain Campbell rejects the idea that preaching is just Bible teaching. If the minister is going to internalize the message, the message should come from his heart and, therefore, be a unique presentation of the truth.

> Others have sold out to the view that preaching is simply explaining the meaning of a passage of the Bible. Now, it is no less than that; but if that is all it is, the meaning of the text can probably better be found in commentaries or Bible-study manuals. The sermon has to be more than the sum of the meaning of the Bible words.[620]

Campbell affirms that good preaching is doctrinal.

> This is not always a given in contemporary evangelicalism. We seem to have trained our preachers well in locating their texts in the history of the Bible; they know where to place them on the timeline of redemptive history. But the glaring omission, it seems to me, is in precise and powerful theological preaching that can unfold any given text within the wider theological context. After all, the end of preaching is not simply that people will know their Bibles, but that people will know

---

[618] Iain D. Campbell, Pray, plan, prepare, preach: Establishing and maintaining priorities in the preaching ministry (Leominster, UK: Day One Publications, 2012), 13.
[619] Ibid., 13.
[620] Ibid., 67.

their God. All our worship, including our preaching, is a response to his self-disclosure; preaching that is less than theological is like a meal without a main course.[621]

Campbell recognizes the importance of having a theme. "When it comes to preaching the passage, it is important that we grasp the theme, for it is the theme of the passage that will be echoed in the theme of the sermon."[622]

Preaching must be Christ-centered:

One reason for this need to recognize the them is simple: every theme of Scripture is related to Jesus Christ. It may be related to him by way of historical detail (as in the Gospels), or by way of exposition (as in the letters), or by way of prediction (as in the prophets) or by way of symbol (as in some of the legislative material of the Old Testament). Even the areas of Scripture that deal with personal, subjective experiences are intended to draw us to Jesus Christ as the remedy for every need and every circumstance.[623]

Campbell recognizes the need for preaching to develop concepts.

So what is the preaching of the Word of God? It is the opening up of the Scriptures, the telling out of their meaning. It is not an imposing of a meaning on the Bible; it is the faithful declaration of the meaning of the text itself. That requires particular skills that are gifted to those God calls to the work: the skill of dealing with words and concepts, of drawing out the correct implications of statements, of understanding the meaning of texts and communicating them intelligibly and clearly.[624]

Application is necessary, and subversive!

It also, however, means addressing the issue of the subversive purpose for which the text of Scripture is given. This Book is given to tear down and build up, to convict and convert, to bruise and to heal. It is given for instruction, for correction, for equipping us to do good works. It is not enough simply to give the meaning of the text; its personal nature and its demands must be pressed home.[625]

---

[621] Ibid., 68.
[622] Ibid., 73.
[623] Ibid., 73.
[624] Ibid., 81.
[625] Ibid., 81.

John Frame has argued that if one gets his interpretation of the biblical text right, he will immediately grasp the application. If one provides the accurate application of a text, this is evidence that one has discerned the heart of the text.

Barry Gritters on Application: Driving the Point Home

Barry Gritters, a professor of practical theology at the Protestant Reformed Seminary, explains the idea of the word apply and how it fits its use. When we talk about application preaching.

> The Latin origin of the word *apply* (to knit to) helps explain what we mean by application. Sermons so address the heart and conscience of the people of God as to knit the text to their heart and conscience. Of course, *actually* to knit the truth to their heart and conscience is the work of the Holy Spirit. Nevertheless, the preacher preaches in such a way that he *addresses* the heart and conscience, speaks in such a way that he *appeals* to their heart and conscience. To use a slightly different figure, application is a *pressing* of the Word onto the heart and conscience of the people of God.[626]

Gritters defends the need for application. He writes that

> Karl Barth denied the necessity of application, even of the possibility of application, suggesting that a minister cannot make application because application is the domain of the Holy Spirit. According to Barth, preaching must be limited to scholarly *explanation* of what the text says.[627]

I am not surprised that Karl Barth played down the importance of exhorting the saints to walk in godliness. He himself is infamous for having a long adulterous relationship with his assistant who even lived in his home with the theologian and his wife. Barth emphasized the saving work of God at the expense of the necessity of the life of sanctification.

Gritters also interacts with the strange idea that has raised its ugly head at times in the Reformed tradition that "if a sermon has *application*, it must not be *doctrinal*."[628] Then doctrinal preaching is "pitted against what is called 'practical preaching.'"[629]

---

[626] Barry L. Gritters, "Application in Preaching." Protestant Reformed Theological Journal. Vol. 48. April 2015. Number 2., p. 53.
[627] Ibid., 54.
[628] Ibid., 54.
[629] Ibid., 54.

Barry Gritters challenges the notion that Reformed preaching does not need to include application. He ran into people who used Herman Hoeksema in support of this anti-application position. Gritters finds it necessary to show how the creeds and subordinate confessions teach the necessity of application. There is the odd idea out there that the minister does not need to provide application because the Holy Spirit will provide it. Under this odd theory it becomes inappropriate for the minister to provide application because then he is trying to do a work that belongs to the Holy Spirit.

It is the Holy Spirit who applies the truth to the hearts of believers. But the Holy Spirit uses the means of the preaching of the Word by ordained ministers. The Holy Spirit softens the heart of the believer so that he is convicted by his sins. The Holy Spirit affects the believer's will so that he desires to do what is right. The Holy Spirit illuminates the believer's mind so he can see what he should do. Peter Y. De Jong writes:

At the same time no preacher may simply leave the application to the Spirit, satisfying himself with an orthodox exposition of the text and telling the people that they are to apply the words for themselves."[630]

I know that in the past there were Reformed believers who thought that if sermons were strong on biblical exhortations to live a new and godly life that somehow this meant that they were not profound or deep. Some people wanted to have more abstract doctrine taught rather than hearing life application. Gritters writes that "Jesus entire ministry was 'truth applied.'"[631] How can application be wrong when "application aims at edification."[632] He defines edification as "the spiritual upbuilding of the people of God in every aspect of their life--their minds as well as their hearts, their emotions in their wills."[633]

Two Templates for Identifying Application that Edifies

Gritters has come up with two templates for teaching and identifying application that edifies. His first template is that a seminary student should learn to edify the congregation in faith, hope, and love. He mentions that this familiar "trio of graces" is found in I Corinthians 13:13 and in I Thessalonians 1:3; 5:8. The congregation "must be strengthened in their faith, quickened in their hopes, and increased in love."[634]

---

[630] Peter Y De Jong, Homiletics, 154.
[631] Barry L. Gritters, "Application in Preaching." Protestant Reformed Theological Journal. Vol. 48. April 2015. Number 2., 59.
[632] Ibid., 61.
[633] Ibid., 61.
[634] Ibid., 63.

The second template he uses is the image of God in the narrower sense. He discusses how the saints need to be conformed to the image of God in true knowledge, righteousness, and holiness.[635]

Good Application

Gritters rightly states that "all texts are able to be, indeed must be, applied."[636] If the minister is preaching on a text that emphasizes a specific doctrine, then certainly the congregation is called to believe in and rejoice in that doctrine and then to live in harmony with it.

Good applications are specific. Gritters provide advice on how the text is to be applied in a specific way. First, he takes issue with the use of "vague, general applications" because they are "seldom effective."[637] Application should be "specific and concrete."[638]

Second, good applications are "exegetically based."[639] "The danger is that the minister tries to make any application that comes to him in a study, rather than on the basis of exegetical study."[640]

Gritters challenges the idea that application needs to be put off until the last point. It is true that the Puritans and some of the ministers in the Netherlands Reformed Congregations taught the meaning of the passage in the first point and saved explicit application for the third point. Joel Beeke preaches in a congregation where historically the minister would present his first two points, then there would be a break. The minister would announce the singing of a Psalter number. After singing the song, the minister would then present the third point which would be mainly application. I am not sure where the custom of singing a song before the third point began. No doubt it started in pietistic congregations in The Netherlands. The pause from the sermon to sing a song certainly woke the church members up for the last point of the sermon. It also let them all know it was time to listen to the application.

In the Netherlands Reformed Congregations the minister would be sure to apply the message to a number of different groups in the congregation, not limited to, but including genuine believers, hypocrites, covenant children, the unregenerated, and those who were spiritually asleep.

---

[635] Ibid., 64.
[636] Ibid., 66.
[637] Ibid., 67.
[638] Ibid., 67.
[639] Ibid., 67.
[640] Ibid., 67.

It is a mistake to put off application until the third point. This is especially the case if the text is one where you find an exhortation. How can you preach about an imperative without exhorting the congregation to obedience already in the first point?

Gritters mentions that he sometimes would be criticized if his third point was too short because then his auditors thought that he had short changed them on practical application. Dutch people like to get their money's worth. They pay their minister's salary.

Good application involves applying the sermon to different kinds of saints. Gritters discusses how application should be provided for different kinds of members of the congregation, whether they are old or young, married or single, employees or business owners. It is good to apply Scripture to different kinds of members, because this will protect you from generic and general application. This helps with specificity. The weary need to be encouraged and the depressed need to be comforted, while those who are hardened need to be rebuked soundly.

P.Y. De Jong's Advice about Application

De Jong provides advice for application. It ought to be concrete and specific: "Ordinarily such application of the Word to the lives of the hearers should be done directly, specifically, concretely."[641] It ought to be done wisely and patiently.[642]

De Jong challenges how Reformed and Puritan sermons in the past tended to have exclusively exposition in the first half of the sermon and exclusively application in the second half of the message. Rather application should permeate the sermon: "During the entire discourse the congregation is to be made aware that the text is directly applicable to their lives."[643]

De Jong challenges the Puritan approach to preaching that created stereotypes in the congregation and felt a legalistic need to address each supposed group in the church in the application of every sermon.

---

[641] Ibid., 149.
[642] Ibid., 149.
[643] Ibid., 150.

It seems so easy, perhaps even appropriate, to address in every sermon such groups as the converted, the unconverted, the weak in faith, the doubters, the seeking souls, the indifferent, the discouraged. But this does violence to the text. Not every text can or may be applied in the same way. How the text is to be applied can usually be discerned from the very words themselves or form their immediate context. And this must be rigorously taken into consideration.[644]

De Jong is correct that the application should flow out of the text. I allow the pastor poetic freedom to bring in application that is not immediately found in the text. We need more prophetic preachers. But the ideal is to draw the application out of the specific teaching of the text. Whatever the unique insights of the text are, whether for doctrine or life, should be the main points of application.

De Jong discusses the benefits of longer ministries in a congregation because the pastor then begins to understand the flock better and can apply the Word in a more fitting way. "What every true preacher needs is a growing understanding of the lives and labors of those whom he serves."[645] He argues that "Despite all the difficulties and even the dangers associated with a relatively long ministry, this is always highly preferable to moving about from one church to another every two or three years."[646]

The preacher must seek to understand the needs of the congregation. De Jong writes:

> To be truly effective preaching is always to be done in the full and rich context of congregational life as the "communion of the saints." This requires faithful visitation of families and individuals in their homes by both pastors and elders. Counseling in a one-to-one basis can take place properly only within such a fellowship.[647]

When the minister is able to provide fitting application to the whole congregation in sermons, the need for personal counseling will be reduced.

> And when the Word is rightly preached, both in the form of exposition and application, the need for such direct, personal counseling may well be greatly reduced. In fact, preaching is the most powerful, persuasive and fruitful form of counseling.[648]

---

644 Ibid., 151.
645 Ibid., 151.
646 Ibid., 151.
647 Ibid., 153.
648 Ibid., 153.

De Jong warns:

> But altogether too many hours are spent in endless counseling today which would be quite unnecessary, were the Word always preached clearly and convincingly and the hearts of those who hear attentive to both the promises and the demands of God's gracious covenant.[649]

Peter Y. De Jong argues that "Always the goal of the sermon is that of urging a godly life, one of obedient love to God and self and others in accordance with the revealed will of Him who calls us to a new and holy life."[650] How can the minister apply God's Word in a relevant and powerful way? "The more a preacher lives with spiritual interest and intensity with his text during the days of preparation, the better able he will be to apply that Word fruitfully from the pulpit to the lives of those who hear."[651]

---

[649] Ibid., 154.
[650] Ibid., 155.
[651] Ibid., 155.

Chapter 41
Preach with Authentic Humility

im Keller has written a booklet about the importance of forgetting oneself. The preacher needs to forget himself. Rather, he needs to work at forgetting himself.

G.K. Chesterton said:

> If I had only one sermon to preach, it would be a sermon against Pride. The more I see of existence, and especially of modern practical and experimental existence, the more I am convinced of the reality of the old religious thesis; that all evil began with some attempt at superiority; some moment when, as we might say, the very skies were cracked across like a mirror, because there was a sneer in heaven.[652]

G.K. adds: "And we all do in fact know that the primary sin of pride has this curiously freezing and hardening effect upon the other sins."[653] Chesterton thought that prophetic preaching against pride would signal the end of his preaching ministry: "If I had only one sermon to preach, I should feel specially confident that I should not be asked to preach another."[654]

Jesus' Hatred of Pride

Jesus was hostile to the proud and friendly to the humble. Jesus had much to say on this topic. The pride of the disciples of Jesus is documented in their pursuit of personal greatness and recognition. Jesus would catch His disciples embroiled in debates about their relative superiority to each other. You can easily document in your own life your own pride. Pride is the greatest enemy of ministers and theologians.

There was the bold request of James and John. They thought that Jesus shared their lofty assessment of themselves. They want to be famous, pure

---

[652] G.K. Chesterton, "If I had only one Sermon to Preach." As I was Saying...: A Chesterton Reader. Edited by Robert Knille. (Grand Rapids: Eerdmans, 1985), 188.
[653] Ibid., 190.
[654] Ibid., 194.

and simple. They want power and acclaim.

Charles Spurgeon rightly said that pride is "a groundless thing" and "a brainless thing."

The disciples were prime offenders in this matter of pride. They were inept and unbelieving, yet strikingly proud. Sounds familiar. Look in the mirror. There is a strange co-existence of ineptness and pride in us. It is easy for us to look down on the disciples and fail to recognize our face in their portrait—but it is there.

Jesus' Hostility towards Pride

At every stage of your training for the ministry, whether it is taking a Hebrew test, or reading an exegesis paper in class, practice preaching, or candidating in a church; pride is your greatest enemy.

As a minister of the Word, whether in preparing sermons, providing biblical counsel, or interacting with catechism students; pride is your greatest enemy. In dealing with church conflicts, your greatest enemy is not the Billy goat in the congregation, but your own selfish pride.

The reason for Jesus' strong and stinging words to hypocrites is because hypocrisy was a mask for pride. At the bottom of pride is: 1) defiance—the desire for self-rule, 2) a sense of merit, 3) delight in feeling superior to others, and 4) craving the praise of men.

Jesus is hostile to your pride because it is a desire for self-glorification. Pride wants to rob God of His legitimate glory. Pride covets the status and position of God. When we are proud, we act like we are gods.

John Calvin said: "God cannot bear with seeing his glory appropriated by the creature in even the smallest degree, so intolerable to him is the sacrilegious arrogance of those who, by praising themselves, obscure his glory as far as they can."

Humility results from seeing yourself as you are in relationship to God. Calvin wrote: "It is evident that man never attains to a true self-knowledge until he has previously contemplated the face of God, and come down after such contemplation to look at himself." I know that it seems odd to quote a Roman Catholic apologist after John Calvin but listen to what G.K. Chesterton says: "If we ask a sane man how much he merits, his mind shrinks instinctively and instantaneously. It is doubtful whether he merits eight feet of earth."[655]

---

[655] G. K. Chesterton, Heretics, 43.

Pride a Service Killer

Pride is loveless. It is not an expression of love for God—since it is an attempt to gain His throne.

Pride does not seek the welfare of the neighbor—because it does not want the neighbor to advance beyond it. "Real conviction and real charity are much nearer than people suppose."[656]

Self-exalting pride is a great service-killer.

The Difficulty of Unmasking Pride

Our self-perception can be as confused as what we see in a circus mirror. In the circus exhibit at the Museum of Science and Industry in Chicago there are circus mirrors. When you stand in front of them they make certain parts of your body shrink in size while other parts grow. Suddenly you look short and fat or tall and skinny.

We do not notice when we are being proud. Often pride tries to manifest itself as humility. When we are being proud, we do not feel that we are being arrogant. We are just celebrating something we did, we try to tell ourselves.

We boast, without realizing that we have runny egg yolk caught in our beard.

Boasting is a response of pride to success.

The braggart says: "I deserve praise because of what I have accomplished."

As proud sinners we constantly fear that our gifts will be overlooked. We fear that others will be placed in positions of leadership. We will languish in the back of the room, while others are active in doing good and get the praise for it.

Then we proudly languish in self-pity. We make ourselves feel humble and low. But our self-pity arises from our stinking pride. We suppose that we deserved far better than what we received. So, we feel bad about the rough situation in our lives. We just feel that given how we have worked so hard and tried to be so nice, that the difficulty was undeserved. We didn't have it coming.

We sinners need to remember that what we deserve is Hell fire, not the limited trial we are experiencing now.

---

[656] G.K. Chesterton, Appreciations and Criticisms of the Work of Charles Dickens.

Your Greatest Friend

In response to the pride of His disciples, Jesus taught them about humility. Jesus teaches that the humble person is childlike. Responding to the disciples vying for power, Jesus says, "Whosoever shall humble himself as this little child, shall be exalted" (Matthew 18:3). Jesus uses a child as the antithesis to a proud, strong, self-confident, self-sufficient, controlling person. Children were not models for imitation in Jesus' day. Children had low social standing. "But ye shall not be so: but he that is greatest among you, let him be as the younger" (Luke 22:26). Children do not live for advancement and higher salaries.

Psychologically healthy children in a healthy family trust their father to care for them. They do not lie awake at night wondering whether they will have food and clothing the next day. Being lowly, children have instinctive dependence and confidence in their father. Children are content to depend on their parents. God's humble children are happily dependent upon their Heavenly Father. The humble person has a spirit of dependence. Humility knows it is dependent on grace for all knowing and believing. The humble person believes what Jesus says about our inability to do anything good without His help. "Without me ye can do nothing" (John 15:5).

Jesus teaches that the humble person is servant-like. True humility involves a willingness to serve others in love. The humble person is like a servant, not a pagan master or Roman senator. Jesus taught this in response to His disciples who were warring with each other about who would be greatest in the Kingdom. At the Lord's Supper, Jesus rebuked the desire to lord it over others and modeled an alternative lifestyle—lowly service. Service means acting in love in ways that are costly to self but aim for the temporal and eternal welfare of others.

Servants did not have high social status in Jesus' day precisely because they were servants. You are to be clothed with a spirit of servanthood. We see a close connection between humility and servanthood. We are to count others better than ourselves. We are to serve one another.

Humility results in a spirit and life of servanthood. Paul writes, "Look not every man on his own things, but every man also on the things of others" (Philippians 2:4). The ransomed sinner does not ask, What can I do to get the maximum applause? Instead he asks, How can I do the greatest good for people who need my help, no matter what the cost? Humility is an attitude that leads to great sacrifices and lowly service in the Kingdom of God.

We are not only servants, but after we have faithfully served Jesus, we remain unworthy servants. The humble servant realizes that he deserves no reward from God because of what he does. "So likewise ye, when ye shall have done all those things which are commanded you, say, We are unprofitable servants: we have done that which was our duty to do" (Luke 17:10).

Humility involves a sense of subordination. The humble person views himself as he is—a purchased slave of Jesus Christ. Humility is a sense of subordination to God. This subordination is a willing submission to the Lord Christ.

Humility in Jesus' Parables

Jesus taught about the need for humility in parables. The humble person is like the tax collector who knew himself to be a sinner. He has an honest view of himself. There are two great things we must know—the nature of God and of ourselves. The humble person has been humbled because he has seen God in His holiness, justice, righteousness and love. Humility results from seeing yourself as you are in relationship to God.

Humility involves a consciousness of the greatness and glory of God. It is a living confession that God alone is Creator and Governor. If the nations are a speck of dust on the balance—what am I compared to God?

The humble man also sees himself as a sinner. Humility recognizes that I am not only a puny creature, but also a sinful and rebellious one! The publican depended on God for grace. He freely acknowledged his need for mercy. The humble person lives knowing how dependent he is upon grace. He feels that grace is a free gift that is undeserved.

The humble person is like the self-abasing wedding guest who takes the lowest seat. Jesus told the short parable of the two wedding guests. The one man proudly sat in a higher seat and was asked politely to move. The humble man is self-abasing. He takes the lowest seat. He has an honest and low view of self. He is content with the lowest seat. He knows that he deserves Hell. Jesus himself took the lowest seat and suffered the most shameful execution imaginable. He descended into the depths of hellish agonies, which is far lower than we ever will have to go.

The humble person does not feel a right to better treatment than Jesus got. "It is enough for the disciple that he be as his master, and the servant as his lord. If they have called the master of the house Beelzebub, how much more shall they call them of his household?" (Matthew 10:25)

There is something truly great about the humble person. Jesus' teaching redefines greatness. It is the opposite of all fallen human ideas of greatness and rank. To be truly great in God's eyes, we must reject entrenched worldly ideas of greatness. "He that is greatest among you shall be your servant" (Matthew 33:11). Jesus said this in response to the love of the Pharisees for the chief seats.

Jesus redirects and purifies ambition. Responding to James and John, Jesus says, "Whosoever will be chief among you, let him be your servant. Even as the Son of Man came to serve" (Matthew 20:27). Humility involves dying to self. The humble person, in his imperfect, weak, sinful work, celebrates the power of Christ.

Motivated by Jesus' Humility

The pre-eminent passage on the humility of Jesus is Philippians 2. In this context, the Holy Spirit is commanding us, "Let nothing be done through strife or vainglory; but in lowliness of mind let each esteem other better than themselves" (Philippians 2:3). Jesus is the ultimate example of humility.

> Let this mind be in you, which was also in Christ Jesus: Who, being in the form of God, thought it not robbery to be equal with God: But made himself of no reputation, and took upon him the form of a servant, and was made in the likeness of men: And being found in fashion as a man, he humbled himself, and became obedient unto death, even the death of the cross" (Philippians 2:5-8).

Jesus became a man in order that God might be glorified. Jesus says, "Learn of Me, for I am meek and lowly of heart" (Matthew 11:29). Jesus felt no jealousy or envy. He could bear to hear others praised and Himself forgotten.

The humility of Jesus is evident from His lowly service. "I am in the midst of you as he that serveth" (Luke 22:26). "If I, then, the Lord and Master, have washed your feet, ye also ought to wash one another's feet" (John 13:14). His most painful service for His people was His death. His humility is evidenced in His dying to self-interest and seeking our welfare and salvation. Since Jesus had humbled Himself before God, it was possible for Him to be the Servant of His people.

Astonishingly, the glorious Christ will remain a servant. He predicts that at His second coming He will again take the lowly and beautiful role of servant. "Blessed are those servants, whom the lord when he cometh shall find watching: verily I say unto you, that he shall gird himself, and make them to sit down to meat, and will come forth and serve them" (Luke 12:37). Jesus will never stop shepherding us.

The humility of Jesus is evidenced in His obedience to the Father's will. "I seek not mine own will" (John 5:30). "I seek not mine own glory" (John 8:50). "The word which ye hear is not mine" (John 14:24). Humility is consent to the Father's will. Jesus found His absolute submission to the Father's will to be a source of ultimate joy. The death of Jesus on the cross is the highest proof of the perfection of humility in Him.

We need more than Jesus' personal example of humility during His life; we need His death. "For even the Son of man came not to be ministered unto, but to minister, and to give his life a ransom for many" (Mark 10:45). "He humbled himself, and became obedient unto death, even the death of the cross" (Philippians 2:8).

His death was a ransom—a price paid to liberate a prisoner or captive. We could not free ourselves from pride and selfish ambition; a Divine rescue was necessary. God executed His Son for proud sinners like you and me. True greatness is not even possible apart from Jesus' death as a ransom. Our small beginning of our future humility is an effect of the cross. It is the fruit of Jesus' humility. Jesus' ransom on our behalf is the possibility of us being liberated from hypocrisy and pride. We needed Jesus' death as a ransom.

God Exalts the Humble

We are to be motivated by the axiom that God will exalt the humble. The Holy Spirit says about the Son who emptied Himself, "Wherefore God also hath highly exalted him, and given him a name which is above every name: That at the name of Jesus every knee should bow, of things in heaven, and things in earth, and things under the earth" (Philippians 2:9-10). God puts down the proud. What folly it is to pursue the highest seat! God abased proud Pharaoh by drowning him in the Red Sea. God humbled proud Jezebel and she was eaten by dogs. Nebuchadnezzar was turned beastlike. King Herod Agrippa I was eaten by worms. God is an enemy to all who exalt themselves at the expense of other people and His glory. An unchanging law, an axiom of the Kingdom is, "he that humbleth himself shall be exalted" (Luke 14:11). God exalted the lowly Virgin Mary. The publican went home fully justified. The humble guest was asked to move to a higher seat. The way of humility is the route to Heavenly exaltation.

Humility draws the gaze of God. "But to this man will I look, even to him that is poor and of a contrite spirit, and trembleth at my word" (Isaiah 66:2).

Charles Mahoney points out, "Humility draws the gaze of our Sovereign God." God's active and gracious gaze is on the humble. 2 Chronicles 16:9 speaks of how God's eyes run to and fro throughout the earth to support those whose hearts are perfect towards God. God does not help those who help themselves. God gives grace to the humble (James 4:6). Mahoney writes, "God is personally and providentially supportive of the humble."

How to Grow in Humility

How can you grow in humility? I will give eight ways.

First, humbly avail yourself of the means of grace by hearing the preaching of the Law and Christ crucified. Study God's Word at home and gather with the saints in Bible studies. Partake of the sacrament of the Lord's Supper with a proper attitude.

Second, pray. Confess your sins honestly. Ask God to expose your secret sins to you. Take time to be thankful. Be grateful for all of God's gifts to you. Pray some grateful prayers.

Third, study the attributes of God. Study the incommunicable and communicable attributes of God.

Fourth, study the doctrines of grace. Pick up a book on Christian theology. Read about election or calling or the perseverance of the saints. Read about the doctrine of Christ.

Fifth, identify evidences of God's grace in others. Instead of being a fault-finder, look for evidence of God's grace in the lives of others. View others as better than yourself. Encourage others. Rejoice in how God is blessing others.

Sixth, view trials as tests. Children do not always like tests, but they are necessary. Suffering is a test to be endured humbly. Never say, "I do not deserve this test." As soon as you talk about what you deserve, remind yourself of the Lake of Fire. So, endure trials and tests with joy—knowing that God is using them to purify you.

Seventh, teach your children the nature of true greatness. Be a model of lowly service to them.

Eighth and finally, meditate on the cross. How can you be proud near the cross? It not only ransoms us and liberates us, but also the message of it transforms us. Dr. Martyn Lloyd-Jones said, "There is only one thing I know of that crushes me to the ground and humiliates me to the dust, and that is to look at the Son of God, and especially contemplate the cross."

The hymn goes like this:

When I survey the wondrous cross
On which the Prince of Glory died,
My richest gain I count but loss
And pour contempt on all my pride.

John Stott states, "It is there, at the foot of the cross, that we shrink to our true size." The cross pops inflated views of self. Carl F.H. Henry says, "How can anyone be arrogant when he stands beside the cross?" May God help us to stand right beneath the cross—for there is no room for pride there.

How can there be arrogance in the pulpit?

How can you be proud as you administer the Lord's Supper.

Preacher, be humble. You are a servant of the servants of God.

Be meek. When others attack you, you do not need to strike back. Imitate Moses. God vindicated Moses when Miriam and Aaron attacked the meekest man in the Old Testament. God will vindicate you someday as well.

Be humble because you cannot cause a single member of the congregation to be regenerated or to grow in holiness. You are just a mere man and a sinful man at that. Humble yourself before a God who graciously chooses to use you for the good of the saints and His glory.

Chapter 42
Preach with Jealousy for Christ's Bride

For I am jealous over you with godly jealousy: for I have espoused you to one husband, that I may present you as a chaste virgin to Christ.
2 Corinthians 11:2

n Zechariah 1:14 an angel says to the prophet: "Cry thou, saying, Thus saith the LORD of hosts; I am jealous for Jerusalem and for Zion with a great jealousy." Your wife belongs to you and no one else. If another man is overly nice to your wife and is always trying to talk with her—you sense that he is trying to steal away her affection. He flatters your wife. You must be indignant when someone causes your heart to burn with jealousy. Who are seminary students training to be? This word of God teaches that you are to be the marriage-friend of Jesus Christ. As the marriage-friend of Christ—you are to be jealous about the faithfulness of the church to Christ.

Your Jealousy over the Bride of Christ

As a minister of the Word, Paul introduces himself as the marriage-friend of Christ. He apparently refers to a Jewish custom in which a bridegroom arranged a marriage through his best friend. He betroths the Corinthian church to Christ: "for I have espoused you to one husband" (2 Corinthians 11:2).

If a Jewish man was interested in marrying a certain woman—he would ask his best friend to arrange a marriage. The friend would woo the young woman by telling her the positive qualities of the potential groom. He would arrange the dowry that the man would pay. The friend would arrange the betrothal ceremony.

Some think that Paul is picturing himself as the father of the church. "For though ye have ten thousand instructors in Christ, yet have ye not many fathers: for in Christ Jesus I have begotten you through the gospel" (I Corinthians 4:15). But in the previous verse he refers to them as "my beloved sons".

John the Baptist, speaking of the church as the bride, uses the same metaphor as Paul does. John refers to himself as the friend of the groom. "He that hath the bride is the bridegroom: but the friend of the bridegroom, which standeth and heareth him, rejoiceth greatly because of the bridegroom's voice: this my joy therefore is fulfilled" (John 3:29).

If Christ has called you to the gospel ministry, then He has chosen you to be His marriage-friend. There is only one Bridegroom of the church—the incarnate Son of God. The church is pictured as a virgin of marriageable age. Through your preaching and pastoral work you are betrothing the church to Christ. Christ will call you to be His marriage friend in a certain congregation. He sends you out as His marriage friend. You woo the church to Christ—by telling her about the excellencies of Christ. His glorious supremacy in salvation and in all the universe! His selfless, hurting, sacrificial love shown on the cross. His present majesty, power, and exaltation. Christ will use you as instruments to unite the church to Christ—and to draw believers ever closer into the arms of their groom.

As the friend of Christ, you are the guardian of the church's virginity. A Jewish marriage-friend would want the espoused bride to show commitment and devotion to her groom—by saving her body for Him.

In the Old Testament a betrothed bride who was unfaithful was regarded as an adulterer. Paul displays his jealousy: "For I am jealous over you with godly jealousy" (2 Corinthians 11:2).

Jealousy refers to the angry and anxious emotions that we feel when we fear that another should be some means supplant us—and take away the love and devotion that we alone deserve from our spouse. You must want the church to be faithful to the one husband to whom she has been betrothed.

This word of God emphasizes monogamy. It is God's will that marriage be between one man and one wife. The church must show a single-hearted devotion to Him. Paul explains the nature of that virginity when he talks in 2 Corinthians11:3 of "the simplicity that is in Christ." The church must cleave to Christ alone, with her whole heart. The passion of jealousy has an intense force—it evokes the utmost wrath. "For jealousy is the rage of a man: therefore he will not spare in the day of vengeance" (Proverbs 6:34). Jealousy is so powerful an emotion because "Many waters cannot quench love, neither can the floods drown it."

Paul's jealousy is his ardor to keep the church safe from the advances of rivals. To be jealous is to "boil over" "to burn" when heretics try to sleep with Christ's bride. It is to become angry when you see the church being attracted to a wicked suitor.

Ministers are to have a "godly jealousy" (2 Corinthians 11:2). In the Old Testament we hear the thundering words of Nahum the prophet saying: "God is jealous and the Lord revengeth, the Lord revengeth and is furious, the Lord will take vengeance on his adversaries, and he reserveth wrath for his enemies."

Ministers possess God's own burning jealousy. God imparts His jealousy to His ministers. God's jealousy flows out of His love. It means that His glory is wrapped up with the church's salvation. God desires the love of His bride.

There is reason for Paul's jealousy. There were heretics in Corinth who were trying to seduce the church away from the gospel of Christ (2 Corinthians 11:3-4).

The whole context of 2 Corinthians chapter 11 is filled with irony. The false apostles boasted foolishly about themselves. "For we dare not make ourselves of the number, or compare ourselves with some that commend themselves: but they measuring themselves by themselves, and comparing themselves among themselves, are not wise" (2 Corinthians 10:12).

The only way that they looked good was by comparing themselves to one another. Jesus warns Peter about comparisons: "If I will that he tarry till I come, what is that to thee? Follow thou me" (John 21:22).

Paul says that he is now going to play the part of a fool, and boast too— although he is defending his apostleship. John Calvin suggests that Paul talks about jealousy because jealousy hurries a man as it were headlong into folly. While the false apostles are ironically called "super-apostles" in 2 Corinthians 11:5, Paul is an authentic apostle who has been commissioned by Christ to be His marriage-friend.

You certainly may not draw the church's attention to yourself and set yourself up as a rival to Christ. The church is not about you. It is all about Christ.

There is reason for you to be jealous. You must do all that you can to keep the church from being corrupted by another suitor during the time of her espousal. The church commits adultery when she buys into heresy or lives in sin. A church that becomes worldly is a cheating church. You must be jealous for the honor of Christ so that you do not allow the suitor of man-centered Arminian free-willism tempt the church away from complete reliance upon their bride-groom for salvation. Warn the church about the suitor of materialism and sexual licentiousness.

When you preach against heresy or sin, your congregation has no reason to be angry with you. You are not trying to injure the church. You are engaging in an act of love.

The purpose of preaching and carrying out Christian discipline is to be able to present the church "as a chaste virgin to Christ." A virgin is a young woman who has never known a man in illicit sex. She has kept her body for her husband. Don't let the church under your charge be corrupted. By the grace of God, you can be used to keep the church in the truth and in the path of godliness so she does not apostatize.

The only way that the church can be presented as a virgin is because of the cross. Christ's blood has cleansed the church of her adulteries. Christ merited holiness for the church and merited for her the grace to persevere.

Ministers have the distinct honor of presenting the church to Christ. That will be the church's wedding day! According to Jewish custom, the role of the marriage-friend was to regulate and preside over the marriage feast. Your ministry looks ahead to judgment day.

Preach with that wedding day in mind.

Chapter 43
Preaching and Listening as Worship

Open thou mine eyes, that I may behold wondrous things out of thy law.
Psalm 119:18

Preaching and Listening as Worship

reaching is not the act of reading an essay. It must be an act of heart worship.

John Piper has a book out entitled "Expository Exultation." His point is that the preacher must exposit the sacred Scriptures and he must exult in God as he does so. Preaching is both the exposition of Scripture and a response to the message that directs glory and praise to the Triune God.

The act of preaching must be an act of worship.

This is the case for the minister and must also be the case for the congregation.

Sometimes church members view themselves as passive when the Word is preached. But their listening to sermons must be an act of worship.

The Holy Spirit teaches us that our preaching and our listening to the preaching of the Word must be an act of worship. It simply is not true that we only worship God when we sing songs in church.

The preaching of the preacher and the listening of the congregation is to be an act of worship because of the fact that there are wondrous things in God's Word. Our response to the glory of Jesus revealed in Scripture is worship! As we hear God's Word, not just with the ears on our heads, but with spiritual ears, we respond to God's revelation with praise and exultation.

Proclaiming the Wondrous Works of God

Preaching is the proclamation of the wondrous things in God's Law. The first thing we learn from Psalm 119:18 is that there are "wondrous things" in God's Law: "Open thou mine eyes that I may behold wondrous things out of thy law" (Psalm 119:18). These wondrous things are to be delighted in. "Thy testimonies also are my delight and my counselors" (Psalm 119:24).

The Bible is full of wonders! The Red Sea crossing and the conquest of Jericho were wonders. The Pentateuch records many wonders. Moses says:

> Ye have seen all that the LORD did before your eyes in the land of Egypt unto Pharaoh and unto all his servants and unto all his land; the great temptations which thine eyes have seen, the signs, and those great miracles. (Deuteronomy 29:2-3)

The same word, "wonders," is used when Moses speaks of "great miracles," because miracles fill the viewer with wonder. The New Testament is filled with wonders. The incarnation is the greatest of wonders. Immanuel is even named "Wonderful Counselor." The crucifixion of His Son was a wondrous act of God towards elect sinners, who were by nature enemies of God. Easter is a wonder, as was the Ascension. Pentecost was a wonder!

Since preaching is the proclaiming of wondrous things out of God's Law and Gospel, it is worship.

Preaching, as worship, is "expository exaltation."

The preacher carefully interprets Scripture and this leads to the exaltation of Christ. The preacher must delight in the wondrous things found in God's Word. Just as heralding was a public event, preaching is a public and passionate celebration of the good news of the King. Wondrous things are truths that amaze. Wondrous things are extraordinary and wonderful things. They are marvelous acts of God. Therefore, such good news about such wonderful acts of God cannot be conveyed without celebration. The celebration of the wonder of the incarnation, the cross, and the resurrection need to be not only taught, but also celebrated. Preaching and listening to preaching is an act of worship; it involves the act of rejoicing in God and His works.

When you see wondrous things in God's Law, the response is praise and thanksgiving. This seeing and this response to this seeing is worship. There are treasures in God's Word. You ought to approach the Bible as a miner during the California gold rush did to a new discovery of gold. The wise man says that his son is to seek after knowledge and his father's wisdom.

"If thou seekest her as silver, and searchest for her as for hid treasure, then shalt thou understand the fear of the LORD and find the knowledge of God" (Proverbs 2:4-5).

The wondrous things in God's Law are like hidden treasures. They are like silver, so act like it. There are treasures in God's Word that mere physical eyes cannot see; therefore, we need the spiritual eye, a heart-eye that sees a Savior.

Preaching is the proclamation of the wonders of the Law and Gospel. God did wondrous things in the Old and New Testament to redeem His people. Preaching must be doctrinal. Men must explain the significance of God's redemptive actions. Paul tells Timothy to "exhort with all longsuffering and doctrine" (2 Timothy 4:2). Today, "doctrine" has foolishly been caricatured as something that is dry and sterile. People act as if to love doctrine is to have a religion that is one of the mind alone. However, there is no opposition between doctrine and life. True doctrine is the basis for a loving life. The preacher must organize and systematize Christian doctrine to show what the Scripture teaches about God, creation, man, the fall, sin, salvation, Christ, the church, and the end times.

The preacher must rightly divide the Word so that he understands the mind of Christ. Preaching is the exposition, the explanation of the Word of God. The preacher must exegete and interpret Scripture. Preaching is not the deliverance of the opinions of a mere man. The preacher must meditate on God's Word to understand it. "I will meditate in thy precepts and have respect unto thy ways" (Psalm 119:15). He must compare Scripture with Scripture. He must rightly divide the Word to understand what it is teaching in its context. Such preaching lets God speak because God's own Word is declared. Redemptive/historical preaching sees the Gospel of Jesus Christ at the center of all of Scripture.

The Law reveals wondrous things about the holiness and beauty of God and the radical life of Christian love to which the believer is called. Preaching is practical. It teaches us how to keep God's statutes. "Thou hast commanded us to keep thy precepts diligently" (Psalm 119:4).

Why does the preaching of the Word have such a prominent place in corporate worship? Why should more than half of our worship service be the reading and preaching and hearing of the Word? That is a remarkable proportion and demands a Biblical explanation.

First, the Word of God is so prominent in public worship because God revealed Himself as the Word through the Word. John 1:1 does not tell us that in the beginning, the "drama" was with God. We are not told that in the beginning was the song. It is tremendously important that Scripture says, "In the beginning was the Word, and the Word was with God." The Son of

357

God is God's communication to the world. One of the greatest wonders is that the Word became flesh.

God chose to reveal Himself by inspiring written words. All Scripture is God-breathed. The word "Scripture" simply means "the writings." Every single verse in Psalm 119 contains a reference to the Word of God.

The Psalm is filled with synonyms. In Psalm 119:18, the synonym for God's Word is "law": "Open thou mine eyes that I may behold wondrous things out of thy law."

Other synonyms for the word that are found in Psalm 119 are: commandments, statutes, precepts, word, testimonies, or judgments. The entire psalm is a celebration of the written word of God in the Law.

Why is Public Preaching the Chief Means of Grace?

There are other things that we can do with the Word, so why is the public preaching of the Word central to Christian worship? For example, we might have a Bible study or we might sing Scripture or we could quietly read Scripture and meditate upon it. So why is preaching, as one form of presenting the Word of God, so prominent in our services? Why should wondrous things of God be proclaimed by a called, appointed minister in our weekly church services?

First, we do have Old and New Testament precedents where wondrous things from God's Law were publicly preached. In the Old Testament, the Law was publicly read and taught by Ezra. Nehemiah 8:8 records, "So they read in the book in the law of God distinctly and gave the sense and caused them to understand the reading." This is an example of the public teaching by a scribe of the wondrous things found in God's Law. In the synagogues during the New Testament era, the Old Testament Scriptures would be read and explained. Therefore Jesus was given the opportunity to preach in His hometown. On his missionary journeys, the Apostle Paul would be invited to preach (Acts 13:14-15).

Secondly, the Word plays a dominant role in public worship because New Testament pastors are solemnly charged, in the presence of Jesus Christ, to herald the wondrous things of God. The Apostle Paul, in very solemn terms, charges the young pastor, Timothy:

> I charge thee therefore before God, and the Lord Jesus Christ, who shall judge the quick and the dead at his appearing and his kingdom: Preach the word. Be instant in season, out of season. Reprove, rebuke, exhort with all longsuffering and doctrine. (1 Timothy 4:1-2)

This is said in the presence of the awesome majesty of King Jesus, who commissions His preachers. Preaching was to be a prominent activity for the minister of the Word.

The word for "preach" is "herald." A king commissioned a herald who made announcements to his subjects. With a loud, clear voice, in the name of the king and with authority, the herald was to bring the king's word.

Timid Timothy must never be afraid to herald the Word. One heralds and spreads gladly good news—and especially news that is wonderful for sinners. One reason why the apostles appointed deacons is because they felt called to give themselves "continually to prayer and to the ministry of the word" (Acts 6:4b).

The Need for Spiritual Vision

The Psalmist teaches us three more things in Psalm 119:18 that have to do with the possibility of seeing wondrous things in God's Law. First, the Psalmist teaches that we cannot see without God's help. Isn't this sad? God has revealed wondrous things in His Law, but we sinful men are too blind to see them. We are like a blind man who is standing outside. A man who is totally blind cannot see the sun, much less anything else around him. By nature, we are spiritually blinded, unable to see what God has done for His people. A blind person who lives in Colorado might try to deny that the Rocky Mountains exist. Or he might deny that the color red exists. Even as Christians, we are dependent on the Holy Spirit from moment to moment for the ability to see wondrous things out of God's Law. If God does not open our eyes, we cannot see wondrous things from His Law. Naturally, we are unable to see the spiritual beauty of the Gospel of Jesus Christ or appreciate what good news it is. The glory of God revealed in Jesus Christ is like the blazing sunshine shining on the face of a blind man.

The Bible says some very realistic things about the minds of fallen men: "Having the understanding darkened, being alienated from the life of God through the ignorance that is in them, because of the blindness of their heart" (Ephesians 4:18). Astonishingly, Moses told the Israelites at the end of forty years, "Yet the LORD hath not given you an heart to perceive and eyes to see and ears to hear unto this day" (Deuteronomy 29:4). These words immediately follow Moses' reference to the wondrous works of God that the *physical* eyes of the Israelites had seen. Yet Moses can say that God had not given Israel *spiritual* eyes to see.

There is nothing wrong with the Word. It has clarity; it is perspicuous. The problem is with us sinners.

There is even a judicial hiding of the Word. The Psalmist prays: "Hide not thy commandments from me" (Psalm 119:19b). Jesus told parables to hide the gospel from the unconverted.

> Unto you it is given to know the mysteries of the kingdom of God, but to others in parables, that seeing they might not see, and hearing, they might not understand (Luke 8:10).

The Word is used to harden many. If the Word of God is not softening, transforming, and producing fruit, then it is probably hardening, blinding, and dulling. Paul writes: "To the one, we are the savour of death unto death; and to the other, the savour of life unto life. And who is sufficient for these things?" (2 Corinthians 2:16)

Secondly, the Psalmist teaches that we need the spiritual vision that the Illuminator alone can give. No one can see God's wonderful things for what they are without the Holy Spirit's help. We take the Holy Spirit's enlightening work for granted. Pray to be filled with the Spirit. We have a desperate need for God's illumination. We need God to work graciously by His Word and Spirit in our lives. We need the mind-informing work of the Word combined with the eye-opening work of the Spirit.

Thirdly, the Psalmist teaches us that we must pray for spiritual sight. We must petition God for understanding by the light of the Spirit. Prayer is crucial for spiritual sight. It is a waste of time for us to read Scripture or listen to sermons if we will not pray, "open mine eyes." Paul wrote a similar prayer for Christians in Ephesus:

> That the God of our Lord Jesus Christ, the Father of glory, may give unto you the spirit of wisdom and revelation in the knowledge of him. The eyes of your understanding being enlightened, that ye may know what is the hope of his calling, and what the riches of the glory of his inheritance in the saints. (Ephesians 1:17-18)

Since we cannot see spiritual beauty or the wonder of God without God's gracious illumination, we should petition our Father for it. Literally, the Psalmist prays, "Uncover my eyes." It is like he has something like scales over his eyes, as Saul of Tarsus had as a new convert. So, pray that your eyes would be uncovered, that you could see wondrous things. As long as we are on this earth, we need to go on praying for spiritual eyesight. We need to read, listen, and pray. The Holy Spirit is sent to illuminate Jesus, and the glory of Jesus is portrayed in the Word. And the Father needs to enable us to see the beauty of His beloved Son.

Prayer for enlightenment is exactly what we find the Psalmist doing in Psalm 119. He prays that God would teach him His statutes (Psalm 119:12b). He prays that God would enable him to understand the Word (Psalm 119:27). He prays that God would incline his heart to the Word (Psalm 119:36). Our Teacher must be God.

Take Heed to How You Listen

Proverbs teaches us to pursue wisdom like a person seeking silver.

You need to hear with your heart-ears. Do not have itching ears. Paul uses a picturesque figure of people who have itching ears:

> For the time will come when they will not endure sound doctrine, but after their own lusts shall they heap to themselves teachers, having itching ears. And they shall turn away their ears from the truth and shall be turned unto fables (2 Timothy 4:3-4).

If your ear itches, you scratch it. In these last days, the ears of fallen men itch for style, oratory, or charisma. They search for a church where their ears will be scratched by preachers who say what they want to hear. Instead, listen with spiritual ears.

The stakes are high—the preaching of the Word is one of the chief means of grace. Hearing with only the ears on the side of your head results in God's Word leaving you as soon as you leave the sanctuary. Hearing the Word without the Spirit flourishes until the love of riches and the pleasures of sin choke it off. Others hear, but only recall it during hard times in life, forgetting that God commands daily heart and mind duties.

Do not be cavalier about reading God's Word or listening to it. Read Scripture as an appetizer. Pray for grace to see wondrous things. You need to hear in such a way that you endure trials, defeat the devil, scorn the pleasures of sin, and walk a godly life. Hearing with faith-filled heart-ears and seeing with spiritual eyes bears fruit unto eternal life

The Fruit

When you listen to God's Word in such a way that you are graciously given to see wondrous things, God will do amazing things in your family! From the beginning of time, God works. God created the universe by His Word. If there were no Word of God, there would be no creation. God regenerates and sanctifies by His Word. "Being born again, not of corruptible seed, but of incorruptible, by the word of God, which liveth and abideth forever" (1 Peter 1:23). God uses His Word to equip the saints.

> All Scripture is given by inspiration of God and is profitable for doctrine, for reproof, for correction, for instruction in righteousness, that the man of God may be perfect, thoroughly furnished unto all good works (2 Timothy 3:16-17).

If there was no Word of God, there would not be any equipped saints. God uses His Word to reveal Christ to us as our justification. We need to look to Christ as our justification.

How can an unbeliever be justified? He needs to believe in Jesus and look to Him for salvation.

> How then shall they call on him in whom they have not believed? And how shall they believe in him of whom they have not heard? And how shall they hear without a preacher? (Romans 10:14)

As we trust in Christ, experience the assurance of our salvation. We know that all our sins have been imputed to Jesus and He has paid for them all. As we see His perfect obedience, we can believe that He is righteous in the sight of God, as well as all those who are in Him.

The Bible teaches that seeing Christ is vital for sanctification. Beholding is also becoming. The wondrous things about Christ revealed in the Bible are so wonderful that they are transforming. The wondrous works of God change us profoundly and empower us to live lives that praise Him and witness to those around us. This is God's work of sanctification! This empowers us -- singles, husbands, wives and children -- to be sacrificial and self-denying.

> But we all, with open face beholding as in a glass the glory of the Lord, are changed into the same image from glory to glory, even as by the Spirit of the Lord (2 Corinthians 3:18).

There is good reason for the Apostle John saying: "He that doeth good is of God, but he that doeth evil hath not seen God" (3 John 1:11).

God reveals Christ's beauty in His Word. True spiritual change comes from seeing the excellencies of Christ in the Word. God sanctifies us as we see the truth about Jesus. Jesus prayed to the Father, "Sanctify them through thy truth. Thy word is truth" (John 17:17). Knowing the Word is crucial for a holy life: "Thy word have I hid in mine heart, that I might not sin against thee" (Psalm 119:11). How do we avoid sin? We avoid sin by treasuring God's Word in our memories. Most things worth doing are not easy. It is hard to fix up an old car. It is hard to play a piece of classical music correctly. It is hard to memorize, but it is worth doing.

So our preaching of sermons and our listening to them must be an act of worship. Delight in what Christ says to you through the ministry of the Word. As you see wondrous things in God's Word, rejoice in these beautiful spiritual realities.

In the act of preaching, the minister needs to celebrate the gospel and rejoice in His God. As the minister exults in the marvelous saving work of God, the congregation is also led into exultation as they see the Triune God in His vast glory. The minister should consciously communicate to the congregation the doxology that is in his heart. Let there be freedom in the pulpit to celebrate and praise God! And let all of God's people say "Amen!"

Chapter 44
Preach to the Church as a Covenant Congregation

One thing that has characterized the Reformed churches is an understanding of the preaching of the gospel as covenantal, that is, it is directed to God's people within the context of the gathered congregation of believers and their seed. This needs to impact how we preach. Today it is vital to emphasize that the preaching of the gospel by God's ordained ministers is an official work of God's ambassadors. In the South (of the United States of America) one often hears the idea that everyone is a preacher. That is why you find untrained, unqualified men attempting to deliver sermons in evangelical or fundamentalistic churches.

We must emphasize the existence of the special office of minister of the Word. But another important issue is that the gathered congregation is God's covenant people. The fact that pastors preach to the gathered covenant people is vital for preaching to the established congregation.

Peter DeYoung underlines the significance of the fact that preaching occurs within the context of the covenant congregation:

> Preaching, as it takes place in the assembly of God's people, as a character uniquely its own. It is not simply a word of exhortation or edification spoken by some individual; rather it is an <u>official</u> service or ministry in and by and for the church as the gathered people of God.

The covenantal context within which preachers preach to established congregations has rich implications for the message and the approach of the minister. Peter Y. De Jong correctly grasped that a distinctive of Reformed preaching is a right understanding of the congregation as a gathering of God's covenant people and their seed. If you misunderstand the nature of your audience, you will make serious mistakes in your preaching. Know your audience (as the saying goes). Then you need to know that the church of Jesus Christ is God's people. They are a holy nation, a kingdom people. They are God's covenant people gathered together with their children for worship.

The minister preaches to covenant children who receive the judgment of charity. Children too are included in the church of God. The minister does not preach organically to the children of the church as if they are "little vipers", even though all the physical descendants of believers are conceived and born in sin.

Covenant children receive the judgment of charity. They are viewed as church members. The gathering of God's people is not just a gathering of adult believers. The church is also the gathering of elect, believing children along with their believing parents.

When the minister preaches to an established covenant congregation, it is not the same as preaching to a mixed crowd of believers and unbelievers in the marketplace (as the Apostle Paul did in Athens).

Within the gathered congregation of the saints, the minister can address the church as "Beloved in the Lord Jesus Christ." This does not mean that every member of the congregation is elect and loved by God, but it does mean that viewed organically they are beloved adult believers and beloved elect and regenerated children.

Speaking to the congregation of believers, the minister can refer to them as God's elect, just as the Apostle Paul did in his address to the Ephesian church (in his epistle). Paul is addressing the church according to her elect kernel. It is true that there are also reprobate hypocrites who are members of the church as institute. But this does not stand in the way of the pastor addressing the gathered congregation of believers as the people of God.

The pastor who preaches to the covenant congregation must exhibit a judgment of charity towards professing Christians and their children (unless their life contradicts their confession). If one is preaching to the children of God, this will shape the message, just as when the Apostle Paul wrote a letter to a church, like the church in Ephesus, this shaped what he would say.

The Netherlands Reformed Congregations and some early American Congregationalist churches made massive mistakes in their approach to preaching to the established covenant congregation.

Jonathan Edwards infamously referred to children of the covenant as little vipers.

The Netherlands Reformed Congregations major in trying to undermine the faith of genuine believers by harping on the possibility of everyone in the congregation being hypocrites. There certainly is room for addressing the problem of hypocrisy, but when ministers preach in such a way as to undermine the assurance of salvation that genuine believers ought to have, we have a serious problem.

The Netherlands Reformed Congregations followed the erroneous idea that assurance is not of the essence of faith. It is true that genuine believers can for a time lose the assurance of their salvation. This might happen if a believer suffers from clinical depression. But the Bible never divides true faith. The one who believes that Jesus is his Savior also has the assurance that this is so. It is the same in ordinary life. If a child believes that his earthly father will give him food, he trusts that this is the case. If we believe that God is our Father, we have the assurance that this is the case. If we did not have the assurance that God was our Father, we would not believe it to be true. If we did not have the assurance that Christ's blood covered all our sins, we could not believe that this was so. Some Puritans and people in the Netherlands Reformed Congregations claim that Christians can have true faith without having the assurance of salvation. They act like this will be the norm among members of their congregations. This turns into a self-fulfilling prophecy.

Peter De Jong on Preaching to the Established Congregation

Peter De Jong, in his homiletics class syllabus used at Mid-America Reformed Seminary, emphasized the fact that the pastor preaches to an established congregation. He writes, "Thus, all congregational preaching must be controlled by the biblical idea of the <u>covenant</u> of which the Lord Jesus Christ is both the Mediator and Surety."

There is a distinction between missionary preaching and preaching to the gathered congregation of believers and their seed. In the Old Testament, we find that God speaks through Moses or through his prophets to the gathered congregation (the covenant people). Therefore, you find the message of grace being proclaimed by God's prophets and at the same time you find a message of warning that is especially relevant within the context of the covenant community.

There certainly is a big difference between a congregation of Jesus Christ and a crowd of unbelievers. The gathered congregation is the kind of group that the apostle Paul refers to in Romans 1:7 as those who were "called to be saints." Paul speaks about the same group of people as "those sanctified in Christ" (1 Corinthians 1:2). Paul writes to the church in Ephesus as "saints" who were "faithful in Christ Jesus" (Ephesians 1:1). Peter uses strong, strong language when he uses Old Testament language to describe the new covenant people saying, "But you are a chosen race, a royal priesthood, a holy nation, God's own people, that you may declare the wonderful deeds of Him who called you out of darkness into His marvelous light. Once you were no people, but now you are God's people; once you had not received mercy, but now you have received mercy" (1 Peter 2:9-10).

The gathering of God's people as the church of Jesus Christ is a gathering of a covenantal people. In such a context, the gospel message can have a particular application. But the same gospel message is preached on the mission field. The people of God hear the gospel message as one that they have affirmed. They are now especially accountable to live the life of the covenant, responding in gratitude to divine grace.

In the established congregation the call to repentance and faith must be made, just as on the mission field. After all, there are hypocrites in the gathered congregation. Members are inviting unsaved natures to church who must hear the gospel. The saints constantly need to be reminded of the great gospel truths. The saints need to rely more and more on Christ and His finished work. God uses warnings to protect and sanctify His people.

On the mission field there soon (by God's grace) will be genuine believers who worship weekly with the missionary. The new converts will need to be built up in the gospel. They will need to be called to ongoing repentance—a life of conversion. Along with them will be unsaved seekers who need to hear the gospel presentation for the first time.

It is important to understand the nature of the gathered covenant community or the local church as institute for the preaching of the Word. If you have a bad covenant theology, you will have a bad approach to preaching. For example, if you have a pure church approach to understanding the covenant (like the Anabaptists do) then you will assume that everybody who is a member of the church is absolutely regenerated. The Puritans began to focus on the question whether they could determine whether a person had gone to the various experiences necessary to show that they had undergone a genuine conversion experience. The reality is that in this life the church as institute or the gathered congregation will include both the regenerate and the un-regenerated.

Some have erred in claiming that by baptism and church membership, a person is in the covenant of grace as much as Abraham was. This will lead to a false assumption that all the baptized and confessing members of local congregation are in a covenant of grace of God with God. But as Paul teaches in Romans chapter 9, not all the children of the flesh are the children of the promise. The promises of the covenant of grace are made to the children of the promise, the spiritual seed of Abraham. Gentiles who believe are true Israelites.

The Netherlands Reformed Congregations are a small pietistic and legalistic denomination in the United States and Canada who view the congregation as mainly a group of gathered un-regenerated persons. They have an approach that militates against the Christian experiencing the assurance of his salvation. This is a radical Puritan approach to the Christian life that implies that every sermon needs to speak to the minority of converted Reformed Christians in the congregation and the larger majority of unconverted members who are all depressed because they have been taught that the experience of genuine salvation is only for the particularly holy few who experienced some type of special conversion experience with the required emotions. In such a context, covenant children are viewed as Jonathan Edwards sometimes spoke of them as "little vipers", rather than as children of the covenant who, yes, include both elect and reprobate, but also include the elect spiritual seed who even as little children already are little lambs of Christ. You need to have faith as one of these little children.

If one does not think that there are covenant keepers are covenant breakers in the congregation, then one will have a naïve view of the church membership. If one presupposes that just by being physically baptized, one is somehow either regenerated or already justified, then one has a wrong understanding of the gathered congregation.

Another danger is having in antinomian approach to church membership, whereby even though members are walking unrepentedly in sin, they still are viewed as members in good standing. Churches where the elders have stopped carrying out Christian discipline are like this. In these churches, the elders are no longer faithful to Christ's command that they place unrepentant sinners outside of the kingdom with the result that people who live in gross sin or teach terrible heresy can remain part of the covenant community. A little leaven leavens the whole lump.

Viewing the Church Organically

The biblical approach to the church as a covenant community is that the gathered congregation is viewed as God's people. But the church is viewed organically and not mechanically. Not every baptized or confessing member of the church is viewed as being truly regenerate and converted. Rather, the congregation recognizes that God gathers His elect in the line of continued generations, but also within the covenant. Reprobate Esaus are born as the physical seed of elect believers. But one views the confessing and baptized members of the church with what is called a judgment of charity. Members who make a good confession and whose lives do not contradict it are welcomed into membership of the church.

Since the elders cannot see into the heart, they are looking for a credible confession of faith. They need to evaluate whether a person's confession of faith is credible and whether their life matches their confession.

Due to the covenant of grace and the fact that God shows mercy and generations, covenant children receive the sign of baptism in their infancy. But the gospel that is preached is the gospel of the kingdom of God, along with the warnings and threats that come with rejection of the gospel message, especially within the context of the covenant community. It is those who have embraced Christ by faith and are living new and godly lives who can have the assurance of their election. Only they can have the assurance that God has established a genuine covenant of grace with them and with their spiritual seed. They alone are the ones who experience the benefits of the covenant of grace.

The hypocrites in the congregation, whether old or young, need to be called to repentance. If a baptized or confessing member of the church shows himself to be an unbeliever, he must be called to repentance and faith in Christ. There are members of the local church as institute who are hypocrites. There are times when that hypocrisy becomes evident in public or private sin. When the person is held accountable by other saints or the elders, their unbelief and ungodliness is exposed. Then they need to be removed from the congregation and publicly declared to be outside of the kingdom of God, if they will not repent.

But for the members of the church who are making a confession of faith in Christ and from all that appears seem to live in a new and godly life, the judgment of charity needs to be followed with respect to them. We need to trust that God show mercy to us in our generations, according to His sovereign will. Then in the congregation the gospel of the kingdom will be proclaimed to believers and to their seed. It is true that the danger of hypocrisy does need to be addressed. Children need to be called to live new and godly lives. They need to be pointed to Christ as the only Savior.

But the assembled congregation is organically viewed as the people of God, even though there are dead branches that in time will be exposed and will be broken off in their generations. But the covenant people are the main audience of the gospel message proclaimed in the church as institute. Gospel preaching in the gathered congregation is addressed to believers and their seed. The minister preaches to many who are converted and living new and godly lives.

And there is a big difference between addressing the gospel to already converted Christians who are striving to live a new and godly lives and preaching to unbelievers who are unsaved.

The genius of Reformed preaching is that it recognizes that a proper view of the covenant needs to define preaching within the sphere of the covenant of grace.

A proper understanding of the covenant means that the pastor as evangelist or the missionary in his missionary proclamation is going to understand that he comes as a messenger of the covenant God gather lost elect sinners and their households into His kingdom in order that He might show mercy to new generations of people.

But in both contexts, whether in the congregation or on the mission field, the gospel call is the same: Repent of sin, look to Christ in faith for justification, and live a new and godly life.

The Warnings

God uses warnings to keep his covenant people faithful.

He sovereignly uses warnings to cause elect believers to fear Him and to dread the consequences of sin.

Those who grow up in the sphere of the covenant will have greater punishments than those who did not. If a person was a member of a church and yet rejects Christ, he will suffer in a hotter place in Hell. Jesus warned that Jewish cities that rejected Him would have a worse punishment than Sodom and Gomorrah.

People who grew up in the church will have greater responsibility for rejecting the gospel than pagans who never heard it. Where much light is given, much is expected.

Within the context of the covenant that there are strong warnings that come to those who grow up in the church and then reject what the writer of Proverbs calls the law of their father or the law of their mother. Jesus gives strong warnings to those who grow up in the church and then reject the faith.

Everyone who hears the gospel preach, hear similar warnings. When pagans on a mission field hear the gospel preach and reject it, they will have greater culpability than pagans who never heard a missionary.

The Covenant of Grace Established with the Elect

One wrong view of the covenant is that all baptized children or all adults who are confessing members of the congregation are in the covenant of grace as if the covenant of grace with its promises is established with the reprobate Esaus who are present in the covenant community or the sphere of the covenant. It is true that the law of God with all its demands comes to all of those were born into the church of Jesus Christ. All children who are born into the church ought to and must confess that Jesus is Lord and they must turn away from their sins. They hear the same message that salvation is for all the spiritual sons of Abraham who believe in Christ like father

Abraham did. The demands that the reprobate who are born into the covenant hear are the same demands that come to wicked unbelievers on the mission field. They hear the same demand to turn away from all their sins and to trust in Jesus as King and Savior. Therefore, the warnings and demands that children who are born into a Christian family ought to hear are the same as what unsaved people need to hear.

There is nothing particularly covenantal about these demands in the sense that the same demands come to people who are outside of the covenant. The difference for children born into the covenant is that they have the benefit of hearing the gospel and the call to repentance from their youngest years. They are also counted as members of the church as institute. They have the benefit of growing up in a family and church where they can hear the gospel from their youngest years. But they will have a greater penalty if they do not repent and trust in Christ.

Klaas Schilder held to the idea that all the promises within the covenant of grace are merely conditional promises. If that is all that the promises of the covenant are (merely conditional covenants), then, of course, the same conditional promises come to unbelievers on the mission field. Unbelievers on the mission field hear the conditional promises, "If you believe, you will be saved" or "If you reject the gospel, then you will perish."

When a minister preaches to an established congregation of faithful saints, he is speaking to the gathered people of God. He preaches within a covenantal context. If a preacher becomes the pastor of a church that is going apostate and where many believers are cultural Christians, he will need to call the members to repentance and faith in Christ. He will need to warn the members of the judgment that will fall upon them if they do not acknowledge Christ's Lordship. And the minister will need to work with the elders to exercise Christian discipline on confessing members who teach heresy and are living worldly lives.

In a true church of Jesus Christ where the congregation holds to orthodox doctrine and is struggling to live a holy life, the preacher will preach to them as God's covenant people. He can call them God's "beloved." He can refer to them as God's elect who were called into the kingdom of Christ. He exercises the judgment of charity. He does not preach as if he is addressing a mixed multitude of half pagans and half Christians.

The faithful preacher knows that might be adult hypocrites in the congregation and that there are also unregenerated children and teens. Therefore, the minister will adapt the gospel message to these various groups. But fundamentally the gospel is going to be proclaimed to the saints as the people of God. They are an imperfect people of God who need to grow in their understanding of the gospel and need to live more and more holy lives. The minister is to believe that the invisible church, the body of the predestinated, has come to visible manifestation in the local church as institute.

The minister will need to administer the Word not only to Christians who are mature but also to children who might be spiritually immature. Since the promise is for believers and their spiritual seed, the gospel is to be addressed to children as well.

It is not as if when preaching to the local congregation that the minister only sees a positive use of the Word. God uses his Word to harden the hearts of the reprobate wicked and to soften the hearts of His elect people. Just as this happens on the mission field in evangelistic preaching, so it occurs in the local congregation. God's Word distinguishes between believers and unbelievers. If the Reformed preacher is preaching to a gathered congregation of God's people, then his approach will not be that of an Arminian evangelist. Arminian evangelists act like everyone in the gathered congregation needs to either accept Jesus as Savior for the first time or reaffirm their faith. The Reformed pastor will recognize that, as a rule, God graciously brings covenant children gradually to conversion. They might not be able to recognize one point in their life when they first trusted in Christ. That certainly is the case with me. The Reformed pastor will recognize that just as children grow and mature physically and psychologically, that the spiritual morphology of a covenant child also will involve a gradual maturing. Just like a child can suddenly go on a growth spurt during the three months between his junior and senior year in high school, so there can be times when a covenant child suddenly grows and matures spiritually.

Not all covenant children have the same consciousness of their sin and guilt and their same awareness of the beauty and love of Jesus. Not all children understand the Old Testament Bible stories and their significance as well as others.

The Goal of Preaching

Whether preaching is done in the local congregation or on a mission station, the first and ultimate goal is the glory of God and the spreading of the fame of the name of Jesus Christ. The preacher needs to live and preach by the motto of Soli Deo Gloria. Maybe he should write that on his manuscript, like Johan Sebastian Bach did on his musical manuscripts. If a minister is preparing a sermon for the glory of God this helps to free him from fear of what people will think. The goal of his preaching is not to establish his name or to make him popular in the congregation, but to communicate something of the majesty and glory of the triune God who is revealed in Jesus.

Secondly, the calling of the minister of Jesus Christ is to announce the gospel of the covenant of grace. I think that the announcement of the good news of the covenant of grace is closely intertwined with the public proclamation of the kingdom of God. Both the idea of the covenant of grace and that of the kingdom of grace are themes that run like a golden thread through all sacred Scripture. God granted Adam the authority to have dominion over the creation. When man rebelled against his Creator and King, God establishes a covenant of grace with Adam and Eve to reestablish His gracious reign over the new humanity. In the covenant of grace, God commits Himself to being a faithful King to His people. From the very beginning, the covenant of grace and the reign of God are intertwined.

God establishes His covenant with David which involves David reigning as king of Israel as a type of the head and mediator of the covenant, the messianic king. Therefore, the content of the preaching of the preacher is the glory of God as manifested in His gracious covenant and gracious kingdom.

The preacher's goal in bringing the Word to the gathered congregation is to re-announce the covenant of grace and the life of the covenant to which God calls his people.

This message is the announcement that King Jesus has paid for the sins of his people and now calls them to submit to his royal law.

Given the weaknesses and sinfulness of God's covenant people throughout all of the ages, the preacher needs to constantly proclaim the faithfulness of God to His covenant people. The Eternal King is the One who not only establishes the covenant of grace, but He maintains it.

He established the covenant of grace by making a solemn vow that he would be a God to Abraham and to his spiritual seed. He established the covenant of grace by sending his beloved Son into this world as the covenant head of his people. At the cross, God causes the sanctions of the covenant to fall upon the King of the Jews. God now maintains that covenant of grace as the Apostle Paul teaches in Romans chapter 9. The Apostle Paul addresses the concern that somehow God's promise came to naught, because many of the Jews had rejected the messianic King. But Paul's argument is that God's promise has not failed. God's promise is an effectual, powerful word that is creative and brings into existence a covenant people in every generation until the return of Jesus Christ. By His Word and through His Spirit, God continues to carry out His decree of election as He shows mercy in generations. God graciously maintains His covenant. He graciously has mercy on those upon whom He will have mercy.

This message of covenant grace needs to be proclaimed from the pulpit. The preacher needs to preach the pure and sovereign grace of the covenant of grace. Every minister is a messenger of the covenant. God has chosen to establish His covenant of grace with elect people. This choice was not conditioned on anything good in them but found its source in His sovereign good pleasure. The fact that God continues to gather His elect in families and in generations is good news that needs to be proclaimed. Along with this gospel message comes all the warnings that we find attached to this message of grace. God calls upon church members and their children to repent of their sins, believe the gospel, and live holy lives.

So, while the first aim of preaching in the congregation is the glory of God, we can say that secondly, and closely connected to that is the exultation of the grace of the covenant God and a magnification of God's supremacy as the King of kings.

A third aim of congregational preaching is the proclamation of God and His saving work in Jesus Christ as well as a faithful presentation of the Law. In other words, the preaching of the gospel needs to involve both Law and gospel.

The preacher needs to be very aware of the first use of the law, which is its function as a prosecutor that indicts sinners. The Law is like a mirror that exposes our sinfulness. The Law exposes our sin sickness. The preacher also will recognize the third use of Law; its function as a path for grateful living for justified believers.

In the established congregation the minister proclaims both Law and gospel. He proclaims that part of the good news of the gospel is that Christ is our Sanctification. Once Christ has justified us, He also sanctifies us. So, while the first use of law in some sense stands in sharpest contrast with the gospel, the third use of the law flows out of the gospel, which is a rich gospel that involves the good news that God not only justifies us but also sanctifies us.

The preacher will focus on announcing God's saving work in Jesus Christ. Notice how I don't focus on just a second article theology that emphasizes Jesus as Savior alone. I write about how the Triune God has saved us in Jesus Christ. It is true that the apostle Paul talks about how he wanted to proclaim only Christ and Him crucified on the mission field. And it is important that ministers preach Christ and Him crucified. But Paul is using this to refer to the whole saving message of God in Jesus Christ. For example, if you think that preachers are limited to preaching Christ crucified, then technically this would not allow them to trumpet the resurrection. Paul is not limiting the minister to a narrow presentation of only the death of Jesus on the cross. Paul certainly trumpets the resurrection and ascension of Jesus as well. Paul did not preach a truncated gospel.

Paul users a synecdoche in which the part stood for the whole. Christ's saving work in the crucifixion is representative of all the Triune God's saving work in Jesus Christ. Paul proclaimed all of Christ's saving work, whether it was His active and passive righteousness or his death, resurrection, or ascension.

Why does the minister preach Christ and Him crucified and the saving work of the triune God? The goal is the salvation and building up of believers and their spiritual seed. That is the positive purpose.

Negatively, the minister knows that the message preached will also be an odor of death unto death for the reprobate hypocrites in the congregation. But the positive goal is the salvation of lost sinners. Within the established congregation, the preacher calls believers to a life of daily repentance. Martin Luther emphasized the importance of the life of repentance in the life of a genuine Christian. The Heidelberg Catechism also emphasizes the need for ongoing, daily conversion. Therefore, the preacher will proclaim the gospel in such a way to build up believers in the holy faith, to encourage them in holiness, and to call them to repentance of their sins.

At the same time, the minister must not neglect the call to repentance and faith for the first time. The minister must recognize that there are very possibly adults in the congregation who are hypocrites and unbelievers and who need to be called to repent and to trust in Christ for the first time. The minister will also get to know children and teenagers who do not give evidence of spiritual life.

Just Planting and Watering

It is not the calling of ministers of the word to preach people into the kingdom of God. I know that this bad practice can happen at funerals where an unbeliever dies and family members apply pressure upon a minister to act as if the dead loved one was actually a genuine Christian. But I mean that a minister of the word cannot somehow coerce or convince anyone by his own power or rhetoric or words to enter the kingdom of God.

In His kingdom parables Jesus makes the point that the kingdom of God is like a farmer who simply scatters some seed. In the absence of the farmer, suddenly the seeds germinate and grow. The farmer doesn't know how this occurs.

Preachers are farmers who scatter seed, but it is God the Holy Spirit who causes life to sprout. The minister needs to believe deeply in his heart that God uses the preaching of the gospel as the means of grace to work faith and strengthen faith in God's people, even if he doesn't seem to see a lot of fruit. It is the minister's calling to be faithful in proclaiming the Word; he merely plants and waters, and it is God who must give the increase.

Chapter 45

Preach and Evangelize as a Pastor-Evangelist

Therefore they that were scattered abroad went every where preaching the word. Then Philip went down to the city of Samaria, and preached Christ unto them.
Acts 8:4-5

How then shall they call on him in whom they have not believed? and how shall they believe in him of whom they have not heard? and how shall they hear without a preacher?
Romans 10:14

Some preachers seem to honor their office of preaching so much that they think that it is legitimate for them to spend most of their time in their study preparing sermons to preach. And they do not seek out lost sheep. If lost people come to church, they will have an opportunity to hear the preacher preach. The preacher almost seems to leave the impression that going out from the church building and bringing the gospel to lost people outside the doors of the church is for lesser preachers. That is the job of bad preachers who have small churches. The dignity of his office of preaching seems to preclude him getting his hands dirty with evangelistic outreach. He is content to prepare sermons mostly for the saved congregation—although there is an evangelistic element to his preaching when the text warrants it

The preacher is called by Christ to be a pastor-evangelist. The title "pastor-evangelist" emphasizes two truths. The preacher is called be an undershepherd to the gathered flock. He is to feed them with the Word. But he is also an evangelist who is called to proclaim the good news of the gospel to lost people. Christ expects the preacher to be used to bring lost sheep into the fold.

Homer C. Hoeksema wrote that "Preaching is the supreme task of the minister. That is expressed already in his very name, *Verbi Dei Minister*, "minister of the Word of God."[657] Hoeksema explains that the minister is also a pastor and liturgist, "But among all these tasks, the preaching of the gospel occupies the chief place."[658] He writes:

> All other things being equal, the minister cannot be a successful catechete, or pastor, or liturgist, except he be a faithful and successful preacher of the Word. In all his work he remains always *Verbi Dei Minister*. Above all he is a homilete."[659]

Herman Hoeksema defined preaching as "the authoritative proclamation of the gospel by the church in the service of the Word of God through Christ."[660]

Each Christian pastor should view himself as a pastor/evangelist. By that I mean that he must be obey the Great Shepherd by both feeding the sheep who are already in the congregation as well as gather lost sheep into the fold.

Every pastor has the calling to seek out lost sheep. Therefore, there is no essential difference between the calling of a pastor in a traditional church or a missionary pastor.

On the mission field, for example, a missionary might begin work with a small group that has been formed. But he places great emphasis on bringing the gospel to the lost--so that the group might grow and a church might be established.

The only difference between a missionary pastor and a pastor in a local church is that the missionary is in the process of establishing a church institute. But the callings of both the missionary and the local pastor are the same. They must both be obeying the Great Commission within their own context. In other words, there is no room in the church for a pastor who is not missionary minded, except if by this is meant that a man does not feel that he has the gifts to learn a foreign language and move to a different culture and country. But every pastor must be willing to transmit the gospel of Jesus Christ across cultural, economic, social, and racial boundaries. In the twenty-first century most Christian pastors live in cities or towns where there is a diversity of cultures and races. A minister may not decide that he is only going to reach out to whites in a community and ignore Laotians or

---

[657] Homer C. Hoeksema, "Homiletics Syllabus," Published by the Theological School of the Protestant Reformed Churches. Grandville, MI. Reprinted 1993., p. 2.
[658] Ibid., p. 3.
[659] Ibid., p. 3.
[660] Cited in Ibid., p. 3.

Hispanics. If there are lost Hispanics or Laotians in your neighborhood, they are proper objects of your outreach. The Apostle Paul is an example for Christian pastors in that he constantly crossed cultural boundaries in taking the gospel from Jerusalem to Gentile communities around the Mediterranean basin. He recognized the need to be all things to all men so as to win some. He was willing to be flexible so as to communicate the truth of Jesus Christ to people from different ethnic, religious, and cultural backgrounds. He did not water down the gospel or deny the fundamentals of the faith, but he was willing to do what was necessary in order faithfully to transmit the gospel across cultural boundaries.

The Word Preached is the Word of God

It is fair to say that the Reformed tradition has emphasized the importance of Paul's teaching on missionary preaching in Romans 10:14-15. Paul writes:

> How then shall they call on him in whom they have not believed? and how shall they believe in him of whom they have not heard? and how shall they hear without a preacher? And how shall they preach, except they be sent? As it is written, How beautiful are the feet of them that preach the gospel of peace, and bring glad tidings of good things! (Romans 10:14-15).

This passage has been mined for a biblical understanding of the importance of missionary preaching by officially called and sent missionary preachers. The Reformed have emphasized the Greek text of Romans 10:14. While the authorized King James Version reads "and how shall they believe in him of whom they have not heard?" the Greek text does not include the preposition "of". Therefore, the passage should read "and how shall they believe in him whom they have not heard?" The implication is that to call on Christ, one first needs to believe in Him, and to believe in Christ, one must first hear Him. The sinner must hear Christ personally. Christ is heard through His preachers. As God's ministers faithfully bring God's word, the word preached is the Word of God. So, sinners need not just to hear about Jesus, but they need to hear the Good Shepherd calling out to His sheep through His preachers.

This is a high view of preaching. Missionary preaching enables Christ's sheep to hear Him as the Word is preached. Preaching is not merely a man lecturing about Jesus. An officially called and sent ambassador of Christ does not merely talk about Christ--but Christ speaks through him. The preacher is an ambassador of Christ. The preacher as a unique man with a unique personality--as he faithfully exegetes, explains, and applies Scripture becomes the mouthpiece of Christ.

This was the doctrine of preaching rediscovered at the time of the Reformation. The Reformers taught that the word preached was the Word of God. The Second Helvetic Confession rejects the error of the Donatists who claimed that the preaching and administration of the sacraments was either effectual or not, depending on the good or evil life of the minister. The Second Helvetic Confession states:

> For we know that the voice of Christ is to be heard, though it be out of the mouths of evil ministers; forasmuch as the Lord Himself said, "All therefore whatsoever they bid you observe, that observe and do; but do not ye after their works: for they say, and do not" (Matt. 23:3).[661]

In other words, Jesus Christ can even speak through an unregenerate minister.

The same confession teaches that God uses ministers for gathering the church. "Therefore ministers are to be considered, not as ministers by themselves alone, but as the ministers of God, by whose means God does work the salvation of mankind."[662] Yet the minister of the Word is only like a farmer who sows the seed, God needs to give the harvest. "Therefore let us believe that God does teach us by His Word, outwardly through His ministers, and does inwardly move and persuade the hearts of His elect unto believe by His Holy Spirit; and that therefore we ought to render all the glory of this whole benefit unto God."[663]

The Reformation creeds emphasize the importance of the official preaching of the gospel as a means of grace. The Canons of Dort state in the First Head of Doctrine, Article 14:

> And as it hath pleased God, by the preaching of the gospel, to begin this work of grace in us, so He preserves, continues, and perfects it by the hearing and reading of His Word, by meditation thereon, and by the exhortations, threatening, and promises thereof, as well as by the use of the sacraments.

The Westminster Shorter Catechism asks: "Q. 89: How is the Word made effectual to salvation?" The answer:

> The Spirit of God maketh the reading, but especially the preaching of the word, an effectual means of convincing and converting sinners, and of building them up in holiness and comfort, through faith, unto salvation.

---

[661] Second Helvetic Confession, XVIII, 18.
[662] Ibid., XVIII, 1.

The Canons of Dort connect preaching and missions in Article 3 of the First Head of Doctrine right before it quotes Romans 10:14-15.:

> And that men may be brought to believe, God mercifully sends the messengers of these most joyful tidings to whom He will and at what time He pleaseth; by whose ministry men are called to repentance and faith in Christ crucified.

When the Canons in the Second Head of Doctrine, Article 5 speaks about the publication of the gospel promise, the implied reference is certainly to missionary preaching:

> This promise, together with the command to repent and believe, ought to be declared and published to all nations, and to all persons promiscuously and without distinction, to whom God out of His good pleasure sends the gospel.

The Westminster Larger Catechism is representative of the Reformed tradition in stating that "The Word of God is to be preached only by such as are sufficiently gifted, and also duly approved and called to that office" (Question 158). The Westminster Larger Catechism explains how the Word of God is to be preached:

> They that are called to labor in the ministry of the Word, are to preach sound doctrine, diligently, in season and out of season; plainly, not in the enticing words of man's wisdom, but in demonstration of the Spirit, and of power, faithfully, making known the whole counsel of God; wisely, applying themselves to the necessities and capacities of the hearers; zealously" (Q.159).

Jesus was an example of a preacher who brought His Father's word to His audience, taking into consideration the "necessities and capacities of the hearers." He was a culturally relevant preacher. His parables were a culturally relevant way of communicating truth about the kingdom of heaven. The messages that the Apostle Paul preached had in common faith in the crucified and resurrection Jesus Christ, but his method of preaching was flexible. In his preaching he tried to become all things to all kinds of people whether Athenians or Jews.

The word preached is the word of God. But this certainly does not imply that when a missionary teaches error, whether doctrinal heresy or simply presents bad exegesis or misapplies a passage, that this is the word of Christ. But in as much as he does speak the truth in Christ and does faithfully teach

---

[663] Ibid., XVIII, 2.

the Scriptures, Christ in a mysterious way speaks through him. This is something that the church must believe. Roger Greenway states:

> The supreme agent of conversion in the New Testament is the Holy Spirit and the means is the Word. Without the Holy Spirit the whole missionary enterprise could not even begin (Luke 24:44ff) and without the Word there is no faith (Romans 10:17).[664]

Explaining Romans 10, Greenway writes:

> The salvation of men and women everywhere is taught to be utterly dependent on the missionary vocation, the sending, the going, the preaching, and the hearing of the Word of God, which make up missions.[665]

As a result, what the Apostle Paul did as a missionary was simply this--preach. He proclaimed the message of Christ in the urban centers of the Roman Empire.

Officially Sending out Missionaries

The Reformed tradition has also emphasized the necessity of officially sending out missionaries. The proof text widely used is Romans 10:15: "And how shall they preach, except they be sent?" This sending out is to be done by the church. Not an individual. Not a synod. Not a parachurch organization. In Acts 13 we have the history of the sending out of Paul and Barnabas by the church in Antioch on their first missionary journey: "And when they had fasted and prayed, and laid their hands on them, they sent them away" (Acts 13:3). Some Reformed churches have decided that their domestic and foreign mission committees must work through a calling church. Therefore, a missionary is sent out by a local church and is under the oversight of that consistory--as well as the mission committee.

The Reformed churches do consciously send out missionaries--with a service where prayers are offered and the word is preached. But there are two apostolic practices that have not been followed. First, fasting seems to be a lost spiritual discipline prior to sending out a missionary--even though our missionaries today face similar challenges and obstacles and dangers to those of Paul and Barnabas. Second, the ceremony of the laying on of hands is not practiced during a commissioning service. The laying on of hands of Paul in Acts 13 cannot be a sign that he is being called to the ministry--since

---

[664] Roger S. Greenway, An Urban Strategy for Latin America (Grand Rapids: Baker Book House, 1973), 80.
[665] Ibid., 80.

he had already been laboring as a preacher of the word. After all he was called by Jesus Christ to the ministry. This laying on of hands symbolized a prayer for the Holy Spirit to equip and bless the missionaries and their work. These practices probably should be normative in the churches.

Abraham Kuyper on the Sending out of Missionaries

In a popular lecture, "Missions According to Scripture," Abraham Kuyper attempted to inspire the local church to carry out her calling in missions.

He especially wanted Reformed believers to be willing to give their sons for the missionary cause.

He spoke of how in the past the Reformed Church had been asleep: "Missions did not come from her spirit." He added: "Accordingly to this tendency towards impersonal spiritual association the main need became money." It is interesting that Kuyper refers to the church as having an "impersonal spiritual association" with missions. This certainly is a danger in the Reformed churches. This results when local churches view mission work as solely the work of a denominational mission committee. Or the mission of the church is viewed as only taking place in another country. Visiting mission fields is something that certainly fosters a personal spiritual association. Kuyper believes that more is necessary than money and prayers for missions:

> The congregation may not remain at this point of the sending of her messengers. More needs to be done. Many who support the work of missions are giving a lot, indeed an awful lot; but who gives himself with the sacrifice of all he has. Who gives his Isaac, his son, the only one he loves? It is to this point that the congregation has to come. The congregation must send her sons. The spirit of mission must envelop her as congregation, and infiltrate and sanctify her in such a way, that she will plead with God that he will give her children. Children, that is those exceptional men in whom is found the essence of the spiritual power of the congregation....
>
> The congregation must grow from her womb men who are born for missions and who are put in the cradle for that purpose, who are not good for anything else.

Kuyper spoke of the benefit of sending out missionaries two by two: "These men must not go alone. Paul and Barnabas and later Paul and Silas went together." One difficulty that many home missionaries face is that they are sent out alone and as a result ministry in isolation from supporting churches—sometimes 500 miles away from the overseeing consistory.

The Office of All-Believer

A perceived weakness in the Reformed churches has been the passion of the laity to witness by their words among the gospel. A small proportion of Reformed Christians invite lost men and women to Bible studies or church services. There is a sense in which the laity need to recover the doctrine of the priesthood of all believers.

The laity played an important role in the spread of the gospel in the Roman Empire and the laity have a vital role today. Believers should not need to be commanded to spread the good news of Jesus Christ. It should be natural for a Christian to testify of what God has done for him. The missiologist, Roger Greenway asks an interesting question:

> Do we hear the apostles pleading for missions, urging Christians to bear witness to their neighbors, asking for help in evangelizing the Roman Empire? Why this silence on a subject which obviously was very dear to the apostles, and about which today we feel compelled to say so much? The answer, I believe, lies in the fact that the congregations back then were spontaneously carrying out their missionary obligation and needed no urging or correction on this matter.[666]

Yet many Christians today do need to be commanded and do need encouragement to carry out their prophetic calling.

The doctrine of the priesthood of all believers means that every Christian has the authority and right to tell others about Jesus Christ. Roger Greenway writes of the role of the laity in the early church:

> It is important to observe Paul's typical approach to a city. He was concerned to search out active collaborators, not passive recipients. It was on people like Aquila and Priscilla, to whom religion was not a mere appendage, that the gospel made its greatest impact. Paul was a trainer and coach as much as he was a church planter.
>
> The spread of the gospel, in Paul's estimation, was not a responsibility resting mainly on the shoulders of outsiders like himself, but a joint effort among all of Christ's disciples and a local responsibility. Paul never left the impression that the evangelization of a city or an entire region was his task alone. On the contrary, his converts were told to tell

---

[666] Roger S. Greenway, Cities: Missions' New Frontier (Grand Rapids, Baker Books, 2000), 47.

others, win others, and continue what the missionary had begun.[667]

In the early church ordinary believers were spreading the good news about Jesus Christ. It would be odd if Christians did keep the good news about Jesus to themselves. Dr. Luke records in Acts 8:1 the pressure that unbelieving Jews and Saul of Tarsus put on the apostolic church:

> And at that time there was a great persecution against the church which was at Jerusalem; and they were all scattered abroad throughout the regions of Judea and Samaria, except the apostles.

Notice that the apostles were not scattered. They remained behind in Jerusalem and continued to minister there. It was the ordinary believers who were scattered. Acts 8:4 describes what the scattered believers did: "Therefore they that were scattered abroad went everywhere preaching the word." The translation is unfortunate. These scattered believers were not preachers. Literally we read that they were "evangelizing"; they were telling the "good news" about Jesus. In other words, the Bible uses the word "evangelize" to refer what ordinary believers do as they spread the message of Jesus. In the very next verse in Acts 8, in verse 5 we find a different verb used to describe what Philip did: "Then Philip went down to the city of Samaria, and preached Christ unto them." The verb used here is "keerusso." It carries the connotation of an official announcement. In contrast to Philip who officially preached, the ordinary believers spread the good news of Jesus.

So, it must be today. Pastors as pastor-evangelists should herald the gospel while believers spread the good news about Jesus Christ.

---

[667] Roger S. Greenway, Cities: Missions' New Frontier (Grand Rapids, Baker Books, 2000), 45.

Chapter 46
Did Christ Call You to Preach?

How can a preacher endure in the ministry? He needs to have a
strong sense of call. He needs to know that the Lord Jesus Christ
personally called him to the ministry.
Did Christ personally call you to preach the gospel?

When I was a around a junior in high school, a professor of the
Protestant Reformed Seminary visited my home town of
Edgerton, Minnesota to speak on the need for preachers. The
seminary did not have very many students. The denomination had around
6,000 members. Not many students were attending seminary and there were
not even a lot of pre-seminary students. Therefore, the board of the
seminary decided to send out the professors around the United States to visit
the churches and speak about the need for qualified young men to pursue
the ministry of the Word.

I listened to the talk. At the time I thought that the professor, in this
case, Robert Decker, was a very impressive man. He had white hair. He spoke
with eloquence. He was highly respected and loved by the members of our
congregation. I began to want to be a minister, but I had mixed motives.

Due to my background and the grace that was given to me, I was the
sort of young man who should have been considering the ministry. But I
always was impressed by how much respect and honor a professor received
and thought that it would be great to have a job where people showed this
kind of respect and love for you.

We can have mixed motivations in pursuing the ministry. What young
man really understands the implications of pursuing the ministry?

I did not share with any one my thoughts about entering the ministry.

After all, my brother was a senior in high school. He was one year older
than I. He had openly declared his interest in attending seminary. People
joked with him about it. He planned to attend Dordt College and pursue a
pre-seminary degree. Meanwhile Allen wrote a letter to one of our first
cousins in Grand Rapids, Doug Kuiper, in which he let Doug know that he was
planning to go to seminary. His letter passed a letter by Doug in the mail.

Doug had written a letter informing my brother that he was going to pursue the ministry! The two were the same age so they ended up in class together at the seminary for four years.

Since my older brother planned to attend seminary, it seemed to me that my interest was robbing me of my individuality. I didn't want people to think that I was a clone of my brother. So I kept quiet.

But I would lay awake at night and think about what God wanted me to do. The idea of becoming a preacher of the Word began to give me great joy. I would stay up late listening to Hooked on Classics, a classical music tape, and imagine what it would be to pursue the ministry of the Word.

My brother and I grew up in a family where life was centered around church and school. We lived across the street from the church. My father often served on the consistory. My parents were spiritually minded. They raised us in the fear of the LORD. They wanted us to put God first. We attended a small Christian school, the Free Christian School, that was exactly one block from our home. This school had about 35 students in two classrooms. Later they added a third classroom just for the kindergarteners.

Our extended family on both sides were committed Reformed Christians. They would not have thought of skipping church or not going to an evening worship service. I was part of a large extended family.

My mother is a Kuiper from Grand Rapids, Michigan and had 11 siblings. I had 70 cousins on that side. My father had seven siblings and I must have had 45 cousins on the Brummel side. Almost all of my cousins attended Christian schools. Their parents were willing to pay expensive Christian school tuitions. No one was rich. But the family was rich in the blessings of the covenant.

My brother and I came from generations of Dutch Reformed believers. Covenant mercy had been shown to many of our ancestors. There was a piety rooted in our families. The Bible was read at the dinner table. Prayer was offered. Parents attended Bible studies and church events. We children attended catechism that was mostly taught by the minister. We started catechism in the first grade.

Both sides of the family were characterized by a concern for Christian piety. Since our families were not made up of intellectuals, you could say that they were more influenced by the Afscheiding tradition. The Afscheiding (Separation) was a reform movement out of the apostate Dutch Reformed Church in 1834. Most of the members of the Afscheiding were poor, yet they were pious and affirmed the doctrines of the Reformation. The Afscheiding encouraged personal and family piety. Yet there was also a keen interest in accurate Reformed theology in my family, like what characterized the Doleantie. The Doleantie (Aggrieved) refer to the reform movement led by Abraham Kuyper that involved people leaving the apostate Dutch Reformed Church in the 1880's. So my brother and I grew up in a family, church, and school context where personal holiness was valued and where a loved of the truth was given great weight.

If families and churches want to be places that can be incubators of future ministers, they need to do three things. First, they have to stand for holiness in an antinomian age. Parents, ministers, and Christian school teachers (who teach in the place of parents) need to strictly teach the Ten Commandments. They need to act like godly Puritans. They need to apply the Law of God to all of life to (1) convict covenant children of their sins (so that they flee to Christ) and (2) show covenant children how to live a godly, grateful life. Second, they have to teach children to love Jesus and His truth.

The warm piety of the Afscheiding needs to be evident in love for God and His Son Jesus Christ. Parents need to read their Bible and read theology so that they can teach their children the great doctrines of the Christian faith. If parents do not value theology, why should the children? Third, they need to show children what is truly important in life. If parents live for the things of this world or only get excited about their job, their children will not put first the kingdom of God. If parents are unwilling to pay Christian school tuition or to homeschool their children, children will learn that God does not come first. Children must be taught by example that all of life needs to center around the glory of God. We need to acknowledge the supremacy of Christ in our jobs and in education.

It is true that Christ calls to the ministry of the Word converts who were never raised in a Christian home. He calls some men to the ministry who never attended Christian schools. Even though the grace of God can be powerfully poured out on such men, yet they minister under a severe handicap. Such a preacher will always sense his poverty. Much grace is necessary to overcome their shortcomings. We need to appreciate how formation for the ministry of the Word begins with covenant boys in their childhood. A lot goes into the formation of ministers of the Word. Their formation does not begin when they start taking their first class in seminary. Their formation begins when their parents pray for them in their mother's womb and when dad and mom are teaching a two-year-old to memorize his first Bible passage. Formation occurs in the catechism room. Christian school teachers play a crucial role in character formation and in the development of latent talents. How the boy's dad and mom conduct themselves in the home, how they resolve conflict, how much they love each other, how they love the imperfect members of their local congregation, how they support the ministry of the Word by their local pastor; all shape the future minister.

When I meet ministers of the Word and see the gifts and graces that

God has showered upon them, I always look at them through this covenantal grid.

Why is it that ministers of the Word can have such striking piety, such a deep knowledge of the Bible, such wisdom in how to act towards others, and such a love for the truth? The long answer is that God was forming these men from their childhood and youth.

He used covenant parents and faithful Christian school teachers along with godly ministers to develop the ability to love, an awareness of the great narrative of redemptive history, and an ability to think through complex theological issues.

Ministers are not made in a day.

Or a month.

Or a year.

God usually takes decades to make a minister. That is why we are sometimes startled by the gifts and maturity that a seminary graduate of 26 years of age possesses. His three or four years of attending seminary are only a partial explanation for this maturity. His dad and mom played a crucial role in raising him. And God blessed the boy beyond the parent's best hopes. God is the one who uses the weak instruments of dads and moms, faithful ministers, and sacrificial Christian school teachers (who live in poverty) to pour out surprising gifts and blessings upon young men whom Christ wants in the pulpit ministry.

So there I was a senior in high school. What would I do? What did my future hold? Even though my dad never went to college and my mom only attended for a short while, my parents always expected that I would go to college. They always expected that I and my siblings would go to college. My dad even told my sisters that it would be wise for them to go to college in case they didn't get married and needed to support themselves or if something happened to their husband someday and they would need to support their family. My parents always encouraged my brother and I to go to college. We never thought about not going to college. The only question was, where would we go.

My brother decided to attend Dordt College that was 60 miles from home—located in Sioux Center, Iowa. As my senior year came, I had a friend in high school who planned to attend Calvin College in Grand Rapids, Michigan. I decided that I would like to go there as well.

Two things drew me. First, I knew that much of my mother's side of the family and some of my father's relation lived in Grand Rapids, Michigan. Second, I knew that Calvin College and Seminary were more at the heart of the intellectual debates in the Christian Reformed Church.

I thought it would be interesting to be at the center of the debates going on in the Reformed community. The Protestant Reformed Seminary was also located in the Grand Rapids area, and this was the school that I was thinking about attending someday.

But I didn't let anyone know at this point what my thoughts were. I started Calvin College in the Fall of 1988. I signed up for a Religion 103 class. The first day of class my professor attacked the doctrine of inerrancy. He rejected verbal inspiration. He taught that the Bible was only infallible with respect to some redemptive message. I was astounded during this semester as I watched him shred the Old Testament. He founds errors, contradictions, and inconsistencies everywhere. In his class I was taught that the Bible was put together in an incomprehensible way by editors. Apparently only higher critics could even begin to understand anything in the Old Testament. Even when a prophet explicitly said, "Thus saith the LORD", my professor would sit in judgment about whatever God said.

I had thought that the big issue between the Christian Reformed Church and the Protestant Reformed Churches of which I was a member, circled around common grace. I was naïve. During the January interim I took a class on Genesis 1-11. There I was introduced to the Frame-work Hypothesis of Genesis and theistic evolution. Suddenly I was amid a big debate that was going on at Calvin College and in the Christian Reformed Church about the teachings of Howard Van Til who had written a book about the fourth day of creation in which he defended theistic evolution. He also used Meredith Kline's arguments in defense of the framework hypothesis of Genesis 1.

Another burning issue was the matter of women in church office. Leading voices in the Christian Reformed Church were advocating for the opening of the special offices to women.

One day as I was walking through the common area outside of the library I discovered that supporters of homosexuality were sitting behind a fold-up table. They were handing out bracelets for people to wear showing that they supported homosexual behavior and the gay rights movement.

Then there was the time that the neo-Kuyperians at Calvin College thought that they should have a showing of "Jesus Christ Superstar" in the auditorium. This film portrayed Jesus as committing adultery with Mary Magdalene. But these Kuyperians (who had abandoned the antithesis) thought that it was fitting to show and watch this video so that the Calvin College community could interact with the culture. They had no fear of God.

It was in this context that I felt a burning need to stand for truth and righteousness. I felt the need to speak out. I could not be silent about the gospel and God's truth.

People learned that I planned to pursue the gospel ministry when I enrolled in Greek class during my sophomore year. I had started taking Dutch already and now I started driving across the city to Grandville, Michigan where the Protestant Reformed Seminary was located. The seminary offered Greek as a pre-seminary class.

After a year of Greek, I also signed up for Latin. The seminary required two years of Dutch, Greek, and Latin for entrance into the seminary. Hebrew was part of the actual seminary program.

Christ gave me a desire to pursue the ministry of the Word. He gave me a prophetic soul. He made me burn for the truth of the gospel. He caused me to hate heresy and depravity. I cared about Reformed theology. I was angered to discover that most of the philosophy professors at Calvin College were semi-Pelagians. I was grieved by the fact that the Calvin College community rejected the authority of Scripture and denied the historicity of Genesis 1-11. I was stunned by the hypocrisy of the faculty who signed agreement to the Three Forms of Unity (the Heidelberg Catechism, the Canons of Dort, and the Belgic Confession of Faith) and then taught contrary to them. And there was no accountability.

There was no accountability for Howard Van Til who later apostatized from the Christian faith. At least he was logically consistent in two crucial ways: (1) If one does not need God to explain the origin of the species, why postulate Him? (2) If the Bible is an erring human document, why believe what it says about origins or anything else (including the resurrection of Christ)?

I had a deep sense that Christ Himself was calling me to the ministry of the Word. It wasn't that I simply wanted to be a minister. I believed that Christ from Heaven wanted me to be a minister of the Word. I never would have endured the four-year boot camp of seminary if I had not known that to be the case. Why endure the stress of internships and synodical exams and classical exams, if Christ is not calling you to the ministry of the Word?

Why suffer in the ministry of the Word, if Christ has not called you to your office?

The Internal Call

There are two important elements in the call to the ministry. The first element in a call to the ministry of the Word is the internal call. This is a deep sense in the soul of a qualified man that Christ wants him to preach the gospel. I came to know that Christ wanted me to be an ambassador for Him. I never heard Jesus speak verbally to me from Heaven, like the Apostle Paul had happen.

In fact, if a person claims that this happened to him, he is not ministerial material. He is claiming that he received an extra-biblical revelation in a time when God speaks only through the Scriptures. Such a man is a liar and deceives himself and tries to deceive others. But I did have a deep sense in my soul that Christ wanted me to proclaim the gospel. I had this sense as I prayed, read my Bible, and listened to God's preachers. This sense was confirmed as I saw in my life the qualifications necessary for the ministry of the Word.

The External Call

The second element in the call to the ministry of the Word is the external call. This involves the call of Christ through the church. I could not have even entered seminary if the local church that I attended had not written a letter of recommendation.

This letter affirmed that I had the godly qualifications necessary for pursuing the pulpit ministry. Later my professors needed to affirm that I had the gifts for the ministry of the Word. They had a good chance to get to know me because I was the only student in my class over a four-year period. They licensed me to exhort. Then the entire synod of the Protestant Reformed Churches examined me before I became a candidate who would be available for a call. A crucial part of the external call is the reception of a call from a local congregation. Christ calls men to the ministry through a call from a local congregation. A new daughter church was formed in Dyer, Indiana and this church extended a call to me. I then had a classical exam after which I was finally ordained to the gospel ministry.

So Christ directly calls a man to the ministry in the internal call and then makes this public through the external call.

How can you know that Christ is calling you to pulpit ministry? I think that you can ask yourself the following questions:

First, do you have a love for the Bible and a desire to communicate its doctrines?

Second, do you believe that Christ Himself from Heaven wants you to pursue the ministry?

Third, are you walking worthy of the gospel?

Fourth, do you have the gift of public speaking?

Fifth, can you interpret texts?

Sixth, do you love the people around you?

Seventh, are you a merciful person?

Eighth, do others recognize that you have the qualifications to pursue the pulpit ministry?

Ninth, do you care about the mission of the church? Do you want to share the good news with lost people?

Tenth, do you feel the desire to stand up for the truth of the gospel in these days of apostasy?

Eleventh, do you love God and His Christ?

Twelfth, are you able to learn Greek? They used to say at Calvin College that in pre-seminary Greek classes the Holy Spirit would reveal who was and who was not called to the pulpit ministry. If you couldn't learn Greek, apparently God had other plans for you.

Thirteenth, do you have a maturing prayer life? Do you desire to talk with God? Are you growing spiritually?

Fourteenth, if you are married, do you have a wife who supports your pursuit of the ministry?

Fifteenth, do you like to study? Are you a good student?

Sixteenth, do other people recognize that you have the gifts for the ministry of the Word?

Seventeenth, do I have a sense of the desperate need for faithful gospel preachers today?

Eighteenth, do you love your Bible? Do you find yourself constantly reading it?

These are crucial questions for the man who is considering the ministry of the Word. No man has the right to pursue the ministry of the Word, if Christ has not called Him. No man has the right to make himself into a minister, if the church does not call him (since Christ calls men through His church).

Has God give you a burning zeal to proclaim the message of the gospel? Do you have a desire to support the mission of the church through overseas missions?

Those whom Christ calls, He qualifies. That is an encouragement to the young man who faces four years of college and then four more years of seminary. If God has called you to the gospel ministry, He will equip you by the Holy Spirit. If Christ has called you, then no human barriers that wicked men erect can stand in the way of your entrance in the pulpit ministry. Sinful, sectarian professors cannot stop you. Liberal presbyteries that try to stop Bible-believing seminarians from entering the ministry will not be able to stop you. If Christ has called you, He will open the door for your ordination. Demons will not be able to get you disqualified. Christ loves and upholds those whom He calls to the ministry of His Word.

Evaluating Your Gifts

The Christian man who feels a call to the ministry needs to take inventory of his gifts. First, does he have the gifts of personality necessary for pastoral relations? Not everyone knows how to relate to people. When I was in seminary the faculty informed a man who had attended seminary for four years that they would not endorse him for his synodical exams. The reason: he had a quirky personality. Some men do not know how to relate to people well. The potential minister needs to be able to communicate with people across social and economic levels. He needs to have the social gifts necessary for interacting with the saints. If a man has psychological challenges, he might not have the psychological strength for interpersonal relationships and the conflicts associated with them.

Second, the potential preacher needs to be honest about his intellectual gifts. If a man does not like to read, he might as well pursue the ministry as much as a man who doesn't like physical activity would join the marines. If you have no desire to run, don't attend marine boot camp. If you don't like reading texts, don't imagine that you are ministerial material.

Third, the man needs to take inventory of his study habits. If you do not have good study habits and the ability to work hard, Christ is not calling you to the ministry. At Calvin College they used to say that the Holy Spirit revealed in pre-seminary Greek whether or not a man was called to the ministry. If a pre-seminary student could not learn Greek, this was evidence that God had not given him the gifts for the ministry. God does not give everybody the necessary gifts.

If a student is unwilling to discipline himself to learn a biblical language, he will not demonstrate the ability to discipline himself to prepare biblical sermons.

Fourth, the potential minister must take a spiritual inventory. Does he pray? Does he love God's Word? Does he have a wonderful thirst for Scripture? Does he love the truth? Does he want to defend the truth? Does he love the people around him? Is he a godly husband? Is he devoted to teaching his children God's way? Is he growing in faith? Is he faithful in sexuality? Is he walking worthy of the gospel? Is he pursuing after holiness?

To attend seminary, a man must have a letter of recommendation from his consistory. The elders need to take inventory of the potential student's faith and life. They should see that the man is living in godliness. They need to evaluate whether the man affirms the doctrines confessed by the Reformed churches. Does he have a good reputation? Is he faithful in his family relationships? Does he have the intellectual abilities to study Scripture and Christian theology? Does he love the church? Does he love the

Word? Has he shown spiritual leadership in the local congregation?

Elders ought to be proactive in their evaluation of potential seminary students. The office-bearers in the local church should encourage young and older men with the qualifications for the ministry to consider this holy calling. Elders not only should pray that the Lord would provide ministers for the harvest of souls but should support the identification and encouragement of potential ministers.

The elders should discuss whether young men or older men in the congregation are demonstrating the graces and gifts for the ministry of the Word. God uses the encouragement of ministers, elders, and the saints to challenge a young man to consider the ministry.

But it is Christ alone who can call a man to the ministry. God might give a young man tremendous intellectual gifts, godliness, and spiritual maturity; but might want the man to be a medical doctor or politician.

Men often approached Charles Spurgeon to express their desire to attend seminary. Spurgeon tells the story of a man who informed the famous preacher that he had failed at several vocations and now thought that maybe he should try the ministry. Spurgeon's response was to the effect that Jesus does not call failures to the ministry.

Another piece of advice that Spurgeon gave potential ministerial students was that if they could find contentment in any other vocation, they should pursue it. I think that if Christ calls a man to the ministry, He will make him discontent with any other vocation.

The potential minister should say with the Apostle Paul: "I am compelled to preach. Woe to me if I do not preach the gospel" (I Corinthians 9:16).

John R. Sittema believes that the potential ministerial student can be "confident" that he is called by God to preach if

1. you have been equipped by the Father with the requisite intellectual, physical, emotional, and spiritual gifts; and
2. the church of the Lord has confirmed your self-evaluation based on her knowledge and observation of your doctrine and life; and
3. you have experienced within your heart the powerful moving of the Spirit of God, coercing you by divine influence so that you cannot live unless you preach.[668]

---

[668] John R. Sittema Called to Preach: Pondering God's Commission for Your Life (Mid-America Reformed Seminary, 1989), 31.

The Mystery of the Internal Call

Joel Nederhood admits that it is a bit difficult to write about the call to the ministry. "One reason is that so few people actually have it, it might almost fit under the subject of abnormal psychology. Another is that it is totally subjective, and those who possess it in its strongest form find it difficult, even awkward, to express exactly what it is for them."[669]

Today preachers receive an internal call from Christ by the Spirit and then an external call from a local church. In Bible times we find that God directly called men to the ministry of the Word by a spoken revelation. God spoke to Isaiah and Jeremiah, calling them to the prophetic office.

It is true that when God called them, the prophets also volunteered to be sent. But God personally initiated the call and communicated it through a special revelation. The Angel of Jehovah called Moses to his prophetic task at the burning bush. Jesus specifically called Andrew and Simon to leave their fishing boats to become fishers of men. Christ chose 12 men to be disciples, and as Mark points out, to be apostles. Famously the Apostle Paul was called to the prophetic office by a personal visitation from the ascended Jesus.

Today it is different.

Sometimes a new convert feels an immediate and strong call to the pulpit ministry. The call is genuine. Other new converts mistake their first love for Christ for a call to pulpit ministry. In times it becomes evident that although God gave the convert a great love for the Word, He was not calling him to pulpit ministry.

But for most men who are called to the ministry, the internal call is something that slowly rises and matures in their consciousness as they grow in grace. Most of these men grew up in the church and received and experienced divine grace from their youngest years. Joel Nederhood writes that "So far as the call is concerned, there is a development of one's consciousness with respect to it."[670] As a rule the internal call is experienced as a growing force. That is why you see that some young men resist a call to the ministry during their college years and then in their late twenties or early thirties realize that they need to quite their job and pursue the ministry. "For most ministers, however, their becoming called to the ministry involves a development over an extended period of time."[671] While the call might at first be questioned, in time it becomes "the most dominant

---

[669] Joel Nederhood "The Minister's Call The Preacher and Preaching: Reviving the Art in the Twentieth Century, ed. Samuel T. Logan, Jr. (Phillipsburg, NJ: P & R Publishing, 1986), 33.

[670] Ibid., 42.

[671] Ibid., 42.

force in their lives."[672]

A married man with children will quit his job, sell his house, and move hundreds of miles off to attend seminary. He will go from an affluent lifestyle to one of poverty and dependence. The call makes a man willing to pursue pre-seminary studies in college. Such a man is willing to deny himself, driving old (almost broken down) vehicles and living with only a few hundred dollars in his checkbook. He will work second jobs and live in sparse accommodations because he has a goal. He will pursue an expensive education, racking up college debt. The call has a dominant effect on the man's life because he senses with the Apostle Paul: "Woe is me if I do not preach the gospel" (I Corinthians 9:16).

What Christ is Calling the Future Preacher to Do

Nederhood writes that the call is to a special office in the church. The calling of the minister of the Word is to preach the gospel and administer the sacraments. Therefore, the call is to preach the Word. Nederhood defines the internal call as *"one's conviction that God would have him faithfully proclaim the Word of God."*[673] Since this is the case, Nederhood rams the significance of this home: "The ministerial call is that and nothing more, and those who want to serve God in the ministry must make sure they have it; and those who have this call must make sure they obey it."[674]

Interior Events in the Psychology of the Called Man

"Certain interior events," which Joel Nederhood identifies as sacred, occur within the consciousness of the man Christ calls. The first interior event is the man's conversion. He knows that Christ saved him. He experiences free and sovereign grace. Second, he loves Jesus and has a deep sense that Christ personally has called him to the gospel ministry.

Nederhood writes that it is "especially necessary for the minister" to "have a personal relationship with the Savior."[675] This includes recognizing that Jesus your Commander has called you to be a soldier of the cross as a gospel preacher. Third, the man with the internal call can't stop reading the Bible. You will find him reading and studying his Bible when other Christian young people would not consider doing so. If you came into my dorm room when I was a student at Calvin College, you might find me lying on a couch reading my Bible. You will find the man reading and studying his Bible

---

[672] Ibid., 42.
[673] Ibid., 44.
[674] Ibid., 44.
[675] Ibid., 47.

instead of doing class assignments. He prefers his Bible to his Mathematics textbook.

Nederhood writes of a "Fascination with the Bible" that characterizes such a man. I experienced this recently when I oversaw a ministerial intern. He manifested the same fascination. When he should have been studying Greek or preparing lessons, he was reading and studying his Bible. He had a burden to inspire other young people to read their Bible and engage in daily devotions. He wanted to share his joy in the Word with others.

The Necessary Gifts

A man whom God is calling to the ministry will have the internal call confirmed as he discovers that he has the gifts for the ministry. Nederhood believes that those whom Christ calls He equips "with the necessary intellectual capacity."[676]

He describes what these intellectual gifts will enable the man to do. "He will provide the person with intellectual capacities sufficient to enable him to handle the general course offered by an accredited seminary. This involves study in the original languages of the Scriptures, systematic study of church doctrine, and studies of the Old and New Testaments."[677]

Nederhood concludes that "if a person cannot handle this material satisfactorily, we should assume that he is not being called to the work of the gospel ministry."[678]

A potential minister needs to have the gift of self-discipline. A man can be bright, but unable to discipline himself to bring his studies to a victorious conclusion. Some men have the ability to learn but will not be taught by others.

Nederhood, a radio and television preacher on "The Back to God Hour" of the Christian Reformed Church in the latter part of the 20th century, emphasizes the necessity of the gift of communication. "What is needed is an ability to attract people's attention as one speaks, and keep that attention, and succeed in transferring from the mind of the minister to the mind of the hearer a certain amount of information."[679]

After three years of seminary studies, the faculty informed a student who roomed with me, that they did not think that he had the gifts of communication necessary for the pulpit ministry.

---

[676] Ibid., 50.
[677] Ibid., 50-51.
[678] Ibid., 51.
[679] Ibid., 51.

Nederhood also emphasizes that the called man have the gift of judgment. He is thinking of two things, the wise judgment that can help to resolve conflict and the wisdom to navigate the many personal and social relationships in a church. Nederhood even talks of the need for the minister "to maintain a certain degree of emotional distance from other people and the circumstances in which he finds himself."[680] How can a man do this? "The only kind of person who can maintain such distance is a person who is at ease with himself, has a proper amount of self-esteem, and possesses self-confidence."[681]

Among the attitudes that a potential minister should find in his soul, according to Nederhood, are a willingness 1) to obey the Lord Jesus, 2) to engage in "levels of self-discipline and self-sacrifice beyond those required of other Christians,"[682] and 3) to be self-giving and to engage in self-control.[683]

---

[680] Ibid., 53.
[681] Ibid., 53.
[682] Ibid., 54.
[683] Ibid., 55-56.

Chapter 47
Be Qualified
I Timothy 3:1-13

The seminary student needs to manifest the qualifications for office. Even though the seminary student might be young, he needs to grow in maturity so that he does possess the qualifications for the ministry of the Word. After all, he might be ordained as a teaching elder at the ripe old age of 26! I get a kick out of the fact that one of the New Testament words for "elder" emphasizes that such an office-bearer is an older, wiser person. A new minister does need to have wisdom beyond his years!

The minister of the Word needs to live such that his life does not disqualify him for his office.

Not everyone has the qualifications for church office. Christ calls only qualified men to the authoritative offices of minister, elder, and deacon.

The Scriptures are clear that office-bearers are to be qualified men in the church who are above reproach. The Scriptures are clear about something else, the marriages of office-bearers must be above reproach.

In I Timothy 3 where the Apostle Paul, inspired by the Holy Spirit, gives teaching about the qualifications of office-bearers, he does not just talk about the potential man. He also speaks about the qualities of a man's family life that qualify him for service in the church. He also writes that there are qualifications for an office-bearer's wife. The complete portrait of a qualified elder or deacon includes a portrait of his wife and their marriage. Paul teaches that the marriage of an office-bearer must be above reproach.

The Apostle Paul describes spiritually beautiful men and women in the church. He is interested in presenting the qualifications for office-bearers. Therefore, first we should think about what Paul is saying about our pastor, elders, and deacons and the marriage and family life that God expects.

The high ideal that Paul has, the qualities he expects from office-bearers, are what God expects from every Christian man. This is a portrait of what the marriages and homes should be like of potential office-bearers and present office-bearers, but of every Christian. The church needs men who have the qualifications for the office of elder and deacon. Spiritual young men are to desire these offices in the church (I Timothy 3:2). The Holy Spirit gives encouragement to qualified men to pursue these offices (I Timothy 3:13).

Christ does not call perfect men to the special offices in the church. He calls redeemed sinners. If Christ chose only to use morally perfect men, there would be no office-bearers to serve. So, God does not use perfect men, but He uses men whom He sanctifies by His Word and Spirit. He uses men who are great sinners who are saved by great grace. He uses men who still fall into sin and constantly need to rely on grace to live new and godly lives.

A Marriage Above Reproach

God wants husbands and wives in their married lives together as one flesh—to be together above reproach. Paul writes about husbands and wives who must be above reproach. The prospective elder must have a favorable testimony from two groups: insiders, that is, church-members, and outsiders, that is, those who are outside the church. A good reputation within.

The first item "blameless" we could translate "above reproach": "A bishop then must be blameless." This item is a kind of caption or heading. As far as his standing is with the members of the church is concerned, the elder must be above reproach. The word used in the original literally means "not to be laid hold of" hence unassailable. Enemies may bring all kinds of accusations, but these charges are proved to be empty. According with the rules of justice this man not only has a good reputation but deserves it. Such should be the elder's reputation, that no one is able to bring a substantiated charge against him in respect to anything in the following list!

High qualifications indeed!

For that reason, deacons are to be "proved": "And let these also first be proved; then let them use the office of a deacon, being found blameless" (I Timothy 3:10). An elder must be proved too: "Not a novice, lest being lifted up with pride he fall into the condemnation of the devil" (I Timothy 3:6).

The language is expressive. The words "lest being lifted up" refers to being "filled with smoke" A conceited person is "full of hot air", we might say. Humility seasoned by experience is an indispensable qualification for eldership.

He needs to have a good reputation without. This is connected with the witness of the church. You might be surprised that Paul says that there is an evangelistic element to the offices of elder and deacon. "Moreover he must have a good report of them which are without; lest he fall into reproach and the snare of the devil" (I Timothy 3:7).

His reputation again!

This takes us full circle back to the matter of one's reputation with which the passage began. A "good reputation" is literally a "beautiful witness." He needs a life that has a beautiful symmetry that adorns the gospel. A married couple should be above reproach in their home life: they should have a home-life centered around the gospel. They need to be teaching their children God's law and the gospel throughout the day.

The first way in which he is "above reproach" is in his marital relationship. It must not escape our attention that the very first and the very last of the eight positive requirements describe the qualified person's relation to his family. Paul, and the Holy Spirit speaking through Paul, must have regarded this family relationship as being of great importance. A number of caveats about the fact that the elder is to be a one-woman man. This cannot mean that an elder must be a married man. Rather, it is assumed that he is married-as was generally the case. Office-bearers have God's blessing on the single life or married life. The Apostle Paul remained single. The Apostle Peter took around a wife.

The assumption throughout is that the office-bearers are qualified *men*. The church fathers like Tertullian and Chrysostom were wrong in claiming that Paul is here referring to men who, having become widowers, remarried. The Apostle Paul did not oppose remarriage after the death of the spouse, though under certain specified conditions he considered continuation in the unmarried state to be wiser than marriage (I Corinthians 7:26,38). It is stipulated that in this marital relationship he must be an example to others of faithfulness to his one and only marriage-partner. Adultery was a sin of frequent occurrence among the Jews and certainly among the Gentiles. An elder must be a man of unquestioned morality in his marital relationship. He must love his wife and sacrifice for her.

Winston Churchill once attended a formal banquet in London, where the dignitaries were asked the question, "If you could not be who you are, who would you like to be?" Everyone was curious about what Churchill would say, who was seated next to his beloved Clemmie. When it was finally his turn, the old man rose and gave his answer: "If I could not be who I am, I would most like to be"—and here he paused to take his wife's hand—"Lady Churchill's second husband."

A one-woman man is a man who has eyes only for his wife.

A one-woman man finds delight in his wife, and she knows it.

A one-woman man spends time with his wife—so she knows that he treasures her.

A one-woman man protects his marriage by avoiding any situations where he would be tempted to impure thoughts or actions.

The marriage above reproach is one where the wife supports her husband as he exercises loving, wise rule over his family.

Paul says that the office-bearer must rule his home well: "One that ruleth well his own house, having his children in subjection with all gravity;" (I Timothy 3:4). Husbands, you are to rule your homes! Your children are to know that you rule your homes—and they are to be in subjection to you. There ought to be fitting consequences for disobedient children. You are to exercise your rule "with all gravity".

The Christian man's wife, recognizes that her husband is the head of the home. Therefore, she will do all she can to foster his leadership. She will never slander her husband to the children! Never! She will submit to his will, even though she might know that if she wanted to she could manipulate him to do her will.

The Christian husband also exercises loving, sacrificial headship over his wife. He does this with sacrificial love, so his wife has a husband she can easily follow.

But he is called to show leadership and he must be the spiritual leader. We need to underline that today.

The man who is office-bearer material is such because he is a spiritual leader in his home.

He makes sure his children know their catechism.

He reads and explains Scripture to them daily.

He goes to Bible studies—he doesn't just command his children to go to a Bible study like Catechism or Young People's Society.

He wants to grow spiritually in fellowship with other Christians.

He reads. How can he grow in his understanding of the Christian faith, if he does not read? If he is not growing in his understanding of the faith, he will not have anything to teach.

He shows leadership to his family—by his desire and willingness to spend time in community for the welfare of the church family.

As a spiritual leader he prays for his wife and children and teaches them to pray.

Self-Control

The husband and wife are to be characterized by Self-control. The man with the qualifications for the special offices in the church must be self-controlled in his use of alcohol. Christians may drink wine. The Psalmist speaks of how it makes the heart glad. The Apostle Paul recommended Timothy to drink a little for his stomach's sake.

Jesus turned water into wine.

But the office-bearer and his wife may not abuse alcohol. They may not try to drink away their sorrows—or avoid dealing with life by going to the bottle.

Twice Paul writes about self-control with alcohol—both as a qualification for elders as well as deacons. Paul states that the potential office-bearer must not be given to wine (I Timothy 3:3). Literally the Greek reads that one should not be "lingering beside wine" or sitting down too long at the wine. Drunkenness was an ancient blight just as it is today. Today we have added to it the abuse of methamphetamine and cocaine. But in ancient times people already abused opium. Today we have a terrible problem with the abuse of opioids in the United States. The potential office-bearer may not abuse opioids.

I recently had a student in prison ask me what it was like to drink alcohol and not get drunk. He admitted that he had always abused alcohol when he was out of prison. He always drank to excess. He didn't even know what it was like not to abuse alcohol. Once the guys in his gang began drinking, it was always to excess. He honestly wanted to know what the difference was between enjoying a glass of wine to make your heart glad and getting stark raving drunk.

In Corinth some Christians were in the habit of getting drunk at the Lord's Supper! (I Corinthians 11:21). The Apostle Paul writes that church leaders must not be "given to much wine" (I Timothy 3:8).

This must be taken to heart by church leaders in a culture that romanticizes drinking. Recently there have been Reformed pastors who glorified drinking beer. And then a well-known preacher is caught driving drunk.

Preachers need to have a balanced presentation of the subject of alcohol. If a preacher only wants to laud the benefits and the joy of drinking premium beer but does not recognize the potential dangers in the abuse of alcohol, he will have an unbalanced ministry. And they will have congregants who will continue to abuse alcohol but feel that they have the imprimatur of their pastor for doing so.

The abuse of alcohol is a spiritual flamethrower.

The office-bearer's wife may not abuse alcohol or drugs. The Apostle Paul writes that the deacon's wife is to be "sober" (I Timothy 3:11).

The office-bearer needs to be self-controlled with respect to his emotions. He needs to be self-controlled in the face of opposition, attacks, and temptations to anger.

The office-bearer and his wife learn how to kindly resolve disputes.

A man who beats his wife is to be immediately removed from office.

Not a Striker

The office-bearer may not be a "striker" (I Timothy 3:3). He may not use brute force to get his way. He can't be punching people. Instead an office-bearer is kind and gentle—in other words a peace-maker!

Churchgoers in Fyaras, Sweden, dragged furious choir director Sven-ake Fagerkrantz away from sour-singing Ercia Bengtsson as he whacked her back and legs with his cane. His explanation? "I just went wild because she kept singing off-key.....She was tone deaf and I begged her for years not to sing so loud!"

Whatever could be said about Mr. Faberkrantz, he definitely was not elder material!

The office-bearer is not to be a giver of blows. I think that this also rules out a sinful pugnaciousness in personal relationships. Pugnaciousness is good in a boxer, but not in an elder. Gentleness is the elder's approved style. Jesus was meek and lowly in heart. Gentleness is a fruit of the Spirit (Galatians 5:22-23). Paul writes:

> And the servant of the Lord must not strive; but be gentle unto all men, apt to teach, patient, In meekness instructing those that oppose themselves; if God peradventure will give them repentance to the acknowledging of the truth" (II Timothy 2:24-25).

The wise man writes: "He that is slow to anger is better than the mighty; and he that ruleth his spirit than he that taketh a city (Proverbs 16:32).

The elders needs to be self-controlled in his pursuit of his daily bread. An office-bearer and his wife are content with the money and possessions that God has given them. "Not greedy of filthy lucre" (I Timothy 3:3).

Money, specifically, one's attitude toward it—plays a big role in both the qualifications of elders and deacons. Some of the richest men I know are not lovers of money. But the truth is, it is hard to have a lot of money and not love it.

It is also hard to be poor and not love money.

Whatever the case, one cannot love money and be qualified for church leadership.

Tongue Control

The deacon must not be "double-tongued" (verse 8). He does not talk one way out of his mouth about a person who is in his presence, and another way when he is talking to others. He does not gossip. He is honest. Likewise, the wives of deacons must "be grave, not slanderers, sober, faithful in all things" (verse 11). The deacon and his wife together fight against and stand against slander. They do not talk badly about a brother in his absence. If the deacon or his wife even come to learn about confidential needs, you can trust that the secret will be kept with them.

Hearts of Service

The office-bearer must be someone who shows hospitality. The word for hospitality literally is the "love of strangers". It is a telltale virtue of the people of God.

Paul writes in Romans 12:13: "Distributing to the necessity of saints; given to hospitality." Peter needs to warn us: "Use hospitality one to another without grudging" (I Peter 4:9).

Today's elder must be a ready and joyful host. He must invite people to his table. An elder should not be a distant, austere man. His home must be open. Hospitality is all over the New Testament. The writer of Hebrews offers an enchanting motivation: "Be not forgetful to entertain strangers: for thereby some have entertained angels unawares" (Hebrews 13:2).

Why an Office-bearer's Marriage must be Above Reproach

A first reason why the marriage of an office-bearer must be above reproach is that the man needs to demonstrate in his marriage an ability to lead. How can he lead the church, if he cannot even lead his wife?

The Apostle Paul is very clear about why he gives the qualification for an elder that he must rule his own house well. "For if a man know not how to rule his own house, how shall he take care of the church of God?" (verse 5) The man who fails in ruling his family cannot be expected to succeed in ruling the church.

The commonsense application is straightforward—and its disregard has brought great trouble to God's people over the centuries, beginning with Eli of old. If a man is faithful to his wife, others can expect him to be faithful as an elder or deacon. If a man rules his own house with wisdom, love, and tact, this character will come out in his rule as an elder in the church. Christian service and leadership is without a question a matter of character. In the 90's—the matter of character was much discussed in the realm of politics. Is character important for leadership? In the world, character is important for good leadership.

In the church of God, one's Christian character is everything in church leadership.

A second reason why God considers a marriage above reproach necessary for office-bearers, is because failure in marriage is one of the most often and most damaging sins of office-bearers.

I do not know what the statistics are for ministers who have been unfaithful to their spouses, but they are devastatingly high.

The devil takes advantage of the power of the sex drive for his devious ends. In the world that is evident—by the large number of cases of sexual abuse of girls. So the Holy Apostle gives these qualifications for office-bearers to press home the necessary of sexual purity and marital faithfulness.

Satan knows that the failures of leaders in the church can have a domino effect. Therefore, God protects His people from leaders who are not totally dedicated to their mates and as a result will damage the church's reputation and hinder the cause of God's kingdom.

God protects the church by calling for her to select godly, faithful men, whose life in their marriage, as well as in the rest of their life is above reproach.

There is a final reason why God has high standards for church leaders. It is a sober fact that as goes the leadership, so goes the church. With some commonsense qualifications, it is an axiom that what we are as leaders in microcosm, the congregation will become in macrocosm as the years go by. Of course, there are always individual exceptions. But it is generally true that if the leadership is Word-centered, the church will be Word-centered. If the leadership is mission-minded, the church will be mission-minded. If the leadership is merciful, the church will be merciful. Elders and deacons, be godly leaders! You and I must be the first ones to be excited about telling lost people about Jesus.

We must be the first to invite people to church.

Be the first ones to extend hospitality to visitors.

Be the first ones to show mercy to orphans, widows, or inmates.

This is also true negatively—exponentially! Unloving, narrow-minded leaders beget unloving, narrow churches. Theologically illiterate leaders beget churches that want no creed but Christ. Paul wanted the church to have leaders whose lives would grace the church and adorn the gospel before the world. So much is at stake. What our leadership is in microcosm, the church will become in macrocosm. And what the church is has everything to do with the welfare of the covenant people and the progress of the mission of God.

The Possibility of Qualified Office-bearers

It is a wonder that we have any qualified men in the church. It is a wonder of grace!

We see the power of the cross of Jesus Christ to save. Apart from grace there would be no men with the qualifications to be office-bearers. Christ suffered to purchase men whom He would give the qualifications to be office-bearers.

We are all foolish, helpless, sinners. But God graciously forgives and sanctifies sinful men, so that they have a small beginning of the new obedience. It is a wonder of grace that we have marriages in the church that are above reproach. We are thankful, we are humbled, we are glad that the crucified Christ who governs us, has chosen to give us office-bearers—for our good and His glory.

Chapter 48
Manifest the Characteristics of a Gospel Preacher

hat are the sort of characteristics that need to be found in a gospel preacher? First, a gospel preacher must have a deep conviction that the Scriptures of the Word of God. When I was a freshman at Calvin college, my religion professor began the first day of class by rejecting the infallibility and inerrancy of the Scriptures. He was part of the neo-orthodoxy that argues that the Scriptures were written by human authors and, therefore, fallible. He claimed that there was some type of infallible redemptive message in the Bible. The challenge was to find where the biblical authors had actually taught these truths. The professor spent the rest of the semester shredding the Old Testament as only Higher Critics can do. He claimed to find error upon error in all of the biblical writers and editors.

The Higher Critics have all kinds of fanciful ideas of the origin of the Pentateuch and the editing of the prophecy of Isaiah. It was only when the Lord assured me about what the Scriptures actually teach about themselves that I once again had a zeal to pursue the ministry of the Word. If the Scriptures can be broken, how could I proclaim "Thus saith the Lord" from a pulpit? Why is there such weakness, triviality, and nonsense in the mainline pulpits? It is because the ministers do not think that there is a clear word from God. I affirm that all Scripture was God breathed and that holy men of God spoke as they were moved by the Holy Spirit.

While my professor could come up with all kinds of elaborate explanations of what the book of Isaiah was teaching. The Holy Spirit causes me to understand that when the Prophet Isaiah said, "Thus saith the LORD" that what he then wrote was not Isaiah's fallible private opinion, but the very Word of the living God.

The first thing a minister of the Word needs is a sense of the truthfulness, purity, and clarity of the sacred Scriptures. Since his calling is to study, interpret, and apply the sacred Scriptures; the preacher needs to have a deep sense of their truthfulness, veracity, and authority.

The second thing that needs to characterize a minister of the Word is that he must have a sense that the Lord Jesus Christ has personally called him to the sacred ministry. I could have never completed my seminary studies or functioned as a minister apart from a sense of this divine call.

It is true that a synod and classis examined me and decided that I was qualified for the gospel ministry. It is true that I was called by a specific congregation to be a minister of the Word. But fundamentally I was called by Christ. I knew that and felt that. He was my Master.

I was able to endure the boot camp that was seminary because Christ called me to the office of minister of the Word. I had the power to struggle on, study on, and endure because I knew that Christ had called me to a holy vocation.

The Christ who called me was my Master. I think it is vital for ministers of the Word to identify with the Apostle Paul who declared that he would not be judged by humans. He didn't care what his critics said. Paul knew that he reported to Christ. Ministers will stand before the judgment seat of Christ. With this solemn future reality in mind, any fear of human councils or courts lose their fearfulness. The authority that ruling elders have in the church is merely derivative from Christ. Christ is the head of the church.

Third, the minister must believe that Christ has commissioned him to be an ambassador. Then the minister will preach with authority. Prophetic utterances will come from his lips.

The preacher knows that he has the right to bring the Word of the King. He will recognize that he is merely an ambassador and that will keep him humble yet the same time, he will have a holy boldness because he has come with a message from his Savior, the one who called him to the ministry, Jesus of Nazareth.

Since the minister views himself as the messenger and not the king, he will humbly bring the Word of the King. But he will also speak with great authority and preach with prophetic boldness because he knows that He is bring the message of a great king.

Fourth, a minister of the word must love the sacred Scriptures. He needs to be a biblical theologian. He reads God's word. He meditates on God's word as a pre-seminary student. As a seminary student he knows that the main textbook in seminary is the sacred Scriptures. He loves God's word and he meditates on it day and night. He has learned the stories of the Bible and he understands the unfolding covenant of grace which is like a flower bud that opens wider throughout the old covenant and comes to its full glory in the new covenant. He understands the history of redemption and the history of salvation.

Fifth the minister of the Word is characterized by love for Christ. He loves Christ his Savior who not only redeemed him but called him to the sacred ministry. If he grew up in a denomination where the focus fell on the economical work of the first person of the holy Trinity, or the third person of the holy Trinity, such that Jesus was neglected; he pours over the gospel account so that he can see Jesus in His Majesty. He celebrates Jesus' triumph over the Pharisees and is glorious resurrection from the dead. The minister loves Jesus as revealed in both the Old and New Testaments.

Sixth, the minister of the Word is characterized by a love for communicating with his God. He prays. Even though his faith is weak yet he calls upon the name of God, the God of his life, and he bears his heart to God. He talks to God as a friend to a friend. He cries out to God as his "Abba, Father." He experiences intimacy with His God. He rejoices in his God.

Seventh, the minister of the Word is characterized by a love for the truth. God expects that His ministers would not only believe the truth, but love the truth.

Ministers trained in apostatizing denominations and grew up in an atmosphere where there was the widespread teaching of error. They can respond in two ways to this background. First, they might be willing to put up with a lot of false teaching because they did not learn to love the truth. Second, they might have a great passion to defend the truth because they saw firsthand the devastating consequences for a church made up of people who loved the lie.

In the last days confessing Christians will lose the love of the truth. If a minister does not love the truth, he will rest on his laurels instead of developing the truth and growing in his understanding of it. If he does not love the truth, a minister will not want to trouble himself or cause waves in the churches by standing up against and opposing false teaching.

Eighth, a minister of the Word will love the saints. He will love his wife and children. He will love the members of the congregation. In seminary he will be remembered due to his love for the faculty and fellow students. He loves lost sinners. This love will manifest itself in care for those around him.

Ninth, the preacher of the Word has a shepherd's heart for hurting sheep. Martin Luther thought that in order to become a good theologian, a minister needed to suffer. God often sends His ministers through times of suffering because He wants to equip them to mourn with those who mourn. Paul Brand wrote about the fellowship of those who suffer great pain. How can a minister care for hurting sheep if he doesn't know what it is like to hurt?

Tenth, a minister is characterized by hospitality. He loves to show mercy and love by taking the needy into his home. His home is open for those who need a meal, a bed, or Christian fellowship.

Eleventh, a minister of the Word is characterized by a desire to carry out the mission of the church. He rejoices over the repentance of members of the congregation. He rejoices with the angels in heaven at the salvation of a lost sinner. He is like a midwife who rejoices at the birth of a new baby. A minister of the word is not content to feed the sheep in the gathered congregation on Sunday morning: he wants to bring the message to people who are on the outside. When he walks by the home of a lost neighbor, he prays evangelistic prayers.

Twelfth, the minister of the Word is characterized by a dependence upon the Holy Spirit for studying the Scriptures and having sufficient wisdom to apply the Word to his hearers. He is dependent upon the Holy Spirit to bless the Word preached whether it is in the established congregation or in the local jail.

Thirteenth, the minister of the Word encourages confessing Christians in their reliance upon Christ and their pursuit after holiness. He strives to help the believers to grow in the assurance of their salvation and the joy of living a new and godly life. At the same time, he is faithful in the warning unbelievers about their sin and calling them to the necessity of repentance and faith in Christ.

Called to the Special Offi2ce of Minister of the Word

The Word is administered by a an ordained minister of the Word. Preaching is the official act of an ambassador of Jesus Christ. The minister does not invent a message to give to the congregation. He administers the Word. He is a steward who has been entrusted with the treasure of the gospel.

God does not appoint just anyone to bring His kingdom message. He appoints men whom He calls and equips to this holy task. The Apostle Paul tells Timothy and Titus what the qualifications are for one who administers the word. We live in a day when the idea of office is under attack. In the United States we have a radical egalitarianism within our democratic system. We view every American as equal to the President of the United States. We do not want kings, princes, or dukes.

With this sense of the equality of people within a democratic political system, Americans can have a weak view of office and the authority of an office-bearer.

The idea that God appoints only certain qualified men to the special office of minister of the Word is offensive to a radical egalitarian. Inmates in prisons imagine that if they think that they should be a minister of the

Word, that, presto, they are!

But it is nothing new that God calls and commissions qualified men to a specific office among His covenant people. In the Old Testament God did not call everybody to be the leader who led Israel out of bondage in Egypt. He called Moses. Miriam and Aaron challenged this. Miriam received leprosy. Korah, Dathan, and Abiram challenged this. The earth swallowed them up.

God explicitly called Joshua as the replacement for Moses. God called Samuel to be a prophet. God had Samuel anoint David the shepherd boy to be king. In the New Testament. Jesus chose twelve to be apostles. He sent out the seventy disciples in groups of two. The Apostle Paul did not lightly lay hands on men. He informed Timothy who was in Ephesus about the qualifications for an elder in the church of Jesus Christ. God, through the apostles, chose seven men to be deacons in the early church.

What should characterize the minister of the Word? If a man has no intellectual abilities or ability to read, why should we expect that he is going to be called to study the sacred Scriptures and to present sermons? If a man cannot speak fluently and with clarity, we should not expect Christ to call him to administer the Word. Christ calls to the ministry men who are characterized by a love for his Word, growing understanding of the doctrines of the Christian faith, and by wisdom and a godly lifestyle.

Christ, by His Spirit, works in the hearts of qualified men so that they have a desire to pursue the ministry of the word. As a pre-seminary student I studied various languages including Dutch, Greek, and Latin. At Calvin College I majored in philosophy. One of the strengths of studying philosophy is the focus on reading and deciphering difficult texts. The Scriptures are texts. As the Apostle Peter comments about some of the writings of the Apostle Paul, some of the Scriptures contain texts that are difficult to understand.

A Bible college or seminary curriculum is one that prepares students to administer the Word of God. That is why the focus falls on learning and studying the sacred Scriptures whether learning the biblical languages or studying the text of Scripture. Systematic theology classes are vital because they look at what all the Bible says on a particular topic. Seminary students need to grow in spirituality and godliness.

We live in an odd day when shysters will pay a few dollars and then send for a mail-order diploma that claims that they are a minister of the Word. I know of chaplains in the Department of Corrections who bypassed the requirement that they go to seminary and become ordained in a specific denomination, by paying money to get a little piece of paper that said that they were ordained ministers! There are too many street front churches where someone simply decides that the they are going to be a minister or with even more pride "an apostle"!

In the Old Testament, men were not allowed to intrude into an office to which God had not called them. A man from the tribe of Ephraim could not claim that he was a priest of God. Only the descendants of Aaron functioned as priests.

God spoke to His prophets and called them to become ministers of His Word.

In Angola prison, a potential student will only be accepted into the Bible College if one of the self-supporting and self-governing churches provides a letter of recommendation. It is the same on the outside. One cannot get into a reputable seminary without letters of recommendation from one's consistory with respect to doctrine and life.

It is Christ who through the local congregation calls a man to the actual office of minister of the Word. The Apostle Paul famously says that ministers of the Word are earthen vessels, clay vessels. God's ministers are imperfect sinners who have feet of clay. It is only by the power of God's grace that they can have the biblical qualifications for office. Only by the Holy Spirit's power can they love, understand, and communicate the gospel of Jesus.

The minister of the Word is a herald. He must publicly announce to the church and the world the message and summons of King Jesus.

The preacher is also a pastor. He is an undershepherd of Christ's flock. He needs to warn, protect, and comfort the sheep. He must feed the flock with the Word of God.

The minister of the Word is an evangelist. He is responsible for bringing the gospel to lost sheep. He must get out of his study and out of the church building to pursue the lost.

The ministers also a steward of the mystery of the gospel. He must administer and dispense these treasures.

The minister of the Word is a prophet. He must fearlessly brings messages of warning and judgment. He must be willing to speak truth to power.

The minister of the Word is a scribe. He needs to bring out of his treasures things old and new.

The minister of the Word is a witness. He may not be a false witness—by contradicting what the apostles witnessed to and saw. He must be a faithful and true witness to teaches what is recorded by the holy prophets and apostles. He must witness to the death, resurrection, and ascension of Jesus. He needs to bear testimony about the second coming of Jesus.

Chapter 49
The Role of Women in the Mission of the Church
I Timothy 2:9-15

n I Timothy 2:9-15, the Apostle Paul begins with some teaching on how the heart of a woman who wants to worship God, will dictate her dress and appearance. He emphasizes the need for spiritual beauty in contrast to a woman who tries to show off her outward beauty: "In like manner also, that women adorn themselves in modest apparel, with shamefacedness and sobriety; not with braided hair, or gold, or pearls, or costly array" (I Timothy 2:9). Paul's confronts women who wear gaudy, ostentatious hairdos that would distract attention from the Lord and worship. Jewelry was and is often used as a way of flaunting a woman's wealth or calling attention to herself in an unwholesome way. Paul forbids a preoccupation with jewelry and dress in the place of worship. When a woman dresses for the worship service to attract attention to herself, she has violated the purpose of worship.

Another way that women in Paul's day flaunted their wealth and drew attention to themselves was by wearing costly garments. This could also stir up envy on the part of the poorer women. Some Christians were dressing themselves like showy pagan women. They were happy to catch the attention of men and women. John Chrysostom was sensitive to the apostle's concerns, given the wealth and flamboyance in Constantinople when he was patriarch:

> And what then is modest apparel? Such as covers them completely and decently, and not with superfluous ornaments; for the one is decent and the other is not. What? Do you approach God to pray with broidered hair and ornaments of gold? Are you come to a ball? To a marriage-feast? To a carnival? There such costly things might have been seasonable...You are come to pray, to ask pardon for your sins, to plead for your offences, beseeching the Lord.

Paul calls upon women who profess godliness to support their testimony by their appearance—and also by their good works. Then he moves on to his teaching about the role of women in church office, an issue of great significance in our day.

The Apostle Paul writes that in public worship Christian women are to learn in silence with the fullest submission to church leadership.

The Apostle Paul prohibits women from teaching with ministerial authority in the church. They are to be silent: "Let the woman learn in silence" (I Timothy 2:11). Paul explains: "But I suffer not a woman to teach,...but to be in silence." (I Timothy 2:12). Paul wrote the same thing in I Cor. 14:34: "Let your women keep silence in the churches: for it is not permitted unto them to speak; but they are commanded to be under obedience, as also saith the law."

In the service of the Word on the day of the Lord a woman should learn, not teach. Kistemaker states: "She should be silent, remain calm. She should not cause her voice to be heard." Paul does not mean that women must remain perfectly silent during church. Paul is not referring to singing. He is referring to being quiet in the sense of not preaching.

Christian women must learn! That was not necessarily the position of the Jewish rabbis in Jesus' day. But the Bible teaches that women must attend public worship to learn! Paul writes: "And if they will learn anything, let them ask their husbands at home: for it is a shame for women to speak in the church" (I Corinthians 14:35).

The Apostle Paul prohibits women from authoritative teaching. Paul does not forbid women from instructing others in regular discourse. Indeed, it is expected. Paul told the Christians in Colosse (and this would include the women): "Let the word of Christ dwell in you richly in all wisdom; teaching and admonishing one another in psalms and hymns and spiritual songs, singing with grace in your hearts to the Lord" (Colossians 3:16). The Apostle Paul expects women to teach other women and to teach their children. In his letter to Titus, Paul exhorts the older women to teach the younger women.

Priscilla along with her husband Aquila taught Apollos in their home. Apollos learned his theology from both. Dr. Luke writes about Apollos: "And he began to speak boldly in the synagogue: whom when Aquila and Priscilla had heard, they took him unto them, and expounded unto him the way of God more perfectly" (Acts 18:26).

When Paul writes that women are not to teach, he uses "to teach" in the sense of careful and authoritative transmission of biblical truth. In the Pastoral epistles, "teaching" always has the sense of authoritative public doctrinal instruction (cf. I Tim. 4:11-16; 2 Tim. 3:16; 4:2). So what is prohibited is preaching, such as is enjoined in Paul's charge to Timothy:

"Preach the word; be instant in season, out of season; reprove, rebuke, exhort with all longsuffering and doctrine" (II Timothy 4:2).

Also prohibited is the teaching-elder role of authoritatively defining and expositing the apostolic deposit. This is the realm of male elders who "are able to teach" (I Timothy 3:2). Paul must then be understood to be prohibiting women from exercising the type of official teaching in the church that places them in a specific kind of authority over men—that is, the authority to be the official teachers of the church. Women must not be authoritative teachers of doctrine in the church.

The Apostle Paul calls Christian women to an attitude of submissiveness to godly leadership: "Let the woman learn in silence with all subjection" (I Timothy 2:11). The issue is not about male or female superiority. Many boys quickly learn that the girls in the classroom mess up the grading curve! Paul's statements have nothing to say about male and female equality. Such equality was established from the beginning, by God creating Adam and Eve in His image.

The issue is not about mere spirituality. Many women show more piety than their husbands.

Furthermore, church leadership is not about wielding power and throwing one's weight around—it is about exercising servant leadership by sacrifice and suffering for the good of the flock.

The issue is one of authority: who has the right to rule and to speak authoritatively in the name of Jesus Christ.

We must all submit to God's rule through His office-bearers, in all things lawful. I am not saying that everyone should necessarily agree with everything that a teaching elder or ruling elder says. We must never forget that preachers are fallible human beings, and they can make mistakes. But when they speak and rule in the name of Christ—justly and in truth—one must submit to their rule. And even when they err, we should respond with love and respect.

Paul forbids a hectoring, argumentative attitude. This learning in silence should not be with a rebellious attitude of heart, but "with complete submissiveness." It is not by way of exercising dominion over men but by way of submission that a woman reaches the state of true freedom and blessedness. Paul is looking for "entire" submissiveness in all things lawful. This emphasizes the complete subjection called for. Christian women must submit to church leadership by qualified men with all submissiveness.

Attempts to Dodge the Apostolic Prohibition

There are many attempts to dodge the apostolic prohibition against women ruling and teaching with authority in the church.

First, some simply argue that Paul is wrong. He supposedly echoes a rabbinical misinterpretation of the creation account of Genesis 2. In other words, Paul misunderstands Genesis 2 and 3 and therefore has a wrong view of the role of women in the church.

A second attempt at blunting Paul's teaching is to give the Greek word translated here "usurp authority" in verse 12. The Greek word is given a negative meaning such as "*to domineer*" or "to control." Therefore, some evade the force of Paul's prohibition by arbitrarily supposing that Paul is only speaking of *abusive* authority. This would allow women to exercise authority over men as long as it was not done in a controlling, domineering way.

Two things need to be said in response to this. First, the word "authority" cannot mean "domineer" here. The word "or" which connects "to teach" and "to have authority" always requires that both words be either positive or negative. If they were negative the phrase could read: "I do not permit a woman to teach error or to domineer over a man." But this cannot be the translation because the word "to teach" is always viewed positively.

Second, in the time of Jesus this Greek word simply did have the idea of authority. A study of the extrabiblical uses of the word "authentein" make clear that the word in Paul's day meant authority. It no longer carried a negative connotation.

A third attempt to deflect Paul's prohibition is to claim that the word for "silence" simply means "calmness." In verse 11 the word for silence is said to be one that connotes peacefulness rather than total silence. Evangelical Feminists argue that the word for "silence" means a "meek and quiet spirit." Women, they contend, can preach and rule if they do it with the proper attitude. But the fact of the matter is that the word does refer to silence. In I Corinthians 14:34 Paul explains that this silence means that they are not to speak: "Let your women keep silence in the churches: for it is not permitted unto them to speak" (I Corinthians 14:34).

A fourth attempt to deflect Paul's prohibition is to hold that references to "woman" and "women" in this passage refer to *wives*. The subject is not women in the church being in subjection to men there, but of wives to husbands. Paul is correcting improper conduct of wives towards husbands. Women were not showing respect to their husbands. Thus the teaching is domestic, applying only to the home—to how wives should act in relation to their husbands in public worship. But the Apostle Paul is teaching about the special offices in the church in this passage—as is evident by his reference to teaching.

Finally, a popular way to discount Paul's prohibition is to misinterpret Galatians 3:28 and then to use that to erase what Paul says here. Galatians 3:28 reads: "There is neither Jew nor Greek, there is neither bond nor free, there is neither male nor female: for ye are all one in Christ Jesus." This passage is a massive and glorious statement about our spiritual status in Christ. Every believer, whether slave or free, Jew or Gentile, male or female, he is in Christ and fully inherits the Abrahamic promises by grace apart from works. He is justified by faith alone. Male and female are "fellow heirs" of God's grace and eternal life. Before the cross of Jesus Christ—we all—male and female—stand as sinners who need the blood of Christ to cleanse us. This is a statement of our radical spiritual equality whatever our status in life. Evangelical feminists argue that the Galatians passage is a *breakthrough text to which all others must bow.*

But this statement does not do away with lines of authority that God has created in the world and in the family and in the church. The passage is not about offices in the church. The fact that Paul says that male and female are one in Christ, does not take away the role differences between men and women in marriage and in the church. The essential equality between believing citizens and a believing ruler does not do away with lines of authority in the civil sphere.

The Misinterpretation of Paul's Reasoning and Motives

Feminists misinterpret Paul's reasoning and motivation to undermine his clear teaching.

First, evangelical feminists claim that Paul forbids women to teach merely because of the aggressiveness and abuses radical feminists who were trying to dominate men. As a result, they became so aggressive and abrasive in their demands for equality, that in grasping for the prestige of teaching and leadership, they caused dissension. This behavior is the only reasonable explanation for Paul's prohibitions. Influenced by false teachers and feeling themselves emancipated by their freedom in the gospel they engaged in noisy, disruptive, and offensive behavior in church. They paraded their new status in a usurping, domineering attitude toward men.

But there simply is no evidence in the text that the women referred to were teaching false doctrine.

Second, evangelical feminists claim that Paul forbids women to teach lest cultural sensibilities about a woman's role be offended. Out of concern for the gospel, Paul did not advocate an assertive defense of women's liberty in a male-dominated society of the Jews and Gentiles of his day. The dominant cultural position among both Jews and Greeks assumed male superiority and a woman's subservience. Paul's motivation is like how the assembly of the apostles and elders decided in deference to the strong social mores of the Jews to tell Gentile Christians to abstain from the meat of strangled animals and from blood. (Acts 15:20) Just like Paul knew what the implications of the gospel were for the institution of slavery, but did not seek to eradicate it, he had the same approach to the role of women. Paul knew the violent response that revolt of slaves could ignite in the Roman Empire. So out of expedience for the sake of the gospel, Paul orders slaves to accept their status and be obedient to their masters. Christian would face an insurmountable obstacle if the gospel was identified as a feminist movement.

The argument continues that today, however, social conditions have changed. In the twenty-first century, if women are not allowed the right to be deacons, elders, and pastors, the church will give offence to society. Since the original reason for Paul's prohibition is gone, it is not relevant for our cultural context. Therefore, Paul's prohibition is not to be understood as a universal, timeless prohibition against women serving as elders and ministers.

The problem with this claim of feminists is that the Apostle Paul does not give this as his reason for the prohibition.

The Apostolic Reasoning

Let us look at the apostle's reasoning.

First, Paul grounds His prohibition in the creation order. The most telling reason why we can see that Paul is not just dealing with a difficulty in the Ephesian church—because his reasoning is not based on cultural expectations.

Paul does not appeal to a cultural situation that might change, but to an unchanging creational order. He refers to the creation order: "For Adam was first formed, then Eve" (I Timothy 2:13). Firstness connotes authority throughout the Scriptures. God could have created Adam and Eve at the same time, but he did not. He created Eve for Adam. She was created to be his "helper." God desires the order of creation be reflected in His church.

Evangelical feminists reject the idea that God created Adam as the head of Eve. They claim that the fact that Adam was created first does not in itself argue for man's priority over women. That the woman is called "helper" does not mean she is subject to the man. Rather, she is a co-worker or enabler who serves as an equal partner. Feminists argue that creation from Adam's rib suggests a side-by-side relationship, and not one of hierarchy or subordination. I wonder how many evangelical feminists today really believe in the creation of Eve from the rib of Adam. Probably not very many—most would hold to some evolutionary view of human origins.

But the Apostle Paul assumes throughout that the man who was made first is the head of his wife. In I Timothy 3 where Paul explains the qualifications of elders and deacons, he states qualifications that only men can have. For example, Paul states that an elder must be first of all a man who rules his own house well. If a person does not know how to rule his own house, how can he rule in the church of God? Paul assumes that the husband in the home is the head who has the authority to rule. Speaking about the elder and later the deacon, he states that they must be "one-woman men."

Paul connects this creation order with the law. In I Corinthians 14:34 he states that he cannot permit women to teach, because God's holy law does not permit it: "Let your women keep silence in the churches: for it is not permitted unto them to speak; but they are commanded to be under obedience, as also saith the law."

Second, Paul grounds his prohibition in the fall of Eve: "And Adam was not deceived, but the woman being deceived was in the transgression." (I Timothy 2:14) We miss the point if we think that Eve was more gullible than Adam, and that is why she was deceived and became a sinner. Eve's sin was not naivete but a willful attempt to overthrow the creation order. Instead of following Adam's example and leadership, Eve chose to lead. Instead of remaining submissive to God, she wanted to be "like God." Eve's sin involved overturning the order of creation. Adam's sin came from listening to his wife and being taught by her—to eat the tree. I doubt that the Apostle Paul's teaching on this point holds much weight with evangelical feminists since many of them would deny the existence of a literal fall into sin and would reject the reading of Genesis 3 as historical.

Despite Eve initiating the Fall, and Adam's sinful abdication, his headship was still recognized by God. After their eyes were opened God first held Adam responsible. Paul grounds his prohibition in the creation order again: Eve violated it when she usurped authority. Women in the church, unlike Eve, should submit to the qualified male office-bearers whom God places in authority over them.

The Significance

Only qualified males are called to be missionary preachers. Only qualified, called, and ordained men must exercise leadership in the church. They must exercise a godly, spiritual, loving, servant leadership. They must die to self and sacrifice for the welfare of the congregation. The missionary pastor needs to have a passion for spreading the gospel of Christ, a willingness to defend the faith, and the courage of a prophet.

He must exercise spiritual authority and power in the name of Jesus Christ. Elders must use the authority that Christ gives them to encourage the saints in godliness and to warn sinners of the subtle snares of the Devil. Deacons must exercise their authority to comfort the needy.

Paul's teaching on women in church office is directed to the sphere of the church as institute. It must be noted that these instructions have nothing directly to say about teaching and authority in the marketplace or academy or public square. They are about order in the church. Neither do these directives allow any man within the church, by virtue of his gender, to exercise authority over women in the church. Such more generally explicit authority only exists within the sacred covenant of marriage and family, and then it is only to be exercised with the self-giving spirit of Christ.

I do not believe that the Bible teaches that there is a headship of all males over all females that extends to society in general. Some do hold to the idea that a woman may not hire male employees to work under her. That is why some Reformed Christians have argued for male principals in schools. Also, it is why some Calvinists in the past were against women rulers. John Knox, for example, wrote against a woman as queen of Scotland. Could you vote for a female president? I do not think that there is a principle reason why you could not vote for a qualified woman for president. Some who hold to this position logically conclude that women should not have the right to vote in local or national elections.

Others wrongly claim that a woman may never pray in the presence of a man.

The Apostle Paul teaches that women of God are blessed as they carry out their God-given roles: "Notwithstanding she shall be saved in childbearing, if they continue in faith an charity and holiness with sobriety" (I Timothy 2:15). Most likely Paul refers to childbearing because it is a universal example of the God-given difference in the roles of men and women. Men do not give birth to children—and most women in every culture do. By not seeking a man's role, women of God will remain in the heart attitude that brings down the blessings of the covenant.

The curse of painful child-bearing is changed into a blessing by the grace of God. Child-bearing meant salvation—because the seed of the woman would come from Eve. In bearing children the Christian mother by faith in God's covenant promise looks forward to the joys of Christian motherhood unto the glory of God.

Paul is not saying that child-bearing as such procures salvation. God does not keep a woman on the way of salvation without exertion, diligence, and watchfulness on her part: "if they continue in faith and charity and holiness with sobriety" (I Timothy 2:15). The strength to persevere in the faith is ever from God, from Him alone.

God's plan for women is for their benefit. There is blessedness in living out God's order. We must not deduce from this passage that women have no part to play in the life of the church. Far from it.

The issue here is about fidelity to God-ordained authority in our lives. The issue is about fidelity to God's Word as we carry out the mission of the church. The issue is whether we will allow God's Word to shape the mission of the church or the powerful winds of an ever-changing culture.

Chapter 50

Rest and Grow: Sabbaticals and Ongoing Education

I have come to understand ever more deeply the value of sabbaticals. In some denominations the idea of a minister having a sabbatical isn't even on the radar of the consistories. A sabbatical is viewed as an extended vacation. But aren't the members of the congregation paying the salary of the minister? How are they getting their money's worth if they give their minister a three month or six months sabbatical? People in other vocations normally don't take sabbaticals.

It is true that landscapers might be very busy in the spring summer, and fall and then enjoy a relaxed winter. And farmers might not be so busy in the winter. who mainly work in the spring, summer and fall and have very quiet winters. But few members of Reformed congregations are professors in colleges or universities where sabbaticals are regularly offered after a number of years of teaching. So the concept of a sabbatical is not familiar to many congregations.

After six years in the ministry, I felt that for my long term ministry it was best for me to have a sabbatical. I approached the congregation where I was the pastor about the idea of doing a sabbatical to work on a doctorate. The idea was shot down.

But there too many ministers who spend years and even decades as pastors without getting an extended break. In the Reformed churches most elders have three year terms. Then they get a break from the challenges, trials, and stresses of serving as ruling elders; even if they might get voted in a few years later. Deacons also have three year terms. But ministers do not get a break from the pressures of pastoral ministry.

As a pastor it took me two weeks on vacation to even begin to forget the pressures of the ministry. I received three weeks of vacation time a year.

I think that the ministry of the word is as difficult today as it has ever been in the history of the church. This is due to the professionalization of the ministry and the fact that members in local congregations can listen to a wide variety of radio and television preachers who might place their own pastor in a bad light. There is also the psychologizing of the ministry so that the minister is perceived to be a counselor and psychologist. The minister is a pastor who is on call 24-7.

The pastoral difficulties involved in long-term ministry are profoundly challenging. I think that men in other vocations can much more easily and readily change their jobs than ministers. The minister might experiencing conflict in the congregation without there being new avenues for him to explore a call elsewhere.

I am bringing up this topic of sabbaticals within the context of discussing the importance of the minister's development after he graduates from seminar. When a student graduates from seminary it is true that his gifts of exegesis, homiletics, and communication are better than those of many active ministers. That is an absolute reality. I am always reminded of how John Calvin as a rather young man and young minister did a lot of wonderful theological writing. We also find young men in their 20's and 30's doing ground breaking work in the hard sciences. Some men come out of seminary with magnificent gifts. Even so, these gifts cry out for further development.

The new minister might feel like he didn't study a specific topic enough. For example, he might feel that he is a lot more to learn about a biblical theology or preaching Christ from the Old Testament. Or he might find that his training in biblical counseling was lacking. When I went to seminary there was only one class in pastoral counseling over a four year period of study. The minister might feel that he has not read widely enough in Christian theology.

The new minister also might find that he doesn't have the same logical mind as his professors when it comes to putting together unified and orderly messages. I think one problem with many new ministers is that they have weaknesses in reading and interpreting texts. Their seminary education addressed this great lack, but the problem was not solved. Weaknesses were not overcome. The minister is going to have to read a lot of good English novels and nonfiction to develop his ability to wield the English language more effectively.

The minister might be aware of deficiencies in his understanding of Greek and Hebrew, so that he could use a refresher course in one of them.

One weakness many new ministers experience is a lack of ability in grasping the main idea of the text. This is related to a weakness in being able to synthesize and process information. The danger is that the new minister or even the experienced minister has a weakness when it comes to seeing all the details in the text and how they can fit together in a unified message.

Another minister might feel a weakness in his ability to provide effective, relevant application.

How can the minister continue to grow?

The answer is that there should be continuing development in the minister's training after seminary.

It should be quite clear by now that this continuing development is not only for the benefit of the minister, but also the church.

The better a minister knows and expresses theology, the better off the church. The better a minister can interpret the Greek and Hebrew Scriptures, the better the congregation can be fed. The more that the minister knows about pastoral counseling, the better for hurting members of the church.

Seminary can't teach the minister everything he needs to learn. Seminary is like boot camp for the minister. Once a soldier graduates from boot camp, no one supposes that he has the qualities of a Green Beret. He is not a Navy Seal. He has only finished boot camp.

Seminary is intense discipleship, but in some sense it merely equips the student to teach himself. It is shows him how he can continue to learn by organizing and discovering new ways for him to continue his education. Since the heart of the minister's vocation is the interpretation and proclamation of the Word of God, he needs to take care to grow.

The minister needs to grow in godliness and spirituality. He needs more zeal for the Word of God. He is going to have to come to understand more deeply the mission of the church and how to carry out the mission of the church in word and deed in the local context, whether in the organic life of the church or in the church as institute.

But our concern here is with the organization, preparation, and presentation of the sermon.

Ongoing Self-Education

Ministers should do more to encourage and assist each other in this ongoing training. While in seminary, I had the opportunity of delivering sermons before all of the faculty and student body. This was intimidating. My professors were effective preachers and leaders in the denomination. They were not shy about giving constructive criticism. I remember students who gave practice preaching sermons in the seminary and never came back. I watched as a fourth-year seminary student basically broke down before he could deliver one of the last sermons of his seminary career. He was intimidated and frightened by the potential criticism. It was a good custom that the faculty also required us to watch our presentations since they were taped on video. This was humbling and important.

There is a reason why radio personnel wear headsets as they record their messages or speak live. The headsets allow the speakers to hear how they sound. Listening to headphones that are connected to high quality microphones help you to hear yourself as others hear you. This allows self-criticism.

How did Walter Cronkite develop his skills as a television communicator? He was active in radio before he got big time into television. His involvement in radio led him to focus on how he sounded, his cadence, and several other complex factors that played a role in how he was heard by his audience.

I found as a minister that it was helpful from time to time to listen to audio or to watch a video of my own sermons. I never enjoyed it. I always felt like I would never want to listen to myself as a preacher after watching myself deliver a sermon. I noticed funny things about my pronunciation. It was interesting that when I would preach in some churches, people would often catch on to the fact that I had an accent.

Growing up in the Midwest of the United States I thought that I lacked an accent. People with accents lived in the South and in New Jersey! People guessed that I was Canadian. I grew up in Minnesota, which is as Canadian as you can get, especially in the love that Minnesotans have for playing hockey. But hockey was strong in the central and northern parts of the state. I lived in the southwest corner of Minnesota. After having left Minnesota behind, I notice some unique accents when I go back home. I notice that some people are lazy with their consonants. They talk slower that people in urban areas. What I'm getting at is that every minister learned how to speak wherever he grew up. If he listens to his family members talk he will get a sense of some of his strengths and weaknesses in wielding the English language. Your entire education affected your vocabulary, pronunciation, and use of English.

The fact that I attended Calvin College for four years and then went to graduate school in philosophy in Wisconsin impacted my use of English. I heard how different professors communicated at the Protestant Reformed Seminary and Calvin Seminary.

As a pastor I took voice lessons so that I could learn how to breathe better and how to use my voice more safely and effectively.

Since the minister is involved in oral communication and his concern is to communicate the gospel of Jesus Christ to the hearts and minds of his hearers, he cannot be ignorant of the use of the voice and matters of rhetoric.

In seminary I was struck by the difference between what our professors expected of us in practice preaching and how the professors actually preached. They had one standard for what they wanted to see from us in practice preaching and a different standard for their own preaching.

They were like an English professor who tries to instill basic principles and rules of writing in freshmen students in contrast to how the same professor uses great license with the English language in her fiction. The professor has a license to play around with the English language in a way that the freshman student doesn't yet have the right to do (or ability).

The minister needs to be aware of the relevance of his voice, his pronunciation, and his rhetoric as a communicator. I know that in the 20th century in evangelical churches so much emphasis fell on exegetical preaching that the importance of a unified message, logic in the sermon, and effective rhetoric was deemphasized.

Today I observe that ministers and seminary students do not try to develop an effective oratorical rhetoric. They somehow think that learning how to communicate with power and effectiveness is showiness. There is a lack of an attempt to communicate well and powerfully. Sermons become the reading of essays in the same tone. Sameness characterizes the delivery of students and ministers who imagine that they are just being themselves.

There is a difference between the rhetoric of an essay and the rhetoric of an orator. In the boring sermons I am talking about there can be times when there is wonderful rhetoric in the sermon. The minister does have choice words to say.

The problem is that the act of preaching is not the same as the act of reading a written essay. The preacher is a verbal communicator above all and needs to have a rhetoric that fits his call to publicly communicate the gospel orally to the congregation.

What Preachers can Learn from Walter Cronkite

Walter Cronkite one of the formative communicators in the history of television. He was concerned with both rhetoric and the content of what he communicated. At CBS News he was famous for his emphasis on getting the news right. He didn't want give his own private interpretation to the news of the day. It was only later that television anchors more and more be a began to give their own slant on the news. Walter Cronkite avoided doing this.

Even when he famously came back from Vietnam after the Tet Offensive and publicly expressed his view that things had come to a stalemate in Vietnam (which had a massive impact on American public opinion) he did not give that personal commentary on his CBS evening news program. He made sure that this commentary was given on a separate hour-long special. Cronkite tried to exegete the news. He wanted to communicate the headlines of the day without bringing his own personal, private opinions to bear on the topic. In other words, he was trying to engage in an accurate and objective exegesis of the various news accounts both in the United States and around the world.

But that doesn't mean that Cronkite wasn't concerned with how to communicate in an effective way. In fact, people who have written on the life of Cronkite are convinced that even apparently spontaneous gestures were thought out ahead of time. For example, when Cronkite famously announced that Kennedy had died from his wounds, he took off his glasses and dangled them with clear emotion. Cronkite understood the importance of gestures.

Cronkite also majored in simplicity and in clarity. His genius was his ability to take the complex events of the day and present them in a simple, organized, and clear way that ordinary Americans could understand.

But Cronkite also focused on his voice and on pacing. He understood the importance of repetition. The very way that he closed every one of his evening news broadcasts by saying, "And that's the way it is," points to his understanding of the power of rhetoric.

How much more the minister of the word should strive to communicate effectively. You should know the strengths and weaknesses of your voice.

Should we be surprised that some of Augustine's writings have passed the test of time? Like my professor said, "If you do not write well, you have no right to expect that people will bother to read you." How could Augustine write well? It was because he spoke well. The ancients viewed communication as an oral event. That is why most of the time that when a person read a document in the first centuries of the Christian era they would read it out loud. Christians in Milan were astonished to discover that Ambrose would read documents without saying them out loud. Augustine tells us that he did the same to save his voice. But this was odd to the ancients.

An Ear for Good English, Effective Rhetoric, and Poetry

Augustine learned Latin rhetoric by studying the written speeches of the ancients. He read Cicero who gave speeches that were oral events even though the great orator would later write out the speech (after improving and editing it) and publish it. But the written speech was grounded in oral communication. Today if you read books by the leading literary authors, like Marilyn Robinson, you will find that the power of their fiction comes from the recognition of the fact that language is an oral event. They have developed a marvelous ear for language which makes their writing alive, realistic, living, and powerful.

The minister should improve his ear for the English language. He should read well-written books like those of Marilyn Robinson. Read Mark Twain out loud. Read Abraham Kuyper's speeches. You will be stunned by the marvelous rhetoric with which Kuyper expressed profound ideas.

While my seminary professors emphasized good exegesis, correct doctrine, the development of concepts, and a logical sermon; in the pulpit they were masters of rhetoric. Herman Hanko was a master of communicating in a way that was powerful, passionate, and that used wonderful metaphors. The two most passionate preachers that I have ever heard are John Piper and Herman Hanko. While Robert Decker read too much of his sermons, his preaching stood on the shoulders of the marvelous rhetoric developed in the Reformed tradition.

Mitch Dick, a minister at Sovereign Grace United Reformed Church in Grand Rapids, Michigan is a preacher who incorporates a powerful use of rhetoric, imaginative language, and poetry into his oral communication. There is a startling originality to his rhetoric. Like John Piper, he shows how Reformed theology can be expressed in a poetic way. Mitch Dick is one of those rare ministers who has found his voice. Christ wants His ministers to be themselves and to communicate the gospel in a fresh and distinct way.

Among an older generation of Reformed pastors, Rev. Gerrit Vos, a Protestant Reformed minister, was famous for his poetic approach to communication. He was well-known for his ability to use humor in the pulpit in a reserved way so that the congregation never actually broke into laughter, although they were on the edge of laughing. You can still read his devotionals which show this marvelous poetic approach to Christian piety and Reformed theology.

A good writer will tell you that one thing you need to do as an author is to develop your own voice. If you sit down and read *Dubliners* by James Joyce you will not mistakenly think that you are reading Ernest Hemingway. Each minister should try to find his own voice, which really means that he has appropriated Reformed theology, the Scriptures, and Reformed spirituality into his own heart and soul.

The Best American Preacher

I sometimes think that John Piper is the best preacher in the history of Christianity, not counting the Apostle Paul.

I think the best American preacher of the 20th century is John Piper. I think that Piper's approach to exegesis and to communication is unique and fresh. Only John Piper could have produced his book *The Pleasures of God*. If you read his sermons, you will see that he has a marvelous ability to exegete a passage in such a way that exposes the astonishing reality there and then communicates it to the reader or listener in such a way that it can impact his heart. Jonathan Edwards finds an effective disciple and Piper.

Edwards' sermons are marvels of logic, even though sometimes his logic is a too scholastic and detailed.

John Piper stands against the spirit of the age with his focus on communicating what the arguments are in the passage. He is also not shy about giving exegetical arguments for a right understanding of the passage. And his concern for a Calvinistic theology is always tied to a surprising zeal for inspiring Christians to pursue after holiness and to carry out the mission of the church.

Always Growing at Effective Communication

When a man graduates from seminary and takes up his call, for example, on a mission field in two-thirds world country; he has a lot to learn. He studies a new culture. He learns appropriate methods of communicating effectively. I think of a minister like Rev. Wilbur Bruinsma who wrote about how as a missionary in Jamaica he learned that his way of delivering sermons needed to be modified. That was good and right and proper. When he first became a minister, he mentally tried to satisfy his professors's expectations. He says that during his first years in the ministry, as he did his exegetical work and his homiletics, he felt that his theological professors were peering over his shoulder.

In Jamaica he discovered that when he preached like he did in the United States to establish congregations that the message flew over the heads of his auditors. He needed to shorten and simplify his sermons. He felt the need to use more illustrations. There are many ministers in the United States who would benefit from their congregations if they simplified their preaching and used more homely illustrations.

I think of another minister who was visiting Jamaica and, while there, was asked to preach at a funeral. This Dutch Reformed preacher suddenly became far more emotionally on fire than he ever would be in his home church. As members of the congregation said "Amens!" and verbally responded to the message, this led him to new heights of emotion and rhetoric.

Recently I preached at Westville Correctional Center in Westville, Indiana. About 140 men came to the service. Half came there to worship God. They sat in the front. The other half came to talk to their buddies and fellow gang members. They sat in the back. As I preached I knew that I had two audiences. One was made up of men who were hungry for the Word. The other group were hardened men who lacked the fear of God and did not want to listen to the Word preached.

The faithful minister in this context needs to do two things. First, I needed to understand that I was there to feed and encourage the men who were repentant and wanted to live a new and godly life. On the other hand, I needed to warn men who came for wrong reasons.

I am still startled when I preach in prison hear applause ring out throughout the congregation. I think of a time when I was preaching on the life of King Manasseh. I talked about how when King Manasseh was incarcerated in Babylon by the Assyrian king, and that Manasseh then humbled himself and called upon God and that God heard him. When I came to the part where I emphasized that when sinful men humble themselves before God and repent, that God will hear from Heaven and forgiven; applause rang out in the congregation.

The godly prisoners were excited about the idea that an incarcerated man could humble himself before God and find mercy. They could see the beauty of God's grace and rejoice at the mercy offered to the penitent.

Then I came to the part about how God took Manasseh (now an old man) and brought him back to Jerusalem and sat him on the throne again. I told them about how the Bible says that then Manasseh knew that the LORD was God. This idea once again excited the congregation and so they began to cheer. This responsiveness surprises me because I mostly preach in Reformed and Presbyterian churches where verbal responses are rare. I have never preached in a Reformed or Presbyterian congregation where clapping was a response to preaching.

Notice how this chiefly African American congregation in prison wanted vocally to participate in the sermon event. They consciously and actively wanted to respond to the message of the gospel. And they would've been surprised at a Reformed congregation where these realities were being preached and yet every member of the congregation sat quietly.

Ongoing Education Through Ministerial Interaction

I think one benefit of ministers working together on improving their preaching is that they place themselves in a context where there is mutual criticism. The difficulty of a preacher receiving feedback from the elders and the congregation is that the elders suppose that they can give criticism without receiving any. This dynamic can make feedback from elders unhelpful. There is additional problem that many elders really do not understand what good Reformed preaching is.

There are benefits for ministers getting together for mutual exhortation and support. When it comes to their preaching is that they are all going to take turns delivering messages or presenting examples of their sermons and therefore there are in a context where there will be this type of mutuality. The dynamic in this is that the ministers will know the sensitivity of critiquing others. They know that soon they might be critiqued by the gathered men. Since one's writings or sermons are very much an expression of one's own heart and self the ministers know the fragility of their own egos.

Writers talk about how when you write good fiction you are in some sense, bearing your naked soul for everybody to see. That is why writing and preaching takes great humility because you are exposing your heart for other people to hear, consider, and perhaps criticize. Therefore, I think that there are marvelous practices out there like when ministers get together and work on a common text. I think that this is a wonderful practice. I have heard of pastors will get together weekly and what they do is they all agree on the text that they're going to all preach on in their own churches.

Then they each do their individual research and exegesis and then having figured out what the main point is an application they come together for discussion. This gives to these ministers since they now are able to benefit from the criticism, feedback, and insights of all the other ministers. I am certain that ministers who do this together must all benefit from having a far richer approach to the text, a better sense of how Christ in the saving work is revealed in it, and what the various options are for personal application. I can only commend ministers during their busy vocations to do this kind of thing. I think that if the ministers were even get together for two hours a week to do this kind of thing.

It would prove to be such an encouragement to them and give them also the type of psychological support necessary for stepping into the pulpit. They would know that they have come to had have a deeper understand the text through their mutual labors together and that they are going to be proclaiming Christ from the text and are going to have a clear sense of what some of the many applications might be. And I think one challenge for ministers is simply the lack of confidence they have going into the pulpit that they have a message worth the members hearing. I realize that some ministers could be lazy and therefore begin to use others as a crutch, but once again, I think that the ministers in a group like this could encourage others not to do that.

This the benefit of ministers of the word doing this together is that they have all gone to seminary. They have had classes on homiletics. They have read Brian Chappell on preaching. They have read the old homiletics. They are in a situation of being able to help each other in pursuing a balanced approach to homiletics, exegesis, and preaching.

Chapter 51
Throw Your Paper Away!

Your paper belongs in the garbage can rather than as a barrier between you and the congregation.

One time Herman Hanko preached a practice-preaching sermon in seminary. In the follow-up to the message, Professor Hoeksema told him that the sermon was so bad that he should throw it in the trash. The next day the professor informed the student that he would need to fill the pulpit in a church in Wisconsin. The student responded that he did not have an available sermon to preach. His professor told him to preach the practice-preaching sermon.

He didn't have to throw it away after all.

Maybe it would have been best if he did throw the paper away, and simply internalized the message and preached without notes.

Professors and ministerial advisers need to take the paper away from seminary students.

Seminary students need to have more opportunities to give brief presentations. They need to learn how internalize a message. They need to learn how to communicate with an audience. So take their paper away. I mean it.

In a homiletics class in seminary, have the student put together a sermon, but then tell him that he can have no paper while he gives the message. Tell him you do not care if he misses important details. It doesn't matter if he gets some of the logic of the message mixed up. But he should internalize the major argument of the sermon and the flow of logic.

He needs to internalize the major concepts and ideas that he has developed.

Then he needs to get up there and talk.

And communicate.

He may not memorize his sermon word for word. He must rather internalize the message.

The student will learn that he must simplify his oral communication. He will begin to value what he is able to internalize.

And congregations will be delighted. And seminarian messages will have an impact.

Breaking away from your over dependence to paper. But you say, "I have been reading my sermons for three years, how can I break this habit now?"

You have a question. I have an answer.

Start by studying your outline and then on Friday or Saturday climb into your pulpit in the empty auditorium and give whatever of your sermon that you can remember. Preach without notes. This is good practice anyway. I find that when I verbally communicate what I have been reflecting upon, I immediately get new and fresh ideas that add to what I have already seen.

If you find it impossible to say anything about your second and third points, which should not be the case, then just focus on trying to speak extemporaneously about your first point. As you begin to speak extemporaneously, your confidence can grow.

Pray. The reason why you think that you must read your sermon is because you are either a perfectionist (you make yourself doing things just right into a god), you have the fear of men (you are intimidated by people), or you are proud (you are fearful of people thinking ill of you). So pray that God would humble you. Pray that the Holy Spirit would help you to internalize the gospel message so that you could celebrate it extemporaneously.

But you object, "I might be able to have freedom in the pulpit when no one is there to intimidate me, but if there are people in the pews, I can't do it." Then start by internalizing just the introduction to your sermon. You always should have done that anyway. Once you have learned to internalize the introduction to your sermon, do the same with the first part of your first point. Practice not using any notes for the first part of your sermon. As times goes on, you can continue to add further sections. The congregation will notice and they will appreciate it. Finally, you will be able to internalize the third point as well and apply the passage extemporaneously with passion (and, therefore, eloquence).

This takes hard work. Internalizing your message is hard work. But it is rewarding. And it makes preaching fun. Extemporaneous preaching is arduous work, but rewarding work.

Made in the USA
Middletown, DE
10 December 2020